CW01562007

Automobile Year

AUTOMOBILE YEAR 1995/96

CONTENTS

Our questions answered:
The readers reply – Jean-Rodolphe Piccard 5

European industry:
Improving – but slowly – Jacques Farenc 7

International overview:
How far can Korea go? – Jacques Farenc 23

Aesthetics of the mechanism:
Looking good under the hood – Robert Cumberford . 29

Open-topped Fiats:
A sporty subculture – Wim Oude Weernink 37

Art and the automobile:
"My dad had one like that" – Jacques Boguel 45

Highlight of the year:
A festival for the fans – Ian Norris 53

US industry:
Is the handbrake still on? – Paul E. Eisenstein 63

Only in America – 1:
Hot rods, now and then – John Lamm 75

Japanese industry:
Living with a strong yen – Peter Nunn 85

Japan's minicars:
A unique breed – Peter Nunn 97

Automotive history:
The roots of Auto Union – Alain van den Abeele 103

A photographers' tribute
Fangio – Günther Molter 112

Formula One World Championship:
Schumacher wins in a team game – Mario Luini and
Ian Norris 119

World Rally Championship:
Bad rules, good sport – Keith Oswin 157

US racing:
A season of newcomers – Rick Miller 177

Only in America – 2:
Dry lakes speedsters – John Lamm 195

European Touring Car Championships:
National strength, international ambitions –
Pierre Dieudonné 205

GT/Endurance and International BPR Series:
McLaren forms a strong foundation – Michael Cotton 215

International F3000 Championship:
Super Nova marks the end of an era – Eric Briquet .. 225

RESULTS

International F3000 Championship 231

Formula One World Championship 232

F1 Grand Prix 233

Touring Car Championships 250

World Rally Championship 251

World Rally Championship – Constructors' Cup 253

Ladies' Cup 254

FIA Cup for Production Cars' Drivers 254

24 Heures du Mans 255

International BPR Series 256

IndyCar World Series 257

European Hill Climb Championship 260

European Championship for Rallycross Drivers 260

ACKNOWLEDGMENTS

The Publisher is grateful to the following photographers and organizations for the illustrations in this edition of *Automobile Year*: 2-3: D. Reinhard – 6: Renault Presse Produit – 7: Rover Group – 8: Italdesign – 8-9: P. Vann – 9: Ferrari SpA – 10: P. Vann – 10-11: P. Vann – 11: P. Vann – 12-13: P. Vann – 13: Bertone – 14: Mercedes-Benz AG – 14-15: Renault Presse Produit/P. Vann – 15: Opel, Opel, Renault Presse Produit/P. Vann – 16: BMW – 16-17: P. Vann – 17: BMW – 18: Opel/W. Drehsen – 18-19: Mercedes-Benz AG – 19: Ford – 20: Renault Communication, Fiat/A. Marzoli – 21: Fiat, Rover Group, Ford – 23: Hyundai – 24: Hyundai Electronics Industries, J. Farenc, Hyundai Heavy Industries – 25: Citroen, J. Farenc, Fortune/Time Inc. – 26-27: L. Debraine – 28: Hyundai (4), Kia (2), Daewoo (3), SsangYong (1) – 29: Automobile Quarterly Photo & Research Library – 30-31: Automobile Quarterly Photo & Research Library – 31: Foto Zumbrunn – 32: General Motors – 33: Citroen, General Motors – 34: T. Andrew/Bay View Books – 34-35: J. Lamm – 35: J. Lamm – 36-37: J. Lamm – 37: Fiat Centro Storico, J. Lamm, J. Lamm, Fiat Centro Storico – 38-39: Fiat Centro Storico – 40: Bertone – 40-41: Fiat Centro Storico – 42: Fiat Centro Storico, Industrie Pininfarina – 43-44: Centro Storico Fiat – 45-52: J. Boguel – 53: Goodwood Festival of Speed/P. Hearsey – 54: P. Burn – 54-55: P. Burn – 55: I. Norris – 56-58: P. Burn – 59: P. Burn, I. Norris – 60: I. Norris, I. Norris, P. Burn – 61: P. Burn – 62-63: Ford Motor Co. – 64-65: Ford Motor Co. – 66: General Motors/Chevrolet – 66-67: General Motors/Buick – 67: General Motors/Buick – 68: Chrysler Corp., Ford Motor Co., Chrysler Corp. – 69: Chrysler Corp. – 70: J. Lamm – 70-71: General Motors/Saturn – 71: General Motors/Pontiac – 72: Chrysler Corp. – 73: J. Lamm – 74-83: J. Lamm – 84: Nissan – 85: Toyota – 86: Toyota – 86-87: Nissan – 87: Toyota – 88: Mazda, Toyota – 88-89: Mitsubishi – 89: Toyota, P. Nunn – 90: Honda – 90-91: Tommy Kaira, Toyota – 91-92: Mitsubishi – 94: Honda, Nissan, Mazda – 94-95: Mazda – 95: R. Hatshimoto – 96: Mazda, Toyota Museum, Toyota Museum – 96-97: Subaru – 97: Toyota Museum – 98: P. Nunn – 98-99: Mitsubishi – 99: P. Nunn – 100: Car Graphic Collection – 101: Suzuki – 102-108: P. Casse – 109: Auto Union, Archiv G. Molter/K. Wörner, The Klemantaski Collection – 110-111: Sutton Photographic – 112-113: Y. Debraine – 114-115: J. Alexander, B. Cahier – 115: B. Cahier – 116: G. Molter – 117: The Klemantaski Collection – 118-119: Sutton Photographic – 120-121: ARC – 122: F. Kräling – 123: B. Williams, D. Reinhard, ARC – 124: Sutton Photographic – 125: Photo 4, ARC – 126: Sutton Photographic, G. Berthoud – 126-127: ARC – 127: P. Nygaard – 128: Sutton Photographic – 128-129: ARC – 129: Photo 4, ARC – 130-131: Sutton Photographic – 132: Sutton Photographic, S. Domenjoz – 132-133: G. Berthoud – 133: ARC – 134: Photo 4 – 134-135: Sutton Photographic – 135: D. Reinhard – 136: ARC – 137: Sutton Photographic – 138: ARC, Sutton Photographic, Sutton Photographic, Sutton Photographic, Sutton Photographic – 138-139: Sutton Photographic – 139: ARC, Sutton Photographic – 140: P. Nygaard, ARC – 140-141: ARC – 141: P. Nygaard – 142: Sutton Photographic – 142-143: Photo 4, Sutton Photographic – 143: Sutton Photographic – 144: S. Domenjoz, Sutton Photographic – 144-145: G. Berthoud – 145: Sutton Photographic – 146: ARC – 146-147: G. Berthoud – 147: Photo 4 – 148: ARC – 149: ARC, ARC, Photo 4 – 150: ARC – 150-151: ARC – 152: Photo 4, Sutton Photographic – 152-153: Photo 4 – 153: Photo 4 – 154: ARC – 154-155: Photo 4, ARC – 155: Photo 4 – 156: ARC, S. Domenjoz, ARC – 157: A. Marzoli – 158: M. Holmes – 158-159: ARC – 159: A. Marzoli, ARC, A. Marzoli – 160: A. Marzoli – 160-161: M. Holmes – 161-162: A. Marzoli – 163: A. Marzoli, M. Holmes – 164-165: A. Marzoli – 166: A. Marzoli, M. Holmes, M. Holmes – 167: M. Holmes, A. Marzoli, A. Marzoli – 168-169: A. Marzoli – 170-171: Linear Photographs – 171: A. Marzoli – 172: M. Holmes – 172-173: A. Marzoli – 174-176: A. Marzoli – 177: M. C. Brown – 178: M. C. Brown – 178-179: M. C. Brown – 180: M. C. Brown, Sutton Photographic – 181: N. Kinrade – 182: N. Kinrade – 182-183: N. Kinrade – 183: N. Kinrade, F. Mormillo – 184: R. Miller – 184-185: A. Patrice/Vandystadt – 185: R. Miller – 186-187: M. C. Brown – 187: R. Miller, A. Patrice/Vandystadt – 188: R. Miller – 189: Photo 4, F. Mormillo – 190-191: M. C. Brown – 192-193: M. C. Brown – 194: A. Patrice/Vandystadt, R. Miller, R. Miller – 195-203: J. Lamm – 204: A. Marzoli – 205: A. Marzoli – 206: G. Dawkins – 206-207: A. Marzoli – 207: Photo 4 – 208-209: A. Marzoli, G. Dawkins – 210-211: Photo 4 – 211: G. Dawkins – 212: Photo 4 – 213: Photo 4 – 214: Photo 4, A. Marzoli, G. Dawkins – 215: Photo 4 – 216: Photo 4 – 217: ARC – 218-219: ARC – 220: ARC, L. Sanson, L. Sanson – 220-221: ARC – 221: Photo 4, L. Missbauer – 222-223: G. Dawkins – 224: J. Overton, L. Sanson, L. Sanson – 225-228: Photo 4 – 229: G. Dawkins – 230: ARC, Photo 4.

Publisher: Jean-Rodolphe Piccard
Editor-in-chief: Ian Norris

Automobile Year is published in French under the title *l'année automobile* and in German under the title *Auto-Jahr*.

Published by EDITIONS JR, J.-R. PICCARD
Rue du Clos-de-Bulle 8
CH-1004 Lausanne / Switzerland
Phone: 41 21 311 67 33   Fax: 41 21 311 67 34

Copyright © 1995 by EDITIONS JR, J.-R. PICCARD
Printed in Italy
ISBN 2-88324-038-8
All rights reserved. No part of this publication may be reproduced, stored in a retrieval system, or transmitted in any form or by any means, electronic, mechanical, photocopying, recording or otherwise, without the permission of the copyright holder and publisher.

OUR QUESTIONS ANSWERED

THE READERS REPLY

Each copy of last year's edition of *Automobile Year*, together with its French and German sister publications, contained a questionnaire which readers were invited to fill in and return. It was the first time that such research had been carried out among the readers of our annual, and the results outlined here will help us to better understand and satisfy our audience. We also hope that by reporting on some of our findings, we may encourage other readers to communicate with us, expressing their wishes and suggestions as freely as did those who replied last year.

The response to the questionnaire was very impressive, and we must thank all those who expended time and thought on sending their replies. Over 12% of the forms were returned, a level of response which is excellent by conventional market research standards. We would have liked more responses, but only for base commercial reasons – since 74% of the respondents were interested in buying books and guides, and 20% were potential buyers of multimedia products, with a few hundred more names and addresses we could have created a viable mail-order business immediately!

It was surprising to find that readers in those countries in which the largest sales of *Automobile Year* take place were not necessarily those most interested in taking part in the development of the publication. The figures speak for themselves: 15% of our buyers in France and Belgium returned forms; while 14% of the readers in French-speaking Switzerland responded, as did 14% from Australia, 12% from Germany and Austria, and 11% from Britain. There was another 11% made up of replies from purchasers in miscellaneous countries, but just 7% from the USA. Amazingly, 20% of the New Zealand buyers responded, as did 26% of the German-speaking Swiss buyers, a degree of support which speaks highly of the devotion and interest of our readers in these two areas!

The wide geographical range which the three language editions cover is underlined by the number of countries from which we received replies. In alphabetical order, they were Abu Dhabi, Argentina, Australia, Austria, Belgium, Brazil, Canada, Columbia, Denmark, Finland, France, Germany, Holland, Hong Kong, Ireland, Italy, Japan, Jordan, Luxembourg, Malta, Mexico, Monaco, New Zealand, Norway, Paraguay, Portugal, Slovenia, South Africa, Spain, Sweden, Switzerland, Thailand, Trinidad, United Kingdom, United States and Zimbabwe.

Of the total number of responses, 32% came from readers living in France, 27% in Switzerland, 13% in Germany and Austria, 7% in Belgium, 4% in the United Kingdom, 3% in the USA, 2.5% in New Zealand. 8.5% of the replies came from countries which the computer decided to join together as 'miscellaneous'.

It was fascinating to see how faithful our readers are: 47% of you have been buying *Automobile Year* in one of its three languages for thirty years or more, 36% for twenty or more and 10% for ten. Only 4% have been reading the book for five years, and we must hope that as we take steps to capture younger readers, our older readers will join us in our endeavours by recommending it or considering it as a gift for young enthusiasts.

As one famous journalist said in 1995, "*Automobile Year* is an addiction." The truth of the statement is underlined by the fact that no less than 13% of our respondents owned a full set of the publication. 27% had more than 30 copies, while 30% had between 20 and 30, and 27% between 10 and 20. The addictive quality is evident from the fact that no less than 80% of our respondents wanted to complete their collection. However, those who own examples of the rare early editions may rest assured that we shall *not* reprint them – although we are looking at alternative, paperless, ways of making them available.

Although 89% of our respondents were happy with the current content of the annual, 11% did want to see changes. Of these, 20% wanted to see greater coverage of the industry, while 56% wanted more sporting coverage – they will be happy to see the Formula 1 coverage of this edition has been expanded!

Even if the level of approval is satisfactory, we will not use it as an excuse for complacency. *Automobile Year* will continue to evolve in form and content and will reflect the tastes of its readers. In terms of the industry and its products, these are – in decreasing order of preference – history, technology, styling and design. In motor sport, Formula 1 is most popular, followed by historical subjects, ahead of endurance racing, touring cars, rallies, IndyCar and NASCAR, and Formula 3000.

The position of *Automobile Year* as a reference work is shown by the fact that of the 51% of respondents who do read other annuals, the majority read only one. Our readers are very interested in the world of cars and motoring, however, for 79% of them are regular readers of specialist motoring magazines.

Many of the responses were accompanied by letters, and it was a pity to read in some of them that there were gaps in our distribution system. We are constantly trying to convince the trade of the value of carrying *Automobile Year*, and we can only say that if you have trouble in finding a copy locally, please complain to your local bookshop or to the distributor in your country – customers are the most listened-to people in any business, and the results of our survey have us listening to you very hard!

JEAN-RODOLPHE PICCARD

EUROPEAN INDUSTRY

IMPROVING – BUT SLOWLY

After a disastrous year in 1993, when sales of 11,469,000 passenger cars were 15% down on 1992, Western Europe saw a noticeable improvement in 1994. Sales were up 6% and registrations reached 11,898,000, but they were still far off the record figure of 13,508,000 reached in 1992. It was not unrealistic to expect a better year in 1995, a year marked by an expansion of the European Union from 12 to 15 member countries with the inclusion of Austria, Sweden and Finland. The only countries of traditional Europe which now remained outside the economic community were Switzerland and Norway. Nevertheless, the ideals of a unified Europe had been somewhat soured by the problems of European Monetary Union and its 'snake' of linked currencies. Britain had dropped out of the dance, to the displeasure of its European purists and the relief of its exporters, but Portugal, Italy and Spain had been forced into devaluations which meant that prices for the same vehicle could be double in one country when compared to another. (The lowest pre-tax prices were to be found in Denmark.)

All manufacturers were looking forward to a noticeable increase in sales in Western Europe in 1995. Their expectations were of between 3.0 and 3.5% growth, but when the figures for the first quarter came in they showed that private car registrations had risen by a mere 1.4% – despite an atypical 7.7% increase in France, which until mid-year benefitted from a government programme giving cash rebates to new car buyers. In the major markets, which made up more than three-quarters of total European sales, the figures were very little better: Spain was up 1.5%, Germany was up 1.2%, but Great Britain and Italy were both *down*, if only by half a percentage point. Only in Scandinavia, where sales rose by about 10%, was the view more encouraging. It was clear that the 15 million sales target which had been foreseen for the mid-Nineties was not going to be achieved.

One of the most important developments in the European Union in 1995 was the renewal, for seven years, of the 'selective' distribution system which governs the retail motor trade. The automobile market is therefore treated as one which operates under different commercial rules from those accepted in classic free-market situations. Principals, be they manufacturers or importers, in each country have the right to sell their products to distributors and dealers, who operate in strictly-defined geographical areas, at prices set by the principals. The result is that the status quo continues, despite Union regulations which call for a free market and are based on the purest principles of the Treaty of Rome. In a move to remove the retailers, who are in the main private entrepreneurs, from a position of servitude, the Commission in Brussels introduced some additional safeguards. These took the form of a minimum contract period between principals and retailers of five, rather than four, years; a minimum notice of termination of contracts of two years rather than one, to give the smaller operation more protection; the possibility for the retailer to hold multiple franchises; the freedom to buy spares, so long as they are of comparable quality, from sources other than the manufacturer; the right to refuse to accept abnormal conditions of sale and a number of other minor changes. The measures contained a number of anomalies which were pounced upon by consumer bodies, but in the end there was no avoiding the fact that business is run according to the rules of supply and demand, and whatever the new rules may say the business was heavily influenced by discounting and – in Continental Europe if not in right-hand drive Britain – 'grey imports'.

As far as relations between Japan and Brussels were concerned, it will be remembered that Japan had expressed a wish to import 993,000 'Japanese-made' vehicles into Europe during 1994. The worldwide downturn in demand for their products meant that they were only able to sell 818,000 – 17.6% short of the target. Japanese penetration of the European car and light commercial market reached a peak in 1992, at a level of 12.6%. It slid minimally to 12.5% in 1993, but it was down to 11.3% in 1994, and by mid-1995 the figure was 10.9%. It has to be said that the rise in value of the yen (or as some would have it, the yen's rise to a more realistic level coupled with the fall in value of the dollar) has hit Japanese industry hard, but there is also the question of competition from other Asian countries such as India, Malaysia and the like. The most spectacular rise in 1995 came from the South Korean manufacturers Hyundai, Kia-Asia, Daewoo and SsangYong. On the other hand, the Malaysian Proton brand, which had achieved a mod-

JACQUES FARENC

1995 was certainly the year of the roadster. Among the best of a plentiful crop was Renault's mid-engined Spider (opposite). Powered by a 150hp 2.0-litre four, it had an aluminium chassis and composite bodywork. It was, however, a limited-production concept vehicle, destined to support one-model race series; Rover's MGF (above) was a real-world sports car. An all-British design, it owed nothing to Honda or BMW, and flew in the face of MG tradition by having a mid-engine with a unique variable valve-timing system, interlinked Hydragas suspension and the option of electrically-driven power-steering. The result was a sports car which, unlike some others, set standards for the Nineties rather than perfecting those of the Sixties.

The Lamborghini of tomorrow as seen by Giorgetto Giugiaro. The Cala design study, first shown at Geneva, was the first of a series which are due to explore varying possibilities for a smaller Lamborghini powered by the company's V10 engine. Giugiaro's targa-topped proposal is mid-engined – of course – with an aluminium chassis and carbon-fibre bodywork.

Despite its age, the Porsche 911 refuses to behave like a 'classic'. 1995 saw the reintroduction of the Porsche with the mostest, the Turbo. A more rigid chassis was the mount for a twin-turbo version of the 3.6-litre flat-six producing 408hp, driving all four wheels through a six-speed gearbox. With a top speed of 290km/h (180mph) and capable of a standing-start kilometer in just 23 seconds, the 911 Turbo Evolution sets new standards.

icum of success in Britain, failed completely in its attack on the rest of Europe. The Japanese also failed to capitalise on their 'non-quota' production, from their transplant factories (mainly in Britain and Spain). Total production from the European overseas sites was 504,629 in 1993, and it rose only slightly, to 516,033 in 1994. It is unlikely that by the end of 1995 more than 560,000 vehicles will have rolled off the end of the transplant lines.

Putting aside the impact of Korean imports, there have been a number of influences on the current position of the European industry, but none has been greater than the disorder caused by the variations between national currencies. It is a situation which caused Jacques Calvet, president of Peugeot-Citroen, to say that the establishment of a common European currency – theoretically due in 1999 – "could take ten, fifteen, perhaps even twenty years" to achieve.

The legacy of M. Balladur

In France, 1995 saw the ending of an unusual sales-promotion campaign which has left behind irreversible changes in the country's retail car business. The process started in February 1994, when Prime Minister Edouard Balladur's government introduced a scheme which would reward new vehicle buyers who part-exchanged a car over ten years old with a $1000 rebate on the cost of the new model. The programme came to an end at the end of June, 1995, by which time it had achieved its aims of lowering the average age of the French vehicle park and kick-starting the industry to the extent of selling the enormous number of 729,500 extra vehicles.

However, the scheme had also set in motion a bitter commercial war, as manufacturers and importers vied with each other to attract the new customers. The result was manufacturers' discounts of between $2000 and $2400 per vehicle, which were in addition to the state-funded rebate. The cars thus sold came to be known as 'Balladurettes', and the success of the scheme aided not only the manufacturers, but also their component and sub-assembly suppliers. Around 35% of the Renaults, Citroens and Peugeots registered during the period were Balladurettes, but the increased sales did not bring universal satisfaction. Because of the level of discounting which was being encouraged, many retailers were forced to sell cars at a loss. In addition, the cyclical nature of sales (June 1995 sales were 50% up on June 1994, while August 1995 was 10% down on the previous year) created an anarchic situation in the market after the Balladur bonus was withdrawn. The result was that discounting, never a major element in the French retail business, had become a fact of life for car dealers. Nevertheless, the manufacturers came out of the period smiling, with the balance-sheets for the first half of 1995 well in the black.

At Peugeot-Citroen, the major talking-point of the year was over the succession of Jacques Calvet, who is expected to step down as boss of the organization some time in 1996 or 1997. The absolute president of the group, he has been in charge at PSA for more than eleven years. His crown-prince is seen as Jean-Martin Folz, who was recruited by the Peugeot family after a successful period with Eridania-Béghin-Say, an agricultural industry group. The 48-year-old Folz is likely to come up against competition from Jean-Yves Helmer, who is currently director of PSA's automobile group. Like Folz, Helmer is a 'polytechnicien', a product of the elite French educational system.

After its divorce from Volvo, Renault collected $520 million in alimony and started life as a single all over again. Louis Schweitzer, the company's president, summed up the affair with Volvo as an opportunity, but not a necessity, and certainly not a tragedy. By the end of the first quarter of 1995 Renault had a well-established 11.2% of the European car and light commercial market, a share which put it alongside Fiat. The most important event of Renault's year was the launch of the Megane, its replacement for the 19 in

the lower end of the mid-size market. Schweitzer did not want a 'car for all people', a product aimed at the average needs of the average family. Individuality is the key, with a widely-varying range of cars: two and three-box saloons, a true sports coupé, a full convertible and a first for the market segment, an MPV – or as Renault more accurately describes it – a 'monospace'. The one-box Megane underlines Renault's lead in the European 'monospace' market, which it led with the Espace and daringly expanded with the Twingo. However, the MPV concept has not been as

The successor to the incredible F40, the Ferrari F50 (above and left) continues the style of applying race technology to an 'ultimate' road car. Every aspect of the car shows F1 influence: the carbon-fibre monocoque body has the engine and fuel tank mounted centrally, for ideal weight distribution and handling, the suspension has wishbones and inboard springs actuated by rocker-arms, and the 520hp engine is a direct descendant of a Ferrari Grand prix engine, but with its capacity enlarged to 4.7 litres to give better characteristics for road-driving. Top speed – not for road driving – is 202mph.

To most non-Italians, Alfa Romeo saloons are Italian police cars. So although there was interest in the 155 and the 145/146, what the world at large really wanted to see was the new generation of sporting cars from Milan. When it came, in the shape of the GTV coupé (above) and the Spider (right), there was no disappointment. Once again, it was Pininfarina which was responsible for the styling, and the swooping elegance of the cars was worthy to be compared with earlier examples of the collaboration between these two great names of the Italian industry.

successful in Europe as some people predicted – sales for 1995 will be of the order of between 200,000 and 250,000 units, against somewhat optimistic predictions of 400,000 to 450,000. Renault's problem, as it prepares for a process of privatisation, is the fall in the value of its shares. Issued in August 1995 at $33, they had fallen to $28 just a month later. This meant that privatisation of the company before the end of 1995 would not be a profitable operation for the major share-holder, the French state.

Round about the time of the Detroit Show, in January, when the Americans seemed to be having doubts about the future of the electric car, the French were putting them into production. Around 50 electrically-driven light vans had been delivered in 1994 to purchasers who were not major public fleet-operators, and in spring of 1995 the authorities announced sweeteners to encourage further sales. These took the form of a premium of $1000 payable to the purchaser, in addition to one of $2000 which would go from Eléctricité de France, the state power company, to the vehicle's constructor. Unfortunately, despite all these encouragements, a Peugeot 106 Electric still retails for $16,000 – plus between $100 and $150 per month for its rented batteries!

It is almost fifty years since French cars held a dominant position in the European market, and today France's motor industry finds itself more constricted. 1994 production figures for cars and light vans from Renault (1,850,000) and Peugeot-Citroen (1,752,000) were up by 8% and 14% respectively, but the proportion of the total which was produced outside Europe was laughable. Just 8.2% of the total production – was assembled overseas. Worse, this figure showed a drop of 17% over the previous year.

Technically, the two new Alfas were fully up to the minute, with a multi-link rear suspension which gave excellent handling. But it was the looks and the details which gave pleasure. None of those details was more attractive than the unique headlamp treatment.

This does not mean, however, that France's two leading groups are not active in foreign parts. Renault, which had been linked in erroneous – or premature – reports with Mercedes-Benz, confirmed its involvement in Argentina with Mercosur, a South American common market which has found favour with automobile investors. The company has also announced a study into a Brazilian operation which foresees an investment of around a billion dollars which would produce some 100,000 Meganes a year by 1999.

Peugeot, in association with Premio-Automobiles, is setting up a plant in India which will have the capability of assembling between 40,000 and 50,000 309 models a year by 2000. The company also has a project under way in Pakistan to produce diesel versions of the same car. There had been talk of a return to the US, with a factory and a complete product line, but at the end of 1995 the idea seemed to be fading. What was certain was a project in Vietnam, where a $30 million investment in Hanoï will produce 5000, rising to 10,000, vehicles a year.

PSA's biggest investment in China, which will run alongside a modest Peugeot project in Canton, is to be a collaboration between Citroen and Dong-Feng. A massive factory in Wuhan will come on stream in 1996 and be capable of producing 150,000 ZX cars a year in 3-door, 5-door and booted versions. Later, production will rise to 300,000 vehicles a year. The enormous programme, which will require a total investment of $1.4 billion, will involve scores of French and European suppliers, who will collaborate with Citroen on a large-scale exercise in the transfer of technology. Another event in the French motor industry was on a more personal level, but nonetheless it was of great importance. It occurred when 69-year-old François Michelin named his son Edouard (40) as his replacement in a calm and agreeable succession at the head of the tyre empire.

Jaguar stays in Britain!

Shaken over the years by a variety of political and economic crises, the British motor industry is today on a much better footing, a state of affairs symbolised by the fact that BMW considered Rover worthy of being

The new generation of sporting Alfas are front-wheel drive, with the engines mounted transversally. There is a choice of a 150hp, 16-valve, 2.0-litre 'Twin Spark' four, with twin balance-shafts and variable valve-timing, or a 192hp 3.0-litre V6 (above).

Giugiaro became involved in the Daewoo phenomenon as the Korean manufacturer concentrated its efforts on European markets. The stylist's contribution came in the shape of the Bucrane, a sporting front-drive coupé with space for four in comfort. The lines of the car are realistic rather than futuristic, and the only elements which would be unlikely to meet with the approval of the accountants and production management of a mass producer like Daewoo are the doors. They are split, with the lower part opening normally while the windows lift 'butterfly' fashion.

taken over. Because it had gone into recession earlier than continental Europe, Britain came out earlier, and sales for 1994, at 1,911,000, were 7.5% higher than the 1993 figure of 1,778,000. 1995 should maintain the 1994 level, but sales are still well below their high mark of 2 million in 1989/90.

Rover Group, with a good Honda-based technical background and some astute British marketing skills, was showing good growth, lifting its share of the European market from 2.9% in 1993 to over 3.0% in 1994, but in 1995 the process reversed, and during the first quarter of 1995 Rover's market penetration dropped to 2.4% in Europe after a 16% fall in sales. It was hard to find an explanation for the state of affairs, but Munich decided to do something about it when Wolfgang Reitzle, No 2 at BMW and a strong product engineer, took over as chairman of Rover from BMW boss Bernd Pischetsrieder. Reitzle confirmed BMW's desire that Rover should be repositioned in the market, abandoning the mass fleet segment in the UK and moving up-market in both home and overseas territories. BMW will co-operate with Rover to renew the whole of the British company's range, starting with the 600 saloon, over a period stretching to the end of the century, when a new Mini is to replace the original – on or around its fortieth birthday!

Rover is making good progress on overseas developments, with a project under way in Indonesia to produce a vehicle specifically for that market. In addition, the Montego and the Metro, British Leyland designs no longer made in Britain, are about to start production in India and Bulgaria respectively. Rover is said to have committed itself to an investment of some $3.2 billion between now and the end of the century to raise its production potential to 520,000 vehicles a year, including a new small member of the Land Rover family, and to completely renew its engine range up to and including a new V6.

Rover's decision to let others fight over the fleet market is indicative of the influence of the 'company car' in the British market. Around half of the passenger cars sold in Britain are bought by companies or leasing fleets to be given to employees as part of their salary package, and naturally such bulk purchases are made at a discount. It is said that some firms receive

ever, to playing the old American game of hardball. The real growth for Jaguar lies not in its large saloons, or in the replacement for the XJS due in late 1996; the money-maker will be X200, the 'small' Jaguar which is due round about the end of the century. Building that car will need massive investment on the part of Ford, and the company didn't hesitate to let it be known that so far as it was concerned, a Jaguar did not have to be built in Britain. There were lots of arguments for X200 to be built in the USA, admitted Ford sources from chairman Alex Trotman down – unless, of course, the British government would be prepared to make a contribution which would ensure Jaguar stayed in Britain. The political game worked, and in late summer the authorities announced a $120 million package which would keep X200 production where the traditionalists believed it should be.

A more distant member of the Ford family is Mazda, in which the American company has a 25 % financial stake and a large say in management policy. Japan's number three manufacturer has been having a hard time in Europe, and has seen its market share collapse from 2 % in 1992 to 1.4 % at mid-1995, so it will start selling a British-built Fiesta under a Mazda badge in Europe early in 1996. The project is yet another example of the link between Britain and the Japanese motor industry. Honda, precipitately freed from its links to Rover by BMW, is fighting back with a further investment of $320 million – on top of an initial spend of over a billion dollars – in its Swindon factory. Honda-UK's objective is to raise capacity from 100,000 cars in 1995 to 150,000 by 1998. Toyota and Nissan are also expanding, and both announced substantial investments in their UK plants during 1995. Finally, we should record a further triumph for prag-

such a large reduction on the list price that they are able to sell their employee cars after three months and make a profit. These facts have not gone unnoticed by private buyers, with the result that they are staying away from the new car showrooms in droves, preferring to buy ex-fleet cars second-hand at a healthy saving. This change in buying habits is likely to affect the retail market as long as Britain maintains its policy of encouraging companies to subsidise their employees' motoring. What is more, it is likely to have a permanent effect sales of those low-end models traditionally bought by the less-wealthy 'blue-collar' worker; a new entry-level Escort has limited appeal alongside a well-maintained ex-company Mondeo, less than a year old and selling at the same price.

Jaguar, which finds almost all its UK sales in the corporate sector, found new success with the launch of its retro-styled saloon range in late 1994. Sales are up all over the world, and the company is looking to repeat and improve upon the glory days of the mid-Eighties. The prospect is even better today, for the Coventry company now has the support and resources of Ford behind it. Ford was not averse, how-

Bertone's Kayak design study (left and below) is based on the new Lancia Kapoa luxury saloon, but takes the form of a two-door coupé. Soft and rounded without falling into the trap of being too 'organic', the Kayak offers much more comfort than its namesake. There was a time when prototypes such as this foreshadowed production vehicles from such manufacturers as Lancia, but modern production economics probably mean the idea is impossible today.

matism over tradition in the technical link between Rolls-Royce and BMW announced at the end of 1994. The new association will give the British company full access to BMW's experience, knowledge and facilities for power-unit development, and the result will be two new engines for a new Rolls/Bentley saloon car due around the end of the century. There will be a luxury V12 unit for Rolls-Royce, and a forced-induction V8 for Bentley's more sporting needs. There is no agreement for BMW to participate further than in engine development, but it is likely the company would be happy to talk if Vickers should ever want to sell the jewel in Britain's automobile crown.

Clouds over Germany

The German automobile industry had a fair amount of media exposure during 1995, but not all of it was welcome. VAG (Volkswagen Audi Group) gained kudos for the way in which Audi renewed its complete line in a single year, after losing $100,000,000 and 25 % in sales during 1993. At Skoda, the newest member of the family, the pressure was on to expand production at the Mlada Boleslav factory from 200,000 units per year to 340,000 by 1997. This will be achieved by adding a second model, similar to the Passat/Toledo. Volkswagen took the decision during the year that the 'new Beetle', based on the Concept 1 show-car, would go into production as a prelude to the new century.

Less acceptable publicity came from the continuing power-struggle within the group, which saw president Ferdinand Piëch fire his financial director, Werner Schmidt, whom Piëch blamed for the crisis at SEAT

Geneva saw Mercedes-Benz introduce its VRC (Vario Research Car), an interesting project in the world of multi-purpose vehicles. A base chassis and lower body was adapted to carry interchangeable superstructures which could be mounted to provide the advantages of a saloon, estate car, coupé, pickup or convertible. The idea is that customers would buy the base and top which fulfilled the majority of their needs and then hire alternative units when they were necessary.

Renault's Initiale (right) is an example of something of which the French motor industry has little recent experience – a luxury car. Local tax laws have killed the production of such vehicles, but Renault see this as a possibility, powered by a detuned version of the V10 F1 engine.

which had led to losses of $1.2 billion in 1993. A leaked letter caused embarassment for the president by taking issue with his dictatorial management methods; Piëch, it was said, ran the group like a medieval fiefdom. Nevertheless, VW's turnaround continued in 1994, despite continuing losses at SEAT and Skoda. The total workforce had been reduced from 273,000 to 250,000, and productivity had improved to the extent that working hours per car, which were at 33 for the first Golf, came down to 14 for the latest Polo. VW's new minicar would, it was claimed, take up only 7 hours of the workers' time per car. The figures were given by president Piëch himself, who also claimed that VAG would be producing 5 million cars a year by 2000.

Opel, which had been at daggers-drawn with VW over the Lopez affair of the stolen secrets, saw a successful launch of the new Vectra. The new version showed every sign of helping to maintain the GM subsidiary's position as No. 1 in Europe, with 12.7% of the market.

From Ford-Europe's point of view, one of the major events of the year, although distant, was the breakdown of the collaboration with VW in Auto-Latina, the joint-venture (5% VW and 49% Ford) it had joined in 1987 to operate in Argentina and Brazil. 1995 saw another Ford/VW collaboration come into operation in the shape of the plant built in Portugal to produce the Galaxy/Sharan MPV twins.

BMW saw a settling-down period in its relations with Rover, which it had taken from under the nose of Honda in 1994. In the autumn, Wolfgang Reitzle took over as BMW's man at the head of the Rover board, to oversee the next generation of Rover products. If they are as good as the new 5-series, launched at Frankfurt in the autumn and seen as a Reitzle product, Rover should be happy.

Just as BMW stole Rover from Honda, it also caused a shock at the end of 1994 by signing an agreement with Rolls-Royce to provide power-unit know-how. The aggrieved party in this case was Mercedes-Benz, which had been seen as the favoured partner. BMW's move was a prelude to a year of shocks for the three-pointed star. Stuttgart was to be the scene of yet another battle among top management in the industry, with continuing accusations of mismanagement from former Daimler-Benz finance boss Gerhard Liener against Edzard Reuter, D-B's former president. Current president Jurgen Schrempp garnered the wrong kind of headlines when he, together with another executive and a female secretary, was briefly held by police after an excessively merry evening stroll in Rome. His business acumen was also called into question when the share price fell from $800 to less than $500 after a pessimistic profit-forecast. The forecast was for a loss in 1995 of no less than $2.2 billion – after profits of $740,000,000 for 1994, mainly driven by the automotive division.

Opel's multi-purpose MAXX is seen as a modular design which can be built to accommodate quite specific customer tastes. A lightweight city-car, the MAXX is seen as a four-door saloon (left) or a two-door semi-coupé (below). Both utilise the same front-drive power-pack configuration, with three- or four-cylinder engines of 30 to 50hp. The car was shown at Geneva as a concept, but by the end of the year a running example was in existence.

In view of the success which French luxury goods manufacturers enjoy on the international market, it was natural that Renault should combine with one of the best-known, Louis Vuitton, in the design of the Initiale. The unique hingeing system for the boot-lid should make sure the suitcases remain unscratched.

The fifth edition of BMW's mid-range car, the 5-series, was launched at the Frankfurt Show. The changes were subtle, but they made an already superb car even better. There are no mould-breaking new developments; it is just that everything about it – styling, body, engines and running-gear – has been improved, and that is enough to keep it competitive with its strongest rival, the new E-series from Mercedes.

The president of Mercedes-Benz AG, Helmut Werner, oversaw the launch of the new mid-range E-class, representing an investment of over $2 billion. Mercedes was also involved in a number of 'overseas' projects in Turkey, South Africa, Brazil, and above all India, where the project was worth 20,000 cars and 60,000 engines annually, and Korea, where the MB 100 van is to be produced. Mercedes had also been chosen by the Chinese authorities to collaborate with South China Motor Corporation to build 60,000 MPV's and 100,000 engines a year. Bouyed up by the success, Helmut Werner – who was changing the concept of 'Made in Germany' to one of 'Made by Mercedes' – declared that the company's automobile capacity, currently running at 500,000 units annually, would be doubled by the end of the decade.

The most unusual project was that underataken with Nicholas Hayek, presented as the man who saved the Swiss watch industry by inventing the Swatch. His Swatchmobile concept, originally picked up by Volkswagen and then dropped for lack of money, came to fruition in the shape of MCC (Micro Compact Car) AG, a Swiss company owned 51% by Mercedes and 49% by Hayek's company SMH, big in electronics and watchmaking. The company is to build the tiny (less than 100 inches (2.5 m.) long, with room for two seats and a crate of beer) car at Hambach, in the French area of Lorraine. The Swatchmobile name has been dropped in favour of 'Smart', and there will be no sign of a three-pointed star when it appears in mid 1998. The investment is worth some $530,000,000, and production is seen as being in the order of 200,000 units a year. According to Mercedes, the Smart will sell for 20,000 marks and it will be unusual in that it will be sold by MCC AG not through the normal motor trade channels, but through 90 'regional centres' which will be assisted by 'satellite sales units'. Mercedes expect this format to appeal to supermarket and shopping centre operators.

Fiat – A world power

Today, more than ever, Italy is Fiat; but Fiat is no longer exclusively Italy. In the words of Giorgio Garuzzo, chairman of Fiat Auto, chief operating officer of the Fiat Group and president of the Euro-

Audi, having launched its new 'A' naming system in the shape of the A8, A6 and A4, gave a hint of the new Golf-sized A3 when it showed the TT coupé (opposite) at Frankfurt. Based on a shortened A3 floorpan, the TT uses a turbocharged version of the A4's five-valve four driving all four wheels. It could be ready for production in short order if the interest is there, but reactions to its styling were not all glowing.

BMW's new sports car, the Z3 (below), is a fascinating example of the the mid-Nineties automobile. Designed and conceived by the German company using the engines and dimensions of the 3-series, it will be built in the United States, because that's where the market is and that's where the most economical manufacturing costs are currently to be found. It will not go into full production until 1996, but by the end of 1995 its marketing campaign will have already started, when the American-built German car has a supporting role in a British film (Goldeneye) about an English secret agent (James Bond) played by an Irishman (Pierce Brosnan). Small world, isn't it?

The renewal process of Mercedes-Benz' mid-range E-Class showed itself most prominently in the styling of the nose (opposite). The elliptical headlamps gave the instantly-recognizable Mercedes prow a new look which was not to everyone's taste, but – as with all things under the three-pointed star – their technology was impeccable. A general smoothing of the body's shape lowered the Cd to 0.28, and continuing development of the available engines (four- and six-cylinder petrol, both with four-valve heads, and a five-cylinder turbo-diesel) led to a significant improvement in fuel economy.

Opposite, bottom: Ford's new MPV is the Galaxy, the result of a relationship with VW consummated in a plant in Portugal. VW's Sharan is the Galaxy's twin, born a couple of months after its brother, and SEAT's Alhambra will follow in 1996. More car-like than some of the 'vannier' MPVs, the Galaxy has met with a high degree of praise for its easy handling and comfort, and in the first months of its life it outsold the mother of all monospaces, the Espace. Power comes from a Ford-built 2.0-litre four, VW's 2.8-litre VR6 V6, and a 1.9-litre Audi diesel due in early 1996.

The Opel Ascona became the Vectra in 1988, when the most recent version of GM-Europe's mid-size car was introduced. 1995 saw a new generation, and with it the Vectra name spread to the British Isles, as Vauxhall dropped its Cavalier tag. The Vectra is one of the hard-working boys or homely-looking girls of the motoring world. Comfort, reliability, performance and economy are all better than the preceding generation, while looks are – well, homely. Until you look at the mirrors and the way they are styled into the car as a whole...

pean Automobile Manufacturers Association, "From now on, Fiat is going to sell 65 % of its automobiles, 78 % of its trucks and 93 % of its agricultural tractors outside Italy. And with the fall of the lire, we shall do it with a high degree of competitiveness. But beware, for the Italian currency has gone from being overvalued to a state where it is seriously under-valued; currently it is at a rate of 1250 lire to the Deutschmark, but in my opinion its true level is somewhere between 1100 and 1200 to the mark."

Looking back at the recent history of Fiat's automobile activities from the standpoint of 1995 is still a cause for astonishment; the Italian group, which has cut its workforce by 25 % in four years, has been 'clinically dead' twice in the last decade and a half (firstly at the beginning of the Eighties, and more recently in the early 1990's). The latest miracle recovery is due to the ability of Giovanni Agnelli, president of the group for the last 29 years, to find the funds necessary for the restructuring of the automobile sector of the business by delivering new products or new working practices. After a long period of tecnical lethargy, in 1995 the group launched the Cinquecento Sporting, the Barchetta, the Ulysse MPV, the three and the five-door Bravo/Brava 'twins'. From Alfa came the 146 and the GTV Coupé and Spider, while Lancia launched the Delta HPE/HF, the Dedra station wagon and the Kappa luxury saloon.

Fiat's turnover in 1994 was $42 billion – half that of Ford, No. 2 in the world – showing an increase of 20 % and reducing the company's debt by almost 60 % to a figure of $1.4 billion. In his message to shareholders, Agnelli pointed out how profits had risen from less than 1.5 % of turnover in 1993 to more than 4.0 % in 1994, with a tripling of self-financing capability and an acceleration in the move towards internationalisation with 37 % of the workforce now employed outside Italy. In 1995, with the Punto among the top-selling cars in Europe, Fiat is looking to create 3000 new jobs on top of the 9000 which were filled in 1994. Net profit is set to double, from a $1.2 billion loss in 1993 to a $1.3 billion surplus, all thanks to the automobile sector and the devaluation of the lira.

What is the secret of Fiat's turnaround? "We have reinvented the company" is the chorus which comes from the still extensive cadre of senior directors in

Turin. To be more precise, it is Alberto Pianta, the Director of Production, who is conducting the real revolution of the 'fabbrica integrata' (integrated factory) from the new plant at Melfi, surrounded by the 21 'on-site' factories of its suppliers. According to Pianta, "We have left time and motion study and strictly-controlled workers behind and moved to become an organisation where people use resources in the service of cost-effectiveness, productivity and quality." With employees working in groups of between 10 and 40, there is an emphasis on individual creativity within the workforce and the group. To show the system works, he quotes figures which show the Melfi operation is around 30% more productive than the European average, and backs them up by statistics compiled by the prestigious MIT. According to these results, which count the number of hours required to build an average-size mass-production car similar to the Golf or Escort, Japan leads with 16.2 hours. Melfi is not far behind, with 16.9, while Japanese transplant factories in the US and Europe require 17.6 and 18 respectively. A more traditional Fiat plant at Cassino, built in 1986, takes 20.3, the average 'Big Three' plant in the US

Names or numbers? The uncertainty continues. While Audi and Peugeot retain a numbers-only policy, Renault replaces the 19 with a name, Mégane, in the shape of a five-door saloon and a two-door coupé (right) on a wheelbase shortened by 11cm (4.3ins) from the 413cm (162.6ins) of the saloon. These two are only the beginning, however. In the months and years ahead there will be a four-door three-box saloon, a 'monospace' and a convertible, making this kernel of the Renault range something to appeal to all tastes.

Alfa's two-door 145 displayed a quirky styling which was in the truly individual Alfa tradition. The 146 four-door (right) is the car for those who found the 145 too quirky. Just 16cm (6.3ins) longer than the two-door, the 146 shares its 1.4-litre and 1.7-litre engines with its more individualistic sibling.

Opposite, bottom: Ford's latest Fiesta is not radically changed from the model introduced in 1989, it's just better all round. The front and rear styling changes make it more attractive, the reworked suspension gives it better handling, and the 1.25-litre Zetec engine completes a revivifying package.

needs 21.9, and the average European facility requires 25.1. Northern European plants are at the bottom of the list with 29.2 hours.

"Melfi is the first automobile plant in the world to operate a 100% 'just in time' system," says Pianta, "and we have achieved Japanese levels of productivity. With the 'fabbrica integrata', the return on capital invested, when compared with the cost of Cassino twenty years ago, is between 35 and 115%, depending on the circumstances." The other miracle is the way in which Fiat is no longer a 100% Italian-oriented organisation. According to Gian-Battista Razelli, director of international operations, "in future, more than 50% of Fiat's production will be worldwide-based". In 1970, 1,550,000 (94%) of the 1,645,000 vehicles Fiat produced were built in Italy, but in answer to the question of how Fiat will globalise itself, Razelli predicts: "A production of 1.5 million vehicles outside Europe in around five years, but not before. By that time, total Fiat production will be over 3 million units a year."

The means to achieve that end is a vast programme, involving 18 countries across the world, based 'Project 178', a medium-sized 'world car' which will be modern but at the same time capable of being produced and sold in developing countries. In addition there are medium-term projects based on the Mercosur free-trade area in South America, which will account for 700,000 units annually, 300,000 in Poland, 250,000 in Turkey, 50,000 in India, and a vast programme in China which envisages between 150,000 and 300,000 units.

The philosophy behind this globalisation of Fiat-Auto is expressed by Razelli as: "For real success, it's necessary to take appreciable risks; starting at 10,000 to 20,000 units a year is never going to put you into a leading place in the local market. We can only the big projects of between 100,000 and 150,000 by using the 'fabbrica integrata' concept as we have at Melfi, with the assembly plant and a group of suppliers on the same site."

1995 has confirmed the long-awaited miracle in Turin, but it's not the first time Fiat has been on the crest of the wave. Back in the mid-Seventies, the group was No 1 in Europe, with a 15% share of total sales against the 11.3% achieved in mid-1995 with more brands. If Fiat has remained strong because of its exceptional European-based corporate culture, it must not be forgotten that currency fluctuations could destabilise Italy tomorrow and reverse the advantages held today. And although the investigations and incriminations of the 'mani pulite' regime have become less obvious, there still remains one major consideration for Fiat's future: who will be the next in the Agnelli dynasty. The 'Fabbrica Italiana di Automobili Torino', which was formed on July 11, 1899, has only known five presidents. The current incumbent, Avvocato Gianni Agnelli (grandson of Senator Giovanni Agnelli), has been in place since 1966, and is 74 years old. His term, together with that of the powerful and ambitious Cesare Romiti, the 71-year-old number two of the group, expires in mid-1996. If the important Mediobanca group has its way, financier Romiti will take over sole control in Turin; the family, it is said have other ideas. They would prefer another Agnelli, the 31-year-old Giovannino Agnelli, another heir of the Piaggio motorcycle business and the son of Umberto, Gianni's brother. As things stand at the moment, only one thing is certain; that whoever is installed as president, be it on a permanent or a temporary basis, Paolo Cantarella, head of the automotive business and the man behind the renaissance in Fiat's products, will take over as the second most-important man in the group.

Spain and Portugal – an era's end?

There was a time when Spain and Portugal, both on a tide of growth, were seen as the 'Korea of Europe'. The image brought a wave of investment in their automobile industry, with Renault, Peugeot, Citroen, Ford, GM-Opel, VAG wearing the skin of SEAT, and a group of Japanese led by Nissan. Now, however, things have changed, with vehicle production having reached 1,890,000 in 1993 and 2,267,000 in 1994. There has been a constant 'dialogue' between VAG and the Catalan authorities about how much government aid is needed to put the SEAT operation back on its financial feet. It ha reached the stage where the European Commission in Brussels has started an inquiry into the question of whether the aid – of almost $500 million – breaches European Union competition laws.

Juan Llorens, the Catalan who is president of SEAT, has refused to accept that VAG's policy towards its Spanish operation is anything less than positive. Seat continued to make a loss (of $250 million – despite $120 million in 'tax credits') in 1994 even though it sold its Pamplona plant for $160,000,000 and its commercial operations for $65,000,000. After negotiations over the cutting of 1200 jobs, Llorens hoped that SEAT would sell 360,000 vehicles (an increase of 6%) in 1995 and come back into profit in 1996 as a result of increasing export sales from 70% to a record 75% and cutting back considerably on purchases made in DM. There was, however, no progress on the plan to build a 'peoples car' in Shanghai on the basis of the Cordoba.

Another surprise development in Spain during 1995 was the divorce between Santana (which had started as an assembler of Land Rovers) and its partner Suzuki, which had seen local manufacture of Samurai and Vitara 4x4's. After a year of searching for someone to take over its partnership with the Andalusian company, Suzuki finally sold its 83.7 shareholding to SOPREA, a Spanish state organisation.

Bravo and Brava are two extremely attractive new Fiat saloons which replace the Tipo. Unfortunately, there is more difference between the five-door Brava and the three-door Bravo (above) than there is between their names. Only Fiat people will be able to remember which is which. After the unhappy break-up between Rover and Honda in 1994, the two continue to drift apart. The Rover 400 (left) is the last product of their collaboration. Dimensionally identical to the Civic built by Honda in Britain, it has styling tweaks and a 1.4-litre Rover K Series engine.

Under the terms of the agreement, the Linares plant will continue to build 4x4 Suzukis for five more years, while financial involvement will come either from Libyan and Kuwaiti sources who are looking to invest some $40 million, or SsangYong, who are looking for a European manufacturing plant.

Ford, which introduced a new version of the Fiesta at the end of 1995, announced an investment of $250,000,000 in Valencia for production of 200,000 units per year of the Ka 'sub-B' minicar. FASA-Renault came out of the red with a $36,000,000 profit which came from internal productivity and the Spanish government's 'Renove' plan which, like the French programme, offered cash incentives ($800 in this case) to turn in 'old cars for new'.

Things were not going so well for Nissan Motor Iberica, in spite of the work they were doing for Ford in producing the Terrano II 4x4 as the Maverick. The Japanese parent, like Volkswagen, called on the Spanish state for aid in a programme which called for Nissan to invest $800,000,000 after cutting 1200 jobs from a total of 7000.

In Portugal, the same manufacturer/government dialogue was going on between Renault-Portuguesa and Lisbon on the subject of the 'mothballing', if not closure, of the company's Setubal factory. Production had fallen from 240 cars a day in 1993 to 100 by mid-'95, and the outlook was not good, for the Clio range is due to cease in 1996. However, thanks to the Ford/VW joint MPV enterprise which is already building the Ford Galaxy and the VW Sharan – soon to be joined by the SEAT Alhambra – Portugal has strengthened its position as a European manufacturing base. Unfortunately the Palmela plant, opened in April 1995 and capable of building 180,000 MPV's annually, has become a source of discord between Ford and VW. There were arguments about build quality, and the European launch of the two vehicles was put back to the autumn.

Volvo regains its balance

For some years now, the Scandinavian countries have been going through a crisis in the automobile business, and sales – of 323,105 in 1993 and 448,225 in 1994 – represented only around 3% of the European total. In 1995, as Sweden and Finland, together with Austria, joined the European Union, the tide appears to have turned. First quarter sales increases were as follows: Finland +20%, Norway +12%, Sweden +7% and Denmark +7%. From an industry point of view, the big question was how Volvio would get on after the last-minute break-off of the marriage with Renault. The figures tell a happy story – in the first half of 1995 Volvo sales in the US were up 14% in a market which had increased by just 1.2%; in Japan, where overall sales increased by 5.5%, Volvo sold 25% more cars, and in Europe, where total sales were up only 1.4%, Volvo sales increased by 11%. The results surprised many industry observers, particularly in view of the fact that the S4, the new medium-size car produced as a joint-venture with Mitsubishi in Holland, did not go into production until the latter part of the year. Volvo executives were unanimous in attributing the success to the company's return to concentrating on Europe, after 30 years of spreading its resources too widely and too thinly across the world. In addition to Sweden, Volvo now has plants in Belgium, Holland and Scotland, and in future will produce two-thirds of its cars and a third of its trucks (which includes the DAF Trucks business) will be built outside the home country. The majority of the car capacity will, of course, come from the joint venture between Volvo, Mitsubishi and the Dutch government at Born in Holland.

The European tendencies of the Swedish group are underlined by the announcement of a $650,000,000 European investment programme which will cover both passenger cars and trucks. The news came in the wake of 1994 profits of $2.25 billion, representing a record 10.5% of turnover, and Volvo's move into second place behind Mercedes-Benz in the truck market. The new policy is a complete turnaround from the programme of diversification led by former president Pehr-Gustav Gyllenhammar, the architect of the link with Renault. By the end of 1996 Volvo will have divested all its outside interests – its associated debt is already cleared – including the share in BCP, the giant food and agriculture company. By the end of 1995, Volvo was expecting to have sold 250,000 units in Europe, 100,000 in the USA, and 25,000 in Japan. The Volvo train is back on the tracks, but those tracks are being laid by the automobile division, with a target

---

EUROPE'S NEW CARS IN 1995

Alfa Romeo 146
Audi A4 Avant, Audi A8 3,7
Audi Coupé/Cabriolet TDi
BMW 3 Touring, BMW M3 3,2
BMW 728i, BMW 5-Series, BMW Z3
Bentley Azure
Caterham 21
Citroën Xantia Activa Turbo, Citroën Xantia Estate
Ferrari F50
Fiat Barchetta, Fiat Brava, Fiat Bravo
Ford Fiesta 96, Ford Galaxy
Jaguar XJ12/XJ LWB, Daimler Double-Six/LWD
Lada 110
Lancia Y
Lotus Elise
MG
Mercedes C 250 TD, Mercedes C Kompressor
Mercedes E Class
Opel Vectra
Peugeot 406
Renault Laguna Estate, Renault Mégane 3-door and coupé, Renault-Sport Spider
Rover 200 and Rover 400
Seat Alhambra, Seat Cordoba 2-door
Skoda Felicia Estate
VW Golf Cabrio TDi, VW Golf Syncro
VW Polo Classic, VW Polo D, VW Sharan
Volvo S4

---

of around 500,000 units a year by the end of the century.

Sweden's other manufacturer, Saab, now lives completely within the orbit of General Motors. It continued the progress it started with the new 9000 by coming out of five years of red ink and reporting a profit of $90,000,000 to close a period which saw total losses of $1.6 billion. The success came mainly on the back of increased sales in the USA, where in 1994 Saab sold 21,500 cars from a world total of 88,700 (60% of which were 900's). However, Saab has only two ranges, the 900 and the 9000, and they are too close together in the market for the tastes of GM (although total sales for 1995 were targeted in 1995). Saab needs a third model, and if it is to be positioned at the top end of the market, making Saab a 'European Cadillac', it will need big investments.

INTERNATIONAL OVERVIEW

HOW FAR CAN KOREA GO?

JACQUES FARENC

In 1980, South Korea's automobile production totalled 123,000 vehicles; in 1994, it was 2.3 million. The aim is to become the world's fourth largest producer by the year 2000, and there is little doubt that the "Land of the Morning Calm" has aggressive economic intentions.

The history of South Korea, which was created in 1948 by dividing the Korean peninsula into two countries, based on the Russian-occupied north and American-occupied south, is influenced by two events: the end of the Korean War, in 1953, and the start of the country's economic growth, in the Sixties. That growth has continued almost without interruption, and has encompassed textiles, automobile production, shipbuilding, petrochemicals and the manufacture of iron and steel in addition to other major enterprises such as cement and electronics.

In 1980, South Korea's motor vehicle production numbered 57,000 cars and 66,000 trucks and busses. In the same year, Western Europe's motor industry, on a roll which had been slowed only by the fuel crisis of 1973, turned out some 10,352,000 private cars. Fourteen years later, Korea's big four manufacturers produced a total of 2,312,000 vehicles; 1,806,000 of these were passenger cars, representing a more than thirtyfold increase. In the same period, Western Europe's car production had risen to 12,779,000, an increase of just 24% over the same period. In France, one of the bastions of car production, the numbers had risen less than 8%, from 2,938,000 to 3,175,000. In 1980, Korea had manufactured just 0.2% of the world's cars – in 1994 that figure had risen to 5.1%. In 1980, France produced fifty-two cars for every one built in Korea; by 1994 that proportion had fallen to just 1.8:1 in favour of the European country. One might well ask just how far this sleeping tiger can go. Despite a recent change of government, the predominantly young Korean population of 45 million has remained hermetically sealed from the Communist North during its economic revolution. As a result of the explosive growth of the automobile industry, the number of inhabitants per car has fallen from 150 in 1980 to 7 in 1993. The growth has been entirely home-produced, for imported cars are not welcome in the country. Nevertheless, despite the lack of overseas input, Korea's roads are stretched to capacity – Seoul is subject to an almost permanent traffic-jam between eight in the morning and ten at night.

In 1980, registrations of private cars in Korea were less than 225,000, but by 1994 the figure had risen to 1,140,000, comparing favourably with that of France, a much richer country with a comparable total population, which had just 800,000 more. Korea's contribution to its own motorisation is shown by the export figures. Although they have grown enormously in numbers between 1980 and 1994 (14,133 to 648,35 respectively), they have not shown a vast expansion in percentage terms, having risen from 25% 0f total production in 1908 to some 36% in 1994. France, by comparison, exports 55% of its car production to its European partners.

Socially, Korea went through one of its most difficult periods in 1987 and '88 when huge public demonstrations preceded the hosting of the Olympic Games. Since then, salaries – which had previously been minuscule – have grown steadily, at a rate of 15 to 20 percent a year. Although the rises started at a very low level, their scale has had an effect on Korea's ability to compete on an international scale. Evidence of the country's uncertain financial policies is the fact that in 1990 Korea's balance of payment went into the red for the first time since the Fifties, and foreign debt has continued to baloon since then. In 1991, it was some $12.5 billion. Inflation has also begun to take off, reaching 10% in 1991, and prices have naturally risen in its wake. For the foreign visitor to Seoul, there is no better measure of inflation than the price of the Oriental speciality of a shirt, made-to-measure in a few hours. In 1987, a traveler would pay $10 for such a garment; in 1995 it cost $60. In short, salary increases between 1984 and 1994 have far out-

The Hyundai Lantra, Korea's second best-selling car (165,000 units in 1994), is number one in the country's export charts, with 197,000 cars having been sent abroad in the same year. The conventional three-box, four-door, Lantra has evolved into this new model (left), known as the Avante in Korea and now available in estate car form. It continues to be known as the Lantra in Europe.

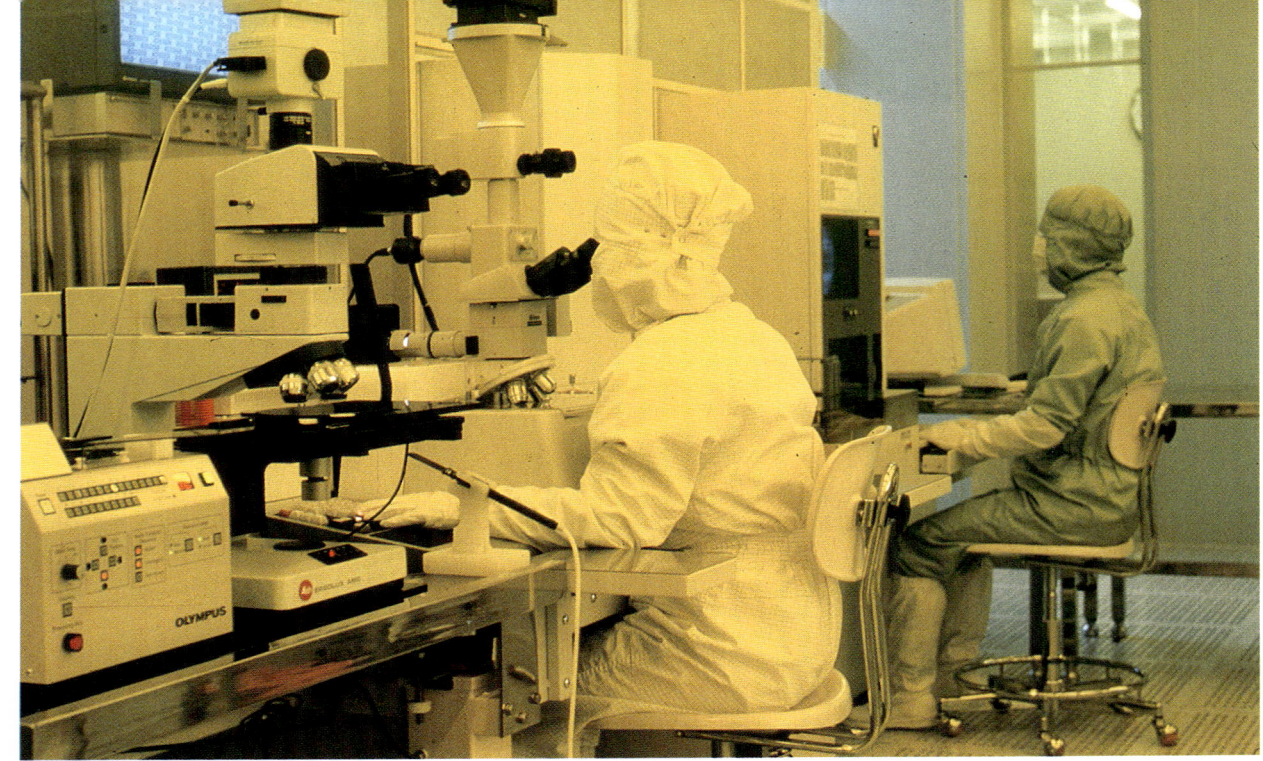

The giant Korean mega-groups, the chaebols, are present in all areas of business and industry, from the biggest supertankers to the smallest microchips, as these two differing illustrations of Hyundai's manufacturing activities show.

The motive power for Hyundai-built ships comes from engines which make car power-units seem microscopic (above). Up to 18 meters (60ft) high, they produce as much as 70,000hp at 110rpm!

stripped industry's improvements in productivity, while the decrease in the official working week, from 65 hours in 1980 to 48 at the beginning of the Nineties, has not helped.

The country's current five-year plan, running from 1993 to 1998, aims to slow down the economy and bring inflation under control, with a target of 3% by 1998, with increased personal taxation as part of the formula. With growth slowed to 5% in 1993, inflation was down to 8% in 1994, but a good export performance ($96.2 billion in 1994) was still not sufficient to balance the trade gap due to imports of $102.3 billion. The government's policy was to cut the deficit of $6 billion to $3 billion in 1994.

Despite an application of the economic brakes, automobile production has continued to rise, with total production of cars and light and heavy commercial vehicles increasing from 2,050,000 in 1993 to 2,312,000 in 1994, a growth of almost 13%. During the same period, vehicle exports rose 15.7%, from 638,000 to 738,000, despite strong domestic demand. Korea's rocketing standard of living, which has seen GNP per inhabitant rise by 395% since 1980, has naturally fuelled local demand for cars, which has grown by some 2500% over the same period.

The effect on Korea's automobile industry has naturally been immense. Groups which were already strong, like Hyundai and Kia-Asia, have expanded greatly, while Daewoo, originally a parts sub-contractor to GM and effectively absent from the market in 1980, manufactured almost 350,000 vehicles in 1994. These three groups, plus SsangYong, take a very dim view of the plans for automobile production announced by Samsung, one of the country's major conglomerates – or 'chaebols', as they are known in Korean – which operate in a wide range of areas. The electronics group has allied itself with Nissan, who will provide technical assistance for a project which has production targets of over half a million vehicles a year by the early years of the next century. The competition's fears are fuelled by the knowledge that Samsung can benefit from 'policy loans', low-interest loans which are only repayable if the project is successful and which amount to a form of hidden subsidy.

Of the four existing Korean motor industry groups, it is SsangYong, the smallest, which currently has the

Formed in 1973, the shipbuilding arm of Hyundai is now the largest producer in the world and represents 25% of the chaebol's turnover.

An importer's nightmare

South Korea's national vehicle park has already passed the seven million mark, and it is growing at the rate of 8 to 10% per year; however, only a minute quantity of those cars are imported, thanks to an effective network of invisible barriers. Officially, the market has been open to foreign manufacturers since 1987, when 11 imported cars – 10 of them Mercedes – were sold in Korea. There is a strong sense of nationalism in the country, so foreign products start at a disadvantage, but natural disinclination to buy imports is backed up by some punitive tax laws. For instance, since foreign cars are classed as luxury goods, any Korean impetuous enough to buy one can expect to have his tax returns carefully scrutinised. On the other hand, although import duties are a not excessive, at 8%, other taxes are incurred which hoist the selling price of an imported car to something like three times the cost of its 'Made in Korea' equivalent.

Among the few vehicles which go into the land of the morning calm, the European contingent is headed, not surprisingly, by the Germans, who sold 900 cars in 1994. France, in the form of Peugeot and Citroen, sold around 250, while Britain exported a mere handful, mainly luxury cars including 19 Jaguars. By comparison, 15,681 Korean cars and 4x4s were registered in Britain during the first six months of 1995.

---

most ambitious plans. This situation is thanks to its position as the favoured far-Eastern partner of Mercedes-Benz. SsangYong Motors was founded in 1954 and has previously specialised in commercial and 4x4 vehicles. The company started its operations by assembling the Korando, a licence-built version of the Jeep CJ6. In more recent years, it took an 80% stake in Panther Cars, the British specialist manufacturer. In 1992, Mercedes-Benz AG took a 5% stake in SsangYong, with an option to buy a further 5% at a later date. As a result of the Mercedes deal, SsangYong is contracted to produce 50,000 MB 100 trucks and an additional 80,000 diesel power units in 1995. These figures will rise to 100,000 and 140,000 respectively by the year 2000, with most of the diesels earmarked for SsangYong's own Musso luxury 4x4. A second joint venture between Mercedes and its Korean partners, in which the German firm has a 51% share, is for the production of the 'V car', a Series E-size saloon to be built and badged by SsangYong. The president of SsangYong's automobile company, Hyoung Dong Cha, is quick to point out that the SsangYong group is the world's largest cement producer and Korea's fourth-largest chaebol, comprising 25 companies employing 24,000 people and with a turnover of $20 billion. "Automobiles are an essential aspect of the group's development", he told us. "In 1986, when the business really started, we produced 5759 vehicles; in 1994 we produced 46,375, representing an eightfold increase in eight years. We expect great things from our co-operation with Mercedes, in terms of both the trucks and the V car, which by 1998 we will be building at the rate of 50,000 units per year."

In view of the fact that in 1994 SsangYong was producing around of 200 vehicles per day, we asked what future plans held. "In five years", Hyoung Dong Cha responded, "we shall have built up to 1500 a day, with an annual target of over 400,000, almost 500,000, vehicles. By 1996, SsangYong will have a presence in all the European markets, with a new short wheelbase 4x4 which will be particularly suited to European conditions and needs."

Hyundai was unknown as a car maker until the early Seventies, when the company, which had bought in British know-how to establish itself in the automobile industry, introduced the Pony. Launched in 1974, on the home market, the small saloon was first exported in 1976, to South America. By 1980, Hyundai was building 70,000 vehicles of all types, and by 1994 that figure had risen to 1,135,000, a sixteenfold increase for the second-largest chaebol in Korea. The world's largest shipbuilder, Hyundai comprises 40 companies, which provide employment for 180,000 people and have an annual turnover of $60 billion.

Despite being just a part of a country artificially split into two, South Korea (population 45 million) has grown into the 13th-largest industrial power in the world. Sung Won Chon, president of Hyundai Motor Co., echoes the thoughts of the other local manufacturers when he says: "Today, the Korean motor industry has truly become a major force, able to stand on its own feet." The independence is not only financial; it is also in the realm of technology, where Hyundai can now manage without its 'tutor', Mitsubishi. "After designing our first 'Alpha' multivalve engine in 1991", the Hyundai president continues, "we developed our new Accent range completely in-house." Speaking of investment, he confirmed that Hyundai will spend $7 billion between 1995 and 1998, on new factories and new products. "Our research and development activity," he explained, "which takes place in three locations across the world and employs 8500 technicians, will benefit from record investment, which will rise from the 4.5% of turnover at which it currently stands to 7%."

President Chon made no comment on the fact that Hyundai's Canadian factory, designed to produce 100,000 cars a year by the late Eighties, had only 14,000 come off the lines in 1992, but he still sees exports as a priority. "We were the first to sell cars outside Korea", he said, "and we exported more than 400,000 in 1994." 125,000 of these went to Europe, marking a 37% rise over the figure for 1993. Hyundai's export targets are even higher, however, with 980,000 vehicles, 190,000 of them for Europe, foreseen by the year 2000.

Where, we asked the president, will Hyundai be on a global scale by then? "In 1991", he responded, "Korea was the world's tenth largest vehicle manufacturing country. By 2000, we should be fourth. Our 'GT-10' plan has the aim of putting Hyundai among the world's top ten constructors, and we are engaged in building three new factories to bring our capacity to

Despite local publicity campaigns like this for the Xantia, Peugeot/Citroen have not made much impact on the Korean market. Of the 244 Peugeots and Citroens registered there in 1994, it is said that only 29 were actually invoiced and paid for.

Ulrich Bez (below) joined the Porsche design department in 1972, and in 1982 left to join BMW as director of vehicle development.

He returned to Porsche in 1988 as a member of the board responsible for research and motor sport. He started working for Daewoo as a consultant in 1991, and in 1993 joined the company as vice-president in charge of new product development.

Woo Chong Kim, the head of Daewoo, is a 59-year-old with exceptional energy and rare charisma. Mr Kim originally founded Daewoo as a textile factory in 1967 – it is now one of Korea's biggest chaebols, with a turnover of over $40 billion. No wonder he made the cover of 'Fortune'.

It's all a question of size, and some would say that Korea's chaebol-based motor manufacturers aim to overshadow the competition as this super-tanker overshadows everything around it. Built by Daewoo, this 300,000-ton leviathan is for Shell, who paid around $100,000,000 – the cost of 10,000 Daewoo Nexia saloons – for it. The car on the floor of the dry-dock – the largest in the world – gives scale to the ship and to the most powerful crane ever built, on the left-hand side of the picture.

2.3 million vehicles a year by 2000; that will give us 4% of the total world capacity."

While Hyundai has ambitions of total independece, Kia – which also owns the Asia 4x4 and truck brand – remains more discreet about such a development. The reason is that Korea's second-largest constructor, which has just celebrated its half-century, has a number of overseas investors. Ford is the largest, with 10% of the equity, followed by Mazda (8%) and the Japanese group C. Itoh (2%). Kia's cars, originally designed by the company, are now Mazda-Ford derivatives. The company plays a large part in Ford's home-market strategy, supplying US Ford dealers with small cars. The Kia-Ford link started with the Festiva, a version of the Mazda 121 sold as the Pride in Korea, which has been replaced since 1993 by the slightly-larger Aspire, sold on the Korean domestic market as the Kia Avella.

Kia suffered serious financial losses (some 1.5% of turnover) in 1994 after paying for expansion of its facilities in Europe and the US. 1994 production of 620,000 vehicles, just 3.3% up on the previous year's, rose to 675,000 when Asia products were included, but the figures still kept Kia firmly in second place behind Hyundai, which produced almost twice as many vehicles.

Kia's president, Sung Hon Kim, sees future priorities directed towards sales in Europe and the United States, "...with ranges specially adapted to these markets – a potential of almost 30 million vehicles – because the Korean market is fast approaching saturation-point". He sums up the company's objectives, not counting the Asia brand, as: "820,000 units in 1995 – an increase of 33% – and we should pass the million mark in 1996. We can do it, because we are commercially active in more than 100 countries".

Having sold 26,000 vehicles in Europe in 1994, Kia has a target of 36,000 for 1995 thanks to its agreement with the German coachbuilder Karmann. Karmann built 9000 Sportage off-roaders in 1994, and with the German company's input Kia is counting on doubling its European sales in 1996. Nevertheless, Samsung's future plans worry Sung Hon Kim: "For the moment, our plans are not in danger," he said, "but ten years down the road Samsung has to be seen as a force to be reckoned with in the Korean market." The talk in

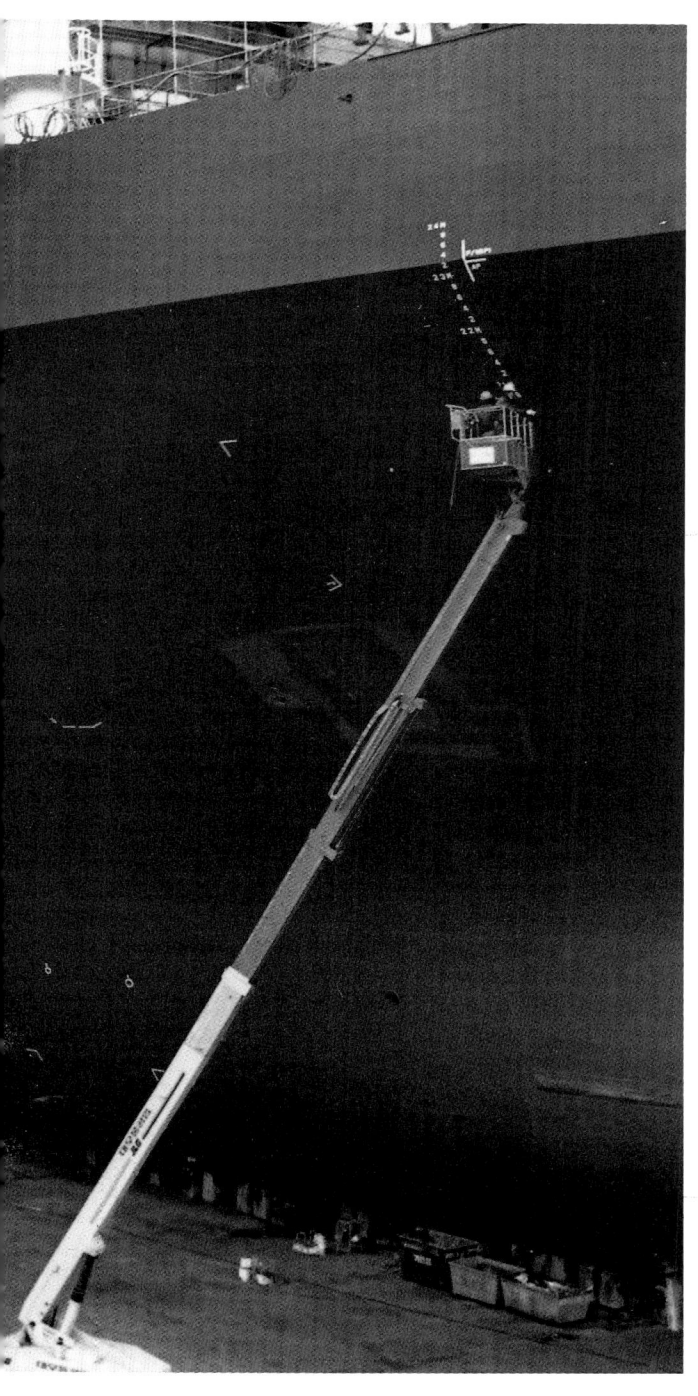

Korean vehicle production by make								
	1980	1985	1990	1991	1992	1993	1994	Growth, 1980/1994
Hyundai								
Total Production	70051	240755	676067	767090	859250	996140	1174041	+1576%
Passenger cars	52961	225970	557683	641350	701654	774949	896592	+1593%
Kia								
Total Production	36039	84931	396325	425296	502227	599904	619875	+1620%
Passenger cars	4753	0	3722	5562	7518	9910	4902	+9110%
Asia								
Total Production	2129	3480	25374	28020	51553	55492	55586	+2510%
Passenger cars	257	0	3722	5562	7518	9910	4902	+1807%
Daewoo								
Total Production	20328	44935	201035	203794	179020	375686	413744	+1935%
Passenger cars	8888	36805	184795	191462	172484	347390	385205	+4234%
SsangYong								
Total Production	4454	3998	22148	24663	21439	22075	46375	+941%
Passenger cars	2158	1683	21426	20894	19057	19256	41829	+1838%

Note: In 1994, production figures of 114,509 from Daewoo Ship Building and Hyundai Precision should be added to the total.

Seoul is that Kia is the most vulnerable to Samsung's attack on the market.

Daewoo is a chaebol which started in textiles and expanded into shipbuilding, where its production capacity of one new ship every nine days puts it in second place behind Hyundai. Driven by its founder and president, Kim Woo Chong, it started in the automobile sector in the late Seventies. Thanks to an accord with GM, it made great strides during the Eighties, manufacturing components as a sub-contractor and assembling versions of the Opel Rekord and Kadett, notably the version of the 1984 Kadett sold in the USA as the Pontiac Le Mans and Racer.

Daewoo produced 340,000 vehicles in 1994, making it Korea's third-largest constructor, but with the end of the links to GM, it is currently restructuring. Between 1996 and 1998 it will completely replace its GM-sourced range with its opwn designs. According to Ulrich Bez, the German who left BMW to head Daewoo's R&D operations, this will mean more than ten new models, from a sub-B mini to a luxury limousine, and will include MPV models. To satisfy local demand, Daewoo has signed a licence agreement with Honda under which it will build the Legend saloon as the Daewoo Arcadia for Korea.

Daewoo projects 809,000 vehicles for 1995, and with the new range in sight, President Kim has expansive plans for the year 2000. "Two million vehicles", he confidently predicts, "with the unique feature that more than half of them will be built outside Korea". Daewoo policy is to expand by what it considers small steps (which would be giant strides for many of its competitors) in the smaller Asian countries and Eastern Europe. This policy is put ahead of expansion in the USA, where Daewoo considers the market to be saturated. "Where there are risks, there is money to be made" is a favourite saying of President Kim. In Europe, Daewoo is supporting its expansion by a major R&D operation, based on doubling the size and workforce of the facility it bought from the British design consultancy IAD when the latter company met financial problems. It has also signed a joint-venture agreement with the Romanian company Automobile-Craïova, which was formerly associated with Citroen in the production of the Oltcit-Axel. The factory is to be renovated with the aim of producing 200,000 Daewoos by the end of 1996. Further examples of this aggressive policy of overseas development are Daewoo's plans in Uzbekistan (200,000 vehicles a year, operational in early 1996), Iran (50,000), the Philippines (20,000), Vietnam, (10,000), India (150,000, in association with DMC, the local Toyota licencee), China (300,000 with First Automobile Works), and Mexico (100,000). Other, post-1999, projects are said to be in Russia and even in Libya.

At the moment, Europe is Daewoo's prime target, with cars built in low labour-cost Eastern facilities, but using novel western selling techniques. In Britain, the company has gone against all motor trade traditions by selling direct to the public rather than through dealers and quoting a fixed, no-haggling, price which includes all servicing and consumables for three years. Using such techniques, by the end of the century Daewoo expects to be selling 200,000 cars a year across Europe.

The Samsung group, Korea's second-largest chaebol, employs 190,000 people and has a turnover of $56 billion, and in 1994 it signed a technical co-operation agreement with Japan's Nissan which foresees automobile production beginning in 1998. The result of

From top to bottom: The Accent (1) is Hyundai's entry-level saloon, while the Lantra (2) is aimed at the heart of Europe's family-car market, competing with the Golf, Astra, Escort and Peugeot 309 among others. The Sonata (3), is a Scorpio-sized car at a Mondeo-sized price, while the Scoupe (4) is a niche-market coupé which utilises Hyundai's 166hp, 12-valve, four-cylinder, Alpha power-unit, which was designed in-house. Kia, aligned with Mazda and Ford, has entered the 4x4 market with the Sportage (5). This three or five-doored sport utility is built in Germany by Karmann, making it the first Korean vehicle to be built in Europe. The Sephia (6) is available in 3,4 and 5-door versions and is conceived as a competitor for the Golf. In Europe, however, it sells for Polo prices. The latest Korean entry into Europe, Daewoo, has broken off its relationship with GM, but the remains of the link show in the company's products. The Nexia saloon (7) and hatchback (8) are based on the old Opel Kadett, but that did not depress sales when they were launched in Europe in 1995. In some countries Daewoo sells on low prices, but in Britain it caused a stir by selling direct from company-owned outlets at a 'no haggling' price which covered three years' free servicing. Both the Nexia and the Opel Vectra-based Espero (9) sold well under the new policy, but sceptics say it will take longer to assess the long-term prospects for going it alone without the dealers. Another 1995 newcomer to Europe was SsangYong, Korea's smallest manufacturer. The Musso luxury 4x4 (10) found ready sales by offering Range Rover size, smooth European styling and a Mercedes power-unit – all at appreciably less than Discovery prices.

the link-up was to put the four other Korean manufacturers on their guard; according to some observers the new operation could destabilise the whole Korean motor industry.

Politically, the move seems to have met with the approval, and Korea's President, Kim Young Sam, appears to be in favour of it. It will, however, require a complete reorganisation of the motor industry's suppliers, and will lead to increased specialisation among the manufacturers themselves. Samsung has already recruited 300 engineers from its competitors, including Myong Han, the man who built up Hyundai's automobile division.

The new enterprise will have cost Samsung $6 billion by the end of 1998, when it expects to be able to produce 50,000 vehicles per year. In addition to the capital investment, the company will have to pay Nissan between 1.6 and 1.9% of the value of each vehicle sold in royalties; this is in addition to the $20 million paid to the No. 2 Japanese constructor for its technical assistance. If Samsung holds out against a competition which is united against it, Korea's fifth player expects to be capable of producing 500,000 vehicles a year within a couple of years of the dawn of the next century.

If one is to believe the president of Hyundai Motors, S.W. Chon, South Korea will be the world's fourth largest vehicle manufacturing country by the year 2000, a position which foresees a total production of some 9 million units. But if one gives credibility to the statements of the heads of the four Korean groups – and then adds in the forecasts of the would-be fifth – one soon arrives at a total of 6.5 million units and a total production comparable with that of the current output of General Motors. In short, the ambitions of the Koreans know no bounds. This is something which was already clear, but it also becomes obvious that they are decidedly optimistic, and share a vision which many European observers consider Utopian. However, it must be remembered that when they go on the offensive, it is not just with the resources of the vehicle constructor, but with all the backing of the whole chaebol, which can be up to ten times greater in size.

There is now a less utopian view of reunification with Communist North Korea, a state of affairs brought about by seeing the problems which have come in the train of the absorbtion of the GDR into Federal Germany.

The days of mass-production of mediocre cars at cheap prices is now over, and will take a little time to overcome that bad reputation. Korea, having come to grips with the problem of inflatinary wage-rises, is now working on resolving problems of vehicle cost by widening its pool of sub-contractors to include emerging Arian countries like Vietnam. Korean industry is also working hard to build up the high-tech engineering resources which will make it independent of Japan, the country's age-old enemy.

The high-cost yen has helped the Korean won to remain competitive, but in the world of the automobile, victory will go to the competitor which is successful in the old Middle empire. When one remembers that the Chinese and the Koreans share the same racial roots, and that there is in China a deep-seated dislike of the Japanese, it seems that Korea starts at an advantage. But the forthcoming battle will be fought on the grounds of innovation and quality, and it will need to attract foreign investors who will not be scared off by the possibility of the theft of technology and intellectual property.

AESTHETICS OF THE MECHANISM

LOOKING GOOD UNDER THE HOOD

For many an enthusiast, there is no automobile engine quite so beautiful as those fitted to Bugatti cars during the twenty years between the two World Wars. Geometrically pure in form and beautifully detailed, Bugatti engines had pride of place in bare, austere engine compartments unencumbered by the myriad accessories cars must accommodate today.

The Type 35, in various guises and displacements, was widely sold for both sports and racing purposes, and with its twin-cam development, the Type 51, it dominated racing in Europe for many years, with amateur drivers winning innumerable competitions, including such triumphs as private owner René Dreyfus taking the Grand Prix of Monaco in 1930. From its inception in 1924 to the demise of European racing in 1939, Bugatti racing car bodies always looked very much like that of the prototype 35, slim, elegant and ending in a vertical knife-edge.

Today's equivalent to that most successful of all Bugattis would probably be the Porsche 911 and its multiple variants. The basic car, from its first-ever motorsports win (GT class at the Targa Florio, with Jean-Claude Killy and Bernard Cahier) on through overall victories at Le Mans and Daytona in 935 form, has been *the* customer race car for the past thirty years, as Bugattis were in their time. The engine has grown from two liters to 3.6, and the power has gone well beyond 750bhp for the turbocharged racers. But when you open the engine hatch on the current Carrera, all you see is a collection of black boxes and one big cooling fan, sitting off-center in a dark hole of a compartment. You almost have to guess that you are looking at an engine. Nothing about the engine room is visually or esthetically stimulating, however, effective the engine may be. That packed compartment is the work of engineers – good ones – apparently bereft of any esthetic sensibility or concern.

It was engineers who created the underbonnet look of cars in the Twenties and Thirties, too. But sometimes, particularly in quality cars, they were concerned with esthetics as well as with functionality. Gabriel Voisin, whose cars were always quirky in concept and execution, put squared-up cast alloy covers over the top of his sleeve-valve engines, thereby hiding the sparkplugs and their associated wires, but there was never

ROBERT CUMBERFORD

Purity of line that transcends and indeed overcomes functionality was the hallmark of Ettore Bugatti's engine designs, never more beautifully expressed than in his classic Type 35 B racing car. The Roots blower was added to the more austere Type 35 to compete when rival makers achieved more power.

the same degree of care for finish that characterized Bugattis.

Perhaps the most impressive passenger car engine compartment in the Thirties was that of the mighty Duesenberg models J and SJ, with a huge seven-liter straight eight block, always painted a rather bright leaf green. Its twin cam covers were beautifully polished, as were the inlet manifolds, access plates and other aluminium alloy parts. Chromed exhaust pipes protruded through the right side of the bonnet on the supercharged cars, adding to the dazzling impression made when the bonnet was lifted. It was certainly the apogee of American underbonnet design, because nothing quite so elaborate has been done with the esthetics of the mechanical bits in the sixty-five years since. Cadillac did use porcelain enamel on the cylinder heads of its side-valve V-8, V-12 and V-16 engines in the Thirties, as did most of the other now-defunct U.S. quality car manufacturers, but looking at them today, one has no impression that any effort was expended to make engine compartments impressive to look at, in the way Duesenbergs were.

Indeed, as more and more functional elements were

The Porsche Carrera has one of the great engines of modern times, but you'd never know that from looking into the densely-packed cavern at the back of the car. None of the visual cues that explain the function of an engine are present, and the multiple black masses have no particular esthetic appeal, although no one can doubt their technical validity. In contrast, the massive twin-cam powerplant of the mighty SJ Duesenberg (right) is almost a three-dimensional diagram of how an Otto-cycle engine works. Every component is clearly delineated, and anyone familiar with the workings of engines can easily decipher how its elements function. The Duesenberg brothers, August and Fred, were deeply concerned that everything they designed be elegantly presentable, good to look at as well as correct for its function, so all alloy parts of the Lycoming-built 32-valve straight eight were beautifully polished.

Gabriel Voisin was an apostle of functionality, particularly in the architecture of his cars, but he was not above a bit of decoration at times. Cast covers on sleeve-valve Voisin engines hid spark plugs and wires, not rocker arms, making the engine look more like those of rival cars. Aeronautical origins of a firm that had built 10,000 airplanes before entering the automobile industry show in fine detailing, and in a studied indifference to the kind of polishing and finishing typical of Bugatti.

added to the engine bay, there tended to be an indifferent carelessness about how those elements were organized, whether in the smallest European economy car or the biggest American highway cruiser. For more than three decades, body styling modes preserved long high bonnets, which provided enormous amounts of empty space above the side-valve engines prevalent in low-priced European cars and most American models whatever their price. In many cars the engine itself was hardly visible with the bonnet open, because it actually sat below the wing valences. All that changed with the introduction of the Jaguar XK-120 at the end of the Forties. It had an extremely tall twin-cam engine which was a delight to see. Polished cam covers recalled the look of the Duesenberg, polished carburetors and stove-enameled exhaust manifolds gleamed in an engine compartment which seemed scarcely able to contain the big engine. It came so very close to the bonnet panel, that the engine itself seemed to leap upward, like the Jaguar's mascot itself, when the bonnet was lifted.

Cars had been steadily reduced in height for many years, but at around one-and-a-quarter meters (4ft), a practical, if not absolute, limit was reached in the Fifties. A sports car like the Jaguar or a monocoque saloon like the first Chevrolet Corvair tended to be of about equal height, and engines were not being made smaller, so some awareness that more easily seen engines should be made more attractive led to painted pressed-tin rocker covers being replaced by cast alloy parts that gave the impression of more substance. But little else was done to brighten up the visual aspect of the engine room.

A particularly unattractive setup was that of the Citroën DS-19, born forty years ago. With the addition of pumps, regulators, hoses, pipes, hydraulic accumulators and other never-before-seen elements running without seeming reason all around the compartment, with the spare wheel added to the underbonnet area, and fabric used for aerodynamic trunking filling up even more space with its alloy bonnet lifted, the car was a visual mess. Never mind that most of what was done made excellent sense; it looked awful, and was horrendously intimidating for mechanics. One wonders whether the car would have been more successful in the marketplace had its underbonnet area been arranged in a more orderly

Compared to the Buick Le Sabre using the same platform and body, the 1984 Cadillac DeVille has a rather messy and inelegant engine compartment – typical for American cars at that time – but it did pioneer color-coding to guide a person performing routine underbonnet servicing in finding the different fluid reservoirs, dipsticks and filler caps. The 4.1-liter V-8 engine, a curious blend of old and new techniques, had an aluminium block, iron heads and dispacement only half of preceding Cadillacs.

This is the engine compartment that inspired Harley Earl to want to redesign all General Motors underbonnet areas. For 1956 the Chevrolet Corvette, GM's fiberglass sports car, had been quite nicely and successfully restyled outside, but the engine compartment was essentially more of the same old American practice: no particular attention was paid to component layout, overall neatness or esthetic appeal. The Corvette had the dimensions of the Jaguar XK-120, but certainly not the underbonnet class.

and practical manner. One can even be permitted to wonder whether a more orderly arrangement might not have eliminated some of the teething problems right at the start. Today's hydraulically-suspended Citroëns probably provide owners the lowest-lifetime-cost, least troublesome suspension systems available, but the company still suffers from a reputation for complexity earned long ago.

In contrast to the DS, consider the under-bonnet layout of Toyota's first luxury model, the 1989 Lexus LS-400, with all its hydraulic lines manifolded neatly, following geometric paths along the firewall. Everyone who first beheld the V-8 installation was amazed at how fine it all seemed, how it visually promised what was later delivered: the best quality, lowest-service-cost luxury car on the market... *any* market.

At the end of the Sixties, engine compartment design was beginning to become really difficult for engineers. Certain items that had been optional add-ons on the most expensive cars became standard even on mid-range models. Pumps for steering assistance, for the circulation of air conditioning, refrigerant vacuum chambers for servo brakes, reservoirs and pumps for washer fluid, batteries, windscreen wiper motors and various other items had to be accommodated, and there wasn't much space left. Following the lead of the DS, many manufacturers had put spare wheels and tires beneath the bonnet. That was no longer feasible, so they were once again banished to the back or bottom of cars, often for space considerations in the form of temporary tires not suitable for speeds above 80kph.

The Seventies brought still more constraints to underbonnet design. Crash safety laws compelled longer noses to provide additional energy-absorbing materials, and strict emission requirements – starting in the United States but soon adopted in all the developed countries – added still more bulky components to the underbonnet mix. Carburetors, when they were still acceptable, got larger to accommodate emissions-control factors, and in many cases fuel injection became the only possible solution, a solution that added still more units under the skin. Then the near-universal adoption of MacPherson strut-type front suspension brought another pair of voluminous vertical cylinders into the engine space. If you look at some engine compartments today, you have the impression that a dropped wrench – even a nut or screw – would never fall out the bottom – things are too densely packed.

Then Mercedes engineers, reporting on their intensive crash safety researches, added another level of complexity to underbonnet design. They talked about the dangers of "stacking" hard components so that they became, in effect, battering rams once the front of the car hit an obstacle. And at that, with their conventional front-engine, rear-drive layout, Mercedes engineers had an easier time of it than those who adopted the Dante Giacosa-style mechanical layout, with the engine and gearbox in line athwart the nose. Alec Issigonis' brilliant Mini at the end of the Fifties had convinced the entire world that a greater percentage of a car's length should be given over the passengers and baggage, but his mechanical solutions were onerous for manufacturers. Once Giacosa's Autobianchi Primula, quickly followed by his Fiat 128, appeared with a simpler and cheaper driveline, the rush was on to convert the whole world's fleet of passenger cars to front drive.

In the Eighties, when General Motors, the world's

largest car manufacturer, finally embraced the Giacosa front-drive layout for its mainstream big sedans, we saw two distinct approaches to underbonnet design. Cadillac, GM's premier marque, was granted a brand new alloy V-8 for its first transverse mounting, but installed it in a traditional manner. The underbonnet area was not quite as messy as in the DS-19, but it was not far off. A tradional round air cleaner body was topped by a cheap pressed-tin wing nut, pipes and wires ran in the shortest paths possible from origin to destination, crossing each other on the way. The MacPherson strut spring seats were left with nuts and bolts exposed around the edges, and – ignominiously – tubular stabilizing struts with flattened ends more suitable to backyard lawn furniture than to an automobile self-proclaimed to be "the Standard of the World" ran diagonally along the sides of the compartment. The one innovative and very good feature was the provision of a color-coding chart printed on the air cleaner trunking identifying each of the six fluids needing verification and replenishment.

Using the same chassis platform and basic body shell, Buick – second marque in GM's rigidly-struc-

tured hierarchy – was stuck with an old iron V-6 with its design roots in the Forties for its Le Sabre. Making the best of it, Buick engineers gave the car a slide-forward and tip-up bonnet cribbed from Saab, and then turned their attention to cleaning up the near-antique pushrod engine and its surroundings. A pair of molded plastic caps covered the spring seats completely, the rocker arm covers were cast alloy, and the induction system in the vee was given a plastic cover carefully matched in color and texture to those alloy covers. The whole effect was stunning: orderly, efficient and practical. Cadillac had the better engine; Buick had the better car. For many years, Buick have been among the best American cars in the annual J.D. Power survey of initial quality, and it is not hard to think that squaring away the mechanical parts must have something to do with that result.

In the mid-Eighties, the Ford Motor Company was on the brink of total disaster. Its cars in the home market were rejected by consumers and critics alike. Management turned to designers and engineers and asked them to make the car they would like to own. The Taurus was the car they wanted, and it succeeded beyond the wildest hopes of the people who allowed it to be made. The underbonnet area was not a model of organization or beauty, but every item that needed regular attention was given a bright yellow cap or handle. It was not as sophisticated as the earlier Cadillac coding, but it was easier to understand, and the engineers had had the wit to put everything on a single plane beneath the bonnet, up high where it could readily be seen, was easy to reach and easy to find in the clutter.

Vehicle designers who *must* integrate function and appearance are the engineers who create motorcycles. So it is not surprising that BMW and Honda, leading manufacturers of both cars and bikes, should have made sensible efforts to put some of the motorcycle esthetic spirit into their cars. Open the bonnet of any current BMW, and you find that the top of the engine is cleanly designed, carrying the company logo and giving you the impression that the engineering that went into the powerplant was serious and dedicated to performance. Renault's odd little sports car, the Argos roadster seen at Geneva in 1994, incorporated engine styling into the overall theme. Even a relatively

André Lefebvre was chief engineer at Avions Voisin before he joined Citroën, where he designed the Traction Avant, the 2 CV and the DS-19. It is hard to believe that the same hand that created elegant simplicity for Voisin underbonnets was responsible for the rat's nest of pipes, wires, ducts and big mechanical elements in the 1955 DS-19 (above). Possibly the technical task of adapting aircraft-style hydraulic systems to the car was so great that there was no time to deal with underbonnet appearance. The 1.9-liter engine, carried over from the 1933 Traction Avant, sat well back in the underbonnet area. For the 1995 Pontiac Firebird, too, the appearance of the engine itself hardly matters: the 3.8-liter V-6 (left) is so far back beneath the windscreen that it is barely visible in the vast underbonnet space. The older car is a more impressive piece of engineering, but the Pontiac certainly is cleaner.

Jaguars were always about style, the company having begun making cars simply as a coachbuilder. So when it was decided, during long nights watching for air raids during WW II, that the company would make its own engine, there was as much concern for style

as for substance in creating the new powerplant. And they certainly got it right; the XK engines, stillborn four and six-cylinder alike, were superb in appearance, good enough to soldier on for almost forty years, and win Le Mans many times.

inexpensive car like the Ford Contour or Mondeo with V-6 engine has a power-plant with exotic-looking inlet tracts that once would have been seen only on a racing engine, so awareness is rising that making an engine look good is worthwhile.

Last April, I drove a Fiat Barchetta from Torino to Calino, where Fiat chief stylist Peter Davis was spending the weekend. He hadn't yet driven the new model he helped design, and I hadn't had a chance to discuss it with him in a relaxed atmosphere. After a tour around the village, he was in an expansive mood, and talked about the various problems his team had had in transforming the Punto platform into a sporting roadster. There were many, but when I noted the elegant fluting on the rubber air trunk across the front of the engine compartment and asked whether the stylists had run into any engineering resistance to their shaping that part, Davis said, "No, that was no problem at all. The engineers were glad to work with us on doing whatever we wanted. The only problem was that no time was blocked out in the program, so we all did what we could and that was that."

There is nothing really exceptional about the underbonnet look of the Barchetta. It is neat and reasonably tidy, no more than that. It could have been better, but it would almost certainly have been worse had the stylists not asked to be allowed to intervene, simply because of that lack of program time. There are those who claim that underbonnet appearance doesn't matter any more, because owners don't bother to open the engine compartment very often, but there is ample evidence that people are interested and intrigued by well-presented mechanicals. At the introduction of the Ferrari F-50 this year, I was struck by how many people remarked on the beauty of the flat-twelve engine, visible beneath transparent plastic panels and approved of its staying visible in service. There is no real problem in making all cars better looking under the bonnet. Engineers and stylists want to collaborate on the process of making their work look its best, and are more than willing to put in the effort. But accountants and manufacturing people have to get on board, as well, allocating working time to accomplish the task. It is not a short-term matter to totally transform the underbonnet look, as some

manufacturers still use engines basically designed in the Forties or Fifties. To do the job right, the architecture of engines must be considered from a visual as well as from an efficiency point of view, which means that it could be years before a unifying design principle can be embodied under the bonnet. It is fairly certain that the engines Ettore Bugatti made could have been a few percent lighter if he had agreed to make his castings less geometric on the outside, but if he had done so, would so many revere his work today? Bugatti could make that decision alone; today there are dozens of people expressing points of view, some embracing elegance, others economy above all else.

There is still a lot to be done on the service side. In 1970, Citroën grouped all the belt-driven accessory functions – steering, suspension and air-conditioning pumps, and the alternator – for the SM coupe on a bar across the front of the engine compartment, which at least gave the impression of rationality. Toyota, on its Previa van, which has its engine even more inaccessibly mounted than did the SM, does the same sort of trick, bringing accessories forward where

In reverting to an elongated powerplant – a straight eight made of two Neon engines – for its Atlantic show car at the Detroit show in January, Chrysler made sure that the engine was as nicely turned out and well presented as were engines in the classic period evoked by the car's retro-modern styling. A single-piece cam cover casting (opposite) hides the fact that there are separate blocks beneath the topside decoration. It's a beautiful engine, but one less convincing than the classic units that inspired it.

AS USUAL, EARLE WAS FIRST!

On a bright Sunday afternoon in June, 1956, I was riding in the first Corvette SR-2, a special version of the Chevrolet sports car that had been made for General Motors Styling Vice President Harley J. Earl's son, Jerry. Harley Earl himself was at the wheel. The car had run for the first time that morning, but its laps around the high speed bowl were interrupted abruptly when the throttle linkage broke. I had been allowed at the test session because I'd done all the body design work on the car, and after repairs were made, Mr. Earl invited me to ride from the Experimental Garage back down to the track with him. It was all slightly illicit, since Vice Presidents were forbidden to drive at the GM Proving Grounds. It made for a kind of intimacy that I'd never before had with the big boss, and never would again, so I remember it well.

"You know," said Earl, "it's too bad this car isn't good looking under the hood as it is outside. That's the next thing we're going to have to do, design the engine. Hell, *everything* under the hood." I thought about that brief commentary when, twenty-seven years later, I looked under the bonnet of the first big front-wheel drive Buick sedan. Its V-6 engine, if not exactly "designed," was certainly *decorated* as though the stylists had been at work.

The luxury car Toyota introduced in 1989 took many people by surprise: it was cheap, very good, with a degree of careful design that had not been seen for years, not least under the bonnet, where pipes were manifolded, run in clear patterns with precise matching bends and held in place with elegant little fixtures. For many, it was the care with which the engine compartment was done that convinced them of Lexus potential. Styling was copied from Mercedes, but the engine compartment was unique.

they can be seen and dealt with. It is to be hoped that by the year 2000, some manufacturers will have put all the fluid fillers and verification gauges in a central area in the engine compartment so that an under-bonnet check can be performed without the need to hunt for color-coded handles all over the meter-square compartment. In some cases, it may be possible to provide a single small hatch that can be used for regular checks, with the main bonnet panel, as in certain German cars, so made as to be able to be removed or swung past its normal hinge limits for major work. That has been the common practice on small piston-engine airplanes for a very long time, and it seems to work quite well from both practical and safety points of view.

Try to imagine what a true Bugatti sports car would be like today had Jean Bugatti not been killed in a stupid accident almost sixty years ago, and had *his* offspring inherited the family flair for design. Forget about the grotesque Italian "supercar" that carries the name, and think of a true spiritual successor to the Types 35 and 55, a serious rival for Porsche. It's a tempting fantasy to think that a car with the purity of the earlier models could exist, but it seems unlikely. Even if its engine block remained as rectangularly solid as a tombstone, it would scarcely matter: as in the Carrera, you would not really be able to see it, lost as it necessarily would be amongst the many appurtenances required in a modern car.

In truth, the better model for today's cars may be the Mercedes Diesel cars which have encapsulated the engine and its accessories in an acoustic shroud in order to reduce noise levels inside and out. It is a rare owner who takes the machinery-covering panels off a TV set, a computer, or any other device today; it is not necessary, and certainly not desirable. Perhaps one day our ordinary cars will finally become what legend suggested Rolls-Royce cars were: machines so good that the bonnet is sealed for life, only the factory possessing the key to open it and gaze upon mechanical beauty bare. It was never true for Rolls-Royce and it is not possible today, despite the advent in the U.S. of cars which require no service apart from oil changes for 100,000 miles (161,000 kilometers), but it certainly is imaginable for the future.

I'd miss the polished alloy, though. Wouldn't you?

OPEN-TOPPED FIATS

A SPORTY SUBCULTURE

Renowned world-wide as *the* industrial giant of typically Italian style and origin – yet sometimes underrated in terms of its detailed disciplines – Fiat is unique. It wasn't founded by a single inventor, pioneering automotive contraptions in a garden shed. Instead, Fiat emerged from the far-sighted minds of a group of *Torinese* – aristocrats and businessmen – who founded their conglomerate to produce automobiles as long as 97 years ago.

Under the charismatic leadership of Giovanni Agnelli, they took the task very seriously, expanding the Fabricca Italiana Automobile Torino to enormous prosperity within just a few years. Particularly after the Great War, Fiat became a serious player, and eventually a giant, within the ever-growing league of Europe's mass-producers of automobiles. Where possible, it diversified, from cars to aero-engines and rolling stock, and into merchandising and financing as well. Fiat was a company which made strong statements, ranging from the pioneering of real compact models to the construction of one of the world's most famous (and at the time most efficient) factories, the Lingotto

WIM OUDE WEERNINK

The Fiat 1100 TV convertible of 1955 and the Barchetta of 1995 may be separated by forty years, but they are similar in concept. The cockpit of the 1100 TV (left), with its column-mounted gearchange, is as typical of the Fifties as is its 1089cc four-cylinder engine (bottom). With two valves per cylinder, it produced 53hp; compare it with the transverse 1.8-litre four of the Barchetta (centre), which – thanks among other things to twice as many valves – develops 113hp. It's obvious that cockpit comfort has also improved in the interim.

The Balilla "Coppa d'Oro" (above) is the ancestor of all Fiat's sports cars; it is the root from which the sub-culture of affordable, open-topped, small to medium-sized performance cars has grown. A superb period piece, combining the fashion of the era with a car of the era (an 1100 TV) and a background which speaks of Fiat's industrial might, as transporter-loads of 600's (left) and 1100's (right) leave the Lingotto factory. The 1100 TV (below) could be equipped with a hardtop, which justified its Italian name of "Trasformabile". It was designed at Fiat by Luigi

Rapi, formerly with Isotta-Fraschini. The 1200 Cabriolet (right) launched at the Geneva Show in 1959, was designed at Pininfarina by Franco Martinengo. Based on the Fiat-OSCA 1500 GT which the styling studio had exhibited at an earlier Turin show, it was, like the 1100 TV, strictly a two-seater.

Plant which is now the home of the Turin Show. Even the way in which Fiat took on motor racing was ambitious, the company competing in Grand Prix racing with a full-backed factory team from 1902 until well into the Twenties. So fascinating and unique is Fiat's history that it can be ranked amongst those institutions of western industrialisation which have given rise to their own internal subcultures. One of Fiat's certainly applies to the culture of creating sporting automobiles for the masses, and the recent Fiat Barchetta is the latest heir to this tradition.

When Vincenzo Lancia, Felice Nazzaro and the other heroes of the early motor racing scene stormed their huge chain-driven four-cylinder Fiats along the dusty tracks of European Grand Prix circuits, the thought of affordable sports cars was still out of the question. But the continuous involvement of the Turin company with motor racing laid a firm base for a spirit of sporting cars and driving which was to become typical for the Italian car industry as a whole. Fiat filled the gap for the broad public after Vincenzo Lancia had started to produce his advanced (but not cheap) cars and Alfa Romeo of Milan had evolved into a full-

the new MGF means the rivalry is likely to continue. As no other model, the 508 C Balilla Sport (and the later ohv CS) sparked an ever-growing interest in Italian amateur motor racing between 1933 and 1937. Its simple and reliable mechanicals inspired an ever-increasing number of specialist engine tuners as well as coachbuilders. The nationalistic Italian movement of the pre-World War II years also played an important role. Italy's efforts in the world of automobiles – and motor racing in particular – brought speed records, overall wins (for Alfa Romeo), class wins (for the small Fiats) and exotic streamlined coachwork, applied in a quasi-scientific manner.

When Italy came out of the war with less damage than other European nations, a continuation of the pre-war regime was natural. By now, the typical Italian relationship between large manufacturers, engine tuners and coachbuilders had been well-established, and the industry knew it could rely on the link between mass-production and artisan craftsmanship. In turn, the specialist firms were assured continuous orders from Fiat, Lancia and Alfa Romeo who – more or less – had chosen their individual market approach.

The 1500 Cabriolet (above) completed the Fiat convertible range in 1960. It was distinguished from the 1200 by the large air-intake on the bonnet, a modified grille and 15-inch wheels, which covered disk brakes at the front. Under the bonnet was an in-line four which came from the OSCA company and produced 80hp (DIN) at 6000rpm.

blooded motor racing specialist, out of reach of the general public. The models filling that gap were the S and SS versions, based on mundane Fiat hardware of the Twenties and seldom bearing any relationship with the pure Fiat racers of the time.

The arrival of the new all-steel Fiat Balilla of 1932 should be considered the starting point for the sports subculture which has lived on at Fiat until today. One year after the introduction of the model 508, alias the Balilla, Fiat adopted a stylish two-seater spider bodywork created by Carrozzeria Ghia for series production. It utilised Balilla mechanicals, i.e. the 995cc side valve engine and three-speed gearbox, but with its light bodywork and slightly higher output, it became the motor racing amateur's delight. Either as the cycle-winged 508 C Balilla 'Mille Miglia' or the more elegant 'Coppa d'Oro' (Gold Cup) model with its streamlined wings, it met with instantaneous success. It could be judged as Italy's answer to the similarly-affordable MG Midgets from Britain. In fact, ever since the Italian models arrived, a certain amount of rivalry has existed between the two makes. The almost simultaneous appearance of the Fiat Barchetta and

The OSCA-designed engine of the 1500 S had a capacity of 1491cc and developed 80hp. For the 1962 model-year, it was bored out to 1568cc, which was worth an extra 10 horsepower and gave it a top speed of 170km/h (105.6mph).

An off-centre bonnet air-intake was the styling modification which differentiated the first version of the 1600 S cabriolet (opposite) from the earlier 1200 and 1500 models. Later, the intake disappeared, giving way as a recognition feature to a second set of headlamps mounted in the outer ends of the grille and the Fiat badge in its traditional form, encircled by laurel leaves. There were mechanical differences too, such as disk brakes all-round and a 5-speed gearbox, but sales were still disappointing.

The car to have for young Italian style-setters in the sixties was the Spider 850 (below). It was designed by a talented young Bertone employee called Giorgetto Giugiaro, and the body was produced in the Bertone factory. Its classic lines, shared by its coupé counterpart, made the Spider a success; nearly 375,000 850s were sold, and almost exactly one-third were convertibles.

Fiat was to retain (and expand) its role as a volume producer of bread and butter models, including affordable sports cars, following the trend which began with the pre-war Coppa d'Oro. Alfa Romeo was the up-market sporting brand, while Lancia opted for luxury.

With continuing development of more elegant bodywork and better performance for the numerous Fiat Balilla and 1500 successors, Fiat entered the innovating Fifties with an important role to play. On the highest level of technology and prestige, in 1952 Fiat came up with the advanced V-8 coupé, based on a brilliant space-frame chassis, independent suspension front and rear, and aerodynamic bodywork around a two litre V8 which was originally intended for use in a big saloon. This chassis was even used for the experimental Fiat 'Turbina' jet-car.

Of much greater importance, and with well-planned commercial impact, was the all-new 1100 model, Fiat's first unitary four-door family saloon with independent front suspension. It was an instant success, and Fiat sold 115,000 examples between 1953 and 1957. This time, the company took the initiative for a sporting two-seater away from the coachbuilders, and Dante Giacosa, who had proven his engineering abilities with the Fiat Topolino and the new 1100, became involved with the project. He used the 1100 platform with 234cm wheelbase, took the lightly-tuned 1,089cc 1100 TV (Turismo Veloce) engine, with power increased from 40 up to 53bhp, and even decided to have the body designed in-house. He gave the job to Luigi Rapi, a talented Italian artist and designer who had worked for Isotta-Fraschini before he came to Fiat in 1949.

With its panoramic wrap-around screen, vertical dummy air-intakes behind the doors, large mesh radiator grille and flamboyant bright work, the Fiat 1100 TV convertible certainly had strong character. But it failed to make an impact on the press and public, maybe because its design was a bit too idiosyncratic, and maybe because its performance and road manners – hindered by a slow column gearshift – lacked a real sports car feeling. But Fiat had at least put itself on the map as a series-producer of sports cars, albeit as a slow starter, with just 571 of the 1100 TV being built before the arrival of the 1200 convertible in 1957. That car differed only in detail from the

original 1100 TV, but it had better torque (and 2 extra bhp) from the enlarged 1,221cc engine – and a floor-shift. To give better access to the narrow interior, it also had swivelling seats. It sold better, too, with 2,363 examples having been delivered by 1959.

By then, Fiat must have felt the necessity to increase its grip on the growing sports car market, to compete with Alfa Romeo and even Lancia, which had developed a good model-mix of open two-seaters and coupés. It was decided that returning to the old relationship with an outside coachbuilder was a better way to create a stronger aesthetic identity, so Pininfarina got the task of styling the 1200 cabriolet. The design was still based on the 234cm wheelbase of the convertible and the 1,221cc engine, but power was increased to 58bhp.

The resulting design – overseen by design chief Franco Martinengo, but with its lines actually drawn by Brovarone – was timeless and without any decorative overtones. A new and sharper interpretation of Rapi's original radiator grille gave the car its identity, but it looked a little too feminine on its small 14 inch wheels. Nevertheless, it was a success, and the company sold around 15,000 between the launch in 1959 and 1963.

Even so, Fiat still did not have the right answer to Alfa Romeo's ever-increasing reputation as a manufacturer of affordable sports cars. While the Milanese Giulietta spider struck a chord with the connoisseurs, Fiat could not get rid of its mundane image. A solution to this problem came from a surprising source, and at just the right moment. By the late Fifties, the Maserati brothers had run into financial difficulties with their small OSCA company in Bologna. They won races as they wanted, but they could not generate enough

turnover from series-production models. It was as a result of this that Ernesto Maserati came to Turin in the summer of 1957 and talked to various Fiat managers, including Dante Giacosa. He suggested that Fiat should use their full-race OSCA 1.5 litre twin-cam engine to give the 1200 convertible (the cabriolet was still in the pipeline) a more sporty character.

The idea was accepted, although Fiat decided for a licence-agreement. The engine had to be reworked, modifying its pure racefeatures (dry-sump lubrication and magneto ignition) into a more practical wet-sump and coil-ignition configuration, but the engine's main features – a four-in-line with stepped chain-drive to its twin overhead camshafts – remained intact. With 80bhp (DIN-rating, as for previous versions), the 1500S had power to match. In addition, a wide bonnet air scoop and larger 15-inch wheels gave the car a much more substantial look.

However, all these improvements could not prevent the original 1200 cabriolet concept losing its grip on the market. Only 80 Osca-engined 1500S versions were sold, to be followed by just 300 1600S cars with 90bhp engines. From 1963, the company tried to attract buyers with a restyled grille and – for the 1600S – a five-speed gearbox and disc brakes all round. As a subtle tribute to the marque's great past, Fiat even decorated the 1500 and 1600S with the traditional round badge surrounded by laurel leaves which dated from the beginning of the century. But it was to no avail, and the cars, the ultimate development of the brilliant 1100 concept of 1953, disappeared quietly from the catalogues. It was the end of an era.

Giacosa had other, more ambitious, plans in mind during the early Sixties when Fiat achieved a high

The Fiat Dino Spider (below) was no money-maker, for it sold in very small numbers, with just 1557 examples being produced in both 2.0-litre and 2.4-litre guises. In terms of image, however, it was a winner. Because of its limited production, it is perhaps even more collectible today than is its coupé cousin. Both cars share the same power-unit, the Dino V6 (bottom), which had its roots in a racing engine designed for Ferrari by Vittorio Jano. It is engineering like this which has made the "Fiat-Ferrari" a classic.

Without a doubt the most important Fiat convertible, the 124 broke many sales records during its long career. It first appeared in 1966 (right), equipped with a 1.4-litre four-cylinder twin overhead camshaft engine which, although up-to-the-minute, developed a somewhat meagre 90bhp. By the time it went out of production, it was known as the Pininfarina Spider Europa (below) and had a 2.0-litre supercharged unit producing 135bhp.

degree of commercial success. After the 850 model had been conceived as an evolution of the Fiat 600, the Italians had surprised everyone at the 1965 Geneva Motor Show with both a compact coupé and cute little spider. Both shared the standard family car's 2,027mm wheelbase and 843cc rear-mounted engine, with its modest 42bhp (SAE rating) power being raised to 52bhp for the coupé and 54bhp on the Spider. With a kerb weight of only 705kg, the Spider topped 145 km/h easily. The sporty two-seater from Turin was a lively and fashionable car in which young men and – in those early emancipation years – women wanted to show off, and both scored immediately at a time when European demand for cars, particularly for special or sports models, was booming – specially in Italy. The open two-seater was produced at Nuccio Bertone's *carrozzeria* to one of young Giorgetto Giugiaro's early designs, and between 1965 and 1972 (including a small face lift), 124.660 Spiders were sold, in addition to more than double that number of coupés.

Fiat had acquired a taste for mass-produced open sports cars during the Sixties, so more were in the pipeline. The company even felt it could take a risk, with a quite extraordinary project which would put Fiat on the map as a maker of real thoroughbred sports cars. The story behind the Fiat Dino, as it was called, was as exciting as the cars. It all started halfway through the Sixties, when Ferrari wanted to enter the new 1,600cc Formula 2. Since the rules prescribed the use of a standard production car engine of approximately similar capacity – of which an annual minimum of 500 had to be built – Ferrari approached Fiat for assistance. The result was two-fold: Fiat not only offered to mass-produce an up-to-date version of one of Vittorio Jano's masterpieces, the famous 65-degree V-6 Dino racing engine, but it also committed to develop and produce both an open two-seater and 2+2 coupé using the engine.

At the 1966 Turin show, the Fiat Dino Spider enjoyed another of those typically surprising Fiat introductions. Who would have expected the Turin giant to get involved with such a delicate sports car project? Of course, its marvellous 2 litre V-6 engine – all-aluminium with twin-overhead camshaft per cylinder bank and 160bhp – proved to be the exotic heart of the matter. But let's not forget that beautiful body, an all-time classic from the house of Pininfarina in which it seemed that everybody in the famous coach-builder's studio got involved, right up to Sergio Pininfarina himself. The car – extremely compact yet well proportioned on a wheelbase of just 2,280mm – expressed a strong Ferrari feeling, with its low, wide, nose and upswept wingline over the front wheels clearly resembling the contemporary Ferrari Dino 166 concept study. If criticism was to be levelled, it might have at the Dino Spider's rather conventional leaf-sprung rear suspension. But at least it was a unique and purpose-built concept, which stood on its own and did not have any technical similarities with the new 124 which had been introduced a year before. Yet it did not sell as it should, probably because the Spider was only marginally cheaper than its more practical sister-car, the Bertone-bodied Dino coupé, which did have some commercial success. Just 1,133 cars, sold over a three-year period, was the Dino Spider's record, despite the fact that it could compete quite well with the two-litre Porsche 911 which was its competition. The Dino achieved a 210km/h top speed easily, and it had a driving character to match all but the best in the contemporary sports category.

The cockpit of – to give it its official name – the 124 Sport Spider. The Pininfarina design changed only minimally during almost two decades of production. Aurelio Lampredi's twin-cam engine found its way not only into every 124 Spider, but also into almost every mid-size Fiat and Lancia for almost twenty years.

Fiat did not surrender, however, and the Spider was completely redesigned for 1969, getting the independent rear suspension it deserved. Its body received such a detailed face-lift that despite almost similar looks, not a single panel could be carried over to the new version. The engine got a cast-iron rather than an aluminium block, with capacity increased to 2.4 litres, which could be used for the enlarged 2,000 cc Formula 2. The production unit produced 180bhp, and mechanical noise was reduced. The Spider became an even more desirable car by virtue of these improvements, but unfortunately they did not pay off: only 424 Fiat Dino Spider 2400's were made – and in the end Ferrari never won a Formula 2 title...

By 1972, when both the full-blooded Dino and the cute little 850 Spider went out of production, Fiat came up with another surprise: the X1/9, in proper Italian "*una barra nuova*". It was a surprise by virtue of its mid-engined concept, at that time the ultimate technology for sports cars. It did not came out of the blue, neither was it a copy of the sensational 1966 Lamborghini Miura. Dante Giacosa, working at the time on the Autobianchi Primula, with its transverse

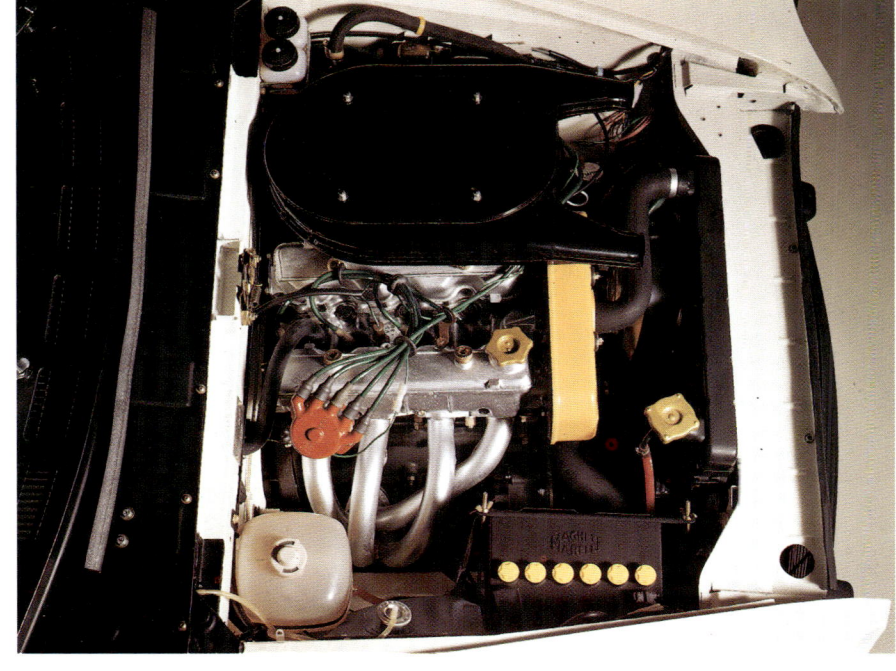

When tuned by Abarth, as in the 124 Abarth Rally (below), it made Fiat a force to be reckoned with in Seventies rallying.

43

engine and front-wheel-drive, had suggested in 1966 the use of the Primula's drive-train for a mid-engined sports car concept. Fiat had even transformed the idea into hardware, the G31 prototype being built that year. Even after his retirement, Giacosa kept a model of this favourite concept on his desk, and he always referred to it when talking about the X1/9's origin.

As a concept, the X1/9 was an all-out sports car, with only the drive-train coming from the new Fiat 128 range, and it outclassed all the contemporary front-engined sports cars. At Bertone, young Marcello Gandini (who had succeeded Giorgetto Giugiaro) performed an outstanding job, the X1/9 expressing exactly the rectangular and trapezoidal lines so typical of his style. With its removable roof-section it was multipurpose (if not a genuine spider) and the targa-look (a stylish roll-over bar) was state of the art. But it only had a mediocre 75bhp available from the 1.3 litre version of Aurelio Lampredi's magnificent single overhead camshaft engine. That proved to be the X1/9's biggest shortcoming throughout its 15-year lifespan, even though capacity and power went up to 1.5 litres and 85bhp respectively by the end of that period. The X1/9 looked like a sports car, but it wasn't. Nevertheless, it had reasonable commercial success during its early years, especially in the USA. Ten years after its public debut, effectively at the end of its life-cycle, Fiat decided not to replace its then-current sports car models. In order to give Bertone some extra work during the difficult Eighties, Fiat allowed the coachbuilder to continue production of the X1/9 under his own name, and in the end – 1988 or so – around 200,000 X1/9's had been made.

Another Fiat two-seater had similar success in terms of

When Fiat introduced the X1/9 in 1972 it broke new ground by offering a mid-engined sports car to the general public. Marcello Gandini's design combined the best of a closed coupé and an open sports car, but the X1/9 always suffered because it lacked power.

production figures, but if one relates the impact of the 124 Spider to the general sports car fan's tastes and enthusiasm, it must be regarded as the most successful and best-loved two-seater Fiat ever made. There is more to the story than the simple figures of 198,000 examples produced between 1966 and the end in 1987. This was Italy's answer to the MGB, winning the hearts of both European and American sports car admirers and performing acceptably well in international competition. It was, one might say, a car with a strong pedigree.

Planned as a successor to the 1200/1500/1600/S range, the 124 Spider was, for obvious reasons, based on the brand-new 124 saloon of 1965. That concept had everything new: engine, transmission and suspension – although Fiat did not go so far as to use front-wheel drive. The 124 featured simple rear-wheel drive and a well-located coil-sprung live rear axle. Unlike the boxy 124 saloon, the Spider was attractive from the outset. Once again, Fiat had commissioned Pininfarina to create and build its bodywork, the design being done by young American Tom Tjaarda, supervised by Pininfarina. He made it a simple and timeless shape, and the 124 Spider still looked good almost thirty years after its debut.

It became the arch-rival of the Alfa Romeo Spider Duetto, also a Pininfarina design, but rather different aesthetically. The 124 Spider could achieve such status thanks to its under-bonnet surprise, a neat twin-cam engine which was to form the backbone of all mid-sized Fiat and Lancia models for around three decades. It came from the drawing board of Aurelio Lampredi, famous for his 'big block' Ferrari V-12 engines as well as the world championship-winning four-cylinder Ferrari Formula 2 engines of 1952 and 1953. Simple as its concept seemed, the Lampredi four featured many innovative details, such as belt-driven overhead camshafts and an intriguing valve-adjustment procedure.

Back in 1966, the 124 Spider was powered by the original 1,438cc version of the Lampredi-four, 90bhp being considered sufficient at the time. But in the power-race which followed during the Seventies, capacity and horsepower gradually increased via 1,608 and 1,856 cc to a full 1,989cc and 122bhp for cars sold in Europe. Describing all the engine variants is not appropriate in this context, but two extremes are worth mentioning. On one hand, the engine was difficult to adopt for the strict American emission legislation of the Seventies and early Eighties, so it ran short on bhp on USA versions, except for a short-lived turbo model. However, Aurelio Lampredi came up with some interesting solutions for the limited-production 124 Spider Abarth versions, including an old idea of gaining extra power for the contemporary Fiat rally cars. He reworked the classic Roots blower concept for supercharging and called it Volumex.

In order to get these blowers homologated for competition use, various Lancia and Fiat models were equipped with them, including what was to be the ultimate version of the 124 Spider. By that time, in 1983, Fiat had handed over production and sales of the Spider to Pininfarina in a manner similar to the way the X1/9 had been passed on to Bertone. Effectively, therefore, Pininfarina was the only company to have marketed the 135bhp 'Spider Europa Volumex'.

For all its life, the 124 Spider remained faithful to its original concept, including the live rear axle, a part from the 124 Spider Abarths, of which a small series was made with 128bhp 1.8-litre engines. These cars even had 16-valve cylinder heads, as well as experimental independent rear suspension. All these developments were for use on the works-entered Abarth rally cars which scored many great results in world championship rallies and paved the way to three Fiat world rally championships with the Mirafiori.

Strange as it may sound, the 124 Spider outlived the decline in American interest in full roadsters and cabriolets in the Seventies, and was only killed by lack of interest from the company itself during the early Eighties. Allowing Pininfarina to continue for another four or five years was just a stay of execution, since a possible successor to the Spider, the larger X1/20 brother to the X1/9, had already been withdrawn as a Fiat and developed into the Lancia Monte Carlo back in 1975.

So, strange as it may seem, after three decades of success, in which it built over 500,000 open cars, Fiat decided to leave the business for exactly ten years. Until, in fact, it heard the cries which went up from enthusiasts all over the world when Mazda launched its MX5/Miata. It was then that Fiat decided to revive its subculture. So, welcome Barchetta, but don't forget your past.

ART AND THE AUTOMOBILE

MY DAD HAD ONE LIKE THAT!

JACQUES BOGUEL

'Mon père avait la même' – roughly translated as 'My Dad had one like that' – was the title you gave your exhibition when it was shown for the first time in Grenoble in 1994. It's a comment most commonly connected with the sight of an old car on the road or in a museum, but for you it always refers to carcasses, abandoned wrecks. Why do these skeletons fascinate you more than living cars?

They have lived their lives to the end. Collectors cars are fine, but apart from those which are still used regularly, their condition is the result of restoration work that's almost like plastic surgery. It's a form of mummification, in a way, and it gives them an artificial air. In Geneva last March, when I was setting up my exhibition at the opening of the new automobile museum, one of the workmen there said to me: "It's strange, but your cars look more alive than those next door." That gave me great pleasure.

My photographs show the real life of cars when their working lives are over – in a way, a kind of life after death.

Renault 4CV (750)

Opposite: Dyna Panhard. Right: Simca Aronde. Bottom: Renault Monaquatre.

Today, the car is often seen as something which disturbs the peace of nature. You, however, have made pictures in which they seem almost a part of nature, something which has always been there. Is that a photographic gimmick, or do you consider the car as something which is now so much a part of our civilisation that it is almost a natural object?

Certainly, the car – like most of man's creations – interferes in the balance of nature. In spite of that, one does find some abandoned cars which in a strange way have become a part of their environment – and that's not just a camera trick, because I find that some of the wrecks are really beautiful. I love the way the old paintwork is washed away by the elements; I love the colour of the rust and the way in which lichens grow on the steel of the body. It's a paradox which has fascinated me – how something which is not a natural part of the countryside can end up integrating into it perfectly. There is an interesting evolution in the way a man-made object decays. It's the way a house which has been abandoned recently has a sinister air, while an older ruin which has been over-

Below: Ford V8.

grown takes on a completely different dimension, with nature and make-believe becoming the most important elements.

Your photographs seem to be meetings with ghost cars. Were these meetings fortuitous or the result of planning?

They were fortuitous in the sense that I never interfere with the scene I am photographing. The most I will ever do is to move a plastic sack or an empty beer bottle. But they are planned in great detail, in that I do lots of research to find the right places. I have systematically studied whole areas of south-east France where it's common usage to abandon old cars in the field behind the house.

Are your pictures taken spontaneously, or planned with an eye to the light and the time of year? Are there some spots where you have been back for another shot?

Many of my pictures are shot the first time I see the

Citroen Traction Avant.

car. When you first discover a subject, you see it with a fresh eye, and often that's when you get the best photographs. But on other occasions I've decided that I must come back another time, to catch a different light, a different mood. As a general rule, I do my research in winter (in summer the cars disappear under the vegetation) and these car-hunting days, be they by car, on my bike or even on foot, have given me at least as much pleasure as taking the pictures themselves.

When you are photographing the wrecks, do the people who live close by tell you their story, and how they came to be abandoned?

Since most of the cars are on private property, I have to ask permission before I take pictures. When I do, I take along a few examples of my work in order to explain what I'm doing. Once the initial coolness has dispersed, people talk to me and tell the story of the car and anecdotes about the people and times connected with it. To be honest, the story of the car has little or no influence on my work, but I must say that I have spent some interesting times having such chats.

An abandoned car is, after all, just another piece of industrial garbage which should be recycled, but on seeing your pictures one gains the impression that to the people who put them aside, they are almost like a religious relic.

That's true; there is a sentimental aspect, an attachment to the object – and then of course there is the fundamental inability of country folk to throw away something which might come in useful some day! I've seen cars turned into chicken coops and rabbit hutches, and I've seen them broken down into spare parts and tools. Once upon a time, farmers would always use the axles for trailers. I've also noticed that these old cars always belonged to the owners of the land on which they stood – either them or their parents. In a way, it seems that although it is a heap of scrap, it is acceptable because it has personal links.

It's striking that all the cars you have photographed

are popular models and often vans or pickups. That gives the impression that those cars which are seen to have value have been better kept, and that in general, common household objects are doomed to disappear.

Yes, that's true. In the course of my researches, I often hoped that I would find a rare model, but I think the car collectors must have covered France with a fine-tooth comb! The only cars which have been abandoned are those which are seen as valueless. If there are any undiscovered luxury cars left, they are well hidden. There's a different feeling about a valuable object – they don't get left in fields.

One looks in vain among your photographs for pictures showing abandoned industrial sites. All the cars you show have been gradually eaten away by time and natural forces, in what one might call a kind of death by natural causes. Since this phenomenon is decreasing, do you feel that your pictures are a record of a disappearing era?

Absolutely. The cars I photograph are the last ones

which our civilisation will allow to be abandoned. Today, the number of cars is continually rising, they are made of longer-lasting materials, and it's obvious that recycling is becoming a vital priority for ecological reasons.

Recycling centres don't interest me, and although I'm sure there's a rich photographic theme there, I don't want to go into the breakers' yards. I'm drawn towards natural death in natural surroundings.

What is your background and your relationship with cars?

I live in Grenoble, where I work in the tourism business, and I was mad about cars when I was a kid. I collected everything I could about them, and when I grew older I took part in a few rallies, but my enthusiasm declined, and today my passion is for photography. But your early enthusiasms colour your later ones, and it was natural that I should find my old hobby impinging upon my new passion.

You have travelled widely in places far from the South of France. Did you take the opportunity to photograph abandoned vehicles when you were in other countries?

In fact, very few. When I was on a trip to the American West, where there were beautiful cars and pickups abandoned all over the place, I found that I was only really interested in the cars I had known as a child.
I think it was there, away from the French countryside in which I had grown up, that I first discovered that the theme of my photographs was more personal than I had realised.

Have you found any cars which were connected with you or your family among those you have photographed?

Yes – and that's why I gave my exhibition its title. My father's first car was a Renault 4 CV, and back in those days, in the France of the Fifties, the country was almost divided in two; you were either Peugeot or Renault, and my Dad was a Renault man!

Opposite: "I had photographed this Ford Vedette in sunshine, but the result didn't please me at all. I never exhibited the picture, but I kept it in my mind. Then I went back on a day of freezing fog – it was perfect.."

Left: Renault Colorale Prairie van. Opposite: Simca 8.

"It would be a little more difficult to take these pictures today. They're really beginning to clean up the French countryside, and many of the cars I have photographed have disappeared."
Right: Peugeot 203.

HIGHLIGHT OF THE YEAR

A FESTIVAL FOR THE FANS

Ian Norris

The event chosen by *Automobile Year* as the 'Highlight of the Year' in 1993 was the 63rd Geneva Salon; last year it was the celebration of Ferrari which combined the 44th Concours d'élégance at Pebble Beach and the 21st Monterey Historic Automobile Races. This year's 'Highlight' is a mere three years old, but it has already built a reputation as one of the most interesting and enjoyable historic motor sports events in the world.

The Goodwood Festival of Speed owes its existence to a uniquely British combination of aristocratic enthusiasm with the national love of cars. The aristocratic enthusiasm is that of the Earl of March, who has inherited the love of cars which made his grandfather a leading figure in British motor sport. His activities started as an apprentice with Bentley and carried on through a distinguished career as a driver in the Thirties. After he had succeeded to his father's title as the Duke of Richmond and Gordon, he went on to create the Goodwood race circuit on his estate in Southern England after the war.

The present Lord March has not inherited his grandfather's desire to race cars, but he has inherited a love of them and an appreciation that in creating the Goodwood circuit, his grandfather built a piece of British racing history. As a member of a family which has one of Britain's most popular and successful horse-racing courses as part of its estate, he is also keenly aware of the commercial realities of aristocratic life in the Britain of the Nineties, where vast country estates must be made to work for their living. Combining enthusiasm with business, in 1993 he decided to bring motor sport back to Goodwood.

The Goodwood circuit, although it is still in constant use for testing and driver training, is not suitable for modern racing, so a race meeting was out of the question. There was, however, an alternative, for in the Thirties a hillclimb had been held on the long drive to Goodwood House, the family's home. The placing of thousands of hay bales, and all the other safety requirements, could make a hillclimb feasible.

It is on this basis, therefore, that the Festivals of Speed have been organised. Drawing on his wide circle of friends and contacts in the world of motor sport, Lord March attracted a superb combination of respected drivers and memorable cars to the first and second events, and by the time the 1995 theme of "Great Racing Battles" was announced, the Festival date in late June was indelibly entered in the diaries of racing car fans across Europe.

The reason for the Festival's success is due to a combination of good commercial sense and a very special social atmosphere. The commercial sense brings in a wide variety of top-level sponsors, and the social occasion ensures that their guests enjoy something truly out of the ordinary in beautiful surroundings. The Festival has become an event which holds closely to the old Brooklands maxim of "The right crowd and no crowding."

The benefits of sponsorship mean the Festival can call upon expert help in all aspects of its organisation. Its Historical Advisor, for instance, is one of Britain's most respected motor racing historians, Doug Nye. It was he who made many of the suggestions for the cars which would represent the Great Racing Battles, the thread around which this year's Festival was woven. Expanding on themes ranging from the Gordon Bennett Cup to Formula 1 of the last decade, the Festival drew cars from museums, manufacturers and private collectors which represented every aspect of almost a century of motor racing. From the earliest days came cars like the Austin 100hp racer of 1908, on a rare outing from the British Motor Industry Heritage Museum at Gaydon, and American George Wingard's immaculate 1914 Grand Prix Mercedes. From the post-war years came a selection of sports cars connected with Le Mans; Blower and Speed Six Bentleys and Mercedes-Benz SS and SSK models, the Bentleys' dark green and the Mercedes' white a reminder of when national glory, not marketing concepts, ruled a car's colour scheme.

The Thirties were represented by a collection of Grand Prix 'monoposti' from Alfa and Maserati, Lagondas and Aston Martins from Le Mans, Alfas from the Mille Miglia, and a dazzling selection of Grand Prix cars built to the 750kg formula. Closing the representation of a glorious decade was a select group of cars which had competed in the 1939 Tripoli Grand Prix, among them the jewel-like 1.5-litre Mercedes-Benz W165 V8, built specially to demonstrate German domination in its one and only race.

The first theme from the Fifties was centred on the Tourist Trophy races held in Northern Ireland, where the Dundrod circuit echoed to the sounds of a British

Peter Hearsey's poster for the Goodwood Festival of Speed combined the theme of great racing battles with the important part played in the event by Mercedes-Benz. The company's support in bringing some of its most important old cars was a major element in the success of the 1995 Festival.

Above: Jack Sears' Paget/Birkin 'Blower' Bentley was first driven by Sir Henry Birkin when he wore down the opposition of Caracciola's Mercedes at Le Mans in 1930. The Bentley broke, but so did the Mercedes, and it was the only one. There were other Bentleys, however, and one went on to win.
Right: The car is Chris Rea's replica of the championship-winning 1961 Ferrari F1 machine. The driver, however, is 100% original – Phil Hill, using the same skill, the same style and the same Herbert Johnson crash helmet he used when he won the title.

Stirling Moss and Denis Jenkinson to their famous victory in the 1955 Mille Miglia.

The late Fifties were represented by cars from a Formula 1 in transition, changing from the traditional, exemplified by the 250F Maserati in which Fangio won the 1957 German Grand Prix, to more modern designs like the 1958 Vanwall and the 1959 Cooper-Climax. This group also included two examples of the last front-engined car to win a Formula 1 championship, the supremely elegant Ferrari Dino 246. One was driven by 1961 world champion Phil Hill, just one of the many famous drivers present for the event.

GT racing of the Sixties was epitomised by Ferraris, Aston Martins and Jaguars which had competed in the Tourist Trophy when it was a fixture in the Goodwood calendar, while 1.5-litre mid-Sixties Formula 1 was brought to life by two BRM's and the Lotus 25 lovingly rebuilt be ex-Lotus mechanic Cedric Selzer as a permanent reminder of Jimmy Clark. There was also a reminder of Clark in the cars selected to represent the competitors in the 1967 Dutch Grand Prix. This was the race in which Clark gave the Lotus 49 and the Ford-Cosworth engine their maiden victories. For

Above: Lord March, dressed for his run up the hill in the Carrera PanAmericana-winning Mercedes 300SL, passes the time with McLaren boss Ron Dennis, ready for his outing in the 1976 McLaren and enjoying a weekend of relaxation with his son Christian.

Below: Seated comfortably on the roll-bar of the CanAm Porsche, Derek Bell signs autographs in a scene typical of the Goodwood paddock. The young fan on the left was not born when Bell scored his first Le Mans win, but he obviously appreciates the occasion!

revival through Aston Martin and Jaguar. The old Goodwood circuit was remembered for its 'anything goes' Formule Libre races, in which Connaught, Cooper-Bristol and BRM gained valuable race experience at a time when Grands Prix were few and far between. Across the Atlantic in South America, racing activity was mainly in the form of long-distance open road events, and an unusual collection of Ferraris, Lancias and Porsches celebrated the Carrera PanAmericana. Once again, the highlight of the group came from the Mercedes-Benz museum, in the shape of one of the 300SL coupés which won the event in 1952. The late Fifties were once more golden days for the Le Mans 24 Hours and the Mille Miglia, and over two dozen cars had been brought together to recapture the atmosphere of the years when sports car racing rivalled Grands prix for the attention of the public and manufacturers. Evidence of the high standards of the event could be seen in the fact that every car had a genuine – and verified – racing history. Highlights of the group were the Jaguar and Aston Martin which won at Le Mans in 1957 and 1959 respectively, and the actual Mercedes-Benz 300SLR which carried

The cars, typified by Herr Ruckwarth's 7.1-litre supercharged Mercedes-Benz SSK of 1930, are the stars of Goodwood, but they are just part of what makes the weekend special. Other outstanding memories were: Seeing the Grand Prix correspondent of a major British newspaper lining up with other fans for Dan Gurney's autograph.
Listening to Mrs Phil Hill and Mrs Dan Gurney enthusing about the joys of being houseguests at Goodwood House.
Walking through a paddock full of classic machinery without a single car being roped-off.
Watching the reverence with which the fans waited for the autographs of Stirling Moss and Denis Jenkinson. Being issued with the elegant metal badge, similar to those used at Brooklands in the Thirties, which gave entrance to the Guests' Enclosure Listening to the sounds of ninety years of progress in high-performance internal combustion engine design.
Reading Denis Jenkinson's comments in 'Autosport' the week after the event and learning he had tears in his eyes as he sat alongside Stirling Moss – you weren't the only one, Jenks!

58

Above: Aston Martin's racing history was featured strongly at this year's Festival, with the company's cars forming a 'guard of honour' in front of Goodwood House. Pride of place went to this, the actual DBR1/300 which won at Le Mans in 1959.

Right: One of the most memorable sights of the weekend was Stirling Moss and Denis Jenkinson, reunited for the first time in forty years with the car in which they won the 1955 Mille Miglia. The photograph shows the inimitable Moss style has not changed at all.

Festival visitors, this group was another highlight, thanks to the presence of Dan Gurney in one of his Gurney-Weslake cars from the Collier collection in Florida.

The giant sportscars of the Seventies were out in force, with no less than 15 examples of the Ford GT40 on show, together with the Ferraris they were designed to beat. The last days of the Targa Florio were remembered, in the shape of Alfa Romeos and Porsche 908's. Porsche had supported the Festival as wholeheartedly as had Mercedes, bringing some cars

Below: Neither Moss nor Jenkinson was 100% fit, with Stirling nursing a leg broken in a motorcycling accident and 'Jenks' battling recent ill-health. Never-

theless, the reception they received on their runs up the hill must have been worth a hundred trips to the sanatorium.

Left: The car is an Italian Alfa Romeo, but there could be little that is more English than this scene.

Right: Cartier's "Style et Luxe" competition was for coachbuilt cars in original unrestored condition. On the eve of the Festival, the protected cars gave the grounds of Goodwood House a surreal look.

John Surtees, the only man to win world titles on two and four wheels, masterminded the motorcycle display at the Festival. Here he warms up his own 1953 1000cc Vincent.

from their own collection which had not left Germany since the end of their racing days.

After the monster 'langheck' 917 Porsches and the even more terrifying CanAm version of the same car, the 'current' Formula 1 cars looked tiny, but when ex-GP and sportscar driver Jonathan Palmer took the experimental six-wheeled Williams-Cosworth FW08C of 1982 off the line on the way to a new record for the hill it was evidence of how Grand Prix technology is king. But although the runs were timed, and many of the drivers were eager to go as fast as possible, the Festival isn't about speed, despite its name. It is about the enjoyment and appreciation of fast cars and those who drive, design and build them. It is a time for enthusiasts to get close to old cars and old – and not-so-old – drivers and for everyone involved to *enjoy* themselves. It is a family day out, not only for the fans, but also for the participants, and there must be many who appreciate the fact that the event has always taken place on a weekend free of other major motor sport. For someone engaged in the world of professional motor racing, Goodwood must be the ideal weekend off!

Right: The Mulberry company publicised its luxurious luggage by sponsoring the Mulberry Challenge, in which grand touring cars like the Cobra, Jaguar XKSS and Ferrari Testa Rossa undertook 'real world' tests – with a full complement of the sponsor's products, naturally.

Opposite: Immaculately preserved sportscar memories of the Seventies – from the rear, a Porsche 908/3 from the Porsche Museum, Nick Mason's Ferrari 512S and Robert Horne's Ferrari 512M.

Lincoln's L2K (opposite) was one of the talking points of the 1995 Detroit Show. The Motor City's own Salon has become a recognised concept car launch-pad, but this car was notable because it was so 'real world'. The power-train is a 3.4-litre V8, putting 250hp through a four-speed automatic to the rear wheels. Nothing too radical there, and for a concept car, the bodywork was clean and modern, rather than Buck Rogers futuristic or the currently fashionable 'Californian cool dude'. It looked as though it could go down the Lincoln production lines tomorrow, and a lot of people expressed a wish it would.

For such mild-mannered people, Dick Buckley and his like are giving ulcers to auto industry executives. With nearly 100,000 miles on his minivan, the retired tool-and-diemaker was hoping to trade it in for a new one. But after looking at the price of a 1995 model, he decided to make the old van last a little bit longer. "It put me out of the car-looking business," Buckley grumbles. In the closing months of 1994, the Big Three were having so much trouble keeping up with surging demand there were shortages of such hot models as the sporty Ford Mustang. But as the new year began, the bottom dropped out. Sales rates plunged, inventories began to build, incentives soared and carmakers began slashing production schedules.

Is this the beginning of the end – at least for this cycle? There have been plenty of headlines suggesting the auto industry is heading for another slump. Why? Well, speculation ranges from sticker-shock to a fear of rising interest rates, and nervous consumers aren't as likely to spend on big ticket items like cars. While the doom-and-gloom scenario does seem plausible, not everyone is conceding defeat. Many observers believe the US new car market could continue growing for at least another year or more. "A slowing down is not a slowdown," emphasizes auto analyst Joe Phillippi, of Lehman Brothers. "We're in the fourth year of a recovery that's not especially robust, but that could mean it's a longer cycle (that is just) starting to flatten out."

Whether it's the bulls or the bears who ultimately prove right, 1995 has certainly turned into a year of uncertainty. And that means more than just trouble at the dealer showroom. The Big Three are facing shake-ups, reorganizations and, in the case of Chrysler Corp., the ongoing threat of a hostile takeover. The Japanese, after decades of growth, suddenly seem to be losing their competitive edge. And while European manufacturers finally seem to have rediscovered their formula for success, they worry that the gains they're making may be no more than temporary.

Where did 1995 go wrong?

Many point the finger at the Federal Reserve Board, the agency which sets US monetary policy. A series of rate hikes in late 1994 and early 1995 put the brakes on an economy ready to boil over. While some steps were clearly needed to prevent runaway inflation, most economists believe the Fed. overreacted. Interest rates only compound the industry's pricing problem. According to the US Commerce Dept., the typical 1995 passenger car now costs about $20,000, nearly double what it went for a decade ago. That means the typical US new car buyer must now shell out the equivalent of 27 weeks wages, up from 23 weeks in 1985 and 18 weeks earnings in 1975. Industry officials dispute the government's numbers. Their own figures place the average price closer to $18,000, a figure they insist is rising at below the rate of inflation. The industry also argues that consumers shoulder some of the blame. Today's typical automobile is likely to be loaded with air conditioning, an AM-FM cassette stereo and power windows, features far less common in the early '80s. And then there's the cost of government safety and emissions mandates, which have added several thousand dollars to the typical price tag. That's a particular problem down at the bottom end of the market, says Paul D. Ballew, chief auto economist for the Federal Reserve Bank of Chicago. Whoever takes the blame, Ballew believes millions of potential customers, particularly in the entry-level segment, have been driven out of the market. And that, he adds, is "why sales haven't hit record levels, even after three years of recovery."

Ironically, in an effort to spur lagging sales, the automakers may have created a Frankenstein's monster. Rebates have been falling out of favor as the industry's tool of choice. These days, carmakers prefer subsidized leases, which now account for nearly three of every ten cars and trucks sold in the US. Leases tend to increase customer loyalty rates, but there's a price. When the lease is over, the carmakers and their dealers have to dispose of the vehicles. And this year, that will mean several million "off-lease" cars and trucks. To turn that glut into an asset, a number of manufacturers, including Lexus and Ford, have launched used vehicle leasing programs. Consider a 1995 Taurus GL sedan with a sticker price of $18,000. Buy it new, and you're facing a monthly note of around $400. Lease a two-year-old Taurus GL, however, and you're down to less than $225. Chicago finance executive John Moss is one of a growing number of people who are trading in new cars for used. "With a program like this, I'll probably never need a new car," he says.

US INDUSTRY

IS THE HANDBRAKE STILL ON?

Whether the problem is leasing, interest rates or simply a weak economy, "The industry is not going to be as strong as we thought," concedes Ford Chairman Alex Trotman. With the final numbers yet to be tallied, US car sales were likely to fall a bit below 1994's mark of 15.3 million – and well below the 16.0 million the most optimistic observers had forecast. What was hot is now not. Take the Mustang. In 1994, you'd have to stand in line to get one. But as the Summer of 1995 drew to a close, Ford was forced to temporarily idle its Dearborn, Michigan, assembly line because the pony car was piling up in dealer lots. Ford wasn't the only one forced to cut back. Chrysler not only had to abandon plans for a third shift at the plant building its previously popular Neon subcompact, it actually had to idle the plant for a few weeks. The automaker also dropped its sluggish New Yorker model. General Motors Corp. finally bowed to pressure and announced it would abandon production of its aging "land yachts," full-sized, rear-drive models like the bulbous Chevrolet Caprice. When production ends in the Summer of 1996, GM will convert

PAUL E. EISENSTEIN

If any one car epitomised the Ford Motor Company's climb back to the heights of the industry, it is the Taurus. Styling which was different, but not so different it frightened customers, a good package, and the quality which the company had worked so hard on combined to make the Taurus America's best-selling car. So when Ford sneak-previewed the all-new 1996 version at Detroit it was a major industry event. The pattern was much the same, with looks – typified by the Taurus sedan (top) – which were smooth but not outré, relying heavily on an oval styling theme which was most pronounced in an unusual rear-window treatment. The packaging and marketing followed the current pattern, with the Mercury Sable saloon and wagon (opposite top and bottom) providing a touch of individuality. Both Ford and Mercury rely on 3.0-litre V6 engines, with 145hp for the entry-level models and 200hp in the 24-valve Duratec version. Both engines achieve 100,000 miles (160,000 km) between services.
Taurus is only the best-selling car in the US. The biggest-selling vehicle is the Ford F-150 pickup, and the Triton (bottom) is a concept showing how Ford aims to keep the Number One spot. It's a big tough 4x4, but it's also a little bit greener than the current best-seller. The Triton's 4.6-litre V8 is 400cc smaller than the F-150 unit, but achieves better power and torque figures – on less fuel.

VIRTUALLY AUTOMOTIVE

"Throughout history, man's imagination has only been limited by his technology. Today, his technology is limited only by his imagination", says Ford designer Tom Scott, a leader in the company's holographic development program.

Laser-generated holograms are 3-dimensional images floating in space. Until now, they've been little more than scientific curiosities. But Scott and his staff are fanning out all over the world hunting down new breakthroughs, like a Russian laser that makes it easier to create full-color holograms, and a Scottish mirror that projects full-size images.

Ford stylists already work on the same computers used to bring movies like Jurassic Park to life. In this virtual world, cars can be run through wind tunnels and crash tested before a prototype is ever built. But the images are projected on flat-panel displays. Soon, Ford hopes to create "fully-interactive" holographic workstations where designers will not only see 3D images, but also be able to "touch" and "feel" the picture-perfect images and shape them much like a sculptor working with clay.

Other automakers also are driving this virtual highway. Slip inside the Mercedes-Benz driving simulator and you'll have a hard time believing you're not on the Autobahn. It works like the flight simulators airlines use for pilot training, but Mercedes' goal is to check out new products before they go into production. "Normally, it takes several years from the time you come up with the original concept until a driveable vehicle is available," explains Hanns-Joerg Schmieder, but "if you can describe a concept in mathematical terms, we are able to recreate the vehicle on our simulator and make it driveable" almost immediately – shaving months off the time it takes to go from concept to production.

That's the same idea behind GM's "Cave". Sit down and slip on a pair of "shutter glasses," and suddenly you're inside a car. It's so real, many participants fall out of their seats when they try to rest their arms on the virtual center console. It's a way of "making people feel comfortable and creative," says Virtual Reality specialist Bob Voiers. Allowing participants to change the virtual design lets GM designers find what consumers are most comfortable with without building solid prototypes.

What's next on the VR front? Ford is developing a full-size holographic projector to let designers present their concepts to management without carving out full-size clay models.

Ultimately, consumers will enter this virtual world. Even the smallest showroom will be able to display every vehicle in a company's line-up. You'll be able to open the hood, sit "inside" the car, and do things you never could do before, like rolling the car over to look at it from underneath, or peeling back the sheet metal to see the suspension. "Until they touch it," Scott says with a smile, "they'll believe it's real."

the Caprice plant in Arlington, Texas, to build trucks. Trucks make up one of the few real success stories of 1995. In recent years, millions of motorists have traded in their passenger cars for minivans, sport-utility vehicles and pickup trucks. In 1981, trucks (including medium and heavy-duty models) accounted for just 21.1% of the overall US motor vehicle market. In 1994, that number grew to 41.7%, or 6.4 million vehicles, according to Chrysler statistics. In 1995, while passenger car sales lagged in the doldrums, light trucks kept racing ahead. The truck share will continue to grow until at least 2010, when it could reach 8.1 million vehicles a year, or 50% of the overall market, "maybe even higher," says Chrysler Corp. Assistant Corporate Economist Van E. Jolissaint. That's good news for Chrysler, Jolissaint stresses. Minivans, sport-utes and pickups account for 60% of the automaker's total capacity. Chrysler has been struggling to break assembly line bottlenecks to squeeze even more capacity out of its truck plants. The Jefferson Avenue plant in Detroit is a good example. Since it opened in March 1992, this Jeep Grand Cherokee plant's capacity has grown by almost

The Cavalier name died in Britain in 1995, when the new generation of Vauxhall's midsize saloon assumed the Vectra label, but in the USA the Cavalier is alive and well. Introduced as a new model for the '95 model year, it is improved for '96 with a new 2.4-litre twin-cam four-cylinder engine which is standard on the Z24 performance version and an option on the LS Convertible (right). This year, the Cavalier and other General Motors cars have gone over to Swedish-style daytime running lights in a move which the corporation says is an aid to driving safety.

Buick's XP2000 concept car (right) is billed as a concept car for the twenty-first century; unlike many dream car descriptions, this one could be accurate. The XP2000 is based on current vehicle technology, in the form of a front-engined, rear-drive four-door five-seater body, but takes its 'things to come' aspects from the world of electronics. In view of the progress electronic development is making in every aspect of our lives, it does not seem impossible that by the early years of the next milennium we will be taking many of the concept car's features for granted. Among them are a 'head-up' instrument display, obstruction sensors which are activated along with reverse gear, and a sophisticated navigation and communications system.

100,000 units a year. And Chrysler's minivan capacity is expected to grow by nearly as much once the new 1996 models are in full production. Chrysler's emphasis on trucks shouldn't be surprising considering "trucks are the most profitable part of the business," according to Bernard Robertson, general manager of Chrysler's Jeep and Truck Operations. By some estimates, the automaker can earn $5000 or more for each of its minivans and as much as $7000 for a heavily option-laden Grand Cherokee.

With those figures in mind, the competition is following Chrysler's lead. Ford Motor Co., for example, recently brought on a second plant to build its Explorer sport-utility vehicle, the industry's most popular SUV. General Motors Corp., which has the lowest truck share of the Big Three, is playing an aggressive game of catch-up. The changeover at the old Caprice plant is only part of GM's strategy to convert under-utilized passenger car plants to truck operations.

The Japanese helped touch off this so-called "crossover boom" in the early 1980s when they introduced a wave of low-priced compact pickups buy they have failed to make nearly as much headway as the Big Three. They've been hurt by the strong yen, high tariffs and critical marketing mistakes, and have yet to introduce successful entries into the minivan and full-size pickup segments. But the Japanese appear to be readying another round of products – and this time, they have a better shot at success. The Honda Odyssey minivan won critical praise following its introduction early in 1995, and the company is considering moving production to the US before the end of the decade. Nissan and Toyota have several new truck models of their own under development and analysts say they have a shot at gaining more share in the next few years.

Many of those new trucks are being targeted at the upper end of the segment. This year will see the introduction of nearly a half dozen new luxury sport-utility vehicles, including the Mercury Mountaineer and Toyota's Lexus LX450. Mercedes-Benz won't be far behind. Its new All-Activity Vehicle, or AAV, goes into production in December. "It's going to get very crowded," cautions automotive marketing analyst and consultant Christopher Cedergren of the AutoPacific

The XP2000's underhood styling is superb. However, under the blanking plate is a very ordinary 5.0-litre V8 linked to a simple four-speed automatic/rear-drive combination – but at least it's driveable, unlike many dream cars. By the year 2000, Buick expect the power unit would be a 3.5-litre V8.

The driver's seat is XP2000's electronic command centre.

Individual 'key fobs' for each driver not only operate the central-locking at a distance – they also set the seats, steering-wheel, mirrors, temperature and entertainment system to the individual's requirements.

The company invented the minivan ten years ago, but with most of the world's other manufacturers now on the bandwagon, Chrysler needed something special for the second generation. In the opinion of most observers, they have it, in the shape of family transportation like the Plymouth Grand Voyager (right).

Group. "The industry is literally intoxicated with the sport-utility concept. Some manufacturers will do well. For others, the products will sit there and die." Cedergren warns that even for those who do well, competitive pressures will force down margins. At the same time, they will be forced to speed up the pace of product development. For some of the industry's smaller players, like Land Rover, that could pose a critical problem. Rover is little more than an asterisk on the US sakes charts. When it entered the market, a decade ago, it sold less cars in a year than GM builds in an hour. But Rover has been able to ride the crest of the crossover wave. Sales hit a record 12,000 in 1994, and as 1995 was drawing to a close, volume was up another 80%. "We were a boutique company with great timing," says Howard Mosher, vice president of retail operations for Land Rover North America. But Mosher admits those it will be difficult for Rover to maintain its pace as the luxury sport-ute market gets more crowded.

Rover isn't the only European import bucking the US sales slowdown. In fact, all the major European brands posted significant sales gains in 1995. A

The Chrysler Town and Country (right) is aimed at the more affluent minivan buyer, who wants luxury as well as a better specification. 'Better' in American minivan terms means car-style features like airbags and anti-lock brakes, but it also means more space, more sliding doors and more cup-holders. Both Chryslers and Plymouths have them all.

decade ago, European imports dominated the upper end of the American luxury car market. The BMW had become a Yuppie symbol and Mercedes found buyers willing to pay anything the company asked just to get the three-pointed star hood ornament. But the bottom fell out when Japan, Inc., launched a wave of new luxury brands. Products such as the Lexus LS400 were thousands of dollars cheaper than comparable European imports. And they offered the essential creature comforts Americans demanded – like electrically operated, telescoping steering wheels and cupholders big enough to hold a jumbo McDonalds soft drink. In 1986, Mercedes sales peaked at 99,314. By 1991, that stumbled to just 58,868. Big Benz wasn't alone. Porsche sales slipped more than 80%, Jaguar dipped by nearly two-thirds. Several European brands, including Sterling and Peugeot, threw in the towel, shutting down their US dealer networks.

But those who remained began to fight back with new products and lower prices. Porsche shaved more than $5000 off the sticker when it introduced a new 911 last year. The newly-redesigned Mercedes E-Class sedans not only offer a telescoping steering wheel, but a set of cupholders. Buoyed by the success of its new 3-series sedans, coupes and convertibles, BMW's numbers have shot up nearly 60% in the last three years. Mercedes and Jaguar have also scored some impressive gains.

So, these days, it's the Japanese who are sweating. Racked by the rising yen, the price of the Lexus LS400 luxury sedan has surged from $35,000 at introduction in 1989 to more than $52,000 today. The division is looking, at best, "for sales to hold about level," according to Lexus Division General Manager Jim Press. And to achieve even that, the company is relying on heavily subsidized leases that are leaving it with little profit margin.

Despite what might appear to be a winning hand, auto analyst Susan Jacobs cautions the Europeans "had better not become too complacent." They may have won the battle, but this is a war that's not likely to play out soon. To counter the tariffs – and the strong yen – Japan has some rabbits it's ready to pull out of its hat. Acura will launch production of its first US-made model next year, and Lexus is likely to move some production to the States. Frantic cost-cutting is starting to pay off. The Q45 was designed to turn a profit at 165 yen to the dollar. The new Infiniti I30 is able to turn the trick at 100. And Toyota's internal goal is to make money at 80 yen to the greenback. It'll be tough, but the experts believe that whatever Toyota sets out to achieve, it has a good shot at pulling off. Any improvement in the dollar's value only would help start the Japanese cash registers ringing again.

The Europeans aren't the only ones watching over their shoulders. Big Three executives are equally concerned about a Japanese resurgence. And that's motivating them to make major changes in the way they design, build and market their products.

There's a noticeably more casual feel in the air at 'Glass House,' the Ford Motor Co.'s world headquarters, these days. Normally a stodgy and conservative place, an employee who made the mistake of wearing a baseball cap to work once could count on a dressing down from his supervisor. Today, that very same boss is likely to show up in a sweater and jeans. The new casual dress code is just the most visible part of a massive reorganization that went into effect on January 1, 1995.

For years, Ford's US and European carmaking operations functioned as if they were independent companies. Now, however, they've been consolidated into the global Ford Automotive Operations, or FAO. And over the next year, Ford will consolidate operations in Latin America, the Mideast and Asia into FAO as well. On paper, at least, the concept could shave billions in product development costs and help Ford rush new cars and trucks to market considerably faster than ever before. But the new organization, developed under the codename Ford 2000, raises a number of troubling questions that could take years to answer. Among the most critical: will a car designed for Germany's high-speed Autobahns also meet the needs of American drivers cruising the country's 55 mph freeways?

Under the FAO structure, Ford has created five Vehicle Platform Centers, or VPCs, each focused on a specific segment of the market. One, based in Europe, will develop the next-generation CDW27. Another, based in Dearborn, will handle products as diverse as the Taurus, America's best-selling passenger car, and the European Ford Scorpio. Ford executives insist that their goal isn't to develop look-alike products, but rather, to

In the land of the concept car, youth today means 'street attitude'. It's an idea which leads to cars like the Plymouth Back Pack (below) and the Ford Fusion (opposite). The Back Pack is part pickup, part utility and part sports coupé, while the Fusion's style is also a mixture of car and pickup, with a soft top at the rear to give the open-air feeling all youngsters seek. As if you hadn't guessed, both funmobiles were designed in their parent companies' California styling studios.

REACHING THE PRICE CEILING?

It should have been a banner year for the US auto industry. The American economy is going strong, yet new car sales aren't keeping pace. Price may be the prime culprit. The average American automobile now costs more than $20,000. That might be a bargain in some parts of the world, but it means prices have nearly doubled in a decade. Even factoring for inflation, the numbers are troubling. The US Commerce Department says the typical buyer is shelling out 27 weeks wages for a new car. That compares with 23 weeks in 1985 and 19 weeks in 1978.

With the Big Three rolling up record profits, it'd be easy to blame greed, but the weak dollar is also a factor. In 1985, the typical Japanese import cost $2500 less than a comparable American car. Because of the strong yen, Asian imports now cost, on average, $2500 more. Customers must also shoulder some of the blame. These days, they demand dual airbags and anti-lock brakes, unheard of in 1985. Air conditioning, CD stereos and power windows are now standard on all but the lowest-priced US economy cars, and then there are the federally mandated emissions and safety systems. Upcoming regulations could add another $1000 to the price tag.

Whatever the reason, the reality is that more and more Americans are being priced out of the new car market.

develop common platforms and to share the type of components that don't matter to consumers. Like door locks and shock absorbers. In the process, Ford will be able to sharply reduce the number of suppliers it has to deal with directly. On the CDW27 program, the pilot for the new organization, Ford has been dealing with only about 200 of these so-called Tier I suppliers. That's down from about 700 on the old Tempo, Topaz and Sierra models which the project replaced.

General Motors is also reshaping its product development process, though you're advised not to use the word "reorganization" to describe the changes. After 11 years of shake-ups and putsches, GM employees are understandably gun-shy about that word. The massive restructuring that began it all in 1984 left the company confused and demoralized – and virtually paralysed it for two years. The boardroom revolt of 1992 led to the ouster of GM Chairman and CEO Robert C. Stempel. And since then, his successor, CEO and President John F. "Jack" Smith, has been tinkering endlessly, trying to find the formula that will turn around the long-ailing automaker. Smith's latest effort is modelled loosely on the Toyota system, where each product program is managed by an all-powerful 'shusha.' At GM, they're called Vehicle Line Executives, or VLEs.

Over the years, the automaker has been carved up into a network of little fiefdoms, and like Middle Ages warlords, many managers have been more interested in protecting their turf than in trying to turn out the right products. The soon-to-be discontinued Chevrolet Caprice is a good example. Market research said potential customers hated the whale-like look of the full-sized sedan, and division executives wanted the

With running gear which has more than a hint of Jaguar's XJ220 in it, a turbocharged V12 designed for 720hp and a calculated top speed of over 200mph (320 km/h) Ford's GT90 (above) is an example of what the company call 'Edge Design' – "a total form that places shapes on top of shapes". If they could link the Stealth Bomber looks to stealth technology, and make it invisible to police radar, they could sell thousands.

When they styled the Pontiac 300 GPX show car (left), the company's designers wanted to combine the sports appeal of a two-door coupé with the practicality of a four-door family car. They achieved that aim so successfully that the casual onlooker needs a second glance to make sure the extra two doors are actually there. We can expect a production car not far removed from the 300 GPX in a year or two.

'95/'96 NEW MODELS

FORD:	F-150/F-250/F-350 pickup
	Mercury Sable, sedan and wagon
	Taurus, sedan and wagon
	Taurus SHO
CHRYSLER:	Chrysler Sebring convertible
	Chrysler Town & Country
	Dodge Caravan
	Eagle Vision TSi
	Plymouth Breeze
	Plymouth Voyager
GENERAL MOTORS:	Buick Skylark
	Chevrolet Blazer
	Chevrolet Camaro RS
	Chevrolet Cavalier RS
	Chevrolet Cavalier Z-24 coupe
	Chevrolet Cavalier convertible
	Chevrolet Corvette Grand Sport/ Corvette Collector Edition
	Chevrolet Express (Chevy Van)
	Chevrolet Tahoe 4-door
	GMC Savana
	Geo Tracker 4-door
	Oldsmobile 88
	Oldsmobile Bravada
	Oldsmobile LSS
	Pontiac Bonneville
	Pontiac Grand Am
	Pontiac Sunfire GT coupe
	Saturn SL1/SL2 sedan
	Saturn SW1/SW2 wagon

Saturn, GM's brave new experiment in a new kind of car and a new kind of car company, launched the first major redesign of its products in 1995. Plastic body panels are maintained, but styling is more rounded and more modern in both the SL1 saloon (opposite, bottom) and its station wagon counterpart. Under the skin, there are innumerable changes, mainly gained through the application of learning from experience and customer feedback, which make Saturns roomier, quieter and more reliable.

The Plymouth Breeze (above) is part of Chrysler's move to revive and reposition the Plymouth brand. Stylish and exciting cars at entry-level prices will, Chrysler hopes, make Plymouth attractive to young buyers who would otherwise go for basic imports or used cars. A 2.0-litre, 16-valve, 132hp engine and stylish cab-forward looks are the way the Breeze fills the prescription.

strategy will help turn around a decade-long slide in market share. The goal is to climb back to 35%, though Rick Wagoner, president of GM's North American automotive operations, or NAO, is reluctant to say by when. "I'm not falling on my sword over market share," Wagoner says, acknowledging that GM executives have repeatedly promised to regain lost ground over the years – only to see share slip even further.

While industry analysts agree big changes are needed at GM, they remain skeptical that this will be the reorganization that finally works. "The big question is how they actually pull it off," cautions Dr. David Cole, director of the Office for the Study of Automotive Transportation at the University of Michigan.

While they're loathe to give Chrysler credit, the number three US automaker has served as a visible role model for the changes at Ford and GM. It reorganized itself five years ago, and its so-called "platform management" system has yielded one of the leanest and most efficient design and engineering systems in the world. But to some, Chrysler still isn't efficient enough.

Caprice radically redesigned. But Chuck Jordan, then head of styling, pushed it through, anyway, declaring it the penultimate statement of his career. The VLEs will be charged with breaking down the barriers between different disciplines, such as styling and powertrain, to get everybody working on the same team. On paper, GM is creating a matrix structure: each employee will have two different bosses. A transmissions specialist, for example, will report to the Powertrain department, but if that person is assigned to work on the next-generation Cavalier, the real shots will be called by the subcompact-car czar. Other VLEs will focus on luxury sedans, such as the Cadillac Seville, and sporty coupes, including the Pontiac Firebird and Chevy Camaro.

There is a human price to these latest changes. GM expects to cut as many as 5000 engineering jobs by January 1997. The impact on the bottom line could be equally dramatic. By some estimates, a carmaker saves a million dollars or more for every day it shaves off the product development cycle. GM expects the new system to cut design and engineering costs by at least 25%. The automaker is also confident the

In April 1995, the business world was stunned when reclusive billionaire Kirk Kerkorian launched a hostile bid to take over Chrysler. Unable to raise the money he needed, the attempt collapsed two months later. But Kerkorian isn't giving up. A master strategist, he has hired on former Chrysler Chief Financial Officer Jerry York. The move gives him additional credibility – and it may signal plans for another takeover bid in the months to come.

With Chrysler potentially still in play, 1996 is likely to be another year of uncertainty. But what of the US auto market as a whole? If it isn't slipping back into recession, where is it headed? Most analysts believe the new car market will remain strong, at least until November 1996. It's in the best interests of the Clinton Administration to do everything it can to prop up the economy until after the Presidential election. But after that, well that's a matter of sharp debate. Many experts believe there's still plenty of "pent-up demand" which "will sustain the market for several more years," according to Chrysler economist Bussmann. But others believe that the US market has already peaked, and that after the election, it will quickly slip into its next recession.

Chrysler's Sebring Convertible (right) has little in common with the Sebring coupé introduced last year except its name. Unusually, it is a convertible from the ground up, and is not based on an opened-up saloon body. It will be on sale in early 1996 as a replacement for the Cnrysler Le Baron convertible, perhaps the only modern American open car to gain a toehold in Europe. It shares the Le Baron's upmarket image, with luxurious trim and a fully-powered top, and is available with either 150hp in-line four or 164hp V6 engines.

Boys of the same generation as Chrysler boss Bob Lutz used to draw cars like the Bugatti Type 57 on their schoolbooks. More than forty years later, Lutz started to draw again, on a menu, and Chrysler styling chief Tom Gale passed the idea – but not the sketch – on to his designers.

The result was the Atlantic concept car, first shown in Detroit in January. With a straight-eight engine made from two Neon fours linked together, dashboard instruments influenced by Swiss watches, and a presence you can't ignore, the Atlantic is the modern equivalent of a 'folly', the miniature castles English noblemen built on their estates two hundred years ago. It may be a folly, but in two hundred years it will still look good!

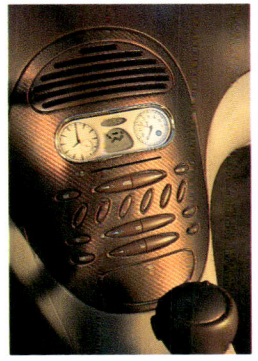

ONLY IN AMERICA – 1

HOT RODS – NOW AND THEN

JOHN LAMM

"Lock up your daughters," the authorities said, the streets are no longer safe. They're juvenile delinquents, James Dean types more interested in going fast in their odd-looking cars than doing responsible things. At least that was the image the popular press gave hot rodders in the 1950s. Movies like 'Hot Rods From Hell' didn't help. Once again an older generation was certain this group of young people would be the ones to ruin civilization. Once again they were wrong.

Their timing was wrong too, for while "hot rods" is a post World War II term, hot rodding has been around since the first time a man tried to make a production automobile go faster, probably back in the days of surface carburetors and tillers. Harry Miller, whose twin-overhead camshaft design so impressed Ettore Bugatti that he borrowed from it, was basically a hot rodder.

Hot rodding as a specific phenomenon began in the late 1920s and was firmly established by the late 1930s. It was a time in America when gasoline was cheap and for the first time there were plenty of inexpensive used automobile. Junk yards were filled with spare parts to replace broken pieces or be adapted to a different car in hopes of adding horsepower. Although men all over the U.S. were trying to coax more power from stock engines, southern California is considered the home of the movement. Its advocates met in garages and raced on back streets, small dirt ovals and several of the dry lakes in the high desert a few hours east of Los Angeles. Those flat, smooth lake beds have names like Muroc, Rosamond and El Mirage, the latter still used for speed meets by the Southern California Timing Association.

After the war years, hot rodders were back on the

A very famous dry lakes hot rod, the Pierson brothers '34 Ford 3-window coupe (left), shares space in Bruce Meyer's Beverly Hills garage with his 275GTB/4 Ferrari and D-Type Jaguar. The Ford flat-head V-8 in the coupe was built at Vic Edelbrock's famous speed shop by legendary engine builder Bob Meeks, who also installed an early Chevrolet V-8 in an ex-Stirling Moss HWM used in the Kirk Douglas movie, "The Racers," to create the road racing Stovebolt Special (below).

Hot rods are properly memorialized in Los Angeles' Petersen Automobile Museum (right) as in this diorama showing a home garage project. A 1950 Mercury coupe is being converted into a hot rod, its top already chopped to lower the roofline. A roof was only lowered too much when an open can of beer or a malt from the drive-in wouldn't fit through the window without spilling. This Merc might well be painted black, lowered close to the ground and known as a "lead sled" because so much lead was used as body filler and any car that was slow was known as a "sled." This would have been a typical scene in garages throughout America in the 1950s, when such home projects were common.

Among the many types of hot rods are Bucket Ts (right), with a Ford Model T body, and also known as "fad Ts" because of their popularity in the late 1960s and early 1970s. This Bucket T is fitted with a supercharged big-block Chevrolet V-8, creating a very favorable horsepower-to-weight ratio and making those monster "big meat" tires a necessity.

While modern hot rods rarely have a Ford engine, a classic rod needs a Ford flat-head V-8 (left). A cornerstone of hot rodding, the flat-head was the subject of much modifying and many speed parts were created for them. Special finned aluminum cylinder heads from Vic Edelbrock, Eddie Meyer or (seen here) Barney Navarro were a must, as were Stromberg 97 carburetors, while this V-8 is also fitted with a rare S.Co.T. supercharger.

put added emphasis on looks and colors. Like the hues that glistened under the sun in Syracuse, New York last summer. A heat wave had settled in for the opening of the Street Rod Nationals, the annual Mecca for hot rods. High temperatures in this part of America bring high humidity with them, so most of the crowd was stripped down to T-shirts, shorts, socks and tennis shoes. It was a colorful group, thanks to the neon reds, blues and greens of the artwork on their shirts, which often declare their preference for Fords or Chevys. There also a lot of pink, freshly burned flesh. Judging by the lack of well-cultured tans and trim bodies, this is a group that works hard all week and is edging up to or past the 50-year-old mark. Family people, the sort that pay their taxes and vote on the conservative side of the slate... a far cry from 'Hot Rods From Hell.'

Hot rodding is a demographic bubble passing through those graying years. Put the age limits between early-40s and mid-60s, but allow for crossover and a lot of disposable income. But don't allow for a lot of young people. While the love of these machines is often passed on to sons (and a few daughters), hot rodding

David Sydorick's automobile collection is varied, two of its main attractions being a pair of cars (below) that are so different and yet strangely similar. In the foreground is a 1947 Ferrari Corsa Spyder with the serial number 002C, making it the oldest existing V-12 Ferrari. Behind Sydorick is one of Boyd Coddington's most famous creations, the Aluma Coupe hot rod that was originally built for Mitsubishi at a reputed cost of $400,000.

lakes, and the sport quickly grew. The aircraft industry had taken hold in Southern California so there was a wealth of both materials and talent for the sport. The speed equipment business soon became a national industry, supplying a sport that was training a cadre of men who not only wouldn't be a detriment to society, but would build championship race cars and staff engineering departments in Detroit... and even run a few automobile magazines.

In the early 1950s, hot rod racing really got organized. Amateur competition on the lakes continued, while Wally Parks and the others who started the National Hot Rod Association, put racing on quarter-mile strips around America and created a new sport, drag racing. With them went hot rods that had raced on the lakes, like a famous car from the 1930s that legendary Art Chrisman turned into what's considered one of the first real dragsters. As with all automotive sports, drag racing became more sophisticated and specialized. By the late 1960s, the term hot rod covered the machines that raced on drag strips plus a new segment, street rods, which retained the sense of high-powered, modified machines for the street, but

When hot rodders returned from World War II, a few made streamliners out of the 315-gallon belly tanks from P-38 Lightning airplanes. The most famous was the So-Cal Special, seen here with a 1938 Ford push truck.

This was one of the most successful flathead V-8 powered streamliners, and had the Ford or Mercury engine mounted behind the driver (below). Several men raced the So-Cal Special on the dry lakes and at Bonneville, but the man most closely associated with the car was Alex Xydias, who drove the car to 198.3mph on the Salt Flats. Bruce Meyer bought the car and had it restored by hot rod specialist Pete Chapouris.

is not a growth industry among the young. Their interests are elsewhere in a world where roads are increasingly crowded, the automobile a villain to some, gasoline ever-more expensive, modern computer-controlled engines difficult to modify and where, quite frankly, they don't care about cars anymore. Graying hot rodders come from a generation that retains some of the initial wonder at automobiles as a replacement for horses. Younger people just accept cars as part of the scenery.

Attendees ambling through the Street Rod Nationals don't seem concerned by all this. They are there for the cars and they'll probably find a favorite among the near 10,000 on display. That's not a misprint, 10,000 cars and owners plus thousands of dreamers congregating in one place to see and be seen.

Workmanship on many of the hot rods at a show like Syracuse would rival that at a highly respected Concours d'Elegance. What's missing is the nit-pick judging that occurs at a classic car show, because there are no rule books for hot rods. Each rod is an expression of its owner's likes and as Ken Gross, former Ferrari and Lamborghini owner now finishing a '32 Ford, explains, "There is no such thing as an incorrect wrong hot rod. There will be some you like or dislike, but they can't be wrong because they are what the owner wanted. He wrote his own rules." Most owner's rules would specify the most desirable of all hot rods, the '32 Ford roadster. If they want a closed car, it would be a '32 2-door, 3- or 5-window Ford coupe (a Deuce Coupe, a la Beach Boys). Next in the pecking order is probably a '33 or '34 Ford coupe or roadster. Then a '28 or '29 Ford roadster. Or a '40 Ford coupe, while the new car climbing the list of desirables is the '37 Ford. This doesn't mean you only see Fords at hot rod meets. There is the occasional Chevy or Pontiac, and variations on two old drag racer favorites, Willys and English Ford Anglia. But for the most part, Fords rule.

Naturally there are variations on stock car bodies, as that's one of the objectives of hot rodding. If the car's roof has been lowered that means it's been "chopped." A car with a body that sits up on the frame is called a "highboy," while if the body has been dropped down over the frame rails its "channeled." When a car builder takes a horizontal strip

Some hot rodders build a car with all the latest equipment, while others prefer a vintage-style rod. The '34 Ford 3-window coupe below is a good example. The body is unadorned and painted a dark color. Instead of low-profile tires on alloy wheels, the car has whitewall tires in a vintage size on steel wheels with standard hubcaps. While a true vintage rod might have a Ford flathead V-8, the fact this one has a small-block Chevrolet could still put it back in the 1950s.

from the height of the body but not necessarily the roof, it has been "sectioned." A "lakester" looks like it might have raced on the dry lakes, while those done for the short oval races run by hot rodders in the 1930s are "track roadsters." Should a car builder create a body style that never existed, like a '37 Ford 3-window coupe, it's called a "phantom." Beyond this short glossary, there is an entire language – hot rod-speak – built around the hobby's terms.

While early hot rods were painted flat, often dark, colors, the hobby has become a rainbow of hues, of rich reds, yellows, greens, or maybe a liquid black accented with flames. Haarm Lagaay, Porsche's design head, recalls leaving a street rod show and noting, "... all the production cars on the road looked dull." If the owner was building a car that resembled those made just after the war, it would be a "retro rod," and would likely have a Ford flathead V-8, possibly with special finned aluminum cylinder heads from Barney Navarro, Eddie Meyer or overhead-valve Ardun hemi heads made by Zora Arkus-Duntov before he become father of the Chevrolet Corvette. A modern hot rod, Ford or whatever, would probably have a

Early hot rods kept their interiors simple, often wrapping the seats with Mexican serape blankets. At the right is more of a custom car job, with modern contoured seats split by a center console and upholstered in a custom-sewn pattern. While the dashboard is basically stock, the car has had electric window lifts, a modern radio and a tilt steering column with a Nardi wheel added. Below is a classic roadster interior, keeping the original shape and simple, upright seats, but brightening it with color. The dashboard keeps a center chrome panel of the sort that originally held a few gauges, but now classic Stewart-Warner gauges are spread all across the dash.

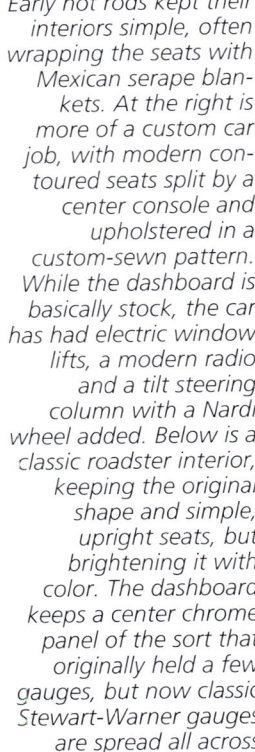

Chevrolet V-8, because overhead Ford V-8s aren't as easy to install and there are catalogs full of proven speed parts for Chevys. You might also find a street rod with a Chrysler hemi V-8, a Buick with its distinctive rocker arm covers or, occasionally, you'll even find a Ford-powered Ford.

To build a hot rod today you could still scour junk yards for parts as hot rodders did in the 30s, 40s and 50s, or you could build a car from new pieces. At any major hot rod show, you'll find displays of brand new frames (classic twin-rail or tube) and metal or fiberglass bodies to mount on them. There are rows of instruments and interior bits and pieces. Full front and rear suspensions are available, along with neat little rack and pinion steering sets. Brakes, wheels and tires are easy. You can even find agencies that will sell you a legal owners' title from the 1920s or 1930s in case your state is sticky about licensing a homebuilt car (most aren't).

If you're handy with tools, you could build a basic hot rod for under $20,000. If not, the tab for such a specialized car would start aroung $35,000 and go as high as you'd care to fly.

In addition to these show cars, tucked away in garages all around America are everyday street rods that usually aren't as pretty, but are used for daily transportation. At the other end of the scale, hot rods are also showing up in top-notch automobile collections throughout the U.S., some being lovingly restored originals, others just as lovingly unrestored. Bruce Meyer owns Gearys, an elegant gift store in Beverly Hills, pure 90210 country. Meyer and his family live nearby in a quiet section of town... quiet except when he starts one of the hot rods in his garage. It could be the mellow pipes of his chopped 1950 Mercury "lead sled." Or the crisp exhaust note of a famous ex-dry lakes Ford coupe. Also tucked away in Meyer's garage? A D-Type Jaguar, a Cobra, a Duesenberg and others.

Gil Nickel and his brother own Far Niente, one of the finest vineyards in California's Napa Valley. Their 1991 cabernet sauvignon is superb. In Nickel's beautifully finished garage with, among others, a James Young-bodied Bentley- a Vignale-bodied Ferrari 340 America and the Lotus race cars he campaigned in Europe during the summer of 1995, is one of the country's preeminent hot rods, a red Phil Cool-built 'glass '32 Ford that took top prize at the prestigious 1978 Oakland Roadster Show.

David Sydorick is another Beverly Hills businessman with a varied stable of automobiles. Cornerstones of the collection are two very different yet oddly similar automobiles, a 1947 Ferrari Corsa Spyder, considered to be the oldest Ferrari in existence (not counting the prewar 815), and the mid-engine Aluma-Coupe, a hot rod created from scratch in California in 1992 by Boyd Coddington, who is another phenomenon in this hot rod craze.

Coddington grew up in Idaho dreaming that the streets of California were crowded with hot rods. When he moved to the Golden State, where he would work as a machinist at Disneyland, Coddington discovered the streets needed a few more hot rods. So he began to build beautifully simple, pure rods modified from stock, eventually designed and built hot rods from scratch... complete automobiles in what Lagaay has called the new wave of coachbuilders. Tacked on the studio walls of Coddington's chief designer, Chip Foose, is a variety of potential hot rods they will create for you for a price of $150,000-400,000.

As a young boy in Idaho, Boyd Coddington (above) would dream of California hot rods. He now has a hot rod mini-industry in the Golden State, selling wheels and other accessories. "Boyd" also creates prize-winning, museum-quality hot rods, often starting from scratch and commanding prices of $150,000 and more.

Hot rod shows are a cornucopia of car parts, whether you're looking for accessories (left) or a custom-made tube frame (below) on which to base your homebuilt automobile

Chrysler's Plymouth division will soon begin selling the first mass-produced street rod, the Prowler (above). The aluminum-bodied rear-drive roadster will be powered by the corporation's 24-valve V-6 and have a rear transaxle. While the Prowler meets all safety and emissions laws, parts like the front bumper will be easily removable. There will be a long list of options to customize the Prowler, since personalizing is at the heart of the hobby.

Praise for Coddington's work isn't confined to hot rod conventions, as his work has been shown in Washington D.C. in America's Smithsonian museum. The best place to see hot rods in their true environment, however, is at the Petersen Automotive Museum in Los Angeles. Not just rows of cars, but a museum that puts automobiles in their proper perspective, the Petersen features several hot rod displays.

Who is Petersen? Robert E. Petersern, born to modest beginnings in Los Angeles and a hot rodder in the late 1940s, "Pete" figured hot rod fans around America would like to read about their passion. In 1948 he co-founded a magazine called *Hot Rod*, which became the foundation for his publishing empire. Throw in real estate and other investments and you have a one-time young hot rodder well up on Fortune magazine's list of wealthiest Americans, far enough up to have donated $15 million to the museum that bears his name.

Then there's Tom Gale. As the man responsible for worldwide design of Chrysler automobiles, Gale knows a thing or two about automobile shapes and colors. Some automotive analysts figure Gale might be the first design executive to rise to the presidency of a major automaker. Gale's automotive roots are in hot rods, he modified Chevys as a kid, and is currently building a supercharged Dodge-powered, '33 Ford-inspired all-aluminum roadster. He carries photos of the car like a proud new father.

But a Chrysler executive who started out on Chevys and is building a Ford? When you get to hot rods, that sort of brand blurring and blending is okay, like Chevy V-8s in Ford Deuce coupes. Hot rods are pure Americana, part of our soul and our heritage and we love them.

Annual meetings like the Street Rod Nationals can attract as many as 10,000 hot rods, like these Ford Model A fenderless street roadsters with their modern overhead valve V-8 engines. Note the lack of cover for the well-chromed powerplants, as they are meant to be seen and admired. There is cover, however, for the driver and passenger, as many of the cars are driven to the event.

Above is a classic hot rod from the late 1940s, a lowered '46 Chevrolet 2-door Fleetline Aero sedan that has been converted into a pillarless coupe. The sides have been modified with "fadeaway" fenders, the headlights "Frenched," with Appleton spotlights to finish the effect. Below is a channeled '32 Ford 3-window coupe from the latter 1960s. There's already plenty of power from a modern V-8 with a GMC blower, so this engine would be built for reliability not ultimate power.

JAPANESE INDUSTRY

LIVING WITH A STRONG YEN

Ten years ago, back in 1985, it was all starting to happen for the Toyotas, Nissans, Mazdas and Hondas of this world. Remember?

Five years later, in 1990, it truly was all happening. Awash with confidence and money, the Japanese had by then pushed production, investment, quality and their competitive edge to unprecedented highs. Pundits talked about world domination and unstoppable juggernauts.

Today, in 1995, the juggernaut has apparently run off the road and the Japanese, we are told, are a spent force, still blighted by their own late eighties excesses, by industrial and social turmoil back home and by the lacklustre design of their increasingly expensive new automobiles.

The auto industry pundits are now talking about Detroit, Europe, South Korea and China. Japan, they say, has lost the plot.

Or has it? The past five years have been some of the roughest the Japanese auto industry has ever experienced. There is still "a plot" in Tokyo, of course. Only it's not the same as it used to be. With the yen soaring ever further into the stratosphere, the number one item on the agenda has been to overcome yen-shock and still stay in the game.

In the scramble to restructure, cost-cutting and risk avoidance have headed the list, which may explain (but not excuse) the unexciting, same-again look of many new Japanese cars (Honda excepted) and the unbelievably bad run of recent Japanese motor show prototypes.

There again, if corporate earnings are any guide, in the aftermath of the bubble economy, Japan's car makers are now finally winning their battle against the killer yen. Hard to believe, perhaps, but true.

Even with the yen/US dollar rate the strongest it's ever been (it surged to a postwar high of 79.75 yen on April 19), Toyota, Mitsubishi, Honda and Suzuki all saw their operating profit for 1994-95 go *up*, not down. Now there's a little teaser for rivals to mull over. After five years of heavy losses, Isuzu and Subaru are also now back in the black.

Yes, Nissan and Mazda are two celebrity casualties that have lost zillions between them since the bubble burst. But after massive internal cut-backs and now with some hot new models in Japan, analysts expect Nissan and Mazda to break even, at the very least, by March 1996. If the yen does them a favour, they could even be back in profit.

Still, once bitten, twice shy. Japan's car makers are no longer taking any chances. Off-shore production is now being pushed even more aggressively than before, especially into South East Asia. The eventual aim for the Japanese is to have a production system that keeps them afloat financially no matter what the yen does in the future.

Thailand, Malaysia, Indonesia, Taiwan, the Philippines and Vietnam are the new Japanese frontier. Japanese majors like Honda are zeroing in on India as well. India is a market (like South East Asia) that looks a lot easier to tackle and profit from than China, which still has the Japanese spooked and, according to those who know, is far from the automotive El Dorado that global automakers make it out to be.

The important thing with China is to be seen to win the race to produce cars there, says a Japanese auto industry source in Beijing. Setting up factories, selling cars and actually making money comes later. For the Japanese, who a decade ago turned down the Chinese approaches to set up local plants, to lose the race

PETER NUNN

There are a small group of mass-market saloons in Japan that sell not so much on practicality or price, but on style and image. Nissan's Presea is one of those cars. Launched in January, this is the second generation Presea (opposite) and it is, in effect, a prettier Bluebird. Twin cam engines (1.5-2.0-litre) and running gear hail from Nissan's parts bin. It's the shapely sheet metal and interior that's unique.

Toyota's Sprinter Trueno (left) has hitherto been one of Japan's best-kept secrets. This Corolla-based front-drive coupe is super-quick and great fun. Revamped for 1995, the Trueno isn't quite as gung-ho as it was (the top 1.6-litre supercharged option has now gone, alas), and styling is a little more bland. But for driver appeal, this is the best and hottest of the new Corollas. Top engine is a five-valve version of Toyota's immortal 1587cc twin cam, packing 165PS.

Toyota lagged behind in Japan's RV boom, but by autumn had made up for lost time through this updated Corolla-based Sprinter Carib wagon (above) and Espace-class Granvia minivan (below). The 1.6-1.8-litre Carib is another lightweight dress-up 4x4, that will probably get its wheels dirty only very occasionally. But then as Toyota knows so well, not everyone wants or needs a chunky-tyred Land Cruiser for real off-road mud-plugging. The big, bulky seven-seat Granvia is another type of RV and will come to Europe as Toyota's HiAce replacement. Sharing some components with the HiLux, the 2.7-3.0-litre rear-drive/4x4 Granvia may not be the greatest looker in the world. But build quality, refinement and attention to detail are all outstanding.

now would be a massive loss of face. So, irrespective of whether the sums really work or not, the lobbying by Japan Inc to get into China shows no let up.

Geographically, Japan is in a perfect location to tap into these emerging, high growth markets. Toyota and Honda are two that are readying cheap 1.3-litre Asian cars for local manufacture. Nissan, Mazda and Mitsubishi are also designing small locally-made ASEAN trucks. Toyota's massive new Australian plant in Altona has been built specifically to supply cars to this seething South East Asian market. Mazda and Ford have set up a joint-venture deal to build trucks in Thailand, which one day could source cars too. And so its goes on.

Not that the Japanese are having everything their own way. The yen is driving the cost of parts shipped from Japan to local ASEAN nations up and up. Fed up with this and what it sees as a Japanese reluctance to transfer latest technology, Proton, Malaysia's number one automaker, has signed a new deal with Citroen. Proton has hitherto operated through strong links with Mitsubishi. But for how much longer?

And then there's South Korea, Hyundai, Kia and

Five years after the original, Nissan unveiled a new Primera in Japan. Europe won't get to see the UK-built edition until autumn 1996. Highlights of the new package include a more supple ride (at last), plus a roomier, redesigned cabin. Punchy 1.8 and 2.0-litre twin cam engines are carry-overs, but there's new multi-beam rear suspension and surprising new styling. Will it make as big an impact as Primera Mk 1?

Toyota announced its 10th generation Crown (since 1975) with great fanfare in the autumn. This (below) is the top ranking Crown Majesta. Not quite visible here is the Majesta's extraordinary Cadillac-like tail end, although the big chrome grille certainly follows Crown tradition. One Toyota exec said proudly the Crown has "no rivals" whether domestic or import. Who would dare disagree?

Daewoo are all on a roll. They continue to cut into Japanese turf (although not in Japan itself), value pricing being their single strongest advantage. Quality and reliability may be a different matter, but when the cheapest new Honda Civic in America costs $12,070 and a Kia Sephia can be had for $3000 less, it's not hard to see where the attraction lies.

Hyundai and Daewoo are also busy setting up assembly plants in Asia, just like Japan. In Europe, more plants and hundreds of thousands of new South Korean cars are also on their way. Whether the world is big enough for all this headlong expansion, only time will tell.

As for the South Korean market itself, this has a tougher reputation for imports than Japan's, and market access was one of the key points of the bad tempered Washington Tokyo auto trade dispute that simmered during the spring, went right down to the wire and finished up in a vague, begrudging accord with both sides afterwards claiming victory.

Angered by Tokyo's perceived inability, or enthusiasm, to close the yawning trade imbalance with America, which in 1994 came to a record $66 billion (more

You see product-sharing more and more in Japan these days. The quizzically-named Mazda Proceed Levante (above) is a Hiroshima-bagged edition of Suzuki's playful Escudo/Vitara/Sidekick 4x4 sport-utility. Mazda and Suzuki are one and the same, except the Levante comes only in 2.0-litre trim (V6 and diesel). It doesn't get the Escudo's 1.6-litre engine or fun convertible option.

than half attributable to the auto sector), Washington threatened to slap 100% tarrifs (worth $5.9 billion) on 13 Japanese luxury cars unless a new "voluntary" Japanese accord to lower the imbalance by importing more US cars and parts came to the table.

In this Heavy Duty dispute, both sides were right and both sides were wrong. The Americans were certainly right to push for a deregulation of Japan's lucrative components market and the notoriously expensive vehicle check system (called the Shaken). The Shaken tradition of using only Japanese approved parts was another worthy US target. For Japanese drivers, the Shaken is one of the most outrageous rip-offs of all time.

But bullying the Japanese to present new parts procurement targets, and demanding flat out the Japanese agree to sell an increasing number of American cars in Japan through mainline dealers was cheeky.

If there was no deal, the sanctions were then to come into force. But they were a double-edged sword. They would hit the Japanese like a stone. They would also effectively put Japanese luxury dealerships in the US –

In the spring, Toyota rolled out the long-awaited five-door version of the hit RAV 4 (right). Differences over the 1994 SWB original include the extra rear doors, bigger back seat area and larger luggage capacity. Styling is also toned down and handling dull but safe. Other than that, it's business as usual.

Mitsubishi scored a massive hit in Japan with the first Diamante, effectively a 5-Series BMW for half the price. This second generation Diamante also wants to be a BMW (the tail lights are the giveaway), but it wants to chase Lexus, too. In Japanese spec, the Diamante centres strongly on Lexus-like refinement, luxury and comfort. Soft suspension and overlight steering make it no driver's car, yet technology and equipment levels are dazzling. Export Diamantes will be built in Australia to beat the high yen. Whether these Aussie Diamantes will get the lavish appointments of Japanese cars remains to be seen.

The Corolla Levin (above) is a sister car to the Sprinter Trueno sports coupé. The Levin, Trueno coupes and Corolla saloon (left) were all re-engineered in the summer, with Toyota putting absolute priority on cost reduction. But the new mainstream Corollas are insipid cars and sales have stalled in Japan. Europe gets a different set of Corollas, with local production getting under way in England from 1998.

True to form, Honda unveiled the new-look Civic at September's Frankfurt Show. First to come are the traditional three-door hatchback (right) and four-door saloon (badged Civic Ferio in Japan). Honda's technology push with the new Civic comes via the new 1.5-litre 3-Stage VTEC engine, offering a peppy 130PS, plus 56.5mpg economy in Japanese tests. The '96 Civic also debuts Honda's electronic MultiMatic CVT transmission, with switchable drive modes (Sports and Economy). To begin with, only Japan gets the 3-Stage VTEC engine. The Civic's body and interior are typically all new. Engines, suspension and running gear are also rethought, yet prices are lower (at least in Japan), and safety equipment levels are higher.

run by Americans – out of business. Not a good idea. Tokyo responded the sanctions were illegal and threatened to take the case to the World Trade Organisation. The Clinton administration had been instrumental in setting up the WTO, but to get what it wanted (a political victory over Japan), Clinton decided to bypass the WTO and wield the big stick. Japan, he concluded, only ever responded to direct gaiatsu (foreign pressure). And even then it was always a fight.

The Japanese were right to accuse the Americans of not doing nearly enough to sell cars in Japan. Not like VW, BMW and Mercedes, for example. The Germans came to Japan with exactly the right attitude and have stuck at it through thick and thin. They are at the centre of the continuing Japanese import boom which shows no signs of losing steam and is expected to do a record 350,000-400,000 units this year.

That the Germans actually had products the Japanese might want to buy, and that were physically suitable for narrow Japanese roads (Detroit has rarely qualified here), was another point of issue.

All the way through, the Japanese refused to give into

Much simpler, and even cheaper, is Toyota's second generation Cynos (right). Known outside Japan as the Paseo, Toyota's pretty front-drive coupe looks sharper than the first edition and now gets an economical 1.3-litre twin cam to match the existing 1.5. Prices in Tokyo for the new Cynos start at a razor sharp 934,000 yen, making it spectacular value for money.

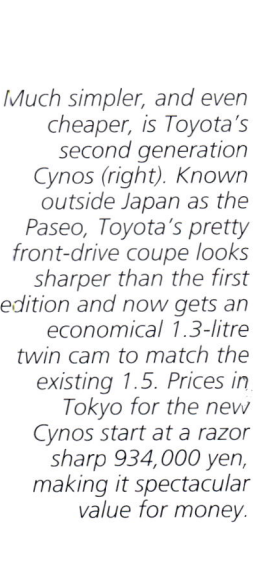

The dream of Yoshikazu Tomita and Kikuo Kaira of Japan's Tomita Auto Co, the Tommykaira ZZ is a sensational, handmade, lightweight sports two-seater. Built around an aluminium monocoque shell, the ZZ mounts a Nissan Primera 2.0-litre twin cam amidships, running east-west. As a purist touch, Kikuo Kaira, the father of the car, has forgone EFi for four Keihin carbs. Suspension is classic double wishbone front and back and weight distribution set at a perfect 50:50. To get around Japanese bureaucratic hurdles, the ZZ may end up being built in England where authorities look more kindly on special-build projects such as this.

numerical targets. Tokyo has issued forecasts before which have been translated by Washington as enforceable committments. The 11th hour Geneva accord didn't mention figures, but the US side has since taken it upon itself to state Japan will set up 1000 new foreign car dealers to handle US cars by the year 2000. Also, that the Japanese auto majors have signed up to increase their purchases of US parts by US$6.75 billion by 1998.

Tokyo disputes those figures. Washington disputes that Tokyo disputes those figures. The row goes on. The pressure is now nevertheless on Tokyo to make some realistic attempt to live up to the market-opening agreement. Otherwise, the US promises the sanctions will be back.

It was Capitol Hill, they say, that spurred on the yen's ballistic rise during the early part of 1995 as a none-too-subtle signal to Tokyo to get its trade surplus (and house) in order. Not that the yen surge was the only crisis of the year. Far from it. Japan has lived through wild times before (the 1973-74 oil crisis, for one). But January-June 1995 must have set some new kind of record for drama and discontent.

The Mitsubishi Carisma (below) is another Japanese car with a foreign accent. Made at NedCar in Holland in conjunction with Volvo, the Carisma starts out as a roomy five-door hatchback with Mitsubishi 1.6-1.8-litre four-cylinder engines. A notchback Carisma follows later. Sensible, well-built, roomy and practical, the Carisma is everything you'd expect. But as a driver, it hardly lives up to its name.

92   *Once again, the Japanese prototypes at the Frankfurt Show left a great deal to be desired. Mitsubishi's were perhaps the best of an uninspiring lot. The GAUS ("an RV for the new age"), above, is a small minivan study that has space and safety as its main pitch. The body, designed around large cross-over frame members, seats four and has a huge lift-up side door, the lower section forming a retractable step. The contentious Mitsubishi HSR show cars go from bad to worse. The best, by far, was the 1991 HSR III. The latest one, this HSR V, reworks the same old formula one more time, but looks cliched and has little new to say.*

This was the period of the terrifying Kobe earthquake and Tokyo subway gassing. There was the Hokkaido aircraft hijack and the first evidence of Tokyo's major banking crisis. Highly disturbing revelations about the Aum Supreme Truth religious cult came out into the open.

More than 5000 people died in the Kobe disaster, which was tragedy enough in itself. If the killer quake had occured later in the day, or in Osaka or Tokyo, casualities and damage would have been incalculable. After Kobe and the Tokyo subway terrorist gassing, for many, complacent notions about Japan being a safe place to live were shattered.

Worries about what else might happen, coupled with concerns over job security in Japan's sluggish economy, were said to be behind the "slump mentality" pervading the nation. People weren't spending money, or buying cars as they were supposed to, and several pump-priming measures initiated by Japan's listless government to kick-start the economy singularly failed to work. By autumn, Japan's economic growth was stuck at the same 1% rate it had been for the past three years.

In September, the yen suddenly crossed back over the 100 yen/US Dollar barrier, which brought much-needed relief for Japan's now whiter-haired exporters. It was the same for company beancounters, who hitherto had banked on a 85-90 yen rate for the 1995-96 business year.

If the yen stays up over three figures, that will put billions back into the system, thank you very much. But it will also raise import prices and for much of the year, there was a welcome price destruction gain for consumers as the yen went skywards. Wine and food importers cut their prices (so did MacDonalds, although a Big Mac in Tokyo was still some 40% more than in California). Toyota and Honda reduced the prices of their US-made imports. Genuine importers (Rover, Mercedes and Volvo) did the same. But not all importers were so noble.

Along with inexorable yen stress, 1995 saw continuations of several other recent Japanese trends: flat domestic vehicle production, falling exports, continually rising imports, reduced graduate hiring.

In July, for instance, due to yen-shock and the desire to cut inventories, vehicle exports plummetted 29.3% to 286,866 units, for the second largest drop in Japanese history. Seven month exports plunged 11.4% to 2,341,309 units. Domestic production for the same period crawled up just a minuscule 0.1% to 6,101,980 units. Imports roared up 29.7% to 248,740 units.

After four years falling output, Japan lost its production record to the US in 1994 with 10.55 million units. With the export downturn now in full swing, JAMA predicts another fall, to 10 million units, for 1995.

When it came to new recruits, Toyota hired 883 new college graduates back in 1992. By 1995, the number of new incumbents was down to 140. A growing number of Toyota designers are being employed on a contract system (no jobs-for-life). For graduates, which university you went to, previously very important, no longer counts. Aptitude, skill and enthusiasm are the qualities Toyota now says it is looking for.

The Japanese auto majors are still having to tread a fine balancing act: trying anything they can to increase sales in Japan, while at the same shifting as much production as possible off-shore without creating the so-called hollowing out of Japan's domestic production base.

Mass layoffs, western style, are still a major cultural taboo in Japan. Radical surgery to deal with the problems of over-capacity and over-manning are still on the back burner. By going gently, an old Japanese philosophy comes into play: everything will be solved in time.

When it comes to new models, Japan is now unquestionably in love with the Recreational Vehicle, whether it be sport-utility 4x4, station wagon or minivan. Hot products in 1995 were the 660cc Suzuki Wagon R, the Honda Odyssey, the Toyota RAV 4 and Subaru Legacy Sports Wagon. All these are just two years old, or less: an indicator that Japanese buyers are losing interest in some of the traditional nameplates like Corolla and Sunny and looking for something new, bright and different.

Within Japan, Toyota made headlines when it appointed Hiroshi Okuda, 63, as the first person outside the Toyota family dynasty to run the company since 1967. Okuda immediately announced he was going to regain Toyota's customary 40% market share in Japan. Or else. Toyota also upped its stake in Daihatsu from 16.8% to 33.4%. Why? Daihatsu's low-cost small car technology and its early entree into local Chinese production must surely have a lot to do with the decision.

Talk to Japanese car company people in Europe, America, Australia, or just about anywhere on the globe, and they will tell you trading conditions in 1995 were very, very difficult. At home, Japan now seems to have learned how to overcome the worst effects of yen-shock. But cost cutting on its own is not enough. Japan Auto Inc also badly needs to rediscover the design flair and confidence it had in the late 1980s. If it can crack that, and the yen, it really will be back on track to former glories.

NEW JAPANESE MODELS IN 1995

January:	Nissan Skyline GT-R Mitsubishi Diamante Nissan Pulsar Nissan Presea
February:	Honda Inspire/Saber 5 cylinder
March:	Honda NS-X Targa
May:	Toyota RAV 4 five-door Toyota Corolla
June:	Mazda Bongo Friendee Nissan Cedric/Gloria
July:	Honda Inspire/Saber V6
August:	Toyota Granvia Honda Integra Type R Daihatsu Move Toyota Sprinter Carib Subaru Legacy Grand Wagon Toyota Crown
September:	Honda Civic Toyota Cynos Nissan Primera Nissan Terrano
October:	Honda CR-V Mitsubishi Mirage and Lancer

Nissan's FEV-II (above) has been designed with 1998 California ZEV regs in mind. Styled at ND1 in San Diego (with one eye on VW's Concept 1?), FEV-II runs with a pack of Sony lithium ion batteries. Viewed by Nissan as the best battery proposal yet in terms of weight, size and output, Sony's new invention gives FEV-II a running range of 200kms (124 miles).

Off-road heroes will hate the Honda CR-V (opposite, top), another family/fashion car-based 4x4 in the Toyota RAV 4 mould. CR-V makes no claim about being a real off-roader. This Civic-derived, 2.0-litre five-seat wagon is designed for "casual" off-road use only (ski trips, camping etc.) and spends most of its time on-road, like most 4x4s.

Mazda's swoopy RX-01 (left and opposite, bottom) suggests the rotary coupé of the future. RX-01, running with a new atmospheric twin rotor Wankel (220hp), is smaller, lighter and more frugal than the RX-7. Since it uses the MX-5 platform, RX-01, displayed at the Tokyo Show, should be cost-effective to build, too. Just like the original RX-7, in fact.

Toyota, not to be outdone, has the MRJ (left). A compact mid-engined 2+2 convertible, MRJ is a return, of sorts, to the glory days of the first MR2. Toyota's show car comes with a 1.8-litre 20-valve engine (170hp) and a swish retractable top. If MRJ gets the production go-ahead, the roof and other exotica probably won't get past the bean-counters. Shame.

JAPAN'S MINICARS

A UNIQUE BREED

PETER NUNN

Rover's planning of a new Mini for the year 2000, coupled with concepts like the tiny Swatchmobile Smart and new sub-Fiesta Ford, shows that the small car is now definitely back in vogue.

But in Japan, where the roads are narrow and space is always at a premium, small cars have never been out of fashion.

Over forty years ago, the Japanese created guidelines for a new breed of inexpensive economy vehicle, a kind of national peoples' car, to fulfil the same kind of role as the Swatchmobile and others like it.

It was dubbed the *kei jidosha* (or light car), and today, this mini vehicle series is not only alive and well, it has blossomed into a highly specialised, action-packed breed all of its own.

In fact, with annual sales in Japan of some 1.5 to 1.6 million units, Japan's minis have become a genuine big-time phenomenon. Putting it into perspective, at that kind of volume, the minis are on a par with the total number of cars sold annually in Britain in recent years...

Not bad for a range of baby cars, trucks and vans that most people in the world probably never get to see. Yes, Japan's mini has come a long way over the past four decades, yet the concept hasn't changed at all. It's a scaled-down version of the real thing: simple, frugal, cheap four-wheeled transport with an engine of around half a litre and a body some 3-metres long. The first cars, launched in the mid-fifties, when Japan's level of motorisation was still at a low ebb, had a capacity limit up just 360cc. At that time, few roads were paved (even in the centre of Tokyo) and driving conditions were poor, to put it mildly. The cars that were around were mostly big, chauffeur-driven imports from Detroit.

To get where they were going, most Japanese rode by bus or bicycle, took the tram or went by foot. Owning a car was simply a dream.

Nevertheless, the government laid down plans for a small basic car and tried to tempt major manufacturers, Toyota, Nissan and others, to get involved. But with very tight restrictions on body size, engine capacity, number of seats, maximum speed, fuel economy and price, the big guns considered the project technically and financially unworkable, and washed their hands of the whole deal.

Not that this stopped small groups of Japanese entrepreneurs like Ryuichi Tomiya from building their own minicar specials such as the extraordinary Flying Feather and Fujicabin. As its name implied, the Flying Feather was extremely light. With simple, spartan body and 350cc motorcycle vee-twin slung between the rear wheels, the Feather was, in effect, a four-wheeled, two-seat, motorised bicycle.

The Fujicabin, which appeared the following year in 1955, was even more way out. Like a fighter cockpit without tail or wings, the diminutive three-wheeled Fujicabin even ran to a full glass-fibre monocoque body. Power came from an air-cooled, two-stroke 125cc single. But like the Flying Feather, this little aero wonder didn't sell and only 85 were made. At that time, those Japanese that could afford cars wanted something better than these curious runabouts.

In penning such tiny, super economy machines (which, in today's world, would be deemed eminently politically correct), some might say the fertile Ryuichi Tomiya was just too far ahead of his time.

Gradually, production of more conventionally-engineered mini vehicles got underway. The Suzulight (Japan's first front drive production car) appeared.

35 years on, the Mazda R360 is still a honey. The first car from Mazda (then Toyo Kogyo), the R360 (below) ran with a tiny air-cooled vee-twin giving all of 16hp. A two-speed automatic box, also rare for its day, was an option. Yet it is for its pert, pretty styling the the R360 is best remembered. Later mini Mazdas were never as much fun as this.

Opposite: As postwar motorisation got under way in Japan, Suzuki came out in October 1955 with the Suzulight (right). Most cars on Japanese roads at that time were big, chauffeur-driven US limos, so the lightweight 3 metre Suzulight was really breaking new ground. Power came from an air-cooled, two-stroke 360cc twin, offering 15hp. With smooth looks, good space and practicality, the basics were OK. Yet the pioneering little front-drive Suzuki somehow didn't take off. Only 43 were made.

So did simple three-wheeled pick-ups like Daihatsu's Tri-Mobile, which could be driven on a motorcycle licence.

But it was the Subaru 360 of 1958 that marked the turning point. Here was the first genuinely successful mini car. Conceived by a team of ex-Zero fighter engineers, the Subaru 360 looked a little odd (it was nicknamed the ladybird beetle). Yet it was strong and light, had a spacious aero-tuned body and its supple torsion bar suspension was capable of countering Tokyo's badly potholed roads like none before it.

"It was the best *kei* car of that era, and a revelation after the Suzulight" recalls respected Japanese journalist Shotaro Kobayashi.

"*Kei* cars were very much favoured in those days. Tax was cheap, it was easy to get a licence and parking was no problem. You could park anywhere, anytime. Even when parking spaces in Tokyo became compulsory, the *kei* car was still exempt, for the government was still behind it."

Into the sixties, the mini car sector began to accelerate fast, as bigger cars like the Toyota Publica and Corona also took off. Mazda (then Toyo Kogyo) entered the race with the R360, a cheeky little vee-twin coupé, in 1960. From Mitsubishi came the 500 (not strictly a mini because of its outsize 594cc engine), but another tiddler built up around the government's basic peoples' car philosophy, nonetheless.

Mitsubishi followed this two years later with the first 360cc Minica. Proving that sometimes some things never change, the Minica name, along with the Suzuki Alto (born in 1970) and Daihatsu Mira (debut 1980), still continues in production in Japan in the nineties.

Similarly, at Subaru, the car they called Rex (launched

And now for something completely different. The amazing cycle-wheeled Flying Feather (below) and ladybird-like Subaru 360 (opposite) both hit the minicar in 1950s Japan. The creation of fertile inventor Ryuichi Tomiya, the Flying Feather was conceived as cheap rudimentary transport. Today, the ultra-basic, lightweight, eco-friendly 350cc machine would be deemed eminently politically correct. So would the Subaru 360. Exceptionally advanced for its era, with small lightweight aero body, roomy four-seat cabin and supple torsion bar suspension, the Subaru was Japan's first successful peoples' car. In the 1990s, the 360 still enjoys a huge cult following in Japan.

Below: The latest in a long line of Subaru minicars stretching back almost four decades, the Vivio first appeared in 1992, replacing the Rex. Hottest ticket is this Vivio RX-R, with intercooled and supercharged 658cc engine pumping out the maximum 64hp minicars are allowed in Japan. Red warpaint, full-time 4WD and boy-racer interior are also part of the package. In the normal range, a Vivio with ECVT box is a big seller.

The new boom in Japanese 660cc minicars is in recreational vehicles (RVs) like this Mitsubishi Minica Toppo (right) and Suzuki's Wagon R. In 1995, the market just couldn't get enough of these baby campers and vans. Attractions include their dual-function ability, compact size, cheap running costs and, not least, the fact they are fun, practical and different from most other cars on the road. From a 1990 start, Mitsubishi is now on its second generation Toppo. This is the original.

in 1972 as a successor to the R2 which, in turn, replaced the ladybird-like 360) lasted a good 20 years until the current Vivio series bowed in.

Japanese vehicle production topped the 1 million mark for the first time in 1963. A year later, amid the glow of the Tokyo Olympics, exports went over 100,000 units and Japan's industrial revolution was well on the launch pad. There's no doubt the *kei* played a major role in the growth of Japanese motorisation, helping to catapult production to over 3 million by 1967 (putting Japan second only to the US).

The year that bought the summer of love also saw the arrival of the buzzy little Honda N360: the first Japanese mini to achieve genuine success in export markets. Since then, minis that venture overseas often have bigger engines than allowed in Japan in the belief they need the extra ccs to cope with faster driving conditions.

By the turn of the decade, minis were really booming. Sales of 507,789 units in 1965 had rocketed to 1,255,913 units five years later.

There were some cracking little cars around then, too (like the Honda Z), proving the mini sector's reputation for ingenuity and unusual, sometimes weird (but never boring) styling was still as hot as ever.

But trouble lay ahead. At the start of the '70s, the *keis* went into deep decline as, as Shotaro Kobayashi remembers, "the price gap between mini cars and basic small cars narrowed and minis suddenly became unfashionable for young people." In 1970, minis had 30.6% of the Japanese market. Five years on, and post first oil crisis, mini sales had halved and their market share crashed to 13.7%.

You might have thought the mini's economy prowess would have been a strong selling point during those dark times around 1973-74. But this was the era of the first Honda Civic with its pioneering low-fuel CVCC engine. Other Japanese family favourites like the Corolla could also be pretty frugal. So why settle for a smaller, cramped, more finicky mini car? Many Japanese must have thought along those lines.

The key to the *kei*'s revival came in January 1976 when engine capacity limit was bumped up to 550cc. Bodies became 200mm longer and 100mm wider. By 1980, sales were back over the million mark again. The early eighties saw the next big trend: the boom in mini trucks, vans and pick-ups (from 839,308 units in 1980 to a peak of 1,596,220 units by 1988). Mini car sales stayed more or less flat around this time, as newly-affluent Japanese decided to spend their money on more glamorous forms of transport than the tiny workaday *kei*.

The sector was supported during this time by Japan's army of farmers, delivery companies and rural dwellers who decided they liked the idea of the mini CVs because of their practicality and low running costs. Right from the beginning, mini vehicles in Japan have qualified for cheaper taxes, insurance and expressway road tolls. For buyers, parking fees (or the lack of them) are another major incentive.

In the country, the carrot is that no certificate (to prove you have off-street parking) needs to be shown to the police when you licence your mini. Having said that, you still have to have off-street parking of some kind (simply leaving the vehicle in the roadway is illegal). But officially, you don't have to show that you do.

In Tokyo and Osaka (and, from 1996, all cities of over 300,000 people), the cops *will* want to see your

parking certificate. And this can turn out expensive. Parking can cost as much as 60,000 yen per month in the centre of Tokyo. In the suburbs, maybe 5,000-20,000 yen.

The other trend of that time was the *kei*'s growing maturity. A car like the 1985 Honda Today was a true smooth operator: a neat, stylish and sophisticated cousin to the City, Civic and Accord. Despite its noisy three cylinder engine, it was suprisingly good to drive, too.

Riotous technology also came to a head as the eighties wore on, as mini makers laid on the techno overkill to boost sales and image.

Superchargers, turbos, intercoolers, twin cams, four valve heads, 4WD and, from Subaru, A CVT box came on line. One car, the wacky 1989 Mitsubishi Dangan ZZ, had all the really good bits crammed into one tiny 550cc package. Except it went one step further: it only happened to be the world's first *five* valve per cylinder car...

There are those (Shotaro Kobayashi being one of them) who consider such hi-tech excesses are pretty much wasted in a tiny 3-metre package which still has

Mitsubishi created history in 1989 with this riotous Minica Dangan ZZ. The Dangan (meaning bullet) was the world's first five-valve-per-cylinder production car. Its twin-cam, intercooled turbo, balancer shaft-equipped 548cc three cylinder engine (64hp) ran to a dizzy 9000rpm red line. Later, an even funkier four cylinder ZZ appeared! And there was humour, too. Also in '87, Mitsubishi produced a tamer Minica with two doors on one side, one on the other. It's name? The Lattice.

WHY SO POPULAR?

The appeal of the *kei jidosha* has a lot to do with its compact size. A length of just 3.3 metres and width of 1.4 metres makes it the perfect, easy-to-manoeuvre city runabout. Threading through Japan's labyrinth of narrow urban and country roads is also a breeze.

Bargain-basement running costs are another attraction. The mini owner gets a significant break on taxes, insurance and expressway fees. If you live in the country, you don't need to provide proof of off-street parking, and that, on its own, can save you a bundle.

Along with cut-price fuel and maintenance bills, all this brings the cost of mini ownership down to rock bottom levels.

Then there's the mini's cute image. Many of Japan's mini cars are bought by young twenty-something Japanese girls who like the fact the mini is small, easy to drive, cheap and (usually) fun-looking.

In Japan's bubble economy era, mini makers tried to widen the mini's appeal still further through funsters like the Honda Beat, Suzuki Cappucino and Mazda AZ-1. But the latest craze is small RVs, with the Suzuki Wagon R exactly what the market wants right now. The Mitsubishi Pajero Mini is another RV in such huge demand that Mitsubishi is having to boost production.

The 1960s produced some of the most special of all Japanese mini-cars, like the glorious Cony Super Guppy (right) and the first Suzuki Fronte (above). The tiny 1961 Super Guppy pick-up was a member of a miniaturised sub-breed below even the 360cc minicar. Capacity of its 11hp single cylinder engine was just 199cc and, with auto box, the Guppy was the cheapest of its kind in Japan. Few have survived, alas. The Fronte, the mid-sixties replacement for the Suzuki's Suzulight, has been a big success for Japan's number one minicar maker. Space was a particular keypoint of this neat Mk 1 edition. Literally dozens of Frontes have followed over succeeding decades. Like Alto and Cervo, Fronte has been one of Suzuki's most enduring nameplates.

to comply with strict limits on engine power and top speed. "Yes, it was very foolish. They only came up with these gadgets and gimmicks to please small numbers of car-crazy guys."

Safety is another contentious point for the *kei*, particularly its ability to withstand side impacts. For this reason, when approached by Suzuki, Mr Kobayashi and *Car Graphic* magazine staff advised the company not to produce the Cappucino roadster, no matter how cute it looked.

"We said that with a width of 1.4-metres, it was just too narrow. The open roof made it even more vulnerable. We told them to forget it, but Suzuki still went ahead. They said it was for the Japanese market only. Later, of course, they changed their minds and sent it to Europe..."

Suzuki, it should be noted, is the dominant force in the Japanese mini vehicle business, with a market share of over 32%. Behind follow Daihatsu, Mitsubishi, Subaru, Honda and Mazda (in that order).

Put another way, a staggering 90% of Suzuki's home sales are attributable to minicars. Hence the company's decidedly less-than-enthusiastic response to recent calls for the sector to be deregulated to allow Eurobabies like the Mini and Cincequento through the door.

Japan's arbitary mini vehicle regs serve no purpose anymore and are irrevelant, the Europeans argued. A nineties supermini like the Cincequento is fundamentally safer, more stable and refined, roomier and probably just as economical as a Japanese mini, they say. It just doesn't happen to have a 3.3x1.4 metre body and an engine below 660cc, the three main constituents that make up a modern day *kei*.

Should they really want to challenge Japan's 660 cartel, the biggest problem for the Europeans seems to be the engine. Developing one just for Japan is just not cost effective, we're told. So what of the future? Shotaro Kobayashi sees a light up ahead.

"The *kei jidosha* could be the base for a future city commuter – basic personal transport for the city and rural areas. There's a need for such a cheap, clean recyclable vehicle: a simple runabout, you might say."

"I'm serious. I see this as a good business chance for somebody. A great opportunity – for some clever man with a dream."

KEI JIDOSHA – A MINI HISTORY

Japan published its first guidelines for its new inexpensive mini car series in October 1954. Amid a tight package of regulations, the main criteria were body length (3 metres or less) and width (1.3 metres or less). Engine capacity was set at 360cc.

The *kei jidosha* was then ostensibly left to its own devices until January 1976 when the regulations were upgraded to make it more appealing following the first oil crisis slowdown. It was decided to add 200mm to body length and 100 to the width. The new engine limit was 550cc.

In January 1990, the latest round of changes was phased in. A further 100mm went on length (taking it to 3.3 metres) and engines up to 660cc were allowed. Limits on engine horsepower (64PS) and maximum speed (120km/h) were left untouched. In order to meet new 50km/h front impact standards due in 1999 (the current test is 40km/h), the mini makers recently put in a request for a bigger engine (700-800cc) and longer body. But boosting the *kei* that way would have brought it up virtually on a par with the 1.0-litre class. Toyota and Nissan, Japan's top two automakers (which don't make minicars) have the Starlet and March/Micra in that class, so duly put their foot down. The mini makers' request was turned down, but a new body length of 3.4 metres was accepted.

One of the best and most stylish of all Japanese minicars, this 1977-82 Suzuki Cervo coupe was also one of the few to receive genuine acclaim in Europe – where, with bigger 970cc engine, its name was SC 100. Back home, the Japanese had to be content with a smaller 539cc two-stroke in the rear of Suzuki's little 2+2 gem. Like all great designs, the coupe hasn't dated. With a minor revamp, it could even be re-introduced tomorrow. There's still nothing else like it.

102

AUTOMOTIVE HISTORY

THE ROOTS OF AUTO UNION

Although Germany was the cradle of the automobile, with the work of Daimler and Benz setting in motion a revolution which was to change the world, it was other countries which took up their inventions and turned them into commercial realities. France had also contributed to the creation of the automobile, but while that country's industry grew, together with those of Italy, Britain – and most of all the United States – the social and political climate of Germany as the nineteenth century turned into the twentieth was not conducive to the development of the motor vehicle business. It was still an imperial nation, with rigid social structures under which the legislation and administration were on virtually feudal lines. With internal and foreign policies which were formed along lines which actively ignored modern technology and thinking, Germany and its empire were not fertile fields for the budding entrepreneurs of motoring. Unlike France, where the natural interest in technology and a sporting spirit encouraged the growth of new technology, Germany was more interested in remaining in the era of the horse.

Nevertheless there were *some* automotive engineers in the country who showed entrepreneurial spirit – in Saxony, for instance, where on February 15th, 1885, Johan Baptist Winklhofer and Richard Adolf Jaenicke formed an agreement to create what was to become the *Chemnitzer Veloziped-Depot Winklhofer & Jaenicke*. The two sold and repaired products of the booming British cycle industry, but by 1887 they had produced a tricycle of their own. In 1896 they had changed the company name to *Wanderer Fahrradwerk vorm. Winklhover und Jaenicke*, and by 1902 there was a Wanderer motorcycle in production. Typewriters and adding machines followed in 1905, and with business doing well, the company went public in 1908 with plans to build a motor car. New reinforced concrete buildings went up in Schönau, a suburb of Chemnitz, with the automobile department on the second of the new headquarters' five storeys.

The first Wanderer car appeared in 1911. A small, economical and well-built two-seater, it soon received the nickname of "Puppchen" or 'little doll'. From the moment it went into production in 1913 it was a success. Powered by an 1150cc four-cylinder engine, it weighed 650kg (1433lb.), had a wheelbase of 2.2m (7ft 2½ins) and a top speed of 75km/h (47mph). Its performance was marginally improved when the engine size was increased to 1280cc just before the outbreak of the Great War. At a time when the average German worker earned 1200 marks a month, the Wanderer cost 3800 Reichsmarks, and its success meant that the 2700 employees in the factory represented one-tenth of the total German industry workforce.

It was in November, 1899, that August Horch founded the Horch company in Cologne-Ehrenfeld. It was originally involved in the repair of engines and the vehicles which they powered, but Horch was very much aware of the burgeoning automobile industry, and it was not long before the company was producing cars bearing his name. Growth meant a change of environment, and the company moved from Cologne to Vogtland in 1902 and thence to Zwickau, in Saxony, where Horch formed *Horch & Cie. Motorenwagen-Werke AG* on May 10, 1904. The first Horch car was built in 1901, a twin-cylinder 4/5hp machine, but with his company's capital enlarged to 350,000 marks, Horch started to produce a larger 16/20hp machine. Eighteen were built, in varying forms, before the move to Zwickau, where the production line was set up in a former spinning-mill. In the new premises, Horch developed three new models, a 14/17hp, an 18/22hp and a 22/25hp. He was a man obsessed with technology and competition, and after a Horch was entered in the first Herkommer Cup competition in 1905, the company went on to win in 1906. Horch designed a new 6-cylinder car for the *Kaiser-Preis*, run in the Taunus region in 1907. But it was less successful, and the other directors reproached Horch for his emphasis on racing and the cost burdens which the wide range of engines being offered were placing on would-be customers. Horch, however, was intractable on the matter. He was convinced that sales would follow success, and rejected any ideas of rationalisation out of hand. In 1909, when the 23/40hp Horch with its specially-designed aerodynamic body failed in the Prince Henry Cup, the directors took a stand and Horch was forced out of the company he had founded with a settlement of 20,000 Reichsmarks. Determined not to give up, he crossed the road, bought a site almost opposite the original factory, and started the company which was to become Audi...

Horch continued to concentrate on large cars until the outbreak of war. Its attempts at designing smaller models were let down by their uncertain roadholding. This meant that when production recommenced after the Armistice they were dropped from the range, which was still overshadowed by the reputation of the marque's creator.

August Horch was born on October 12, 1868, at Winningen on the Moselle, where he worked as a foreman in charge of the construction Carl Benz' first automobile. He was a genuinely creative innovator, introducing aluminium components into his engine designs, developing an improved carburettor jet, and experimenting constantly in the search for more efficient engines and cars. He designed a 'vibrationless' twin-cylinder, and he was the first in Germany to offer a shaft-driven automobile. In 1908 he showed an advanced appreciation of aerodynamics in vehicle design in the shape of his "Torpedo" body, which brought with it a measurable improvement in maximum speed. He made improvements in the position of the valves in the cylinder-head, created the auto-

ALAIN VAN DEN ABEELE

Opposite, top: This was the building which housed the production lines of Horch. in Zwickau. It was photographed shortly before it was demolished, in March 1995. Opposite, below: When he was dismissed in 1909, August Horch bought the land across the road and started up again; by 1910, his company was known by its definitive name of Audi, the Latin translation of the German word 'horch' – 'listen'.

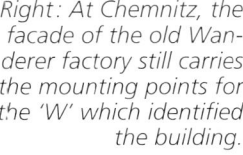

Above: The East German authorities did their best to destroy all reminders of the past, but it is still possible to make out the words 'Horch Werke' on the frontage of the company's old factory building in Zwickau. One wonders how much longer it will stay there.

Right: At Chemnitz, the facade of the old Wanderer factory still carries the mounting points for the 'W' which identified the building.

matic carburettor, and introduced the concept of twin spark-plugs. He was a great believer in the use of high-quality raw materials, using nickel-chrome steel for crankshafts and gears.

If Horch was not ready to compromise his standards for commercial reasons, there was in Jörgen Skafte Rasmussen – who had come to Germany from Scandinavia when he was a little boy – someone capable of reconciling the talents of the engineering purist with the needs of the salesman in a way which would lead the enterprise to success.

On October 14, 1906 he bought a textile mill, close to Schopau in the valley of the River Dischau, and transferred to it his newly-formed company, *Rasmussen & Ernst GmbH*. The company's headquarters remained in Chemnitz, and Rasmussen saw his new acquisition as a means to achieve his ambitious aims of building and selling a variety of engineering products, from steam-boilers to cooking utensils. Reflecting the lofty aims, in 1909 the name was changed to *Rasmussen & Ernst, Schopau-Chemnitz, Maschinen-und Armaturenfabrik, Apparatebauanstalt*, but in 1912 this was simplified to *Zschopauer Maschinenfabrik J.S. Ras-*

registered the name Audi, the Latin translation of Horch, which means 'hear' in German.

Horch started his new company with a completely new range of products. The first Audi was the 10/22hp Type A, but the second, the Type B, was more powerful, and Horch himself drove it to a win in the first Austrian Alpine Trial in 1911. Business was booming, and the new 14/35hp Type C was ready for production. It went on to success in the Austrian Alpine Trials of 1912, 1913 and 1914, making Audi a well-respected name in competitions circles. The Type C was a car designed specially for sporting purposes, and its 40hp engine gave it a speed of over 100km/h (62mph). By 1913 the 18/45hp Type D and the 22/25hp Type E were available, and they were soon followed by the little 8/22hp Type G. The latter completed a product range which had been designed from scratch in just four years! The 2.6-litre four-cylinder engine had its cylinders arranged in pairs, and the camshaft drive of the Type C engine was modified in order to move the axis of the camshaft away from the centreline of the cylinders in an effort to reduce the stress on the pushrods. The combustion-chamber was also modified, with the vertical exhaust valves tilted slightly.

The Type C, which was known as the 'Alpensieger' in honour of its Alpine Trial successes, was Audi's standard-bearer. 1116 Type C's were built between 1912 and 1928, and the total Audi production prior to the war was 2164 cars. During the war, the factory produced grenades and mine-throwers, together with a tracked car and an armoured car.

Germany's defeat and the signing of the Treaty of Versailles which followed it brought about a devastating economic recession in the country, which the motor industry approached in different ways. Many manufacturers decided to concentrate on small economy models, while others – including Horch and Audi – chose to produce large-engined cars for a market which was in recession and a country which was being targeted by foreign manufacturers.

American, French and British cars were being imported in large numbers, and imported makes took some 40% of the German market. In addition, Ford and General Motors had set up European operations in Germany in the Twenties, and GM was to take over Opel in 1929. Technically, the transatlantic

The roots of DKW encapsulated in two engines. Above, the tiny two-stroke, a miniature marvel christened "the child's dream". Below it, the Fahrrad Hilfsmotor an auxiliary engine for pedal-cycles. The DKW name itself came from the German word Dampfkraftwagen, *meaning 'steam-car'. Despite the fact that only one prototype was built in 1915, the name stuck.*

mussen. The factory enfolded in the Dischau valley was not yet involved in automobile manufacturing – during the war it was to produce shell fuses and detonators – but it was extremely busy. The shortage of fuel in wartime encouraged Rasmussen to experiment with a steam car in 1916, but lack of finance led to it being abandoned. It did, however, give the future company its name of DKW, a short form of *Dampfkraftwagen*, the German for steam car. Curiously, it was a miniature two-stroke engine, a children's' toy designed by Herr Ruppe, an engineer from Apolda in Thuringia, which brought success to the company in the immediate post-war years. The engine, christened *Der Knaben Wunsch* (the child's dream), was successively a stationary engine and a power-source for bicycles. In 1928, it finally appeared as an automobile engine.

August Horch, having been ousted from the company he had founded, started *August Horch Automobilwerke GmbH, Zwickau* in 1909, but almost immediately fell foul of a court decision which prevented him using his own name. It was a difficult problem, but he tackled it with intelligence: in November 1910 he

Established in 1932, the Auto Union headquarters in Chemnitz was turned into a hospital by the East German authorities who rechristened the town 'Karl-Marx-Stadt'. The building is still a hospital.

Opposite: The Horch engineers were housed in these villas within the factory grounds at Zwickau. They were decorated with bas-reliefs showing various modes of transport, including trains, automobiles, and here, horsedrawn carriages.

Below: This Auto Union Type C was found in Riga, now in Latvia but formerly part of the USSR, where it had been taken by Russian troops in 1945. It is now in the Auto Union museum at Ingolstadt, and is in completely original condition. The museum is now engaged in the task of putting it back into running order.

models were more advanced than their German counterparts, for American development departments had not been as seriously affected by the war. Times were hard for the German manufacturers, who were at a technical disadvantage, fighting galloping inflation, and under a considerable tax burden. In 1922, the state took 100 marks for a car under 6hp, 200 for those between 6 and 10hp, and 300 for models of 12hp and above. It was not until 1923, with a devalued mark and a load which was taken off war reparations by American capital, that things took a turn for the better. Between 1924 and 1928 the Weimar Republic saw something of an economic recovery, but the damage had been done. Of the 71 automobile manufacturers which were active in 1924, only 19 remained in 1928. Reorganisation saw the disappearance of such marques as Apollo, Fafnir and Röhr among others and the linking of names like Daimler and Benz. Other manufacturers, like NSU, Brennbor and Dürkopp, stopped building cars.

Wanderer produced good results in 1926, thanks to its 6/30hp 4.0-litre Type W10. It was the company's intention to develop a range of small and medium-capacity cars, but the W10 and W11 enabled it to repay some of its debts. Wanderer asked Ferdinand Porsche's design bureau to work on six-cylinder engines of 1.7 and 2.0-litre capacities and a 3.5-litre V8, but in 1931 its financial situation was such that it was necessary to ask the Dresdener Bank to look for possible merger partners.

At Horch, 1926 saw the launch of the 303, equipped with a V8 engine which had been designed in-house by Paul Daimler, the son of Gottlieb Daimler. The car was a large luxury saloon, but the engine was prone to overheating problems, which were solved by Fritz Fiedler, who replaced Daimler in 1927. Horch, which was following a policy of establishing itself in the luxury market, introduced a V12-engined car at the 1931 Paris Salon. It was designed to solve the company's problems, which were manifesting themselves in steadily dwindling sales figures, but it was ill-conceived for the market as it stood. The range comprised 18 expensive models, and some of these variations sold as few as 20 examples. It was soon necessary to reduce prices on the smaller 4.0-litre models to revive sales, and part-time working became a matter of course. In October 1931, the management of Horch

began discussions with Rasmussen's DKW group and the Sächische Staatsbank, which was eager to protect its investment in the Horch company.

As has already been mentioned, DKW's expansion was due to the success of the amazing two-stroke 'toy' engine. It was first used in a moped in 1921, and the same year it appeared in its first true motorcycle application, marking the path for the company's growth. In 1924 DKW was Germany's largest motorcycle manufacturer and put an instalment payment plan into operation to widen its market even further. There was already talk of building cars in the factory where the popular 200, 300 and 500cc motorcycles and the 'Framo' light delivery tricycles were built. The first car duly appeared in 1928, taking the form of a two-seater roadster and a three-seater cabriolet, designated 'P15'. Both were powered by two-stroke engines, very much a novelty in the car world at the time.

At the 1931 Berlin International Motor Show, DKW introduced the first mass-produced front wheel drive car, the DKW F (for 'Front') 1, which was also notable for its floating axle and laminated bodywork. The F1 was followed in 1932 by the 'Sonderklasse', which had conventional rear-drive but stayed with the two-stroke powerplant – in this case a 1.0-litre four-cylinder. But the economic crisis was having a drastic effect on car sales, and the banks were reacting strongly. It was a scenario which was to put Jörgen Rasmussen, to whom we shall return in a moment, at centre stage.

At Audi, post-war production had concentrated on the more powerful models, but with little success in terms of sales, and on June 21, 1920 August Horch was to leave the company. In 1923, Audi launched a new 6-cylinder car, designed to replace the earlier fours. The Type M, as it was known, remained in production until 1928, but its high production costs led to the collapse of the company, and as early as February 1926, Audi was under the control of the courts. In 1928 *Zschopauer Motorenwerke J.S. Rasmussen AG* bought two-thirds of the newly-issued issued capital of Audi, and by 1931 Rasmussen had become the principal stockholder. The take-over made the Rasmussen group one of the main players in the automobile industry, and set the scene for the incredible poker game which would ensure, if successful, the continued existence of the motor industry in Saxony. Audi's range, however, did little to help matters. The 4.6-litre Type M was capable of 120km/h (75mph), but it was handicapped by an overall weight of 2400kg (5291lb.)! The Imperator and Zwickau models followed, each powered by an eight-cylinder engine and carrying a '1' on the radiator cap as a symbol of leadership in exclusivity and automotive technology, but they could not save the marque. In a last-ditch attempt which followed his take-over, Rasmussen tried a new tack and fitted the Audis with a 5.3-litre engine built under licence from Rickenbacker. This was the American company founded by the famous Great War flying ace who was also the owner of the Indianapolis race track. The engine was a special feature of the Zwickau S and SS models, but it did nothing to arrest Audi's collapse.

As Saxony's motor industry set out into the Thirties, the business situation was, thanks to national and international trading conditions, somewhat complicated. Wanderer was in discussions with the Sächische Staatsbank, and despite its affordable model range, sales were not good. Horch was on a knife-edge and DKW was suffering under the effects of Rasmussen's over-enthusiastic expansion plans. The time had come for talks of merging the troubled companies, and after nine months of discussion the beginning of 1932 saw the units of the industry in Saxony start the move towards consolidation. The process was accomplished in two stages. First, Horch, Audi and DKW joined together to form *Auto Union AG*, with its headquarters in Chemnitz. This new entity then bought Wanderer's automobile interests. On June 29, 1932, Audi, Horch and DKW held meetings of their stockholders at which the plans were unanimously approved.

As part of its take-over of Wanderer's car business, Auto Union also took over the contracts with *Porsche AG* for the design of new models and retained the whole of the company's workforce. In total, Auto Union employed some 4500 people in the plants at Zschopau (motorcycles and two-stroke motors), Zwickau (car manufacture), Berlin-Spandau (wood-based coach-building), and Siegmar (car manufacture and steel body-building). The new creation had its own badge, four interlinked rings symbolising the four marques which it had joined together.

By April 1933, the reorganisation which followed the merger was complete, and the factories were in full production in a Germany which had a new leader, Hitler, and a new dream, the Third Reich. The new regime had lowered the tax burden on motor vehicles, and business was improving, putting Auto Union, with 14% of the market, in second place behind Opel among German constructors. It was the start of a period of expansion, in which each member of the group would introduce new models into a home market where car ownership was very low.

Hitler had changed the rules of the game in April 1933 with a programme of national road construction, state support for racing car construction, and the launch of the 'Peoples' Car' programme which was to culminate in the Volkswagen. This state support for the automobile industry was particularly strong in the case of motor sport, where a subsidy of 600,000 Reichsmarks was made available. The motives were purely political, for it was seen that Grand Prix victories would demonstrate German supremacy in a field which had for years been dominated by foreign manufacturers such as Alfa Romeo, Bugatti and Maserati.

So it was that between 1934 and 1939 Grand Prix racing was dominated by the battles between Auto Union and Mercedes-Benz, a rivalry which gave rise to technical developments which were to revolutionise motor racing. Alfa Romeo had to be content with the crumbs left over from the feast, while French manufacturers were left trailing in the wake of technological progress fed by state finance.

For Auto Union, racing was a testing ground for product development, but despite a state subsidy of some 2.7 million marks, the company had difficulty in finding the enormous total of 13 million marks which its racing programme cost. Because of the state intervention, racing decisions were not able to be taken solely by the company; the case for Auto Union's racing car had to be pleaded before Hitler himself, who heard a presentation given on behalf of the company by Klaus Detlov von Oertzen, the chairman of the board of Wanderer, Hans Stuck, the racing driver, and Professor Porsche, the car's designer. His plan was for a car with a centrally-mounted 45-degree V16 engine of 4358cc capacity. A simple design, featuring a single central camshaft to operate all 32 valves, the engine would use a super-

Above: Lost in a garage in the vast Horch factory, this unusual fire-engine was built on an eight-cylinder Horch Type 850 chassis which had been extended after it was damaged at the Nürburgring. A little further away, a similar vehicle awaits restoration.

charger to produce 295hp at 4500rpm. The car itself was to have a tubular chassis and all-round independent suspension, by torsion bars at the front and a transverse leaf spring at the rear.

The P-wagen, as it was called, was a revolutionary design, and before the programme could be approved it was stipulated that a prototype should pass a qualifying test and complete a circuit of Berlin's Avus track at over 200km/h (124mph). The test was passed on January 12, 1934, when the first P-wagen, the A-Type, completed an hour at an average speed of 224km/h (139.2mph) and reached a maximum speed of 257km/h (159.7mph). The run was carried out under the eyes of a number of personalities from the fields of motor sport and the motor industry, but none were more important than the political appointees, led by Major Brückner, Hitler's aide de camp. The result was a triumph for Auto Union, and the car became the major attraction at the Berlin Motor Show, which opened a few days later.

The car made its competition debut on May 27, 1934, again at the Avus circuit. Thanks to minor teething problems, it was beaten by the Alfa Romeos, but the

Above: Nobody wanted the old textile factory in the narrow valley of the Dischau when Rasmussen took it over in 1906. The administration offices are at road level, but there are no less than seven floors below them! This DKW factory at Zschopau did not produce cars until 1928.

potential of the design was obvious. Proof came in the form of a victory for Stuck in the German Grand Prix, run at the Nürburgring. This was followed by a one-two finish in the Swiss GP, with Stuck leading his team-mate, Momberger, home. A final win in the Czechoslovakian Grand Prix made Stuck the champion driver of Germany. This was in addition to the hillclimb champion's title, which he had also won after scoring first place in three major events, and the seven new world records which he had set during the year.

The Type A was modified for 1935 and became the Type B, with wider aluminium bodywork replacing the aircraft-style doped fabric used in 1934. Torsion bars were now used front and rear, and the engine was modified to produce more power by increasing the bore and stroke to give a capacity of 4.9 litres. Better breathing came thanks to shorter exhaust pipes, and the result was a power output of 375hp at 4800rpm. In performance terms, this increased top speed by 15km/h to 300km/h (186mph), but the most outstanding aspect of the engine's performance was its massive torque, which meant that a two-speed gearbox was sufficient for most circuits – on the slow-speed Monaco GP circuit, there was no need to change gear at all!

Varzi, the Italian driver, had joined the team for 1935 and won in Tunis, but soon after there came a new recruit, a talented young motorcycle racer called Bernd Rosemeyer. The youngster soon showed that his combination of youth, talent and nerve made him the only driver capable of completely mastering the B-Type, whose understeering characteristics increased when the engine capacity was raised to 5.6 litres from the French GP. Varzi won in Pescara, but Rosemeyer's maiden victory in Czechoslovakia was witness to his unique skills, and he was the team's lead driver for 1936.

Capacity was raised again for the new season, to 6.1 litres, giving the new C-Type no less than 520hp at 5000rpm. Rosemeyer was dominant, starting the season with a win in the *Eifelrennen* at the Nürburgring in which he raced through rain and fog thick enough to cut with a knife. This win was followed by victories in the German GP, the *Coppa Acerbo* at Pescara, and the Grands Prix of Italy and Switzerland. He won the European Championship, the equivalent to today's World Championship, and also led the results in the Freiburg hillclimb. In addition to Rosemeyer's successes, Varzi won in Tripoli and Stuck set three new world records and four class records on a stretch of the new Frankfurt *autobahn*.

The C-Types were retained for 1937 while design work was in progress on new cars to comply with new regulations due in 1938. Rosemeyer scored victories in the *Eifelrennen*, the *Coppa Acerbo*, the Vanderbilt Cup in the United States, and the British Grand Prix at Donington. Hasse, his team-mate, won the Belgian GP.

According to factory documents which survived the war, fourteen examples of the A, B and C-Type cars were built before they were rendered obsolete by the new rules. The 1938 regulations replaced the 750kg minimum weight formula with a limit on engine capacity, set at 3.0 litres supercharged and 4.5 litres unsupercharged, and a minimum weight of 850kg (1874lb). Porsche had left Auto Union, so the D-Type which was designed to the 1938 rules was the work of a new team, led by engine-designer Robert Eberan von Eberhorst. His new engine was a 3.0-litre supercharged unit with 12 cylinders set in a 60-degree V. Three camshafts operated three valves per cylinder, and thanks to a new gear-driven supercharger, power output was 485hp at 7000rpm and maximum speed as high as 330 km/h (205 mph). De Dion rear suspension was used, and modified suspension, combined with repositioning the fuel tanks centrally, flanking the driver, improved the handling considerably. The new bodywork was wider and more rounded, giving the car the appearance of a giant beetle.

Sadly, the team could not call on the genius of Rosemeyer, for he had been killed in a record attempt on January 28, 1938. His loss was badly felt until mid-season, when the legendary "Flying Mantuan", Tazio Nuvolari, was recruited to the Auto Union team. The Italian swiftly adapted to the car, and won the British Grand Prix at Donington at the end of the season. He continued with the team in 1939, when despite lack of finance, Auto Union achieved regular second places in Grands Prix There were two wins, too, Muller was first in the French event, and Nuvolari won the last Grand Prix of the pre-war era, the Yugoslavian GP at Belgrade, on September 3 1939, the very day on which Britain declared war on Germany.

Eleven D-Types were built by the factory, but details of what happened to them after that fateful day on which Nuvolari won in Belgrade are sketchy. At the end of the war, the remaining Auto Union competition cars were taken and hidden in mines close to Zwickau in order to save them from being destroyed by the advancing Red Army, but as time went by their presence was discovered or revealed and one by one they were taken to the Soviet Union where they disappeared. Fortunately, not all were lost completely, and some cars have been discovered, saved and lovingly restored.

While Auto Union expended large amounts of money and effort on its racing programme, the company's production-car, between 1932 and 1939 show little evidence of having been touched by the the technical or publicity spin-off which is often used to justify racing activity. Many of the cars were the products of combining elements from different member companies of the group. The results were often very good, like the Audi 225 of 1933, for instance, which used a Wanderer six-cylinder engine and DKW front-wheel drive. Similarly, the 1938 Audi 920 combined a six-

Jörgen Skafte Rasmussen, the Danish-born engineer who came to Germany at an early age, built himself this house beside the factory he had established at Zschopau, in the Dischau valley. It was from here that he formed the powerful group of Saxony-based companies, firstly by buying two-thirds of the new capital issued by Audi in 1928. By 1931 he was the largest shareholder, and he then went on to link his original company, DKW, with Horch, Audi and Wanderer under the banner of Auto Union.

A COMET IN THE SKIES OF RACING

In the July of 1935, I was present at practice for the German Grand Prix at the Nürburgring. I found myself at the spot where the cars, after diving into the *wehrseifen* and crossing the bridge over the local road, came into a difficult climbing right-hand turn under full acceleration. After Nuvolari, Chiron and Caracciola had passed, there suddenly appeared an Auto Union. Crossing the bridge on full song, the driver attacked the bend in a full four-wheel drift, coming so close to the edge that he scattered the gravel at the side of the track. It was Bernd Rosemeyer, and I had never seen anything like him before. Although it was his first year of Grand Prix racing, he was in complete control of the rear-engined monster which the 'old boys', used only to front-engined cars, found so difficult to handle.

Rosemeyer was born on October 14th, 1909 at Lingen, close to Germany's border with Holland. His family owned an automobile repair shop, and from his early teens young Bernd worked in it with an enthusiasm born of his love of cars and motorcycles. At 16 he took his new driving licence and his savings and became the owner of a BMW motorcycle.

He took part in his first race on May 30th, 1931, riding a new 250cc Zündapp and taking first place. This race was on grass, but he soon moved to road racing, with a BMW, and his skill brought him to the notice of NSU, which engaged him to ride in its factory team in 1933. After six victories for the team he was recruited for 1934 by Auto Union, riding a factory DKW. Again, he showed his brilliance, but his main target was a drive in the new Auto Union racing car. He badgered Herr Walb, the team chief, constantly until he was given the chance to prove his worth. He was immediately at home in the Auto Union, even though he had never before driven a racing car – let alone one with the engine in the rear. Placed under contract to the team for 1935, he took second place to the great Caracciola in his second race, the *Eifelrennen* at the Nürburgring. At the end of the season he took his first Grand Prix victory at Brno in Czechoslovakia.

In 1936 he became one of the leading names in the sport, taking seven victories and winning the German and European championships. Despite strong competition from Mercedes, Rosemeyer won four grands prix in 1937 and also became the first man to exceed 400kmh (248.6mph) when his Auto Union record car achieved 406.3kmh (250.792mph) on the Frankfurt *autobahn*. On January 28th, 1938, while trying to better the record of 432.7kmh (268.87mph) which had been set by Caracciola, he was the victim of a fatal accident when his car went out of control after being struck by a gust of wind at over 400kmh.

Bernd Rosemeyer was a natural talent and a natural leader. Friendly, charming, open and direct. For him, nothing was impossible, and he was never one to turn away from taking a risk.

Günther Molter

cylinder Horch powerplant in a Wanderer body and chassis. Horch continued to build high-quality cars, notably the 830 V8 of 1933 and the 855 and 930 of the late Thirties which had 3.5 or 5.0-litre engines. The Wanderer tradition was continued by models such as the excellent W21 and W22, designed by Ferdinand Porsche around an Auto Union six-cylinder engine. The later W23 and W24, together with the later W50, marked the high-point of the company's existence. In 1932, 4500 people worked at Auto Union; by 1939 the number had risen to 25,000, and they produced a gamut of cars varying from the 10 members of the DKW range through the 2.3-litre Audis to the Horch 830 and 930, with their 3.8 and 5.0-litre V8 engines. But 1939 marked the culmination of Saxony's strong representation in the German motor industry. After the war, the area which had nurtured Auto Union became part of Eastern Germany; the factories which had been destroyed by the Russians lay idle and Chemnitz became Karl Marx-Stadt. Audi is now linked to VW and has left the area – but is it possible that now there is a new order of things in Saxony we shall see a new beginning?

Above: In the course of a record attempt in an Auto Union V16 in October 1937, Rosemeyer became the first man to exceed 400km/h (248.6mph) on a 'normal' road. He recorded a speed of 406.3km/h (252.47mph) for the flying kilometer on a portion of autobahn near Frankfurt. He is seen here in conversation with Ferdinand Porsche (left), the designer of the car.

Below: His final race was the British Grand Prix at Donington, on October 23, 1937. He won, leading home von Brauschitsch's Mercedes.

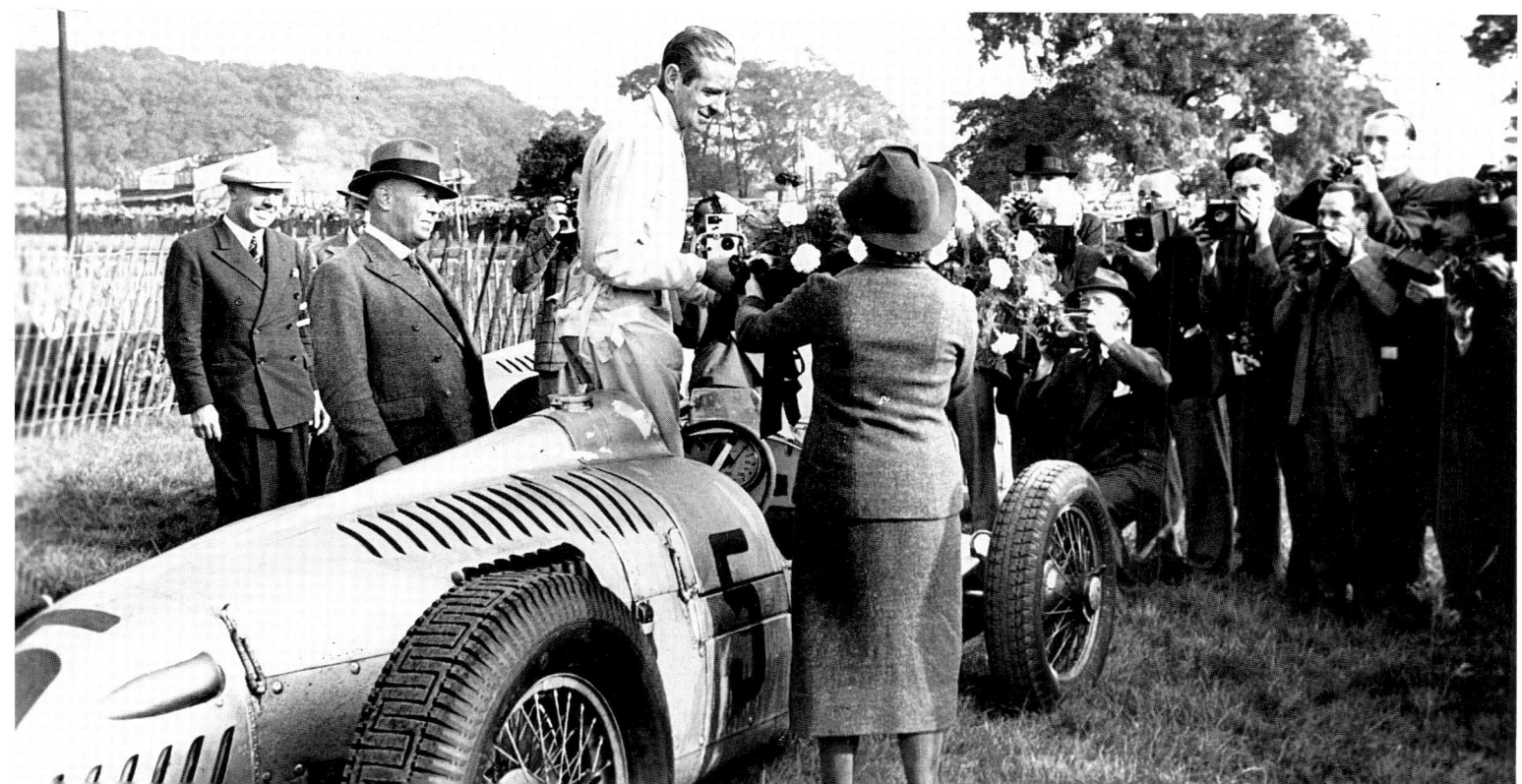

MOTOR SPORT
1995

A PHOTOGRAPHERS' TRIBUTE

FANGIO

Juan Manuel Fangio was world champion five times, in 1951, 1954, 1955, 1956 and 1957, demonstrating in impressive fashion that a man can attain his goals in any walk of life if he pursues them with determination.

Fangio's parents were simple folk; a father who had left the Italian Abruzzi for Argentina when he was seven, and a mother who was a first-generation Argentinean of Italian parentage. For both of them, the new world represented the gateway to a better life. That gateway was symbolised by Balcarce, a

small town on the edge of the pampas which was best-known – before Fangio – for the quality of its potato crops.

The future world champion was born on June 24, 1911, the fourth of six children. He was a sickly child, fortunately blessed with great self-respect. At the age of 14, following a creditable school career, he became an apprentice in the workshop of Maestro Capetini and learned to become a valued automobile mechanic. After his military service, Fangio was offered a scholarship, but he decided to set up on his own. He was 24 when he took part in his first race, in a modified Buick 8 known as 'The Bathtub', and in 1940 he scored his first major win, in the Gran Premio International del Norte, run over a course of some 10,000km. Ten years later, after the war had interfered with what would have undoubtedly otherwise been an even more meritorious career, he won his first Formula 1 race, driving an Alfetta in the Belgian Grand Prix.

As a driver, Fangio was completely without pretension. According to the mechanics who worked with

Juan Manual Fangio died on July 17, 1995 at the age of 84, following a long illness. He had been in poor health since the beginning of the Eighties; in addition to undergoing multiple by-pass heart surgery, he had only one remaining kidney and had to undergo dialysis treatment three times a week. I had known Fangio since 1955, and I published a biography of him that year, having visited his parents in Balcarce. From 1973, when I became head of press relations at Daimler-Benz, it was on a close professional and personal level that I followed his successful career as a Mercedes agent in Argentina and as president of Mercedes-Benz Argentina.

GÜNTHER MOLTER

I had the pleasure of taking thousands of photographs of motor racing during the years I contributed to Automobile Year, but the best one came during the 1957 German Grand Prix. At a Grand Prix, the photographer releases the shutter by instinct, hoping it is the perfect moment, much as a hunter squeezes the trigger. I was lucky enough to be at Brünnchen that day, alongside a minute section of the endless old 'Ring. The sun was shining on Fangio in his Maserati, illuminating his chest, his arms, his face and those eyes, fixed on the finish. The man and the machine looked as though they were cut out of light, silhouetted against the dark background of the forest. Fangio has the look of a great actor, as he flies towards victory. The car is magnificent, you don't see the ground, the light is perfect, and the trees are like a velvet backdrop. That time, I pressed the button at the perfect moment.
Yves Debraine

Reims, July 4, 1954: it was Mercedes' great return to Grand Prix racing, and all the factory's hopes rested on Fangio. This is an 'atmosphere shot' taken just a few moments before the start, and you can see that, as usual, he was totally relaxed, even though the flag was on the point of being dropped. He's wearing his usual polo shirt and has his spare goggles round his neck, and you can see that Karl Kling and his old friend and rival Alberto Ascari, alongside him, look much more tense. The sun was beating down and it was very hot; it was going to be a hard race, but in the eyes of Fangio one can see a great calmness and the confidence of a champion sure that he was going to win – which he did, beating Kling by a tenth of a second.

The other picture (opposite, bottom) was taken at Pescara in 1957, after the final qualifying session for the Grand Prix. For me, it shows perfectly Fangio's incredible eyes, like an eagle's, and the look which made so many feminine hearts flutter. It also shows the charisma and the personality of an exceptional champion, who was the centre of attention wherever he went. Because of his legendary style, kindness and modesty, Fangio was able to make an indelible imprint on an unforgettable epoch.
Bernard Cahier

him, he never expressed idiosyncratic requirements, but merely got behind the wheel and drove. If another driver was faster, he simply put in extra effort to beat him.

He was a great respecter of the car's mechanism, usually driving just fast enough to win. He had, on the other hand, immense reserves of personal determination and stamina, which could be called upon when the occasion demanded. This was never demonstrated more effectively than during the German Grand Prix of 1957, when, delayed to what seemed an impossible degree, he caught and passed the younger Hawthorn and Collins in a classic dash to victory. He won his world titles driving for Alfa Romeo, Mercedes-Benz, Ferrari and Maserati, and his incredible cool-headedness enabled him to overcome any difficulty thrown at him. As long as his car was running, no outside influence would be allowed to get in his way. He drove his races with a sure sense of tactics, often misleading his rivals in a way which was reminiscent of the great Hermann Lang. He would never, however, turn to underhand methods; the thought of taking another driver off would just never have occurred to him.

His personality continued to develop in harmony with his success, with a self-effacing manner which was seemingly in inverse proportion of his increasing stature as a world-famous personality. On the occasion of his 80th birthday, he treated fellow guests of Mercedes-Benz to a speech – made without notes – of which the most accomplished diplomat could have been proud. Juan Manuel Fangio was unique; of all the drivers since the war, he was surely the greatest personality. Today, Grand Prix racing and drivers have changed – we shall not see his like again.

Fangio wasn't happy with the Maserati 250F which he was driving in the 1958 French Grand Prix at Reims, and it was to be his last race. I photographed him as he came out of the hairpin at Thillois, which follows the fastest part of the circuit, a long downhill straight which used the main road from Reims to Soissons. It's one of those 'lucky' shots, because as I was following him in the viewfinder he looked round to see who was following – just as I pressed the button.
Jesse Alexander

It was the 1957 Italian Grand Prix at Monza, in the days when racing cars looked like racing cars, before they were smothered in aerodynamic appendages. Fangio is taking his Maserati 250F through the Curva Sud in a full four-wheel drift. For me, the comparison between the agitation of the photographer and the serenity of Fangio makes for a very dynamic picture

Below: This photograph was taken during practice for the Argentine GP in 1955, which took place on the streets of the capital, Buenos Aires. Fangio is at the wheel of the V8-engined Mercedes-Benz W196, which is reflected in the streaming asphalt. The left-hand front wheel is on the point of aquaplaning as it throws a plume of water in the air. Behind the visor, you can see the strain of intense concentration on Fangio's face.
Günther Molter

117

Practice for the Monaco Grand Prix in 1955, and Fangio is in a Lancia-Ferrari D50. I'd been lucky enough to get a room at the Hotel Metropole which had a balcony giving an unusual view of the Mirabeau corner showing the exact angle of the different cars in the corner, together with the angle of their front wheels. What a difference there was between the different cars and driving styles! In my opinion, Fangio was almost perfect. The unusual shadows caused by the early-morning sunshine add an artistic value to a picture which is also interesting from a technical viewpoint. And in between shots I was able to sip my coffee!
Louis Klementaski

FORMULA 1 WORLD CHAMPIONSHIP

SCHUMACHER WINS IN A TEAM GAME

Mario Luini

The mixture as before – not very original, it's true, but that's the way the 1995 Formula 1 World Championship season worked out. Racing technology has reached such a level that in Formula 1 it is now increasingly difficult for top teams to achieve more than relatively small technical advantages over one another. Progress is slow, and it was not surprising that the beginning of the season saw Williams and Benetton, who had dominated 1994, still at the top of the heap.

Based on the previous year's performance, in which the Benetton B194 and its incredible Ford Zetec-R V8 had taken Michael Schumacher to his first world title, there was a consensus even before it had turned a wheel that the B195 would be the car to beat in 1995. Derived directly from the superb B194, but now equipped with the Renault V10, which had made Williams so strong and was universally regarded as the best engine in Formula 1, the concept of the B195 in the hands of Michael Schumacher had an air of invincibility. Except that such a scenario ignored the fact that the most important attribute of the B194-Ford combination was its balance, something which might not be so easily achievable with the very different power and torque characteristics of the Renault.

Just as Williams had years of experience with the Renault engine, Benetton had a deep knowledge of getting the best out of the Ford. It was astonishing, therefore, that the Benetton technical team under Ross Brawn and Rory Byrne produced a car as good as the B194, itself the result of years of development, at their first attempt. Nevertheless, it was still up to Michael Schumacher to address the fact that although the Benetton was good, the new Williams FW17 was better. It took its place as the best car in the field and was even further ahead than it had been in the latter part of the preceding season. For the whole season, Benetton was playing catch-up, and although each team made continuous improvements it was almost always Didcot which was ahead.

As in 1994, it was finally the drivers which made the difference, with Schumacher proving a worthy champion in the face of a Damon Hill who alternated between being the best and being markedly less than the best. Despite his superb form at the end of 1994, when he was a real threat to Schumacher and only lost the title in the melee of Adelaide, Hill lacked the self-confidence which is the mark of the great champions. Maybe he drew his advantage from a detailed analysis of the flood of information presented to him by the electronics which have become a major tool of Formula 1. But that is not enough when it is a question of making a split-second decision about a move in the heat of a race, or improvising a new fuel-stop strategy born of inspiration rather than reasoning and calculation – in short, when the outcome of events is dependent upon pure talent.

One single Grand Prix – the Belgian – offers a telling summation of the Schumacher/Hill confrontation,

Red lights, green lights and rain: it was a feature of both Brazil and Argentina, when the GP circus returned to Buenos Aires and this damp picture was taken. McLaren was starting a new chapter, with high hopes and engines which were built by Ilmor, but carried the three-pointed Mercedes-Benz star on the cam-covers. Unfortunately, the cold showers they would encounter during the season would not all be meteorological phenomena.

The renaissance at Ferrari continued in 1995, but as ever the final slopes are always the most difficult to climb. The season brought high points, none higher than Alesi's win in Canada, and lows, none lower than the retirement of both cars in Italy. When it rained, the gap to the Renault V10 power of the Williams and Benettons was reduced and Alesi and Berger could shine. It was to no avail, however, for the Scuderia bosses decided that what was really needed for 1996 was not their talents, but those of Michael Schumacher.

BRAZILIAN GRAND PRIX A new season, new cars, a few new faces, but no Senna made it a sad weekend. Hill's pole, ahead of new champion Schumacher, showed the competition between them would again be the theme of the year. This was underlined at the start, when the Benetton shot ahead of the Williams. Coulthard was third, but he and Schumacher were racing under the threat of disqualification. With preparations for the start in progress, the FIA had informed Williams and Benetton that the fuel in the two cars did not conform to a previously posted sample. Appeals allowed the drivers to undertake the risks of racing, knowing that a committee meeting afterwards could render all they did useless, but it didn't seem to worry the German and the Scot as they sandwiched Hill, who took the lead at Schumacher's first pit-stop. More importantly, he maintained the position after his own visit to the pits. Coulthard held on to third, and Hill was untroubled by Schumacher as the field sorted itself out after the first pit-stops. But on lap 30 fate dealt a cruel blow as his transmission failed and he spun off.

Schumacher took over the lead, lost it to Coulthard at his second fuel stop, and then took it back and kept it when the Williams made its own second call for fuel and tyres. Berger, who had been gradually making his way up from sixth place at the start, was third, and that's the way it stayed till the flag fell. Later there was the committee meeting, and Schumacher and Coulthard were disqualified, making Berger the winner ahead of Hakkinen and Alesi. Unfortunately for them, a few weeks later another committee cleverly avoided the need for muddying the waters of the drivers' championship. It reinstated the two drivers, but judged the *teams* guilty. Some said this set the precedent that a driver could score points in an illegal car, but the FIA, having banked over $400,000 in fines from the affair, didn't seem too upset. **MARCH 26, 1995**

confrontation, over just a few laps, the characters of the two contestants for the title were laid bare; Hill – the worker, tenacious and impetuous – was certainly making progress, but Schumacher showed a natural superiority to him in every respect.

One has to point out, however, that while we recall this battle as one worthy of appearing among the classic Formula 1 duels, the Stewards of the race found it necessary to sanction Schumacher for a manner of driving which was excessively defensive. They were working in an environment which two weeks before had seen the FIA introduce new 'rules of the road' for overtaking. Essentially, they gave the advantage to the attacking driver, who had the benefit of priority if any part of his car was level with the rear wheel of the car in front. Apart from the fact that it is impossible for the drivers themselves to judge such a rule, it has the effect of limiting impulsive last-minute overtaking manoeuvres and taking some of the spectacle from the sport. The application of such a rule to a back-marker who is being overtaken is not the same using it between two front-runners battling for the lead. In addition, it opens the door to all sorts

Marlboro-McLaren became Marlboro-McLaren-Mercedes during the close season, and the new MP4/10 sported an unusual winglet on the cover of its new engine. Nobody knew what it was supposed to do, and McLaren weren't saying, but winglets or not, the new car was not as effective as some earlier McLaren designs and Hakkinen (right) could only manage fourth at Interlagos. Possibly the old aircraft design rule of "If it looks right, it is right" also works in reverse.

vintage '95. The conditions were typical of the magnificent Spa-Francorchamps circuit and the Ardennes; too wet for slick tyres, but not wet enough for full wets. On that day Schumacher turned in a performance which would have been worthy of Ayrton Senna, staying on slicks longer than any of his rivals and adapting his driving to the ever-changing conditions on each individual section of the circuit. Hill, meanwhile, lost precious time in a series of tyre-changes, as he tried to match his equipment to the conditions. As a result, the two found themselves in close formation, Schumacher on slicks and Hill on wets, for a duel which would sum up their individual talents perfectly. In the beginning it was the Williams which was best suited to the conditions, but Schumacher made up for his disadvantage by superb driving and car-control, losing the lead to his rival only when he finally ran wide and off the track. It was typical of Hill's luck, however, that a convenient service-road allowed Schumacher to run straight back on again. Nevertheless, Schumacher had gained the psychological advantage, and Hill was almost marked as the loser from then on. In this brief but significant

of subjective interpretations, influenced by the fact that TV images are distorted by perspective and cannot provide a true basis for judgement. But perhaps the rule was all the FIA needed to take a hand in the progress of the championship. The threat of a one race suspension which hung over Schumacher for the four races which followed Spa seemed over the top in comparison with the Hill, who had hit Schumacher at Silverstone – and would do the same at Monza. The Briton was also placed under a one race ban for this latter infraction, but his was only dependent on good behaviour in one race. It might be thought that the more severe punishment should go to the driver who caused two accidents which resulted in the retirement of both cars, and not to he who was merely defending his position as leader, with no other consequences. (*On the other hand, it could be that the punishment was influenced by a continued, deliberate, driving style, rather than momentary lapses into short-sighted over-enthusiasm – Ed.*)

It was another incident of the same type which effectively put paid to Hill's chances of the title. It was some weeks later, in the cold of the Nürburgring,

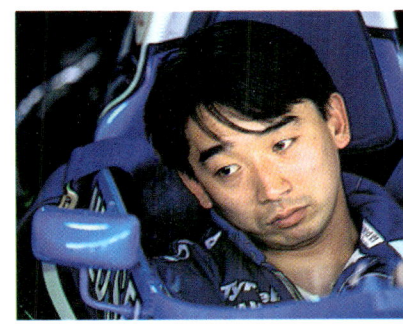

Now with a Renault V10 in his Benetton, Michael Schumacher (left) was in a position to put his competitors in his shadow – undoubtedly, he was the man to beat in 1995. Ukyo Katayama (above) would be suffering no delusions that his Tyrrell-Yamaha was going to make him a threat to the German, but the team was making perceptible progress. On the other hand Jean Alesi (below) could harbour podium hopes; the renaissance of Ferrari was still rolling along.

While Mika Hakkinen and Norbert Haug, Mercedes' Formula 1 representative, could only ponder the new MP4/10's lack of performance (above), Damon Hill and Williams were in sparkling form in front of the big crowd which had gathered for the return of Grand Prix racing to Argentina. A suspension problem had put him out while leading the Brazilian race, but there were no such mishaps in Buenos Aires. With a win for Hill and a first pole position for young Coulthard, Williams were looking in good shape.

Jean Alesi (left) set off on the wrong foot in Argentina, getting entangled in a first-corner accident which forced him into the spare car for the restart. He overcame the problem however, and after a superb race took a second place which saw him menacing Hill in the closing laps. Team-mate Gerhard Berger (below) was not so happy, a troublesome damper meant sixth was the best he could do.

where Hill once again attempted a precipitate overtaking manoeuvre. This time it was on Alesi, who had put his Ferrari in the lead of the Grand Prix of Europe by a daring choice of tyres. The two continued in the race, but Hill's front wing was destroyed, and he had to call in his pit for a replacement. But that was not the total of the damage; his steering was also deranged and a few laps later he was to spin off into retirement. Trapped on the outside of the circuit and unable to return to the pits, he had to stay with his car and watch Schumacher take a win and an all-but unassailable lead in the championship. It was the German's seventh win in fourteen races, and it was achieved in a faultless manner on a treacherous track.

Hill could take consolation in the fact that not all the faults were his. In 1995 the Williams team was notable for its less than perfect pit organisation, which showed in its refuelling stops, which were often much longer than those of its closest competitors, and its pit-stop strategy. Both of these elements were below the standards of Benetton during the 1994 season, but at least there was some improvement in the latter aspect of Williams' performance in that the team at last showed itself able to change tactics during a race. This ability was shown in the management of Damon Hill's race in Portugal, but unfortunately it was to have no influence on the outcome. This year was a severe blow to the team's prestige, for its years of experience in working with Renault had little effect in the face of the spirit showed by the Benetton organisation. That spirit was a the result of an imaginative, non-conformist approach, which went a long way towards overcoming the disadvantage of the fact that the relationship between the team and the French engine-manufacturer was a brand-new one.

It was logical that the Williams was the better car, but the rest of the organisation was weaker, both in terms of the teamwork and the drivers, who seemed less able to withstand pressure. With the benefit of hindsight, some were asking at mid-season whether Frank Williams had taken the right decision in turning down Nigel Mansell in favour of the young David Coulthard. The young Scot, who had put in some excellent performances at the end of the previous season, started 1995 in the shadow of Hill and did not come into his own until the end of the season – by

ARGENTINIAN GRAND PRIX The fourteen years since the last race in Buenos Aires is a long enough period to ensure that there were no current drivers with experience of the old circuit. If there had been, there would have been even more criticism of its preponderance of low-gear corners. Still, there was a job to be done, and in qualifying it was Coulthard who did it, taking the first pole of his F1 career, ahead of Hill and Schumacher. He was unable to take full advantage of it at the start, for as the leaders got cleanly away a mighty *carambolage* broke out behind them, causing a re-start which had people such as Alesi and Barrichello in their spare cars.

Schumacher took advantage of the second chance of making a first impression and slipped past Hill, but he couldn't catch Coulthard. Hill, trapped behind the Benetton, was showing that the Williams cars had a real advantage, but Coulthard lost his after half a dozen laps, when his engine momentarily lost power, allowing Schumacher and Hill past. It picked up again immediately, and he set off in pursuit, but though his Williams had it in it to beat Schumacher's Benetton, mechanical trouble struck the Rothmans car before the first quarter of the race was run.

On lap 11 Hill had passed Schumacher in an overtaking manoeuvre the like of which we see too infrequently these days, and from then on there was little anyone could do about him. He lost the lead at the first pit stops, when Alesi, running a two-stop pattern to the three chosen by everyone else, held it for eight laps, but it was obvious the place at the head of the field was only on loan to the red car. Schumacher could not challenge Hill and settled for third, but Alesi felt he could, and his fighting second place in No 27 was a treat for all those who had some feel for the soul of Formula 1. After some false starts, Ferrari was truly on the comeback trail. **APRIL 9, 1995**

The San Marino Grand Prix at Imola had a particular significance for Damon Hill (right) and the entire Williams team. It was just a year since the death of Ayrton Senna, and the British driver's win, which put him in the lead of the world championship, must have been valued much more than mere points can ever signify.

Nigel Mansell (below) had missed the first two races because the new McLaren was too small for him, and Imola marked his return to Formula 1 in a new 'tailor-made' MP4/10.

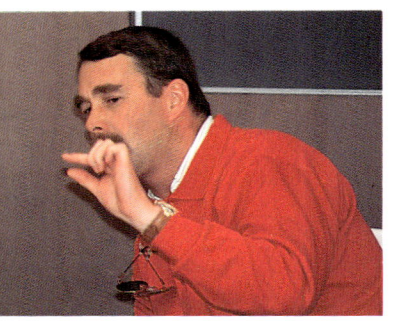

This was not to be a marriage made in heaven, however. Unhappy in a car which was off the pace, his dissatisfaction continued to grow; after Spain, he made his second retirement from Grand Prix racing.

The new Benetton B195 still lacked fine tuning, and even Schumacher was finding it twitchy. At San Marino he had started on wet tyres, like other prime contenders, but when he switched to slicks a patch of damp – or cold tyres – caught him out. After just 11 laps, he began his trip home on foot (right).

SAN MARINO GRAND PRIX Marking the end of the year which started with the death of Ayrton Senna, this race opened a new chapter. As the first European GP of 1995, it was some kind of new beginning, with safer cars and an Imola track which had been adapted, rather than spoiled, to make it less dangerous.

The grid lined up with Schumacher on pole and Berger beside him. A wet second qualifying session had prevented Hill from achieving the time he felt his car was capable of; he was fourth, after Coulthard. The qualifying weather was still around, and most drivers lined up for the start on rain tyres. Berger and Alesi, who qualified fifth, must have been praying for more rain, for in the wet the Ferraris were untouchable. Unfortunately for them, it was not to be, and the two Maranello cars were the first to come in for dry tyres. Schumacher, Coulthard and Hill, lying first, second and third respectively, were still on wets, but by the tenth lap they too had changed and to the delight of the locals Berger was in first place. His position was made more secure when Schumacher crashed, just a lap after his pit-stop. "Too fast on cold tyres" was the obvious verdict, but was the *wunderkind* capable of such an error? "Yes" said some observers.

The *tifosi* didn't care, for there were red cars lying first and fourth, sandwiching Hill and Coulthard. When the time came for Berger's pit-stop, he had enough time in hand to retain the lead but fate was against him. Caught out by a heavy clutch, he stalled, re-entering fourth and letting Hill into a lead he was never to lose. Coulthard had a spin and a 10-second pit-lane speeding penalty, so the Ferraris made second and third, but for Berger it was a case of what might have been. For Hill, the Williams leader for a year, it was a victory to dedicate to his team and to the memory of Ayrton Senna. **APRIL 30, 1995**

which time Williams had decided to replace him for 1996 with IndyCar champion Jacques Villeneuve. Coulthard started to collect pole positions at Monza, regularly out-qualifying both Hill and Schumacher, and in Portugal – coincidentally during the same the weekend in which it was confirmed he would drive for McLaren in 1996 – he took his first Grand Prix win. He blotted his copybook at Monza and the Nürburgring by spinning off before the race had even started, but it must also be pointed out that he lost possible good results in Argentina and Belgium when his car let him down.

For Renault, the Benetton-Schumacher victory was particularly satisfying. It was a superb pay-off for the chances taken in deciding to equip a second top team and throw a strong competitor into the ring against Williams, the team with whom they had collaborated since their return to a turbo-free Formula 1. The result of the effort was an almost complete domination by the V10, memorably broken by Jean Alesi's win for Ferrari in Canada. The rivalry which was created between Williams and Benetton, each with equal engines, could not help but encourage this domination by Renault, and the team, under designer Bernard Dudot, had great cause for satisfaction. 1995 saw the Renault engine pass the landmarks of 250 Grands Prix and 70 wins, a superb record.

The new RS7 V10 was reduced in capacity from 3.5 to 3.0 litres in line with new regulations aimed at reducing power. It was not long, however, before the handicap had been overcome and the engine was once again established as the one to beat. It remained in that position throughout the season, thanks to a constant programme of improvements. An RS7/A appeared at Imola, then came the RS7/B, first used at the mid-point of the championship at Magny-Cours, which gave its users yet more advantages, particularly in respect of the 'Tipo 044/2' Ferrari V12. By the time the championship moved to the high-speed circuits at the end of the season there was yet another enhancement, the RS7/C.

As the engine-designers were improving their products, so too was the Williams technical team, under the leadership of Patrick Head and aerodynamicist Adrian Newey. They introduced the results of their efforts, in the shape of the FW17/B, in Portugal. The new car had a completely revised rear-end, which

Memories of Ayrton Senna burned brightly on the first anniversary of his death, and the Tamburello corner which had claimed him was covered in tributes to his personality and skill.

Johnny Herbert (above) has that quality which the English find so attractive in their sporting heroes – bad luck. 1995 was a new beginning for him, however; as number two to Schumacher at Benetton he had the opportunity to achieve something. Taking second place in a Spanish Grand Prix which Schumacher had led from the start (right) to the finish was proof of his ability and the fact that the team had finally driven the bugs out of the B195.

SPANISH GRAND PRIX If Hill had been disappointed with fourth on the grid at Imola, Barcelona was worse. He was one place further down, behind Schumacher on pole, the Ferraris of Alesi and Berger, and his team-mate Coulthard. The Ferraris had everyone wondering when the team would win, and if there was a sentimental favourite it was Alesi, who deserved a first victory for so many reasons, not least of which was ability. Making things worse for the Williams drivers was the fact that Schumacher's Benetton, a pig in the first three races, underwent an overnight transformation between first and second qualifying. Suddenly, the team had hit on the right formula, and the car which put the world champion 0.6 second ahead of Berger was again the class of the field.

The superiority was underlined when the start came; the German just powered away from the rest, leaving Alesi, a quick-starting Hill, and Berger. The first stops did nothing to change the order, but Hill took over second place when Alesi's engine expired on the 25th lap. It became a team event, with Benetton and Williams leading Benetton (Herbert) and Williams (Coulthard), but with a dozen laps to go Coulthard's gearbox let go. Worse was to come, however, for on the very last lap Hill's car ran out of hydraulics – a mortal failure on today's cars. Locked in fifth gear and with no throttle control, he coasted home, passed on the way by a jubilant Herbert and a grateful Berger. He salvaged fourth, but saw Schumacher take the championship lead. There was a historic footnote to the results in the carefully chosen wording of the McLaren press release following Mansell's retirement on lap 18 of the new car which had been specially built to fit him comfortably. "Nigel had handling problems," the statement read, "and (our italics) *chose not to continue.*" In other words, the British Bulldog had given up. It was the beginning of the end of an era. **MAY 14, 1995**

broke away entirely from the format which first appeared in the FW16 of 1994. Equipped, among other modifications, with a narrower gearbox, the car was much more competitive than its predecessor. Nevertheless, it still did not enable Hill and Coulthard to follow up in the races the supremacy they were to show in qualifying. The car was due to make its first appearance at the British Grand Prix in July, but it was delayed by the transmission reliability problems which handicapped Williams in the early part of the season. The car was meant to be the team's secret weapon, but it probably appeared too late to make the necessary difference. The fact remains, however, that it was the drivers' mistakes, rather than the machinery, which compromised the team's success in the championship double.

In the realm of sporting politics, however, Renault was the loser when Schumacher decided to sign with Ferrari for 1996. In linking itself with Benetton, Renault was forging an alliance with the world champion; the idea of the German superstar quitting the team to explore new pastures was not expected. In fact, Renault underestimated the incredible attraction exer-

Damon Hill (above) was the victim of a double blow in Spain. Unable to challenge Schumacher, he had settled for second place when his hydraulics collapsed on the very last lap. Second rapidly became fourth and Schumacher took the championship lead.

Just outside the First Division of F1, Sauber-Ford and Ligier-Mugen are always among the leaders of Division 2. In Spain it was Heinz-Harald Frentzen and Martin Brundle (below) who battled for places just out of the points.

cised by Ferrari; although Schumacher's head may have told him to stay under the Benetton-Renault colours, his heart led him towards the *Scuderia* and the challenge which it offered. (*It is also possible, with a retainer of $25 million, that his wallet had a part in the argument – Ed.*) For the French company, it was another replay of the situation in which the world champion they had helped to crown broke his links with Renault at the end of the championship season. Nigel Mansell had done it at the end of 1992, when he went to IndyCar rather than play second fiddle to Alain Prost, then Prost himself did it one year later. 1996 will be the third year out of four in which the previous year's champion was in a Renault-powered car – and yet in only one of those four years has the title-holder's coveted number one appeared on a car powered by Renault. Perversely, in that one case (Schumacher, 1994) the title had been won with Ford power!

In a number of ways, 1994 marked the return of Ferrari to the top levels of Formula 1 – even if the return had not achieved complete fruition. In 1995, the team continued its progress towards the top of the heap,

but without the expected victories. A disappointment? Yes and no, if one bears in mind the fact that during the same period of time McLaren had continued its downward slide. Even though it is of no great consolation, everything in Formula 1 is relative. Curiously, the behind the scenes political activity at Ferrari, which seemed to have calmed down with the arrival of Luca di Montezemolo and got even quieter after Jean Todt was placed in power, reappeared just after Ferrari and Jean Alesi had won the best race of the summer, in Montreal. It almost seemed that the success, seen as a form of release by the driver, had given the signal for a new palace revolution to break out at Maranello, a place where such events have always been regular occurrences. It seems the powers that be at Ferrari had not even waited for this pretext, for contacts with Schumacher had been made some weeks before. From the outside, however, it looked as though Alesi's win had liberated the two parties from a tacit agreement and laid the foundations for a new situation which would have cleared away all remnants of the past. From now on, those at Ferrari considered the team was on its way back to the top level of the sport and that it was necessary to whatever had to be done to et the best drivers. While on one side Luca di Montezemolo did not hesitate to proclaim the Berger/Alesi pairing as the best possible one in Formula 1, on the other he was doing everything in his power to attract the phenomenon which is Schumacher, knowing all the while that the arrival of the probable double world champion would split the existing team irretrievably. In doing this, Ferrari took great risks, the first being that of losing its two existing drivers. Worse, it was felt that Berger was more likely to quit than Alesi, and the Austrian was seen as being more compatible with Schumacher. In the end, Schumacher's move was confirmed and both members of the 1995 Ferrari driving team decided to move to Benetton. Alesi was pushed, but Berger jumped, to what seemed to be the consternation of the Maranello management. The choice of Eddie Irvine as number two to Schumacher for 1996 was perhaps the most unexpected development of the entire season. The second great risk run by the Scuderia when it (with help from Shell and Marlboro) hired Schumacher was that with the man universally regarded as the best driver in the world on board, there would be no excuses if the victories did not start to arrive. But that is still some way away, even if it did seem that in the latter part of the 1995 season spirits and ideas at Ferrari were being turned more towards the promises held by the next season.

Once again then, Ferrari has not lived up to the hopes of the *tifosi*, and once more – in spite of three major new versions during the course of the year – the principal blame has fallen on Tipo 044 V12 engine. If the 044/1 which started the season gave satisfaction, the mid-season 044/2 was off the pace in comparison to the Renault RS7/B. It was necessary to wait for Monza, and the 044/3, before Ferrari had an engine which would give it a horsepower advantage over the 700-plus of its French rival. But with an operating regime mainly situated above 17,000rpm, its performance characteristics were decidedly 'peaky', to the point where the engine never gave the performance advantage expected of it – except on circuits like Monza, with its long straights interspersed with corners which need little in the way of smooth power-delivery. Heavier, less fuel-efficient, very powerful but less progressive, the disadvantages of the V12 once again outweighed its advantages, particularly insofar

131

Having inherited the Peugeot V10 engines abandoned so suddenly by McLaren, the Jordan team was starting off on a new footing. The results they achieved were fitting for the best small team in Formula 1. Both Rubens Barrichello and Eddie Irvine (here at Monaco) scored points and podium places, but they also had some bitter disappointments. Jordan outshone Barrichello this year, but it was still the shock of the season when he was recruited by Ferrari for 1996.

Putting a chicane into the old Ste. Devote corner at Monaco has caused more accidents than it has prevented, but at least they occur at a lower speed than they would otherwise have. The 1995 version saw David Coulthard (No. 6) trapped in a Ferrari sandwich between Alesi and Berger, who took to the air when he tangled wheels with his teammate. All three drivers raced their spare cars, with mixed fortunes. Coulthard retired, Alesi got taken off in a bout of over-enthusiasm by Brundle, and Berger scored his fourth third place in five races.

"I hope I don't have to do that when I drive for a major team!" French F3000 star Jean-Christophe Boullion (above) came into the big time as a replacement at Sauber for Karl Wendlinger. Damon Hill (right) scored an unchallenged pole position, but in the race he visited the pits too often. Hill's two stops against Schumacher's one allowed the World Champion to race through his home tax-haven in solitary splendour (opposite).

as John Barnard and his British-based design staff were prevented from making the 412 T2 the chassis it could have been with a lighter and more compact engine.

Did some-one say V10? This was the year in which Ferrari finally took the giant step and set in motion the process of designing and building a V10. This type of is engine generally considered to be the best compromise possible within the framework of the existing regulations, particularly in view of the reduction in capacity from 3.5 to 3.0 litres. This engine – a veritable cultural revolution for Ferrari engine-designers brought up on the siren-song of the V12 – made its first outings in private testing in October and was immediately reported to be showing promise. If the engine does prove to be the answer, the team can express regret for not taking the path earlier. An analysis of the 1995 season shows that Ferrari only missed out on being a real contender for the championship by a small margin. Sharing the points as they did, Benetton and Williams could have been vulnerable to a third force – if that force had been more consistent than Ferrari, which had too many ups and

MONACO GRAND PRIX An almost perfect lap in the final qualifying session by Hill, 0.8 second ahead of Schumacher, was more than anyone could counter. The benefits of pole position on the worst overtaking circuit in the world became evident at the first corner, when Hill and Schumacher were clear away as Coulthard became the meat in a Ferrari sandwich. Both Alesi and Berger energetically tried to take away his third spot on the grid, and all three had to start in spare cars when after the inevitable accident, the red flag was shown and a restart ordered.

Hill profited from his pole again at the second start, but Schumacher was not letting him get away. Coulthard retired on lap 16 when his gearbox broke, and the two Ferraris, Alesi leading, took over third and fourth. As one-third distance approached, bringing with it the time when cars which had chosen a two-stop regime would have to come into the pits, Hill and Schumacher were already lapping traffic. The gap between them was less than three seconds, and when Hill stopped, Schumacher was able to open up a healthy lead over his rival. It turned out, however, that from that point he had no rival, for Benetton had won the tactical war. Choosing to make one stop – no doubt working on the premise that a fast and skilful driver is likely to be overtaken at Monaco only during pit-stops – Schumacher's team had decided to give him the least possible time in the pits. Alesi, on the same schedule (Berger made two stops), could have beaten Hill too, if he hadn't got involved in an accident due to Brundle's over-enthusiasm. As it was, Hill (who, it was found out after the race, had a malfunctioning differential) was second ahead of Berger. But the winners were the Benetton chess-players who planned the tactics. Sadly, with 71 seconds between first and third it was as about as exciting as chess. As a footnote, Mansell did not race, but Blundell took his car to fifth.   **MAY 28, 1995**

CANADIAN GRAND PRIX The grid showed the state of the form-book. Williams and Ferrari had the best machinery, but Benetton had the best driver in a machine which was almost as good, so the order was Schumacher, Hill, Coulthard, Berger, Alesi and Herbert, the two Benetton-Renaults sandwiching the Williams-Renault and Ferrari teams.

At the start, Schumacher used his pole position to advantage, but his team-mate was less fortunate and fell victim to another over-active start by Hakkinen. On the second lap, Coulthard spun off into a gravel-trap, so although the race was following a familiar pattern, with Schumacher ahead of Hill and the Ferraris, at least there was space for a couple of second-division cars to get into the top six. It was the leaders of the second division, Barrichello and Irvine in their Jordan-Peugeots (what a commentary on the 1995 season that McLaren was not even a contender in the second rank) who took up the vacant positions. On lap 17, Alesi passed Hill, but there seemed no likelihood of him challenging Schumacher, particularly since all the leaders were on a single-stop refuelling plan. The thirst of the Ferraris meant Berger's car ran dry within sight of its pit, arriving at pushing pace. Time to completely refill the tanks and restart the engine lost him five places. On the other hand, Alesi was going well. When Hill's hydraulics gave out on lap 50 there was a lessening of tension in the Ferrari pits, but it was nothing compared to the elation eight laps later when Schumacher pitted with gear-selection troubles – cured, 1995-style, by a new steering wheel and a software patch. The German dropped to seventh, leaving the Jordan pair in second and third and Alesi, on his 31st birthday, in sight of his first Grand prix victory. When the flag fell, the outpouring of emotion from the crowd and the pits was nothing less than the first three deserved, but it was a pity the crowd invaded the track.

JUNE 11, 1995

A fault in the gearchange on Michael Schumacher's Benetton dropped the lead of the Canadian Grand Prix right into Jean Alesi's lap. The Ferrari driver (top and right) was overjoyed with his first GP victory and so was the crowd. A car carrying the 27 which will always be associated with Gilles Villeneuve is a natural favourite in Canada, but when it's driven by a man who also drives from the heart – and it's his birthday – it's not surprising there was a track invasion.

Having linked with Peugeot, petulantly divorced by McLaren at the end of 1994, the Jordan team continued to strengthen its position as the strongest pretender to top-team status. In Canada, Rubens Barrichello (above) and Eddie Irvine filled the two lower steps of a pleasantly different podium.

FRENCH GRAND PRIX Damon Hill took pole position for the third successive time at Nevers-Magny-Cours, and for the first third of the race it looked as though he was able to tame the unstoppable force which was Michael Schumacher. Taking the lead from the start, the Rothmans Racer seemed to have his rival under control as the two led Barrichello, Coulthard and Panis, the latter going well on Ligier's home track. After only ten laps, however, Barrichello and Panis were handicapped when the technology-overkill which spots the slightest movement before the green light drew their names to the attention of the stewards. A ten-second penalty which actually loses approximately half a minute because of a trip to pit-lane seems to be a harsh penalty for a millisecond's anticipation, but it fits in with the 'get-tough' policy of the FIA. It lost Barrichello five places and Panis four, and effectively destroyed their chances of a podium finish.

The order was now Hill just ahead of Schumacher, with Coulthard third and Brundle a pugnacious fourth. Schumacher was the first to make a stop, on lap 19 of 72, and Hill went in just two laps later. They were important laps, for when Hill came out he was in the thick of traffic and desperately trying to catch up the deficit on the Benetton. It was not to be, however, and for the rest of the race, including another fuel-stop, Schumacher merely stretched his lead. At the finish it was over half a minute, and the fact that Hill had another 30 seconds-plus on Coulthard, pressured by Brundle in the final laps, could have been of little consolation. Alesi was fifth in a disappointing afternoon for Ferrari; after a malfunctioning fuel-hose ruined a pit-stop, Berger was twelfth. Barrichello and Panis salvaged sixth and eighth respectively, but a three-sprint race handicapped by electronic movement-sensors was not a good advertisement for Grand Prix racing. **JULY 2, 1995**

The Ligier-Mugens were well-fancied at Magny-Cours, but Martin Brundle (above) had to be satisfied with fourth place after after an off-track excursion during qualifying meant he could do no better than ninth on the grid. There was disappointment for Rubens Barrichello (right) too. Fifth on the grid, he was going well before being called in for a penalty for 'jumping the start'. For Michael Schumacher, however (opposite page), it was a trouble-free race. Winning in France for Renault must have brought him and the Benetton team lots of brownie points.

downs. Originally very reliable, the red cars showed their performance to be too influenced by the characteristics of individual circuits. Then, particularly in the latter part of the season, they gained performance but lost reliability. Although Alesi took command in Canada after the Williams and Benetton front-runners dropped out, it was not until Monza that the Ferraris truly came out on top – and then fate dealt the two drivers a truly awful hand to play in front of the home crowd. Alesi was led to surmise that if the points had been calculated on the positions at the time he dropped out, rather than at the end of the race's full course, he would have been challenging Schumacher for the championship, rather than fighting for a podium place with Coulthard, Herbert and his teammate Berger! It's a very theoretical approach, but it does show Ferrari's position in the scheme of things for 1995 very clearly.

Unlike Ferrari, McLaren did not make any progress in 1995. In fact they lost ground, in spite of – or perhaps because of – their link with Mercedes-Benz. After Ford in 1993 and Peugeot in 1994, the Woking firm made a third change of engine-supplier in three years and still continued to slide backwards. McLaren's change came at the expense of a long-term contract with Peugeot, while the German company's new liaison came at the expense of a similar long-term deal between itself and Sauber. It was an opportunistic method of operating which did not find universal praise in the paddock. Formula 1 is definitely a hard-nosed business in which there is little room for sentiment, but there are some courses of action which go directly against the image which those involved want to promote by their very presence in Grand Prix racing. Certainly the critics were not in a mind to look kindly on the arrogant team led by Ron Dennis, which could not use the change of power unit as an excuse for its lack of progress. The preceding year, with Peugeot, which was in its first F1 season, had seen much better results, while in 1993, when the team used 'customer' Ford V8's, Ayrton Senna win five Grands Prix. It is perhaps not a coincidence that the team has not won a Grand Prix since the Brazilian left.

It is true that the change in the regulations, introduced for 1995 and requiring a 5 cm step in the flat surface under the car, made the designers' jobs more difficult. The aim of the new rule was to lift the side sponsons and the bodywork in order to reduce downforce, and it took the design and aerodynamics departments into new territory. Some came out of it better than others, but it was McLaren which dropped the greatest number of bricks in their solution to the problem. The biggest among many was to build a brand-new car which was too narrow for the shoulders of their last minute signing, a multi-million dollar superstar driver. The basic error was probably that of wanting Nigel Mansell at all costs, in order to keep the sponsors and Mercedes happy. It was an odds-on bet that Ron Dennis and the temperamental star would never get on, and few were surprised when the marriage hit the rocks after a few weeks. The union wasn't even consummated, for Mansell had soon decided that the MP4/10 was undriveable in its original narrow form. He sat out the first two races, in Brazil and Argentina, while a new car, wider by three centimeters (just over an inch), was being built. It was ready when the circus returned to Europe for the San Marino GP at Imola, but the Briton soon realised that this modified B-series car was no better than the first had been. Considering the task which would face him if he was to try to turn the car into a potential winner, Mansell threw in the

Damon Hill (above) had little reason to be glum before the race at Silverstone, where he set a fine pole-position time. After the race it was a different matter.

An over-enthusiastic overtaking move on Schumacher (right) had put them both out and started a media-fueled 'feud' between them which would drag on and on.

towel and retired from the team after a Spanish Grand Prix in which even he decided it just wasn't worth carrying on.

McLaren would never recover from this situation, and even though the Ilmor-designed and built 'Mercedes' V10 showed occasional flashes of brilliance, notably on fast 'engine' circuits like Hockenheim, Spa or Monza, it also suffered from a lack of reliability. Thanks to numerous modifications and revisions, the version of the McLaren which finished the season – the MP4/10C – had little in common with the car which appeared in the first races of the year – apart, that is, from a lack of performance, which seemed to remain constant. Mikka Hakkinen did not come out of a tumultuous and disappointing season unscathed, for although he had some good drives, he was also guilty of a number of errors. However, the pressure on him was so great, and so intense was his commitment, that few would reproach him except those innocent parties caught up in his occasional bouts of start-line over-exhuberance. Mark Blundell, the test-driver promoted to take Mansell's place in the team, did little to give the team the justification to keep him on for

BRITISH GRAND PRIX Damon Hill went to Silverstone determined to prove a point. The process started well, with a lap in the dying minutes of first qualifying which decisively took pole from Schumacher. Second qualifying was wet, so nobody tried to improve on their times, making it rather boring TV. This made the powers-that-be say that maybe there should only be one session. This would force the drivers out, no matter how bad the conditions, and would give the people who sell the TV rights (who are powers-that-be, not drivers) a better product to sell.

At least the race was a good TV product, enlivened for the partisan crowd by a good start by Hill and a *phenomenal* one by Alesi, leaping from sixth to second by the first corner. Protected by a Ferrari cork which was keeping the Schumacher genie in its bottle, Hill built up a handsome lead. "Yes, but wait till the pit-stops", said those that had seen this before. Sure enough, as Hill went in, Schumacher, who had languished behind Alesi for 17 laps, took over the lead. When it became clear that Schumacher was going for one stop against Hill's two, it looked as though Benetton's tactics would win out again. But it was not to be; Hill left the pits after his final fill-up right behind the Benetton – with twenty laps to go, the two were on equal terms. Unfortunately, as in Adelaide in 1994, it ended in tears. These two make each other edgy when in close formation, and after just two laps of sparring they went off, fighting over the same few square feet of space. Hill saw a gap that might or might not have been there, and Schumacher tried to take it away from him. With both in the gravel and Coulthard forced to halt 10 seconds for a pit-lane speeding ticket, it was a win for the sentimental favourite, Johnny Herbert, who was lifted shoulder high on the podium by Alesi and Coulthard. It was *magnifique*, but it was not the *guerre* which had been expected. **JULY 16, 1995**

Even after Schumacher and Hill had 'retired' each other, the British Grand Prix was still a race full of incidents. David Coulthard (left) was first choice for a win, but speeding in the pits earned him a stop-and-go penalty which put him out of the running. Then it was time for Jean Alesi to lead. He had stayed ahead of Schumacher for a long time in the race's early stages (opposite page, bottom), but it had perhaps taken too much out of his engine, and he was unable to withstand a challenge from Johnny Herbert which saw the Benetton No. 2 taking a win (above) which satisfied him and the home crowd enormously.

Mark Blundell and Rubens Barrichello enlivened the closing laps with a battle for fourth place which ended with a collision which left Blundell staggering home fifth in a three-wheeled McLaren and Barrichello on the edge of the track, cursing his misfortune.

GERMAN GRAND PRIX After Silverstone, there were different but equally strong pressures on Schumacher and Hill to prove themselves in Germany. Hill took the advantage in qualifying, with a pole time just out of the German's reach, with Coulthard third ahead of Berger. Alesi, however, was down at tenth – on a circuit considered to be V12-friendly.

The Hockenheim stadium was a sea of German flags as the start was given, but it did not worry Hill; he got away superbly, and when the pack reappeared after their swift trip through the woods he was already a couple of seconds ahead of Schumacher. And then the rear end of Hill's Williams-Renault snapped sideways on the first right-hander after the pits. It seemed very sudden for a loss of control, and there was a story that when the car was checked later there was evidence of a problem in a wheel-bearing. Whatever the reason, Hill was a passenger as it careered into the tyre-wall, fortunately without injury. It was the start of just over an hour and twenty minutes of mass adoration of the local – well, local enough – boy, and the end of the race as such. Coulthard pursued Schumacher, and even led for four laps during the first pit stop period (Schumacher was on two stops, Coulthard one), but there was never any doubt about the result. Schumacher simply dominated in the way in which he would control any race which did not have Hill in it.

The thought of any kind of competitive racing went out of the window on lap 5, when Berger was called in from fifth place for a '10-second' penalty after Bernie's Black Box said he had jumped the start. He rejoined fourteenth, and at least gave the crowd something to watch as he clawed his way back. He was third, but still over a minute behind the two leaders. As usual at Hockenheim, the rate of attrition was high, and it was good to see Boullion (Sauber) and Suzuki (Ligier) in the points.   **JULY 30, 1995**

In the sultry heat of Hockenheim, the reverberations of the Silverstone collision between Hill and Schumacher rumbled on. They mixed with the usual transfer talk, which always starts at around this time, to make the German Grand Prix a hot-house of rumour. One man who wasn't influenced by the talk was Michael Schumacher, who got on with the job of winning his first German Grand Prix. His joy (right) was matched by the thousands of fans in the stadium who celebrated with him.

The performance of the Ferraris was disappointing, on a circuit where their V12 engines should have been at an advantage. For Jean Alesi, who was the subject of rumours that he was due to be replaced by Schumacher, it was not a cheerful weekend.

1996. McLaren did have ideas about trying to lure Schumacher for next year, but in the absence of a single element in the deal which would outweigh what was on offer from Ferrari, Ron Dennis exercised his option on David Coulthard's contract instead.

In two years, McLaren has fallen from being a leading light in Formula 1 to a position in which the team has to work hard to take a position at the front of the 'also-rans', fighting off teams with less money, less experience, less technological back-up and less political clout, such as Jordan-Peugeot, Sauber-Ford and even Ligier-Mugen Honda, three other teams who also started 1995 with a new engine-partner. Two of them – Sauber and Jordan – found their new power-units as a direct result of McLaren's link-up with Mercedes. Sauber made a good move, replacing its Mercedes-Ilmors with an arrangement to be Ford's favoured team and receive the 3.0-litre version of the Cosworth-built Zetec-R V8 which had taken Schumacher to his 1994 championship. Peugeot, brushed aside in a deal which at the end of the year seemed to have done little more than get Ron Dennis the possibility of a better road car from his sponsor, found in Jordan a team with whom they could collaborate on a much more human level. Both Sauber and Jordan made real progress in 1995, as, to an extent, did Ligier, working for the first time with Mugen Honda. Ligier's renaissance had started half-way through the previous season, when the team was taken over by Flavio Briatore, the charismatic and entrepreneurial boss of Benetton Formula.

No doubt destabilised by what many felt was treacherous treatment on the part of Mercedes, the Sauber team had a hard time during the first half of the season. It soon became clear that the drivers' fears that the new C14 chassis lacked grip were well-founded. With the changes made under the new regulations preventing them from making direct comparisons, they could not be completely sure of their suspicions, but the first Grand Prix, in Brazil, confirmed the doubts which had sprung from pre-season testing. Practically the whole of the first half of the season was lost as the Swiss team's engineers, under Leo Ress and André de Cortanze, pursued ineffective aerodynamic solutions. At the same time Sauber's legendary reliability, inherited from the team's background in endurance racing, began to falter, while the new 3.0-

Damon Hill made a superb start from pole position in Germany, and he was already opening up a gap on Schumacher when the cars came back into the stadium at the end of the first lap. But on the first corner of his second lap it all went wrong. The tail snapped out, possibly thanks to a mechanical problem, and Hill shot off into the barriers. There was nothing more for Michael Schumacher (below) to do than drive steadily towards an appointment with the man with the flag.

Untouchable in qualifying, the Williams-Renaults of Damon Hill and David Coulthard made up the front row of the grid in Hungary. They held their own at the start (right) and it gave them the key to victory. Overtaking is very difficult at the Hungaroring, and Alesi (27), Berger (28), Schumacher (1) and Irvine (15) were forced to play a waiting game. Only Gerhard Berger would be there at the finish, to take third place behind the two Williams drivers, both happy to head home with their trophies (opposite).

Rubens Barrichello had need for some very soothing music for his Walkman after the race in Hungary. Not for the first time, he was to have a promising result betrayed by fate. This one was the worst, however; his Jordan-Peugeot died on the last corner of the last lap, when he was lying third.

On a track which put the emphasis on handling, the Minardis (opposite) showed their chassis were better than their 'customer' Ford V8 engines. At least the engines were reliable, and they gave Luca Badoer and Pedro Lamy, returning to F1 after his serious crash while testing a Lotus at Silverstone last year, eighth and ninth places respectively.

HUNGARIAN GRAND PRIX   The biggest pre-race news was the fact that Michael Schumacher would drive for Ferrari in 1996 – shifting the one log which caused the jam – now all the other logs could start to flow or crash into their places for next season. On the track, Damon Hill continued his excellent qualifying form, taking pole ahead of Coulthard and Schumacher on a circuit which is second only to Monaco in the importance of starting ahead.

Hill used his advantage at the start, and since Schumacher was initially unable to get past Coulthard, things looked good. The Williams number one was driving at his best, and his lead over his pursuers increased steadily to the point that when he made the first of his three stops on lap 17 – as did Schumacher, Berger, Brundle and Irvine – he was able to get in and out and stay ahead of Schumacher, who had pressured past Coulthard on lap 13. The German driver was not able to catch Hill, and the fact that a faulty refuelling rig had given him short measure on the first stop did not help. His second stop had to be taken well ahead of schedule, and it spoiled the rhythm so important in today's 'series of sprints' Grands Prix. Nothing spoiled Hill's rhythm, however, and he maintained sufficient lead for him to take his two remaining fuel-stops without being threatened by the Benetton driver. Coulthard was holding third comfortably, but fourth place was a popular spot, held successively by Frentzen, Hakkinen, Alesi, Hakkinen again, Brundle, Herbert, and finally Barrichello. On lap 73, with just four to the flag, third and fourth suddenly became second and third, as Schumacher coasted to a halt with a fuel-pump problem. For Coulthard and Williams, it was the prelude to a 1-2 finish; for Barrichello, fate flattered to deceive. The Jordan-Peugeot's engine cut out on the last corner of the last lap, a cruel stroke which dropped him to seventh and handed third to Berger.

AUGUST 13, 1995

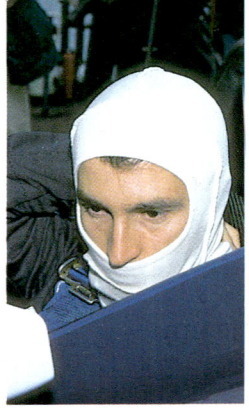

In the cool and rain of Spa, a balaclava was of as much value for warmth as it was for safety. Heinz-Harald Frentzen (above) had his own way of keeping warm, driving a superb race in the Sauber but once again missing the podium finish which most people now realised he deserved. The duel between Hill and Schumacher (right) was also a hot one, the German driving superbly on slicks to hold off a challenge from the wet-tyred Hill. Schumacher was judged to have used too much muscle during the battle and was put 'on probation' for the next races. The crowd, which included many German visitors who had just popped over the border (opposite) probably didn't care too much.

Martin Brundle (below) had a good day despite the weather; third place was well-earned by him and the increasingly-professional Ligier team.

litre Ford Zetec-R, which the Cosworth management had said would be the equal of the 3.5-litre version used by Benetton in 1994, was far from coming up to scratch – particularly where maximum power was concerned.

To make things worse, Peter Sauber was facing a delicate human problem in that it was becoming obvious that Karl Wendlinger – whom Sauber had promised a drive as soon as he recovered from the terrible accident at Monaco in 1994 which left him in a coma for three weeks – was not back to his original form. The only bright spot in a gloomy period was the return of Max Welti, Sauber's right-hand man in the team's endurance racing days, who came back to the organisation as team manager. Another positive point was the continuing improvement in the performance of Heinz-Harald Frentzen the team's number one driver. One of Welti's first tasks after his arrival was to sort out the Wendlinger problem; he did so by hiring the young French driver Jean-Christophe Boullion, the reigning Formula 3000 champion, and giving him the difficult task of starting his F1 career in the Monaco Grand Prix. Two months later, Boullion scored his first

BELGIAN GRAND PRIX Spa again, and a combination of rain-induced spins and mechanical problems put Hill eighth on the grid and Schumacher an amazing sixteenth. The front row was all-Ferrari with Berger on pole; race-day was his birthday, and he must have been hoping to repeat Alesi's win in Canada. The start was dry, but few would have put money on a rain-free race, and As the lights changed Berger found he had problems, in the shape of Herbert, coming through from fourth to snatch the lead, and Alesi, diving into second. Some birthday this was turning out to be – he was out on lap 22.

On lap 4 Alesi was out, Herbert was first again, and Coulthard was second with Hill already behind him. Then a spin for Herbert put the two Williams in front of Berger. Unfortunately Coulthard, who was driving well, had his gearbox fail on lap 13, leaving Hill ahead of Berger and Schumacher, who had been displaying his Senna-like ability to cut through traffic. Then came the rain, as we knew it would. Hill, still ahead after the first pit-stops, went for wets, but Schumacher stayed on slicks and drove superbly to hold off the Briton's challenge. The driving was superb, but the tactics were too robust – perhaps Schumacher learned Senna's bad points with his good – and the way Hill was continually blocked earned the champion a suspended one-race suspension. To compound Hill's woes, the rain stopped, so when he did get past he was unable to take advantage. He went back on to slicks, and then the rain came down again, but stronger. Somebody decided to send out the safety car, so both Williams and Benetton put their men on wets – equal tyres, equal cars, equal drivers and thirteen laps to go when the safety car was called in. The prospects were exciting, except the officials took a hand. Hill had been speeding in the pit lane. The '10 second' penalty gave the race to Schumacher, while Hill salvaged second from a brave Brundle on the last lap.

AUGUST 27, 1995

championship points, at Hockenheim, but his main role was to support Frentzen, a driver whom it was generally agreed was one of the best young talents around. Boullion did have one unique aspect to his career, however. At the same time as being number two at Sauber, he was also following in the footsteps of Damon Hill and David Coulthard and being employed as a test-driver by Williams!

Frentzen confirmed everything which had been expected of him in the second half of the championship, when the C14 had achieved the levels of performance and reliability which were expected of it. The car had gained downforce and lost weight, Cosworth had come up with an improved version of the Zetec-R, and Frentzen thus became able to put himself regularly among the top ten on the grid. He consistently scored points, and at Monza he climbed onto the podium for the first time when he finished third behind Herbert and Hakkinen. Just a few days before, Frentzen had taken a great load from the minds of Peter Sauber and his team by re-signing for 1996 in the face of some very attractive blandishments offered by competing teams. The prospects are good. Sauber

146

Mika Salo (right) was showing great promise in his first full season of Grand Prix racing. The young Finn always made the most of his Tyrrell-Yamaha, and at Monza he scored his best result so far, taking fifth place for a team and engine manufacturer whose determination balanced the lack of a big-league budget.

has an exclusive contract to run the new V10 which Ford and Cosworth are building, and the team had greatly increased its effectiveness in the latter part of this season. These considerations must have played a large part in the young German's decision.

With Peugeot providing its engines, the Jordan team was consistently fast during the season, both Eddie Jordan and Rubens Barrichello regularly being among the top ten on the grid. It was reliability which let them down, and both drivers were denied podium finishes by engine failures. The retirements were made even more hard to bear by the fact that they happened too often during the latter part of the race, when a place in the points seemed certain. For both Jordan, who had used the Hart engine in 1994, and Peugeot, who had scored 42 championship points with McLaren, the season could be summed up by saying that although they were operating on a higher level in 1995, the results were less good because the competition was also on a higher level.

The thing Jordan lacked, in common with all the teams who did not have the resources of Williams, Ferrari, McLaren and Benetton, was time. Adapting to the new regulations was a veritable time-trial in the design offices and workshops; the aerodynamic modifications to reduce downforce and the strengthening necessary for the tub to withstand the new crash tests meant that Jordan designer Gary Anderson had to throw away much of the knowledge gained in the four years Jordan had been in F1. This no doubt helped explain the numerous problems which affected both chassis and engine, together with the hydraulic system and the gearbox, and which prevented the cars of the 'Irish' team showing their true mettle. The best proof of the team's ability came in Canada, one of the races in which the Jordan-Peugeots had a complete and trouble-free run, and which saw them take second and third places. The Jordan chassis turned out to be at its best on high-speed circuits, and it proved difficult to adapt it to varying circuit characteristics. It was not the easiest car to drive, thanks to a centre of gravity which was a little higher than most and which made it twitchy – particularly on bumpy tracks. To the surprise of many observers, the reduction in downforce had the effect of making F1 cars in general more susceptible to unevenness in the asphalt.

Coupled to a semi-automatic seven-speed gearbox

Marlboro McLaren Mercedes did have a big-league budget, perhaps one of the biggest, but the second place at Monza for Mika Hakkinen (opposite) came only after seven major competitors had retired. Some of the gloss was coming off the red and white cars.

Once again, the mixture of Hill and Schumacher on the same section of track had ended in both of them out of the race. This time, the normally imperturbable Schumacher had to be restrained from putting his views to Hill in forceful terms.

ITALIAN GRAND PRIX Pole-man Coulthard was more than a second faster than Hill, who was fourth, with Schumacher and Berger between. The Scot spun off at the Ascari Curve on the warm-up lap, but when five mid-to-tail-enders also went off there on the first lap and blocked the circuit, it meant a re-start in the original grid order with spare cars. Young David was back on the pole he thought he had lost. This time he made no mistake, and for a dozen laps he was an impressive leader; unfortunately a front wheel-bearing let go and put him out, leaving Berger in the lead. The Austrian was in fine form, and there was nothing that Schumacher and Hill, in second and third, could do about it. Schumacher was under pressure from the Williams driver, and on lap 23 the almost-inevitable happened. As the two came to pass Inoue's Arrows-Hart, Schumacher slipped in his usual surgical fashion, and as Hill followed him the Williams hit the rear of the Benetton. That Hill hit Schumacher is incontrovertible – why he hit is another matter. Schumacher was probably trying to arrange it so that Inoue came between him and his adversary, a state of affairs Hill was not ready to accept. The result was both in the gravel and Schumacher reaching new heights of offended innocence. The fans cared little, for there were two Ferraris in the lead, Alesi now ahead. Then, on lap 33, the TV camera attached to Alesi's rear wing fell off. It demolished Berger's front suspension, and the Austrian showed great skill in controlling what could have been a very nasty accident. With eight laps to go the dream ended, as Alesi retired, his rear wheel-bearing perhaps another victim of the new Monza kerbs. And who was there to pick up the lead? Why, Johnny Herbert, as he had been at Silverstone. Behind him were Hakkinen and Frentzen, and Blundell was fourth. Two McLarens in the points! Yes, but only after the retirement of the entire Williams, Ferrari and Jordan teams...

SEPTEMBER 10, 1995

After having hit the Minardi of Luca Badoeer, the Tyrrell of Ukyo Katayama was thrown into a horrifying series of rolls as the field accelerated away from the start in Portugal (top). The Minardi (above) shot from one side of the track to the other, finishing up against the pit wall, while ahead of all this, Frentzen's Sauber was hit by Brundle's Ligier (right) and sent into a spin. The race was stopped, and rescue services worked on releasing Katayama (opposite, bottom). In a tribute to modern safety standards, his worst injury was pain in the neck.

PORTUGUESE GRAND PRIX Once again, it was Coulthard on pole, ahead of Hill, Schumacher and Berger. Surprisingly, Frentzen and the Sauber were fifth, yet more evidence of the *other* young German's talent. The good position was of little benefit, however, for a start-line accident involving Katayama and Badoer, which looked bad but was fortunately injury-free, caused the race to be stopped; at the re-start, Frentzen's engine stalled and he had to start from the rear of the grid. A sterling drive which brought sixth place was little recompense for what might have been.

Ahead of him, the leading players were untouched by the consequences of the accident, and the restart was just like a normal start except that fate – as usual, it seemed – did not help Damon Hill. Coulthard defended his first place, but Schumacher – who had been fended off by Hill the first time – snatched second. Hill, his team-mate *and* his championship rival now ahead of him, must have been having to call on all his reserves of self-confidence. Coulthard, on the other hand, had led both the previous Grands Prix before retiring with mechanical problems, so was no doubt convinced he could do it if the car would hold out. Behind him, Schumacher filled his usual role in a team/driver/car combination now clearly superior to any other. Playing the fuel-stop strategy game perfectly, Benetton psyched Hill and his handlers into believing Schumacher would only stop twice. The Williams crew changed from three stops to two to match, and then discovered the German was making three. It upset Hill's rhythm; after his first stop he was weighed down with fuel, and after Schumacher's third stop he had the fresh tyres which enabled him to take second place from Hill almost as he liked. Coulthard didn't change his tactics, and reaped the benefits in a first GP win and the knowledge that Frank Williams was probably wishing he had not let the Scotsman go.

SEPTEMBER 24, 1995

Tenth on the grid, tenth in the race. On the track, Portugal was nothing special for Eddie Irvine (above left). In the paddock, however, it was a different matter. Ferrari, having unexpectedly lost Gerhard Berger for 1996, were supposed to be talking to and testing all kinds of drivers. In fact, they were signing Irvine in one of the surprises of the year. Eddie Jordan, pocketing the money which bought Irvine's contract and signing Martin Brundle, smiled through his tears.

The Ferraris (centre) were disappointing in Portugal, fighting between themselves for fourth place. The two drivers had chosen varying refuelling strategies, with Berger going for three stops against Alesi's two. Relationships between the French driver and the team, already unsettled, got worse when he ignored team orders from Jean Todt to let the faster Berger past.

designed to exploit its torque range the maximum, and with a modest decrease in maximum revs to compensate for the drop to three litres, the Peugeot Type A10 V10 engine was one of the revelations of the season. It made a major step forward at mid-season, with the appearance at Magny-Cours in early July of the EV2 version. Three weeks later, at Hockenheim, that was followed by the 'EV2 bis' designed for use on high-speed circuits. As far as top speed was concerned, the Peugeot V10 gave the impression that it was giving away little to the Renault V10 and Ferrari V12 in terms of all-out power. An eagerly-anticipated EV3 version was due at the end of the season, but in view of the reliability problems which had shown up during the summer, including high temperatures and excessive wear, notably in the pneumatic valve-operating system, engine-design chief Jean-Pierre Boudy and his team put the project on hold.

On a personal level, Rubens Barrichello found the going hard in the early part of the season. The death of Ayrton Senna and the departure of Christian Fittipaldi for IndyCars had left him as the leading focus for the hopes of Brazil, ahead of his two compatriots from the new Forti team, Roberto Moreno and Pedro Diniz. The responsibility was a heavy one for a driver who is still young. In addition, the introduction of the hand-controlled clutch, leaving just accelerator and brake pedals, had led drivers to use a left-foot braking technique, similar to that which most of them had learned during their early days in karts. Barrichello, however, was one of those – along with Alesi and later Berger – who could not get used to the system. The young Brazilian wasted many weeks before learning from his telemetry read-outs that braking with his left foot was wasting more time than it was gaining. Starting in Canada, he reverted to a three-pedal set-up, and his driving soon returned to its earlier standards. In the meantime, however, Eddie Irvine, in his second season of Formula 1, had gained the upper hand in the team. His new-found status was to pay off later in the season when he, ahead of Barrichello, Coulthard and any number of Italian drivers, was selected to partner Michael Schumacher at Ferrari in 1996. It was a hard knock for 'Rubinho', who, it seemed, was thought to be psychologically too 'fragile' for Maranello.

EUROPEAN GRAND PRIX – NURBURGRING As F1 returned to the 'New' Nürburgring after ten years, the weather was typical of the two finest road-race circuits in the world, Spa and the *true* Nürburgring. It might be cold and it might be damp, but on the evidence of 1995, it makes for the best racing even on an *ersatz* circuit.

Coulthard, on pole again, emphasised his qualifying superiority over Hill, second and showing the superiority of the Williams over Schumacher's Benetton in third. The critical decision at the damp start was tyre choice, and while the majority took wets, McLaren and Ferrari went for slicks. For the McLarens, 9th and 10th on the grid and carrying more wings than the Red Baron's Fokker, the decision was probably academic, but for Alesi, the king of car control, it was a first step to glory. For the first few laps, race order was as it might have been expected, Coulthard holding on to pole advantage and Hill trying to retrieve the second place Schumacher had taken at the start. By lap 6, Alesi was beginning to make progress as the track dried and wet tyres became an embarrassment. On laps 11 and 12 the leading trio all came in, leaving Alesi in the lead.

By the time he made his single pit stop, exactly at the half-way mark, he had enough in hand to keep first place, but only just. Hill was close behind, but on lap 40 an impetuous overtaking attempt by the Briton left him with no front wing. It was a useless manoeuvre, for he was due to pit on the next lap anyway, and it cost him dear. A long pit stop put him behind Schumacher, but the accident had deranged the steering, and with nine laps to go he spun off. Alesi was still in the lead, but Schumacher was on fresher tyres; with three laps to go he unceremoniously bundled the Ferrari aside to take the lead and the win. Hill waved as Schumacher passed on his lap of honour; he was congratulating a rival, but he was also waving his title hopes goodbye. **OCTOBER 1, 1995**

When the 'New Nurburgring' opened in 1984, the comment was made that the only modern convenience it lacked was a roof – and that was what it needed most. From a weather point of view, holding the Grand Prix of Europe there in October was as about as intelligent as holding the same event at Donington Park in April (remember 1993?). And yet, as at Donington, the race was good, even though the warm-up was delayed because of bad visibility (opposite, top). Michael Schumacher saw his grip on the championship strengthen when Damon Hill, who was pursuing Alesi (left), made a mistake during an unneccessary overtaking attempt and damaged his car's nose. Later, Hill added to Schumacher's day by spinning off; after Michael had dealt with the first-placed Alesi in a forceful manner and won, the title was almost his.

PACIFIC GRAND PRIX – TI AIDA With the title safe if he finished fourth or higher, Michael Schumacher went to Japan in confident mood. Even though qualifying left him in his now-usual third place behind Coulthard and Hill, he probably still felt confident. But as the field came out of the first corner he was confident and angry. The reason was that Damon Hill had given him some of his own medicine, and the champion-elect didn't like it. As Coulthard powered away from pole, Schumacher challenged Hill for second in his usual forceful manner. This time, however, Damon 'did a Schumacher', not only protecting his line, but modifying it to such an extent that the Benetton was forced towards the outside of the track. Schumacher didn't get past, but a couple of Ferraris did, and when the cars came round at the end of the first lap Hill was behind Alesi and a seething Schumacher was fifth, behind Berger. It couldn't stay that way, of course, and it didn't. As Coulthard sat comfortably in the lead, the German got past Berger after four laps and then harried Hill, who was still behind Alesi. It all changed on lap 19, when Alesi, Hill and Schumacher all came in to refuel together. They left in the order Schumacher, Alesi, Hill, with the Benetton team taking almost exactly half the time required by the Williams crew. Even given that there was a minor problem with Hill's car, that is still as good an explanation as any of one reason why Schumacher was going to be champion. And that's the way it was. Coulthard adapted his fuel-stop strategy on-the-fly, changing from three to two, but it didn't do him any good. He lost the lead to Schumacher on his second stop, and when the Benetton crew and their man did their stuff at their last rendezvous they made sure the lead didn't slip from their grasp. The victory brought deserved championship celebrations – and yet Schumacher was still complaining about Hill at the post-race press conference. If you can't take it, Michael, don't dish it out. **OCTOBER 22, 1995**

For Michael Schumacher and Flavio Briatore – on the right, above – the finish of the Pacific Grand Prix at Aida marked another triumph. For Benetton's lead driver it was the culmination of a superb season, and the team boss could be proud of the part true teamwork had played in that season.

Called in to take the place of Mika Hakkinen, who was recovering from an appendicitis operation carried out a few days before, Jan Magnussen, the young test driver for McLaren-Mercedes, put up a splendid performance at Aida. In his first F1 race he had no trouble mixing it with such experienced drivers as Rubens Barrichello (opposite) and he finished 10th, just behind team-mate Mark Blundell. Nevertheless, the McLarens had been lapped twice by Schumacher!

The fourth team waiting in the wings was Ligier. Taken over in mid-1994 by Flavio Briatore, the team was completely reorganised, with not a little help from Tom Walkinshaw. Cesare Fiorio, the former Lancia rally and Ferrari F1 team manager, was brought in, but for the 1995 season Walkinshaw took on the 'team owner' position and mid-way through the year Fiorio handed over to Tony Dowe, one of the TWR boss's trusted lieutenants. The team had lost its factory Renault engines when Benetton got theirs, because Renault-Sport did not feel capable of providing an efficient service to three teams. It was not until the last moment, and as the result of one of those deals which have 'Briatore/Walkinshaw' written all over them (remember Schumacher's original move from Jordan to Benetton?) that the Ligier team got its hands on the Mugen Honda engines which were supposed to be the subject of an agreement between Mugen and the Minardi team from Italy. The first result of this last-minute deal was to delay the appearance of the Ligier JS41 Mugen-Honda, a car which some people felt looked a little too like a Benetton B195. Briatore had said he wanted both Benetton and Ligier to benefit from the synergy of their association, but it seemed that the latest business buzz-word was perhaps not the ideal for Formula 1, where the rules insist that each team designs and constructs its own cars. In fact the similarities between the two cars were so numerous, and the murmurings against them so strong, that Briatore was forced to deploy a considerable part of his resources towards proving that the JS41 was more than just a recycled Benetton. It was an important undertaking, for Ligier's major (state-owned) sponsor was said to be considering ending its support if the cars were not a true French blue.

The results were not all they might have been, particularly in view of the substantial budget which the team enjoyed. Despite the 'synergy' with Benetton, the JS41 evolved slowly and suffered from too long delays between the design, manufacture and implementation of new components and systems. Concentrating its testing at the Magny-Cours circuit, just outside its factory gates, the team found it difficult to adapt to other tracks. Main drivers Olivier Panis and Martin Brundle reckoned that they had never been able to get the maximum out of the cars, and development seemed to have become log-jammed before

Starting from his fourth consecutive pole position, David Coulthard looked in good shape to give Williams a win as he led the early laps of the Pacific Grand Prix. But the combination of Schumacher and Benetton tactics and pitwork was not to be denied.

The Champ. Michael Schumacher put on a masterly demonstration of his abilities at Suzuka (right). With the world title safely in his pocket, he took pole position, put in the fastest lap, and won as he pleased, equalling Nigel Mansell's record of nine wins in a season. He did it, as he had on the previous eight occasions, with the help of superb Benetton teamwork, and it was fitting that the win gave them the Manufacturers' title.

Called back by Sauber for the final two Grands Prix, Karl Wendlinger (below) showed some of his old talent in training and qualifying, but in the race he had trouble matching the pace of other drivers who had the benefit of a full season's racing.

Japanese drivers met with mixed fortunes in their home Grand Prix: Aguri Suzuki, who had already announced his retirement, had an accident in qualifying and had to withdraw his Ligier-Mugen. Ukyo Katayama (Tyrrell-Yamaha) dropped out early in the race, but Taki Inoue (right) took his Footwork-Hart through to the finish, albeit in last place.

the season ended. The Mugen-Honda V12 wasn't the best engine in the field, but it wasn't the worst either, as it followed the Japanese philosophy of favouring reliability over outright power. An improved version arrived in time for the Italian GP in September; one race later it was further improved with the adoption of a 'fly-by-wire' throttle, a development which made the driver's job easier and better exploited the engine's potential. The last three Grands Prix of the year, in Japan and Australia, were run with engines which had been improved even further.

As far as the drivers were concerned, Panis gave precedence to the tough and experienced Brundle, but for a number of races the British driver had to give way to the less-skilled, but mega-yen sponsored, Aguri Suzuki. It had negative effects on all three; Panis was perhaps trying too hard to keep his seat, and after having one of the best finishing records in 1994 he went off-track too often in 1995. Brundle was frustrated, and although he scored Mugen's first podium after a great race at Spa, he was also occasionally guilty of going too far, notably when he spun and took off Alesi in Monaco, and when he incurred a fine

after driving almost a full lap on a terminally damaged tyre and wheel at Monza.

The final third of the grid was made up of teams struggling against the handicap of a restricted budget. The best of this group by far was Minardi, whose Aldo Costa-designed M195 was very good, showing some original thinking in its aerodynamics. Minardi had had the Mugen-Honda engine contract taken from under their noses by Ligier, so the small Italian outfit had to make do with a 'customer' version of the Ford ED V8, an engine which was something like 150hp down on the front runners! In these circumstances, Minardi could hope to do little more than prove the efficiency of their chassis on those circuits where power was not at a premium. They succeeded within this framework, for they regularly beat better-sponsored and better-equipped teams like Tyrrell-Yamaha and Footwork/Arrows-Hart.

Great things were expected from Tyrrell at the beginning of the season, and when the young Finn Mika Salo just missed a point after a good showing in Brazil it looked as though the prognostications had been correct. Unfortunately, the team failed to live up to

JAPANESE GRAND PRIX Michael Schumacher said he was coming to Suzuka to enjoy himself. Well, he certainly did. He started by taking pole, ending a Williams run which stretched, with a single break for Ferrari at Spa, for nine races. Alesi was second, and behind the Ferrari was Hakkinen, feeling the benefits of a successful appendectomy and a modified engine. Hill and Coulthard were fourth and sixth – there was no Williams advantage here.
The start, with all the field on wet tyres, was clean, and at the end of the first lap the champion had a useful lead over Alesi and Hakkinen. It stayed that way until lap 5, when Alesi was called in for a ten-second jump-start penalty. Berger was also a victim of the over-sensitive electronics, and came in a lap later. Alesi seemed stimulated by the fatuous penalty, and was tenth on lap 7, sixth on lap 10 and back into second by lap 12. It was driving to stir the heart, and one anticipated a glorious battle between the two. But it was not to be; just before the half-way mark, the Ferrari coasted to a halt with differential failure. The challenge gone, Schumacher was untouchable. He made the first of two stops early, to change to slicks, and lost first place to Hakkinen for just one lap. At his second, on lap 31, Hill got ahead for just four laps, but there was no stopping the Benetton's progress. Hill slipped back to second and then spun as rain fell at the back of the circuit. He called in for a new nose, broke the speed limit in the pit-lane, and was on his way in for a penalty when he spun off on the damp and dust of some-one else's spin. Coulthard fared little better, spinning off, recovering, and then spinning again on the gravel collected in the spin and thrown out of his own car's sidepods under braking! And so it was a victory for Schumacher – and Benetton, who took the Manufacturers' championship – ahead of Hakkinen, a relieved McLaren team figuratively at his shoulder, and Herbert, polishing his CV for potential employers. **OCTOBER 22, 1995**

AUSTRALIAN GRAND PRIX The paddock was in shock when Mika Hakkinen crashed in first qualifying. The first bulletins from intensive care were worrying, but by race-day they were more encouraging, and the atmosphere was the usual Adelaide fever, fanned by a crowd of 205,000, the largest ever for a modern Grand Prix. However, since nobody counts studio audiences, it was to be Adelaide's last F1 race.

Hill was back to his old form, on pole ahead of Coulthard, Schumacher, Berger and Alesi. It was the young Scot who led from the line, however, with Hill ahead of the two Ferrari drivers who had slipped past the champion. By lap 5, Schumacher had disposed of the two red cars, but not before Coulthard and Hill had established a handy lead. By the time Hill came in for the first of three planned stops, the gap to Schumacher was 18 seconds. Coulthard was coming in a lap after Hill when, aided by a glitch in the engine-management system, he understeered off at the tight entrance to the pits. It was not the best way to say farewell to the team.

Schumacher, yet to pit, suddenly found himself in the lead. But when the Benetton came in, two laps later, it left Hill in a semi-comfortable lead. Semi-comfort became cushioned luxury a couple of laps later when Schumacher challenged Alesi for second place. They touched, and although both struggled on for a few more laps, sufficient damage was caused to put them out. Hill was 32 seconds ahead of Herbert, in second place – and Herbert had not yet pitted. The pattern of the race was set; Hill pursued a rhythm which even a 22-second final pit-stop could not spoil, while behind him attrition ran rampant. It was attrition with justice, however, for two laps from Hill at the finish were Olivier Panis and Gianni Morbidelli; for Panis and Ligier, being on the podium was good – for Morbidelli and Footwork, it was wonderful. **NOVEMBER 12, 1995**

Adelaide marked the end of any number of chapters. For the circuit, it was the last race before politics and money take the event to Melbourne for 1996; Michael Schumacher (top right) was getting out at the end of a fruitful relationship with Benetton, and for Jean Alesi (above) it was his last race for Ferrari after five years at Maranello. The two would swap teams in 1996. Neither left their old home in the best manner. Only Damon Hill (opposite) had reason to feel satisfied, he could look forward to a new season with a car and a team he knew and which knew him.

the promise, and its performance slipped in direct relationship to the way in which its unusual 'hydrolink' suspension failed to provide the performance expected of it. Development of the new Yamaha V10 was slow too, so that did not help matters. At Footwork, the new Arrows FA16 was most noticeable for the incredibly compact dimensions of the Hart V8. Coupled with a longitudinal gearbox, it allowed designer Alan Jenkins to create a car which showed superb aerodynamic cleanliness at the rear.

There were two other teams whose budgets condemned them to the use of the customer Ford V8. Pacific, in its second season, and Forti, a newcomer in 1995, both regularly filled the final lines of the grid. Pacific had made definite progress since 1994, but despite the fact that Minardi were using the same engine, the British team were – thanks to lack of development – never even close to them.

Guido Forti was another to make the leap from Formula 3000, a move which he achieved thanks to Brazilian financial backing. The team was the last one to use a manual gearbox, and it made regular progress while design and development was being carried out on its own semi-automatic box. Such a device has become a key element in the performance of modern F1 cars; capable of changing gear in 25 thousandths of a second, it can go through all six gears of a racing gearbox in the time taken by one shift on a manual component. In addition, there is so much interchange between gearbox electronics and the engine management system that an electronically-controlled gearbox allows better exploitation of the engine's power and torque characteristics, which gives better handling, which reduces tyre wear – and so on, in a situation in which the advantages grow like a snowball. Another example of 'snowball' growth is in the never-ending expenditure which has become necessary to keep up in the rush of technology. Among those who fell by the way in 1995 were Lotus, a once-proud team which had become a financial rugby-ball, passed from hand to hand and finally irretrievably dropped. Larrousse dropped out on the eve of the season, unable to put together an adequate financial package, while Simtek, another newcomer in 1994, stumbled and fell at mid-season. The result was that at the end of the season, grids were down to 22 cars, a figure which is likely to fall further.

WORLD RALLY CHAMPIONSHIP

BAD RULES, GOOD SPORT

There may have been only four teams contesting the World Rally Championship in 1995, but as the year drew to a close three of them were still fighting for the title. And with a handful of drivers still in the hunt as well, this had to be one of the closest-fought championships in years.

With only two events to go, the drivers title race was still in full swing. Toyota's Juha Kankkunen was heading the points, chasing his fifth crown. Teammate and defending champion Didier Auriol was in there as well, while Subaru's Carlos Sainz and Colin McRae were the other realistic contenders. Mitsubishi's Tommi Makinen was lurking in the wings, a dark horse ready to pounce.

Toyota looked strong as makes title contenders yet again, but one of the season's high points was the emergence of Mitsubishi as a major player, even if the team did play the rules to their absolute limit. More of that later. Subaru's wipeout in Sweden cost them any realistic chance of the title, although they were still in with a shout at the end. Ford, however, blew it by the end of summer and surrendered early.

Naturally the year had its highs and lows, its happiness and controversy. The latter ran for the season and centred on the new servicing rules. They were designed to reduce cost but only served to create such confusion that no-one knew what they were doing at any given time. Given that penalties for infringing the rules amounted to a fine of around $300,000, exclusion of the whole team from the event and the loss of all championship points to date, it seemed bizarre that the rules were still being clarified while the Monte Carlo Rally was in progress. Not only that, but they changed for Sweden. And for Portugal. And for Corsica…

The concept was simple enough. The teams had argued that a major cost saving could be achieved by reducing the number of service opportunities and, therefore, the amount of spare parts required to support the cars. The easiest way of doing this was to use cloverleaf routes which brought cars back to central service points throughout each leg. That way just two or three service vans would suffice, rather than eight or nine each day.

Some events managed this quite successfully, while others simply ignored the trend and blundered merrily along. For some years now the FIA has asked event organisers to aim for a three-day rally and all but two have now complied. The Monte Carlo still ploughs through the mountains for four days, on top of the two required for that holdover from the Thirties, the Concentration Run. Equally the RAC Rally sticks a tedious opening day into the already drawn-out schedule with its attendant massive road mileage for little reward. The organisers say they can't afford to do anything different as the spectator revenue from the opening day is essential. A properly conceived superspecial – such as that in Australia – run three or four times during the event would have equal benefit.

So, while most organisers fine-tune their events towards routes which solve the service problems, the FIA imposed rules. Badly. Full service was permitted every two or three stages as usual but in between, cars could only be refuelled and re-tyred, providing the spares were on board. It seemed so simple in theory, but in Monte Carlo it was a farce. Thanks to the changing weather conditions, drivers faced the daunting prospect of having to run several stages on unsuitable tyres. Thus we had the bizarre sight of highly paid sportsmen and women pulling studs from

KEITH OSWIN

The cream of the crop line up for a family portrait in Perth. At this point in the season, the question of who would succeed Didier Auriol as world champion was still wide open. It was quite possible, of course, that he would not have a successor, for he was well-placed among the leaders himself. Jostling him for position were Kankkunen, McRae and Sainz. Among the manufacturers, the battle was between Toyota and Subaru – except that Mitsubishi, despite its constrained budget and sometimes unusual sporting priorities, was a shadowy threat. One thing was certain, however, and that was that the championship of makes was strictly a Japanese affair.

tyres with pliers in order that they might have something more suitable for the next stage where the ice was absent. And did it save money? Not at all, for the stupidity of the affair was that the mechanics and their well-stocked vans were forced to stand by and watch the pantomime, unable to even touch the cars lest they incurred the wrath of the authorities.

Sweden was a little simpler. Essentially these mini-service zones were cut to five minutes maximum in which any work could be done by anybody, the theory being that time was too tight for major work. Wrong. All it did was to force teams to build up suspension units beforehand and employ the best – and most expensive – mechanics for these areas while encouraging drivers to speed through service areas to maximise the time available.

The true folly came in Corsica, where Bruno Thiry had led the event more or less from the start, but his Ford Escort Cosworth broke a front suspension unit three stages from his first World Championship victory, cruelly at one of the 'no service' areas. Worse was the fact that it was accessible enough for a full service van to have dropped by. While Thiry struggled in vain to

In order to ensure that competitors respected the new rules limiting service, the FIA equipped all works cars with a sophisticated system (above) which not only used satellite navigation aids to pinpoint their exact position at any time, but was also able to monitor any interference (in the form of opening the bonnet or the rear doors) in areas where servicing was banned. Based on the GPS (Global Positioning Satellite) system, the equipment was first used on the Monte Carlo Rally where the weather proved to be extremely changeable (right).

effect temporary repairs, the parts he needed were a few tantalising meters away, within sight but out of reach. Instead of victory the hugely popular Belgian was forced to walk away. He wasn't the only one in tears that day. It was especially hard on Thiry as he does not yet have the confidence he needs to be a successful gravel driver. With only Corsica and Catalunya on this year's calendar using a completely asphalt route, his opportunities to win were few and far between.

Doubtless the rules will be modified again for next year, hopefully with more structure and clarity. Far simpler would be for 'no-service' zones to mean just that. No fuel, no tyres, no lurking mechanics, nothing. Even better would be for event organisers to open their eyes and minds to the way the sport should develop in future and plan their events accordingly.

Mitsubishi – on the rise

But while there was farce, there was also success. The emergence of Mitsubishi is one thing, the maturing of Colin McRae another. At the beginning of the season, few really gave Mitsubishi much of a chance. Tommi Makinen was quick enough but it looked as though he would have to sustain the title bid more or less alone. Andrea Aghini joined the camp, but was very much the asphalt specialist and decidedly suspect if he had to venture onto the loose. Everyone knew Kenneth Eriksson would be quick enough in Sweden, but did he really still have the edge to run with Makinen? Things went pretty much to form on the Monte, although Makinen was denied third place by Kankkunen when a broken front differential intervened on the final stage. Aghini was sixth on his debut. Sweden, however, proved a revelation, with the team taking first and second, albeit in controversial circumstances. Makinen was contesting the full World Championship, with Eriksson was dipping in occasionally while concentrating on the Asia-Pacific competition in a crucial market for Mitsubishi. Eriksson led at the end of the penultimate day, but Makinen was able to shoot ahead on the final one after an overnight blizzard made conditions tricky for the driver running first one the road – in this case Eriksson. What

The regulations which called on drivers themselves to work on cars in areas where service was banned led to scenes of confusion when some of them were required to remove studs from their tyres or hand-cut their own patterns. Among the victims was Carlos Sainz (above).

The complexity of modern rally cars requires constant maintenance by specialised service personnel like this Ford crew on the Monte Carlo Rally (left, below). The fact that well-paid factory mechanics were not allowed to use their skills was a bone of contention among the drivers, who felt that they should only do the specialist job they were paid for – that of driving.
Michelin's GA tyres (below) played a major part in Mitsubishi's success in Sweden.

Mitsubishi team-boss Andrew Cowan had to impose team orders in Sweden to put an end to the battle for the lead which was going on between his two top drivers. Local favourite Kenneth Eriksson was engaged in a furious duel with Finn Tommi Makinen (right), but the Swede, who was leading by a whisker at the end of the penultimate stage, received the benefit of Cowan's nod.

For Subaru, the Swedish Rally was a disaster, with all three cars, including that of Sainz (below) retiring with similar engine problems.

no one knew was that a decision had already been made by the team management that the result would reflect the overnight positions. Makinen stopped on the final stage and let Eriksson go by for a home win which was hardly greeted with delight, even by the Swedes. The Finns were furious, and should Makinen miss the title by the points he had to give up in Sweden, the incident will not be forgotten for a very long time.

While Makinen struggled home eighth in Corsica, Aghini salvaged his reputation with third, having rolled the brand new Evolution 3 Lancer just hours before its debut. Overnight rebuilding of a test car was rewarded by the contrite Italian and the mechanics forgave him for their sleepless night at last. But that was Corsica. What happened to Portugal? The rules for 1995 demanded that registered teams entered all eight events but Mitsubishi's budgets have always been tight. The 'spirit' of the regulations was that the same team did all events but the 'letter' wasn't quite the same. So Mitsubishi nominated a team to compete in Portugal on its behalf. Instead of the Ralliart Europe's Rugby-based Group A squad, the

trio of Group N cars from Ralliart Germany carried the flag. Ninth for Rui Madeira and tenth for Jorge Recalde (along with the top two Group N places) brought enough points for the team to retain the series lead it had taken in Sweden. Aghini's Corsica result kept them there and things were looking good in the title race.

They might have been even better in New Zealand, as Makinen, the only man capable of halting McRae's progress, stormed the opening stages. But he crashed out of the lead, and the event, on stage 10 and that let McRae through. It also exposed a possible crack in Eriksson's armour. While Makinen was running, Eriksson had a reason to fight, and rumours of a personal battle (even to the extent of it being a rift after the Swedish politicking) gathered pace. Once Makinen was out, Eriksson went off the boil and fifth was scant reward for his early promise.

Australia, however, fired Eriksson to greater heights than ever before. Throughout the event, the Swede battled with McRae, swapping the lead between them no less than six times. They started the final day tied, but it was Eriksson who got ahead, keeping Mitsubishi in the title hunt for both the World and Asia-Pacific manufacturers' titles (the latter now virtually assured) and putting himself at the head of the A-P drivers race. It also brought him into the 'Who goes where' equation for 1996 with Subaru a possible target. Watch this space...

Subaru – two shooting stars

McRae, the former 'wild child' of the sport, emerged during 1995 as a serious title contender. Certainly he crashed out of the Monte, in a situation where his lack of experience might have warned him not to push so hard, but subsequently he got his act together. Sweden was a disaster for the whole Subaru team, as all three cars were sidelined with an engine fault in similar circumstances. Portugal was better and McRae finished third behind team-mate Carlos Sainz and Toyota's Juha Kankkunen. He was disappointed with fifth in Corsica, but then headed for New Zealand and rattled off his third successive win in such style that the result was a foregone conclusion from halfway through the opening day. Any lingering doubts, and

Discontent among the professional drivers continued to rise in Portugal on the subject of servicing (this is Toyota's factory setup). They moved to bring their objections to the notice of the authorities.

Despite the political and practical difficulties posed by the new rules, the competition in Portugal was fierce. The battle between the Subaru of Carlos Sainz (above) and Juha Kankkunen's Toyota went right down to the wire with Sainz taking the decision by just 12 seconds.

For François Delecour (right) things were going much worse. Before the early stages were over, he had first rolled the car and then suffered engine failure.

Reigning champion Didier Auriol (above) could not come to grips with the leaders in Portugal. A roll and an off-course excursion meant he could finish no higher than fifth.

Despite his multiple appearances on the event, Kenjiro Shizuoka was not to become the first Japanese driver to win the Safari Rally. That honour was to fall to Toyota driver Yoshiro Fujimoto (left), in an event which this year was only a qualifier for the 2 litre championship.

Mitsubishi's German Ralliart team fielded three production-class Lancers for (L-R) Jorge Recalde, Isolde Holderied and Rui Madeira.

indeed any challengers, had been dispelled by the end of the Motu stage, an awesome corkscrew of a thing which McRae says is not one of his favourites as it needs a precise style of driving. Nevertheless, no one else has found an answer to that style yet.

A fighting second in Australia suddenly catapulted the Scot into the frame for the title. While he admitted that Catalunya would be tricky for him on his Spanish debut, the season would close with the RAC Rally. It is his home event, and when he won last year he ended an 18-year drought for British drivers on the one event where they should have an advantage over their European rivals. It was a masterful performance and one which convinced British fans that the days of Scandinavian and continental Europe's domination of the sport could soon be over.

Mitsubishi may have been the team that played the registration game hardest but they were not the only team to use 'guest' drivers during the year. Subaru let Sainz and McRae bear the brunt of the effort, but the third driver changed regularly. For the asphalt events it was the Italian Piero Liatti; the former European Champion campaigns a Subaru at home, and that added the necessary ingredient. In Sweden the team might have pulled the coup of the year in signing Mats Jonsson, but the engines let them down and they suffered a wipeout when a walkover might have been more predictable. Possum Bourne is the team's Asia-Pacific driver, so that saw his place assured for New Zealand and Australia, while Richard Burns joined in for Portugal. He became the official substitute in New Zealand when Sainz was injured.

Last year it was Ford's François Delecour who spent a large part of the season on the sidelines after a road accident. Now it was the Spaniard who had to sit out

Mitsubishi's best showing in Corsica came from Andrea Aghini in the Lancer Evolution 3. It was a performance which might not have been expected, in view of the Japanese manufacturer's somewhat uncertain plans at the beginning of the season.

one round after a fall from a mountain bike tore the tendons from his right shoulder. Doctors said that any other sportsman would have been looking for a new career, but Sainz is no ordinary sportsman. A former Spanish squash champion, fencing expert, tennis player, football trialist for Real Madrid and now a more than competent golfer, Sainz is super fit. Nevertheless, New Zealand was a non-start for him and his championship lead was lost to Auriol. But he was back for Australia, very much against the odds and a bit rusty, but back at the wheel. It didn't last long, though – a tree branch punctured the radiator and sidelined him midway through the opening day.

Ford – soap opera

Ford also played the guest star game, although not so regularly. Delecour and Thiry did Monte Carlo alone, but they had veteran Stig Blomqvist alongside for Sweden. Alex Fiorio was brought out of obscurity for Portugal but his lack of experience with the Escort showed, as did the fact that only Delecour had tested

A ridiculous ruling deprived Bruno Thiry (above) of a well-deserved win in Corsica. He had shown skill, talent and maturity which enabled him to dominate the event, and then fate intervened when a relatively minor fault struck him in a no-service zone – with a service crew just yards away!

Although Didier Auriol (left) inherited victory from Thiry, it was a just win. He had never been out of contention, and gave the newest version of the Toyota Celica GT-Four its first victory.

Just a few months short of his fiftieth birthday – on September 29th – Jean Ragnotti (above) showed that he had lost none of his talent or enthusiasm for driving, but in Corsica he had his work cut out with the Renault Clio 'kit-car', and had to give way to team-mate Philippe Bugalski.

Aris Vovros (right) had cause to thank the FIA, who had decided that the Acropolis Rally should be a 2-litre championship event this year. In the absence of the big boys, he became the first Greek in forty years to win his country's premier event.

Erwin Weber (opposite) had a tough job taking his Seat Ibiza to a win in the Formula 2 category, but team-mate Antonio Ruis backed him up to give the Spanish constructor a 1-2 finish.

the two men, so things were becoming complex to say the least...

Ford brought French Champion Patrick Bernardini into the equation for Corsica but seventh place was only marginally better than the eighth that Neil Allport netted in New Zealand. The Kiwi joined Ford for his first event in over a year, his first in a left-hand drive car, and his first with the tricky seven-speed gearbox (while the 'stars' reverted to the six-speeder). What a mess! The team gave up any hopes of the title at that point and began to look for ways to improve things next year. Boreham will have to take full responsibility back again and run things from a single base if it has any hope of regaining any respect among its peers.

Toyota – stability reigns

With all this chopping and changing within teams, Toyota was an oasis of stability. The World Champions lined up Kankkunen, Auriol and Armin Schwarz (who joined from Mitsubishi over the winter) and stuck to its line-up throughout, Yoshio Fujimoto joined in from for the event. The team's curious marriage with Belgium's RAS preparation outfit didn't really work at all this year. Although the team blamed the language barrier, there were rumours on two occasions that the Belgians had not been able to pay their workforce and that Ford had been forced to step in and top up the funds. When cash was tight, Thiry didn't get to test, and since the two drivers have very different styles of driving, what was suitable for Delecour was nowhere close to what Thiry needed. It came to a head in Australia where Delecour opted for Michelin FB71 tyres while every other Michelin team used FB73s throughout the event. When Thiry finally got his hands on a set of 73s he was immediately on the pace. But for three stages only, as the team had no more than four tyres to play with.

By now there seemed to be civil war going on within the team and with the new Ford motorsport director absent from mid-season in favour of Formula 1, there was no one around to calm the waters. On top of everything else, Delecour's co-driver Catherine François is the girlfriend of team engineer Philip Dunabin. It seemed there was soon little love lost between

After the win for Vovros in Greece, the next 'second division' event, in Argentina, also provided a win for a local driver – this time Jorge Recalde – in a Lancia HF Integrale.

François Delecour, here with co-driver Catherine François, never lost heart, despite his lack of a win since his unfortunate road accident in 1994.

time to time for experience, and Schwarz dropped from the nominated drivers in favour of Thomas Radstrom in Sweden, purely as it was Schwarz's snow debut and Radstrom had won the event before.

There was a switch of co-driver, however, following an unpleasant incident in Corsica. One of the hotel waiters allegedly assaulted Bernard Occelli's young daughter and Auriol's co-driver took the law into his own hands. To most people it was an understandable reaction, even if there was only circumstantial evidence. However the team saw it differently and Occelli was sent home before the event. Denis Giraudet partnered Auriol to the win but, while Occelli was expected back for New Zealand, the team decided otherwise and to Auriol's displeasure sacked him forthwith. If Auriol wants a reunion, he will have to leave the Cologne squad to do it, but he says he will only do that for a more competitive car, not just for Bernard's sake. It was Auriol, however, who won in Corsica when Thiry retired, and it was that result which kept him in the hunt for the title. Conversely, failing to finish in Australia may have been the result that cost him the crown.

Kankkunen headed the title race with two events to go. Despite not having won an event so far in 1995, he was still seven points clear of McRae. This was testimony to the consistency of the world's most successful driver, but his only real chance of netting the title in the manner of which he would approve would be by winning the RAC Rally. He knew that Spain would likely be a lean hunting ground as he has never yet won an asphalt round of the series. Most likely he would settle for a solid drive to set up a title bid on an event he knows well. McRae's second place in the title standings came through a better second half of the year, with victory in New Zealand kick-starting his title bid in fine style. But as with Kankkunen, Catalunya would be difficult for him, and he also vowed that a solid finish would be the best target, even though no event or surface holds any fear for the flying Scot.

Auriol, on the other hand, ended Australia (early as it turned out, after a roll) in third place and would be looking to Spain to get him back on track for a successful defence of the title he won in 1994. He led the series in mid-season after Sainz had to miss New Zealand, and knew that his best plan was to make good use of the final asphalt round, as the RAC Rally

A traditional Maori welcome for Didier Auriol (left) was the prelude to a fine performance on the New Zealand Rally. Second place behind Colin McRae put the Frenchman into the world championship lead.

Opposite: Juha Kankkunen is never far from the front of the field, and his third place in New Zealand put him into contention for the world title. Nevertheless, he had now been looking for his 22nd win in a championship event for over a year, since Portugal 1994.

Kenneth Eriksson's fifth place in the land of the Maoris ((left) was not enough to maintain Mitsubishi's lead in the Constructors' Championship. It was a disappointing result for the team, for Tommi Makinen had been leading until he went off the road.

Although he had been fighting for third place in New Zealand, François Delecour (below) had to settle for sixth after a minor accident. As a result, Ford lost sight of any hopes for the constructors' title.

He had been keeping a fairly low profile since his return to the Toyota squad, but Armin Schwartz (left) showed in New Zealand that he was still capable of producing an excellent performance.

would not favour him as much as it would his title rivals. Despite his mid-season problems, Sainz was still in there pitching, and clearly keen to do the business on his home event, even though, despite what many had thought, it was not one he knew well. If his shoulder survived the event unscathed then he, like McRae and Kankkunen, could expect a good result on the RAC. But there was a fear of team orders to be considered.

Last year he knew that if the championship was still open with a few stages to go on the RAC, he would be favoured – even though McRae was leading the event. It was an unsavoury situation for the home fans but, perhaps happily, it came to nought when Sainz crashed on the final morning and let Auriol take the title while McRae took the win. What would happen this time?

Eriksson's Australia win promoted him to fourth but it was a false situation as he would miss Catalunya in favour of the Hong Kong-Beijing event where Asia-Pacific points were at stake. However, Mitsubishi did still have a title hope in the form of Makinen, fifth, providing he emerged from Spain still in contention. One title wrapped up earlier in 1995 was the Formula 2 crown for the 2-litre championship, which, thanks to the rotation system, ended at San Remo. This was the second year of the controversial scheme where events dipped in and out of the championship over a three year period and, happily, it will not be continued after 1996 completes the sequence.

In 1995 we lost the Safari to the F2 boys, along with Argentina, the Acropolis and the 1000 Lakes. Individual events were still won by big-name drivers but unless they were driving a 2-litre, two-wheel drive car they weren't scoring points. The Safari highlighted how many new teams, mainly from the Far East, are looking at F2. It also highlighted how unsuitable the category is for events like the Kenyan classic, no matter how hard the organisers try to make the route user-friendly. Azar Anwar won F2 in 13th place, for Daewoo. The Vauxhall/Opel derivative came, saw and conquered on its debut, but it was through reliability rather than pace, as its rivals all fell by the wayside and it was the lone survivor. Despite earlier fears that the event would not be attended by any top cars, Toyota eventually relented and gave Yoshio Fujimoto the keys to an old-style Celica. He promptly became the first Japanese driver to win the classic. The irony was that he beat Kenjiro Shinozuka who, 20 years earlier, had been the first Japanese finisher. It was a cruel blow for the Mitsubishi driver, who was at the wheel of an old Lancer which had been converted to Evolution 3 specification for its world debut, albeit not at championship level.

SEAT took the F2 win in Greece with Erwin Weber nicking the points in the bright green Ibiza and edging out Skoda, who ran in 1995 with a new car. SEAT would close the season by showing off its kit-car version for 1996 but Skoda had a modified Felicia,

Just two long and twisting stages put Colin McRae (opposite page) in control of the New Zealand Rally and on his way to his third successive win in the event. In a rally where the terrain is particularly difficult, even world champion Didier Auriol could not match the Scotsman's pace.

Always a threat when the going is difficult, Colin McRae (above) gave Subaru its third win of the year, following the success of Sainz on the Monte Carlo and in Portugal. McRae's win rekindled his title hopes, and he could look to Australia, where he had won in 1994, with renewed confidence.

which first appeared in Sweden, and it was a glorious device. Only 1500cc, but it went well and finally shook off the team's dowdy image.

Kit cars were the rage for 1995 as they gave teams the chance to build a more potent machine without having to produce fleets of unsaleable cars first. Renault was first out of the blocks but still stubbornly refused to take part in the championship it had forced the FIA to create – so it was probably justice that the title headed in the direction of arch rivals Peugeot (who also had a stunning kit version of the 306 available during the year) by the time the championship ended in Italy.

Skoda scored its only F2 win with fourth overall in Argentina, an event so badly supported that even Jorge Recalde could win. Normally he can be seen in one of the Group N Mitsubishis, but the veteran Argentinian never quite reached the heights that some thought he might. Home wins for Lancia when no-one is looking are his only reward these days.

The 1000 Lakes Rally should have been a duel for outright honours between Makinen and Kankkunen, but the latter was out on only the first stage with sus-

It was a second consecutive victory on the 1000 Lakes for Tommi Makinen, this time in a Mitsubishi Lancer (above). This year the Finnish classic was a '2 litre event', so Makinen's only major competition came from Juha Kankkunen – and he went off the road and out of the rally on the first stage.

Rally Australia was an important event for Mitsubishi. Victory for Kenneth Eriksson (right) gave the manufacturer a strong grip on its prime objective, the Asia-Pacific Championship. An additional benefit was that the win brought the team to within striking distance of Toyota in the World Championship.

pension failure on his Toyota. After that, Makinen was able to win as he pleased. The F2 contest went to Jarmo Kytolehto's Opel Astra Sport over the likes of Nissan's Alister McRae. It put the GM team at the head of the points table.

However, in a year when GM is pulling the plug on its regional rally activities and diverting the cash towards Touring Cars, it failed to enter a single car on any of the non-European events in the F2 series. That made it ineligible for the title, even if it ended the year as top dog. A bizarre situation, but one entirely of its own making. The victims of the pull-out were not entirely sympathetic...

Changing times

If Formula 2 brought a rich and varied collection of machinery throughout the season, Group N was a predictably dull affair. Mitsubishi's trio of Madeira, Recalde and German lady star Isolde Holderied were the class act, and no one else got a look in, save for Ed Ordynski in Australia, who rattled off his sixth category win on his home event. Mohammed Bin Sulayem had a go with his Toyota but was all too often among the early retirements. There was the occasional Group N Ford in the pack (most famously that of 'Beverly Hills 90210' actor Jason Priestley in Australia) but that was all we had to look forward to. In the opinion of this observer, it's time the category was given the push.

So what exactly does the future hold? The start of the year saw the sport facing some swingeing cuts for 1997 but the FIA performed a major U-turn in mid-season. How does it all pan out? At first it was thought that the current breed of four-wheel drive cars was to be phased out by the end of 1996 to make way for an F2 World Championship. The idea had its merits and the emergence of new teams in 1995 indicates that the sport could be expanded by this route. But the current teams were worried that the sport could be destroyed by such a move. It would be a worse situation than in 1986 when Group B was ditched in favour of Group A, for although the current cars are now faster than those they replaced, the performance gap between them and F2 is massive.

Colin McRae (above) fought to the end in Australia but was finally forced to give way to Eriksson. The duel between the pair was as close as it had been some months earlier in Portugal.

Bruno Thiry (below) continued his apprenticeship in the world class, but was handicapped by Ford's less than total support of its rallying activities. Limited reconnaissance opportunities made things worse in Australia.

Unfortunately, the teams which wanted F2 from the start singularly failed to put their money where their mouths are. Renault led the way, and had a car out immediately, but the company will not get involved at World Championship level while it is in Formula 1. And other potential competitors might be forgiven for thinking that if you haven't beaten Renault then you haven't beaten anyone. So, angered by the lack of support given by those who promised so much, the FIA performed a U-turn in mid-season and announced it was extending the life of the current cars to the end of the decade at least.

However, the kit-car option has been modified to help smaller teams build a car capable of running with the Toyotas, the Subarus and the Mitsubishis. Instead of only allowing performance modifications within the 2-litre, two-wheel drive format, the new super-kit cars – or World Rally Cars as they are to be officially known – will be allowed turbos and four-wheel drive systems off the shelf.

The current top teams are greeting the move with cautious optimism. The problem is that while it embraces the spirit of the kit-car formula as originally intended, it has to be carefully planned, so that teams cannot automatically build faster cars 'on the cheap' after others have gone through lengthy and costly homologation procedures in accordance with the existing rules.

The new formula will almost certainly bring companies like Citroen into the equation and the engineers, led by the people who created the hugely successful Peugeot 205 T16 a decade ago, are already working on the prototype model.

The current 2-litre formula will remain as a championship as well, so there is no obligation to get into the big league if smaller companies don't want to. It all seems fine on paper but, until detailed technical regulations are available for all to see, it could just be a dream world.

Next year's calendar rotation will see France without a round of the championship, the most notable absentee being the Monte Carlo Rally, which drops out to become an F2-only event for one season. Most events have used this opportunity to try out a fresh format but, predictably, not the Monte.

The powers-that-be have opted for the same route as in 1995, which is unlikely to tempt even the biggest teams to try and win the most famous event of them all. Even the FIA is said to be losing patience with the organisers.

There could be a way out in the not too distant future, as the 1997 series could have as many as 16 events – even though teams favour 12 or 13. It was announced in September that Indonesia had been successful in its bid for inclusion next year and the next group of possible candidates includes the Hong Kong-Beijing rally (set to change its format by 1997 to accommodate the service requirements of a clover-leaf design). There are also suggestions that an event in South Africa could be returned to favour now that the political situation in the 'Rainbow Nation' has been resolved and sporting links renewed.

Promotion of events, primarily through television, continues to be a major talking point. While the BBC has filmed every 1995 event for the FIA, there are still many countries who don't get to see the sport on terrestrial channels. FIA president Max Mosley is keen to have the sport televised live, along with in-car action, but in order to do that the events really need to sort out their formats in order that the sport can be made more accessible to the cameras. The fact that televi-

If you wanted a really good view of Rally Australia, it was better to be a koala or a kangaroo. Human spectators were tightly controlled; without the hard-to-get accreditation, the only places to see the cars were in heavily supervised spectator zones on a few selected stages.

Despite Didier Auriol's retirement, the points scored by Armin Schwarz (opposite) for fifth place combined nicely with those which team-mate Juha Kankkunen picked up for third to put Toyota in the lead of the manufacturers' championship after Australia.

Won by the Subaru Impreza of Piero Liatti (above), the San Remo Rally was the last round of the '2 Litre' championship, and it brought success for Peugeot. Success is a relative term; neither of the two 306 Maxi 'kit-cars' entered by the factory for Andrea Aghini (below) and Bernard Béguin finished, but Peugeot became the first winner of the 'Constructors' World Cup'. Opel, which scored more points – but did not enter any non-European events and was thus ineligible for consideration in the final results – must also have been deliberating on 'success'.

sion's requirements and those of teams eager to cut costs by 'service-friendly' routes are almost identical should sound a warning to organisers. With a bit of thought and open mindedness, they could solve two problems in one go.

The year has seen great strides made in relations between the events, the teams and the governing body. There remains a very real fear that while Bernie Ecclestone still has a hand in promoting all FIA championships, anything that isn't Formula 1 will be suppressed in some way. But it is to be hoped that these are false worries. The season proved that the sport is very much alive and capable of producing great entertainment and a close finish to the contest. Now that's something that Bernie would have difficulty in saying about F1 1995-style.

Rallying's future could, therefore, look brighter than for some time. New events, fresh outlooks and new teams, combined with exciting technical developments, may be the key to ensuring success well into the next decade.

But that's all in the future. Till something better comes along, 1995 was pretty good.

THE PATH TO THE CLOSEST FINISH

By the time the championship reached Britain and its final round, the race for both Drivers' and Manufacturers' titles could not have been much closer. How did it get that way?

Carlos Sainz kicked off the scoring with a crushing win on the Monte Carlo Rally. He beat arch-rival François Delecour by over two minutes, but accidents claimed Didier Auriol (on the same stage on which Toyota also lost Armin Schwarz with a blown engine) and Stage 1 leader Colin McRae. For all his dislike of asphalt, Juha Kankkunen took a solid third place, pipping Mitsubishi's new boy, Tommi Makinen, when his Lancer hit transmission trouble on the final stage.

The snows of Sweden beckoned next and it was Mitsubishi's turn to shine, albeit in controversial circumstances (see main story). Kenneth Eriksson hadn't competed in his home event since he won in 1991, but that didn't stop him repeating the feat, this time with Makinen in tow. It was a disaster for Subaru, all three Imprezas sidelined by identical engine failures. Thomas Radstrom headed Toyota team-mates Kankkunen and Auriol in the next three places, with Ford's Bruno Thiry and Stig Blomqvist following.

Portugal saw a frantic battle between Sainz and Kankkunen resolved by just 12 seconds, with McRae third, Schwarz fourth and Auriol fifth, all well spread out behind the leading duo. Once again it was Thiry who topped the Ford pile; Delecour was sidelined with engine failure, albeit after rolling the car in the early stages.

Corsica '95 will be remembered for the bitter blow that befell Bruno Thiry and cost the likeable Belgian his first World Rally win. He spent the entire event fending off Auriol, but in the end the servicing rules beat him and Auriol cruised home ahead of Delecour.

With four rounds gone, Sainz had a clear lead in the series from Kankkunen (12 points adrift), Auriol, Delecour, Makinen, Eriksson, Thiry and McRae, with Andrea Aghini and Thomas Radstrom rounding off the top 10.

The party reconvened in New Zealand, and McRae took his third Kiwi victory with apparent ease. Makinen pushed hard in the early stages and led for a while, but put the car in a ditch on stage 10. The Scot rocketed into the lead from fourth, and if Auriol and Kankkunen had any ideas about sneaking a win, they reckoned without McRae's mastery of the Motu stage. With a time 35 seconds faster than anyone else, the rally was decided on the spot.

Australia threatened to be tougher than New Zealand for McRae, and so it proved. Eriksson hounded him from start to finish, the pair swapping places with almost every stage. They went into the final day tied for the lead, but Eriksson got the advantage. McRae wisely settled for second to strengthen his chance of becoming champion.

But Kankkunen had been picking up steady points all season, despite failing to reach the top step of the podium. The Finn, with four titles already to his name, led the series as it went to Spain with McRae second, Auriol third and Sainz (who had missed New Zealand through injury and then retired with a blown engine in Australia) fourth. Eriksson, although concentrating on (and winning) the Asia-Pacific championship, still had a mathematical chance, as did Makinen, Delecour and Schwarz. But all the possibilities were scrambled in the most dramatic fashion on Catalunya's tarmac. First, Kankkunen crashed and retired. Then the spectre of team orders rose again. At the final overnight halt, Subaru decided on a 'cool-it' policy which would result in a home win for Sainz, 8 seconds in front. But McRae was faster on the final stages, and 'lost' by picking up a one-minute road penalty. Sainz and McRae were now tied in the championship, and nobody was truly satisfied with the result. However, things were much worse *chez* Toyota. Both Auriol and Kankkunen were found to have been running with illegal turbo restrictors; Auriol lost fourth place and, after the FIA had considered the matter, the team (but not the drivers, who were deemed to have been unaware of the infringement) was banned from rallies for a full year.

Going into the final round in Britain, Kankkunen was 8 points behind Sainz and McRae in the Drivers' title, while the early-season outsider Mitsubishi led Subaru in the Manufacturers' listings by just two points. Talk about a climax!

US RACING

A SEASON OF NEWCOMERS

Judging by 1994's record-setting attendance and the even greater crowds at most races this year, IndyCar has never been more popular. And with nine different winners (four for the first time) and 17 drivers on the podium, rarely has it been more competitive.

Consider this grid: 1994 IndyCar and Indianapolis 500 champion Al Unser Jr., Danny Sullivan, Jimmy Vasser and Christian Fittipaldi, Emerson Fittipaldi and Adrian Fernandez. Included are three series champions with four crowns and five Indianapolis 500 wins (Unser, Sullivan, Emerson Fittipaldi), three ex-F1 drivers (Sullivan, the Fittipaldis), and three future stars (Vasser, Christian Fittipaldi, Fernandez).

Except for one problem, all might expect to win the upcoming race. The problem? Each will first have to pass at least 11 faster cars, because they have just qualified 12th through 17th for the 1995 Cleveland Grand Prix.

On pole, series rookie and former F3000 contender, Gil de Ferran. Beside him, Jacques Villeneuve, son of former F1 star, Gilles. Behind them, Bryan Herta and

RICK MILLER

Everything came right for Jacques Villeneuve (below) this year. He took six poles, won four races, including the Indianapolis 500, and booked himself a Formula 1 seat in 1996.

The Flying Fittipaldis – Christian and Emerson – together (right) in the field at Phoenix, where they finished tenth and third respectively. It was new boy Christian's first IndyCar season and veteran Uncle Emerson's twelfth. The high point of the youngster's year was a second at Indianapolis, where Emerson failed to qualify. Unusually, 1995 was not a good year to be a Penske driver, and Emerson could finish no higher than eleventh in the championship.

Teo Fabi. All four drove for medium-budget teams, and only Herta had a teammate; the rest were single-car entries.

Such things are not supposed to happen. Early in the year, teams are unfamiliar with the cars, and mechanical failures can also occur. Sometimes, a surprise winner emerges. As the season progresses, powerful two-car teams like Penske, Newman-Haas and Rahal-Hogan with on-going testing programs and superior resources are supposed to take over. Yet Cleveland was the twelfth of seventeen races.

But the superteams did not have one thing that all four of Cleveland's top qualifiers had – a Reynard chassis. The company's first Indycar had been conservative. The next, it was said, would be radical. What arrived was more like a post-critique R94I. But it was effective on all types of tracks, and all three versions (Honda, Mercedes and Ford) won. If there was a weak spot, it was the gearbox, which failed often until a selector drum problem was rectified.

In April, Ford debuted its Series II motor. New "from the block up," it was claimed to produce 50hp more than the original XB. Shortly after mid-year, however, the Series II was shelved, with unreliability problems unresolved. Meanwhile, Ilmor quietly improved its IC108. But at the season's end, another engine was more desired than either – Honda. The second-generation powerplant which first appeared at Indianapolis stunned the competition. Tasman Motorsports ran it in a car for Brazilian Andre Ribeiro, and three times they had a second Reynard for Scott Goodyear. To test, American Honda chose another new team, Comptech Motorsports, a team which had brought Honda numerous sedan titles and three consecutive IMSA Camel Lights (C2) crowns, and driver Parker Johnstone. Ribeiro had raced in Indy Lights and F3000, but Johnstone had not been in open-wheelers since the early 1980s. After last year's high-profile Rahal-Hogan effort, the rookie drivers and teams took the pressure off engine development. If problems arose, they would take the blame or be ignored. Given success, the engine would be credited. With around 900hp (perhaps a 50hp edge), success came.

This year, just one man was the focus of attention among the drivers: Jacques Villeneuve. In his third year of racing in North America, Villeneuve had learned

Right: Mauricio Gugelmin (foreground) battles with Michael Andretti at Phoenix. Gugelmin said during the season: "In Formula One, it's who you are with; in IndyCar, it's who you are." Andretti, who might – or might not – agree with him, at least knows where he's happiest, even though 1995 was not his best year.

from the best in the business. Engineer Tony Cicale had worked with Mario Andretti, while team manager Barry Green had worked with drivers such as Keke Rosberg, Teo Fabi, Danny Sullivan, Michael Andretti, Bobby Rahal, and both Al Unser Sr. and Al Unser Jr. "In 1993, Villeneuve and his manager had the option to go to run a Formula 3000 program in Europe, which was a pretty good deal for them, but they chose to go with us," Green began. "The plan was laid down that we'd do a year in Atlantic and then two more years of IndyCar. And we would only go to IndyCar if I thought that Jacques was capable of driving an IndyCar. After one of the first tests, we soon realized that this guy's feel for the race car was something special, and he did do nearly all of the setups after that. If you told Villeneuve something, it went down in his memory bank; he is a great student."

His early IndyCar races, like the first Atlantic attempts, were a bit wild. "But then we ran at Indy and finished second last year, and after that he gained a lot of confidence. But certainly as we've gone on and on, to see this guy mature as fast and as well as he has, it is a surprise to me... It would seem that the more pressure

New cylinder heads, pistons and a revised intake system and plenum upped the output of the Mercedes-Benz/Ilmor engine (right) to 850hp. By mid-year, it was on the pace on the high-speed road courses Ford once ruled. The pop-off valve is removed in the photograph.

Above: 25 year-old Brian Herta's Reynard-Ford at Long Beach. Herta took his first pole at Phoenix and finished second in Cleveland. A 120-G practice crash at Indy left him unconscious, and he started last; he still finished fourteenth.

Whether it is high drama or soap opera depends upon one's point of view, but, either way, NASCAR (opposite) is great theatre. The question is, if it is show business, is there a script? And if so, who writes it?

Absent from IndyCar racing since 1974, Firestone (right) won twice this year. The safe, successful return was marked by corporate detente, reached after Goodyear initially insisted on referring to the company as Bridgestone, its Japanese parent.

we put on him, the less mistakes that he does make." How does Green rate Villeneuve? "I had three great years with Michael Andretti, and he's a guy that gives you 110 percent every in-lap, every out-lap, every lap he's in the race car. He's just incredible, but as far as someone to compare, I would compare Villeneuve a lot with Fabi. Fabi had a tremendous feel for the race car and still does, obviously. Not a blindingly fast driver, just very fast, and usually very consistent, because they're able to get their race car set up. Very, very calculated with their aggression, and someone that you don't worry about going out and hitting the wall every other session that he's in."

The exception was Indianapolis, where Villeneuve crashed the day before qualifying began. The car was rebuilt, and he started fifth. Referred to variously as the Indianapolis 505 (for the distance he covered) and the Infraction 500 (for its numerous penalties), many under-informed fans furious with the standards of administration blamed IndyCar, which sanctions the remainder of the events. This blame is somewhat misplaced, since the "500" is run by the US Auto Club. Penalties for passing the pace car early in the race put Jacques two laps down, but guided by Green, he battled back. Using fuel strategy when necessary and hard driving when possible, late in the race he ran second after Scott Pruett crashed out after battling with Scott Goodyear. When Goodyear miscalculated and also passed the pace car, the race belonged to Jacques.

Villeneuve had the series' fastest, most dependable crew. On the Miami street circuit, they had gained him numerous positions – together with the race lead and another win. Mauricio Gugelmin, who led late in the race, remarked: "On the radio they said to me, 'Sorry, Mauricio.' I didn't see any mistakes on our pit-stop, but when I came out of the pits, I saw Jacques three hundred yards ahead."

Initially, that first event seemed destined for Michael Andretti. Again driving for Newman-Haas, he had taken pole and controlled the race. A full-course yellow put him behind Eliseo Salazar, whom he mistook for Christian Fittipaldi, also in a green car. Andretti knew Fittipaldi's skill from F1, but Salazar ignored his mirrors, forcing Andretti against a wall. Laps later, when Michael thought he had escaped damage, his suspension failed.

Andretti seemed on a mission. His new teammate, Paul Tracy (on a year's sabbatical from Team Penske), had, like Villeneuve, received glowing European reviews after an F1 test. Andretti, quicker head-to-head than McLaren's "unexploded bomb" Hakkinen, had been treated shabbily. The mission was: Defeat Tracy: prove them wrong. Indeed, Andretti repeatedly out-qualified and out-raced Tracy, leaving little doubt as to his superiority. The Lola T95 proved difficult to develop, however. After claiming three of the first four poles, the time came when he could not even place it on the front row. Reynards took 13 of 17 poles, including the last 11.

"What can I say? We were gone," Andretti had said of round two in Australia. "Then second gear went out... I use it on every corner but one. I might have been able to hold them off if it wasn't for that last caution." He wrecked trying to keep Rahal behind. More gearbox problems ruined Long Beach and Vancouver, races he also led. The new dual caliper brake system that precipitated his Australian crash caused additional trouble, too.

Off-season personnel changes temporarily weakened Newman-Haas. At Phoenix, the team failed to inform Andretti that he was leading and Robby Gordon was closing. He let Gordon by and finished second. At Nazareth, Andretti crashed after an unsecured wheel fell off. Michael was driving hard, perhaps too hard. Unser blamed him for a collision at Elkhart Lake that eliminated both. Unser had closed rapidly, then, as Andretti's XB reached high rpm, lacked power to pass. As he lingered in Andretti's blind spot, they touched. When Newman-Haas got its act together, Ford's Series II motor (debuted at Phoenix) came apart. Michael topped the "laps led" and "times led" categories, but failed to win until round eleven, Toronto. Afterward, engine failures at Cleveland, Michigan and Mid-Ohio, two of the three while leading at race's end, crushed his title hopes.

Andretti's 1994 experience with Reynard, plus Tracy's Penske knowledge, might have made history. Instead, it resulted in little more than raised-center front wing, developed independently by Newman-Haas to reduce pitch sensitivity. Just two laps into the season, Tracy discovered the new brake problems and crashed out, but he won in Surfer's Paradise after Andretti struck trouble. After finishing fourth in Phoenix, he led

Right: The Monte Carlo of seven-time NASCAR champion Dale Earnhardt in close company with the Thunderbird of Ted Musgrave. Earnhardt quit driving in the junior Grand National series to concentrate on Winston Cup, but poor qualifying (for him) was still a problem.

Jeff Gordon (below) was nicknamed "the Boy Wonder" by Earnhardt, and for good reason. He is a remarkable talent, and it is IndyCar's loss that having risen rapidly through the open-wheel ranks he found his future in stock cars.

the championship, but it did not last. He crashed at Long Beach attempting an ill-advised move on De Ferran, then wrecked at Nazareth trying to pass Vasser. Following a broken motor at Indy, he took his second win in Milwaukee, the seventh race. Down the stretch, second places were interspersed with gearbox and motor failures, and he was critical of the Series II Cosworth. The frustration boiled over at New Hampshire, where he was fined US$12,000 for a rude gesture, grabbing an official and ignoring a black flag notifying him of an oil leak.

Andretti and Tracy each finished just nine of 17 races, fourth and sixth in the points. Villeneuve finished 14 times, Unser, 13. The winning total of 173 points in 17 races was the lowest since 1985, when 15 events were held. Andretti holds the 17-race record with 234 points (1991), and Unser Jr. set the 16-event mark of 225 last year.

By New Hampshire (15 of 17), only Unser challenged Villeneuve. In 1994, the 33 year-old claimed eight races and four poles en route to his second IndyCar title. This year could hardly have been more different. First, Penske blamed lack of testing. Then, it was poor feedback due to fewer cars running than Reynard or Lola. Both, of course, were team choices. It seemed that, after fielding three cars and two engines in 1994, Penske now lacked funds to chart a proper campaign! Astonishingly, having dominated the "500" last year, neither Unser nor Emerson Fittipaldi qualified. Even so, strategy and hard driving won Al Jr. races at Long Beach, Portland, Mid-Ohio, and Vancouver. The Portland result was stripped after scrutineers found the distance between the tub bottom and the sidepod bottom was less than two inches, a rule intended to prevent sidepods being used to improve downforce. Penske blamed the problem on a skid pad worn off during the race, and the appeal process dragged on beyond season's end. Ultimately, the disqualification was overturned and the victory restored, but the decision had no effect upon the final standings. This year, there were no miracles in the Penske budget. Unser's sixth-place at Laguna Seca left him runner-up to Villeneuve, the matter decided on the track, not in the committee room.

Disappointments resulting from the PC95's fickleness (attributed to a mechanical grip problem), also

plagued teammate Emerson Fittipaldi. Leading at Phoenix, a late fuel stop left him third, but he defeated Villeneuve on Penske's home track at Nazareth (after Eddie Cheever's car ran out of gas). In the ten races after Milwaukee, he qualified an average of 17th and finished an average of 13th. The car, he felt, demanded a different driving style than his.

Rahal/Hogan, the series' third major player, produced disappointing results and split at season's end. Rarely was their Lola-Mercedes the best package. Raul Boesel and two-time champion Bobby Rahal were evenly-matched in qualifying, but in races Boesel had a surfeit of problems which were not of his own making. His best finish was fourth at Portland. A veteran of 14 seasons and 214 starts, Rahal was unable to add to his 24 wins this year. Always consistent, he was still capable of great speed when the occasion demanded. He produced eleven results of eighth or better and finished third in points behind Villeneuve and Unser.

The championship had hung in the balance at Mid-Ohio, race 14, with Rahal Villeneuve's closest pursuer. Villeneuve had taken one of his six poles, but, as usually occurred, fell back in the race. De Ferran had gotten past going into the esses, leaving Jacques off-line and slow for the next bend. Rahal drew abreast on the outside, intending to complete the pass as the road reversed. He never got there. As Villeneuve followed the road to the left, three times he jerked the steering wheel to the right. On the last jab, their cars touched, and Rahal shot into the wall. "I guess there's more than one way to win," Bobby remarked afterward. Villeneuve said he made a driving error, adding that had Rahal not been a contender, it would not have looked so bad.

In Cleveland, two races before, another incident that appeared less than accidental deprived De Ferran, a Jackie Stewart protege, of his first win. The Brazilian had taken his first pole and led, only to fall behind Andretti on a late restart. "Michael and Scott (Pruett, two laps behind) got slowed by traffic. I got by Michael and halfway past Scott when he decided to fight for the corner. I was on the inside on the entry when he moved over on me. He fought me like he was fighting for the lead!" Helicopter video suggested that, at impact, Pruett's car was aimed at De Ferran, not the apex.

After 35 tries and many near misses, Dale Earnhardt (above) won the first road race of his career at Sears Point, taking the lead when Mark Martin spun off on oil. The vastly experienced Earnhardt had smelled the oil laps before and avoided it.

Given NASCAR's frequent rule revisions, a skeptic might say that, in NASCAR, you win because you are allowed to win. The fans – like those at Sears Point (left) – which flock to the series' bright colors and doorhandle-to-doorhandle racing do not seem to mind.

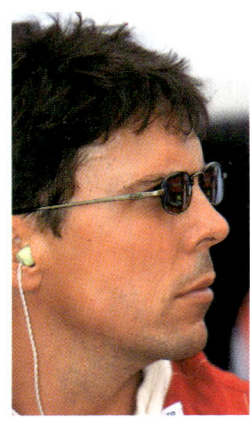

After five disappointing seasons in IndyCar, Scott Pruett (above) spent 1994 winning the Trans Am title and developing Firestone's new IndyCar tires. Using them, he won his first IndyCar race and Firestone's first since leaving the scene in 1974.

Like team-mate Michael Andretti, Paul Tracy finished only 9 races. He won twice, but never seemed comfortable in the Lola-Ford (right). Several crashes and numerous mechanical failures left the talented Canadian sixth in the points.

Danny Sullivan (below) suffered a broken pelvis in a crash during the Michigan 500 after Lyn St. James' motor blew. The 1988 IndyCar champion was replaced by Juan Manuel Fangio II, nephew of the great Argentinian driver.

Paul Tracy (above) will return to Penske next year, but whether his goatee is going along remains to be seen. The "handicapped" sign on the pit trolley refers to his broken foot, suffered near mid-season at a celebrity go-kart event.

185

Al Unser, Jr. (below) had a right to look pensive. For the first time since 1962, there was no Unser at Indianapolis when neither he – nor teammate Emerson Fittipaldi – could qualify the Penske PC24. Attempts in borrowed Reynards and Lolas failed, too, deepening the mystery.

Scott Goodyear's Reynard-Honda levitates at Indianapolis (below). Honda's new motor was clearly strong and he qualified third in the midday heat. On race-day, unfortunately, there was no magic. Penalized for passing the pace car while leading, Goodyear finished 14th.

Despite running well, until the penultimate Vancouver race, De Ferran's best result was seventh. That event, too, started depressingly. Unser, risking much for a championship contender, tried to pass from the outside into a chicane. De Ferran allowed room, but an unapologetic Unser hit the curb, then knocked De Ferran into a tire wall. "When I saw myself flying into the barrier I thought, 'Oh no, another weekend gone.' Then I saw the red flag and I thought, 'Great, we have a chance to run the spare car,'" De Ferran explained. He ran it all the way to second place. At Laguna Seca, he qualified third and dominated the event, taking his first victory and stealing Rookie of the Year honors from Christian Fittipaldi by one point.

Only Scott Goodyear (three races), Parker Johnstone and popular Andre Ribeiro had access to Firestone tires, Honda power, and a Reynard chassis. After Goodyear's near-miss at Indy, Johnstone took Honda/Firestone's first pole at Michigan, running away with the race before rear suspension problems, which befell many, forced long repairs. In New Hampshire, Ribeiro used unorthodox but effective lines reminiscent of Nigel Mansell's oval track style enabling him to take his and Honda's first win (Firestone's second). Robby Gordon recovered from mistimed pitting to sneak by Andretti and win in Phoenix, then took Detroit when a pitstop gamble paid off. Fifth in the championship, his stock did not soar. He deliberately ran into Andretti on the "cool down" lap in Cleveland, believing Michael had twice cut his tires (untrue). Both were fined. During the race, Gordon's wild passing attempts damaged De Ferran's car and his side-by-side lunges at Villeneuve infuriated the future champion. "This is Indy car racing, not the Baja 1000 or off-road racing," Jacques said. "When you're going 170 mph, there's no point in trying to hit the car or push him into the grass." Gordon missed the Michigan 500 after a suspension piece on his Reynard (the 13th R95I built) broke in practice, causing a 116-G crash which left him concussed. He continued to drive off-road races, but his time might have been better spent. Inexperience in circuit racing and difficulty controlling his emotions on track are holding him back.

Scott Pruett scored Firestone's first win since their 1974 departure at Michigan, besting Al Unser Jr. in a

thrilling duel by 0.056 second after 500 miles. Ironically, Firestone's last victory had come there with Al Unser Sr. driving. Having spent 1994 helping develop the tires, Pruett's success was well-deserved. The victory was his first in six IndyCar seasons. Leading in points before Indy, several crashes and mechanical failures demoted him to seventh in the final standings. "When I was Wilson's chief mechanic in Formula One and Christian was a little boy, I told him that I would some day have a race team, and that he would drive for me," Derrick Walker said. And it happened. Fittipaldi, over from F1, teamed with Gordon at Walker Motorsports. Finishes of fifth at Miami and second at Indy (worth US$594,668) were promising, considering he had not seen the tracks. While the car was well-prepared, his driving style was dissimilar to Gordon's. Generally, one would have a good set-up, but not both. Walker had the disadvantages of a two-car effort without the benefits.

Among other new drivers, Parker Johnstone and Juan Manuel Fangio II (nephew of the great champion) quickly proved their merit. Johnstone, Honda's test driver, was deprived of a chance to run the "500"

due to lack of sponsorship after testing there at over 230mph. He decimated the field at Michigan, qualifying 2mph faster with a warm-up lap good enough for pole. Fangio, filling in for the injured Danny Sullivan, sadly made his long-awaited IndyCar debut just weeks after the passing of his uncle. Like Johnstone, Fangio is a quick, clean driver who never received the respect he deserved while racing in IMSA. The 1993 IMSA GTP champion had not raced since 1993 or sat in a car since early 1995, but he qualified 14th and finished 7th in his first race (Mid-Ohio). He is expected to be the cornerstone of the Dan Gurney/Toyota IndyCar effort in 1996.

Some drivers had more than their share of misfortune. Stefan Johansson finished third at Nazareth and fourth at Vancouver after painting the leaves on his helmet blue. "I had green leaves on the side of my helmet my whole career, but I just found out that Al Jr. is repainting his motorhome because it had green on it. I found out that green is bad luck over here. So I changed it for Long Beach, and I had a good result... so maybe there is something to that." In a year-old Penske, he posted six top-10 finishes.

Above: Brazil's Andre Ribeiro explores an Elkhart Lake gravel trap. Apparently, the technique worked – he finished fourth in the race. The 29-year-old ex-law student won an impressive first for both himself and Honda on the New Hampshire oval.

A graduate of F3000 and also from Brazil, Gil De Ferran (below) adapted quickly to IndyCar. One of the best of the young drivers, he qualified on pole in Cleveland and won at Laguna Seca. The 27 year-old will have Honda power next year.

Mauricio Gugelmin, tenth in points, could easily have won a race. Eddie Cheever parted company with A.J. Foyt late in the year after a dismal season. He lost a win at Nazareth and a second-place at Long Beach when his car ran out of gas due to crew errors. Stan Fox, critically injured on the first lap at Indianapolis, is at home recovering.

Teo Fabi's new Forsythe team took a few races to get going, but after it did, he was a constant threat. Early in the season, Fabi predicted his fate: "When the car is good, it breaks," he said. "And when it is not so good, it keeps going." He took the pole at Milwaukee, had a best finish of third, and was ninth overall. Newcomers Carlos Guerrero and Eliseo Salazar found the going difficult. However, Salazar, moving over from IMSA, did finish fourth at Indianapolis.

NASCAR: Benevolent dictatorship

Of course, it is easier to double four million fans than 50 million, but NASCAR racing is still the fastest-growing spectator sport in North America, as the series expands beyond the southeastern US. When new tracks are added, they are targeted for top-10 US markets, and Miami, Dallas and Los Angeles are next in line.

On the track, Chevrolet replaced its Lumina design with a new Monte Carlo body, emphasising the value placed upon NASCAR success. Developing a new car is expensive, and the Lumina was still competitive, so a new shape was the answer in commercial and competition terms. Nevertheless, in 1992, when Ford Thunderbirds won nine straight races, NASCAR intervened. Afterward, the Fords took just two of the next twelve, so spending millions perfecting a body style that could be altered by the stroke of a rulemaker's pen was quite a gamble. Chevrolet won the first seven races of 1995 before a Thunderbird won, on the slow Martinsville Speedway, where aerodynamics are a secondary consideration. Despite ensuing rule changes, Monte Carlos still claimed 11 of the next 15 rounds, and the manufacturers' title was clinched by September.

Any series which continually rewrites rules leaves itself open to charges of favoritism, but constant adjust-

Right: The Trans Am Camaros of teammates Ron Fellows and Jamie Galles at Elkhart Lake. It was here that Fellows, a fast and fair driver who has been the series' runner-up the last two years, was punted off the track by Tom Kendall, a repeat of an incident which happened last year. Last season, Trans Am officials let Kendall keep his win, but removed the points. This year, Kendall instead got a 13-second penalty, which dropped him from first to third, but he kept the 25 points. Like NASCAR, Trans Am rewards finishes, even in low positions, so points decline from 30 for a win to 1 for 25th. Fellows, who did not finish, therefore got none. At season's end, although he won the most races, he lost the title to Kendall by 25 points.

Third overall and first in GTS at the Daytona 24-Hour was the Jack Roush Mustang of actor Paul Newman, Mark Martin, Tom Kendall and Michael Brockman. Newman drove 4 hours and at night, impressing all with his speed – especially because of the fact that the race number denotes his age!

IMSA/TRANS AM: TWO OF A KIND

Adversaries since the 1960s, the Sports Car Club of America and International Motorsports Association (IMSA) have continually fought for the same audience, market, manufacturers, and entrants. Following the disappearance of IMSA's GTP prototypes and the SCCA's high-tech Trans Am cars, however, interest has waned. Nor is their conflict limited to the top series. Both sanction numerous other open-wheel, sedan and sportscar championships. Increasingly, the regulations for SCCA Trans Am and IMSA GTS classes have become similar, and merger may be in the cards. Meanwhile, competitors switch back and forth between them, searching for better treatment and prospects for victory.

IMSA's flagship World Sports Cars championship garners minimal, if improving, television coverage. Most races are shown weeks later, and the best-known events, the Daytona 24-Hour and the 12 Hours of Sebring, are unsuited to live coverage. Trans Am boasts same-day edited coverage, though on a smaller cable network.

Heavy-handed rules administration by both bodies has scared away manufacturers like Toyota and Honda, who have opted for more stable IndyCar rules. Even this year, Porsche withdrew factory entries days before Daytona in a dispute with IMSA. With the corporations go the familiar drivers. After Ron Fellows, Tom Kendall, Dorsey Schroeder and Price Cobb, Trans Am's driving talent evaporates. The WSC line-up usually stops after Fermin Velez, James Weaver, Wayne Taylor and Mauro Baldi.

IMSA billed the WSC as a continuation of the 1960's Ford vs. Ferrari wars. The reference was meaningless to many (in cradles at the time) and unbelieved by the rest. True, there was an expensive Ferrari 333SP "prototype" (in a class conceived as low budget), but "Ford" was simply a Ford V8 in a Riley and Scott chassis, and there were R&S Oldsmobiles, too. In the endurance races, the privateer Porsche of Lassig/Bouchut/Lavaggi/Werner won at Daytona, while the Ferrari of Evans/Velez/van de Poele took Sebring. The WSC championship was won by the Ferrari of Fermin Velez – as if anyone noticed.

In April, a crash at Road Atlanta critically injured Jeremy Dale (then WSC points leader) and Fabrizio Barbazza, and both were still recovering at the end of the year. The wreck occurred after two slower GTS cars in the race crashed, and many faulted IMSA's practice of running the classes simultaneously to fill out the field.

For its part, Trans Am created excitement by inverting the top-five qualifiers, the quickest car starting fifth, and giving the top-three bonus points for their troubles. Few liked the system, and crashes also resulted. In the championship, Ron Fellows' Camaro posted five wins, but one win and bonus points gave Tom Kendall the title – as if anyone noticed.

Two evenly matched World Sportscar Championship contenders: the Ford-engine, Riley & Scott chassis, car of Weaver, Letzinger and Dyson leading the Ferrari 333SP of Fermin Velez at Sears Point. The former had more torque and superior braking, but the Ferrari boasted better horsepower and handling. Billing their encounters as 'Ford v. Ferrari II' was a little disingenuous.

Mexico's Adrian Fernandez (right) and his Lola-Mercedes. The likeable 30 year-old driver posted a career-high third place in the IndyCar championship this year. It was a success which brought a full-time TV crew from his home country to follow his exploits. The car's colour-scheme must have made for dazzling viewing!

and loose weights paid $5000 each. Jeff Gordon's team was fined for racing an unapproved (though commonly-used) suspension part. There is no way of knowing what violations were missed or overlooked. Fisticuffs resulted in fines to Ricky Rudd's crew chief and driver Michael Waltrip. Progress is still frowned upon, and NASCAR vetoed one team's novel impact wrench system. Crewmen wore air bottles to power the wrenches, dispensing with the troublesome and dangerous rubber hoses.

One thing NASCAR cannot stop is rain, but President Bill France, Jr. is not about to let Mother Nature interfere. Rain delayed several races this season, but most were run the same day. Indeed, many fans left the Brickyard 400 after unofficial announcements it would be postponed only to learn it had just started. France is unwilling to settle for good fortune; he wants certainty. This summer, at Watkins Glen, NASCAR took a step toward weather control. Dale Earnhardt and Mark Martin tried hand-grooved Goodyear rain tires. Directional and symmetrical, the tread patterns were based on the company's Aquatred passenger car tire. Use in the two road course rounds is not the only possible application. With 31 races (13 tracks are visited twice) jammed between February and November, time is short. Travelling by transporter, teams are on a tight schedule, and rainouts are a major problem. Television is critical to the series' success, and Monday races, even when possible, are an undesirable alternative. Rescheduling, which necessitates additional travel and may find broadcast times already filled, is worse. Would NASCAR dare race on ovals in the rain? Absolutely. High velocity is the prime component in bad crashes, and who is to say the slower racing might not be safer.

As Dale Earnhardt chased Jeff Gordon for the points lead, he checked off items on his "things to do" list. Item: win my first road race. Accomplished at Sears Point. He won after Mark Martin spun off on oil that Earnhardt had located by smell several laps earlier. Item: win my first Brickyard 400 (worth over $500,000). Accomplished. A purpose-built car with less than 40 test laps did the job. Three lines remained: win the Daytona 500, improve my qualifying performance, and win a record eighth Winston Cup crown. He won three races, bringing his total to 66, but might have won more had he started higher.

1987 World Sportscar Champion Raul Boesel, seen here (opposite) at Portland, had a Lola-Mercedes for his tenth year in IndyCars, but success continued to elude him. Second place remains his best finish in the series and with just sixteenth place in the overall rankings, 1995 was his worst season in eight years.

Hired by Williams for F1 in 1996 well before the IndyCar season was over, Jacques Villeneuve (below) had logged many test miles by the end of the year. Williams will not, it is hoped, repeat McLaren's mistakes with Michael Andretti. Villeneuve will be properly prepared, and his talent will not be wasted.

ments were made to spoiler and air-dam dimensions to equalize the Thunderbirds and Monte Carlos. Even the Pontiac Grand Prix, virtually unaided since its 1988 debut, received concessions which enabled Kyle Petty to win with it. Next year, however, a new Grand Prix body is due.

In April, series officials kidnapped a Monte Carlo, Thunderbird and Grand Prix, bundling them off to a wind tunnel to compare drag, lift and other factors. The results, used to manage competition, were not released, but it is believed the Monte Carlo produces improved downforce and balance with less drag. Credit for the better performance goes to improved front end/hood, rear glass and rear deck profiles, and the difference is said to show up more on long runs than in outright speed.

Fines this year were more numerous and costly than ever. Ricky Rudd was charged a record $50,000 for a hydraulic device that raised his Thunderbird for scrutineering, but allowed the car to be lowered on track. A similar system on a Pontiac drew a $35,100 bounty. Junior Johnson was charged $45,100 for an illegal intake manifold, while teams with illegal air cleaners

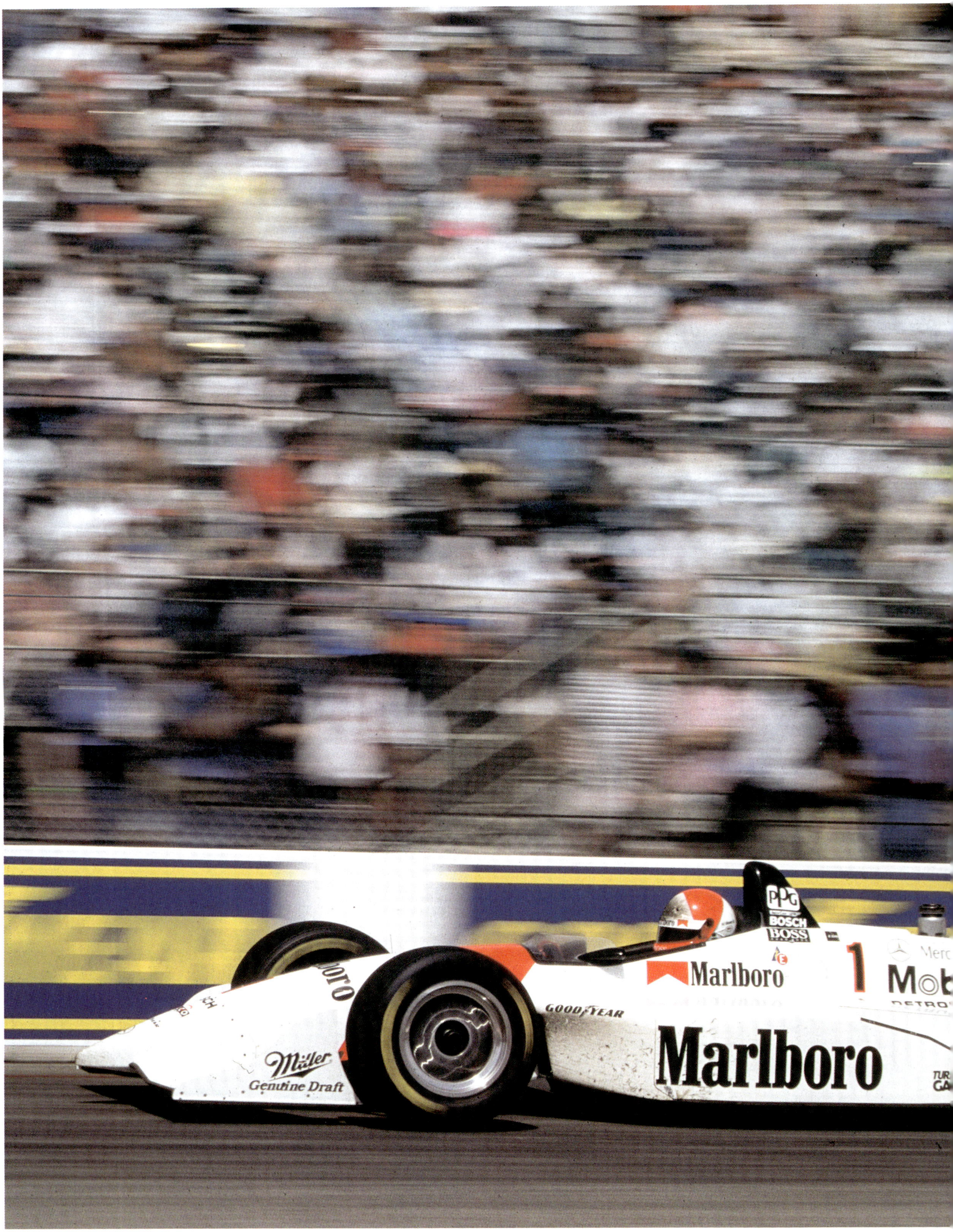
PPG
BOSCH
BOSS
Marlboro
1
Mob
GOODYEAR
Marlboro
Miller
Genuine Draft

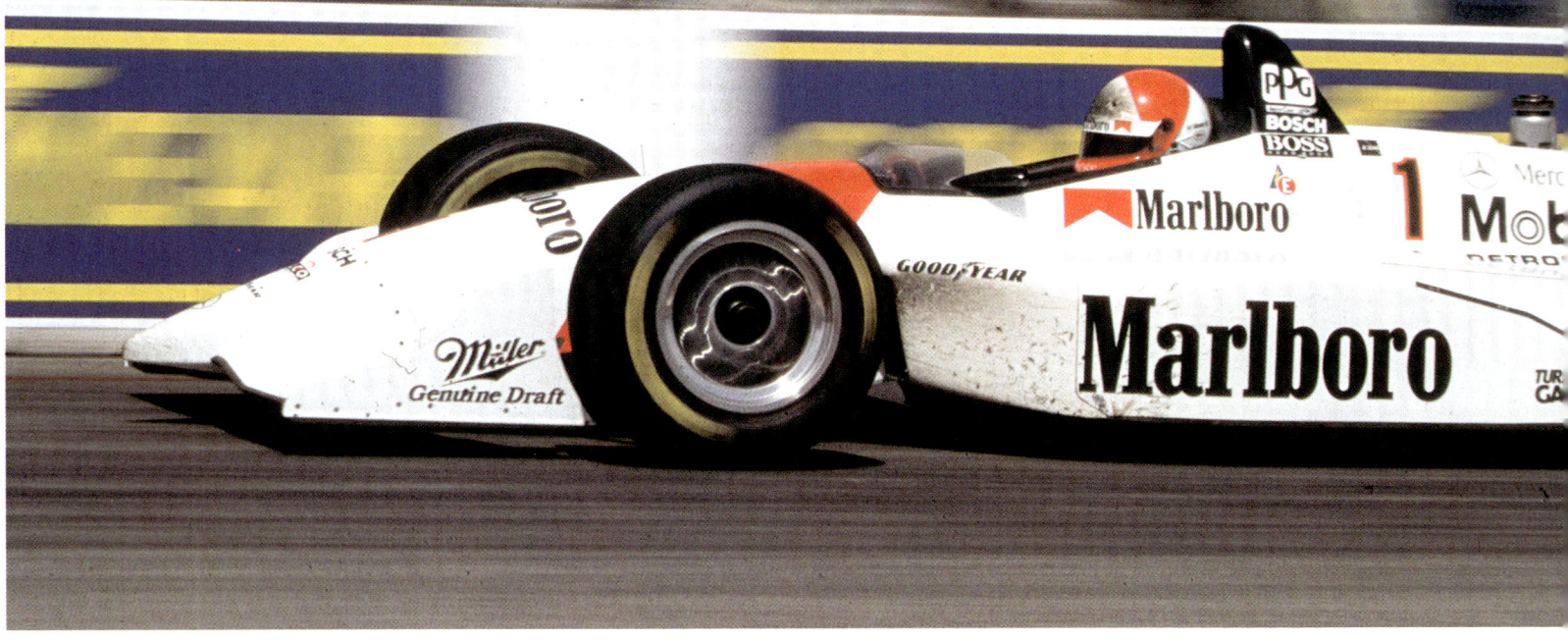

Wrecks and engine failures hampered his chase. In IndyCar, 500-mile races are the exception, and reliability influences outcomes as much as skill. Durability is rarely the issue in NASCAR. There is time to recover from a poor qualifying session if you avoid the wrecks around you. NASCAR's point system contrives to keep otherwise unraceable cars on the track, however, complicating the process.

Earnhardt has never been known as a great qualifier, but by comparison to Jeff Gordon, everyone suffered. No relation to IndyCar's Robby Gordon, and — if reputations are anything to go by — with little in common apart from an ability to drive fast, Jeff had eight poles by September, compared to four for Mark Martin and three for Earnhardt. Moreover, it was rare for Gordon to start outside the top-ten. In view of the qualifying procedure, which usually consists of one lap, that is outstanding. On Friday, the fastest 20 cars make the show, and the rest try again on Saturday.

With Ray Evernham as crew chief, the 24-year-old Gordon, who had his first NASCAR start in November of 1992, seemed to be the best driver in the best car with the best motor. In addition to his great speed, he has already acquired patience and maturity, qualities lacking in drivers twice his age. He won seven races and generally led the points standings, much of his margin resulting from bonus points for leading individual laps and leading the most laps in a race. At one time, he had led 24 of 25 events and mistakes, either by Gordon or his team, were rare. A missed shift on a late-race restart caused a blown engine and cost him one victory, while his crew missed another chance by dropping the car off the jack prematurely in the Daytona 500.

Gordon's Hendrick Racing teammates Terry Labonte and Ken Schrader benefitted from engine builder Randy Dorton's powerplants, too. Labonte won three races, as did his younger brother Bobby (driving for Joe Gibbs), who also used the motors. When Hendrick had problems, they struck luckless Ken Schrader. Unlike Gordon and Labonte, he found it difficult to stay in the top-ten. Worse, the amiable driver lost part of his left thumb while working on his NASCAR SuperTruck. He did not miss a race.

One great disappointment was the departure of Steve Kinser. The sprint car champion left Kenny Bern-

"The Boss of the Beach." This year Al Unser Jr. (opposite) won his sixth Long Beach GP, proving again that he is a truly superb street racer. 14 of his first 19 victories came on temporary circuits, but since joining Penske last season he has diversified, and the figure is now 18 of 31.

Italy's Teo Fabi led seven times this year, but mechanical problems while running well with his Forsythe Racing Reynard-Ford prevented him achieving success. His best finish was third at Long Beach (below). He has five IndyCar wins, the most recent in 1989 with Porsche.

Above: Robby Gordon (above) won here at Phoenix and again at Detroit. Victories in other series came easily, but he is finding the going tougher in IndyCar. Emerson Fittipaldi (left) finished third, having led until a late fuel stop.

A parked Indycar quickly draws a crowd. Jimmy Vasser (right) proves the point as he waits to qualify at Michigan. He finished second in Portland and appeared to have won after Al Unser Jr. was disqualified, but Unser's appeal was later upheld, so Vasser went back in his original second place.

No IRL! Tony George's proposed new oval-track Indy Racing League angered fans and teams alike. Bizarre rules, which guarantee "500" participation to IRL regulars and multiply points by the number of races entered, did not help.

stein's team and returned to his winning ways in the open-wheel series. His talent is unquestioned, and the team was sold at year's end. Bernstein's now-defunct IndyCar and NASCAR teams have tarnished the reputations of other top drivers including Roberto Guerrero, Scott Goodyear and Brett Bodine.

Mark Martin won his third straight race (and second of the year) at Watkins Glen, but his Thunderbird was simply the wrong body style. Rusty Wallace's hard driving wrung two more wins out of the car, and the 1989 Winston Cup winner now has 41 victories. Sterling Marlin's Monte Carlo won three races, and his "Runt" Pittman engines were particularly effective at Daytona and Talladega, restrictor plate tracks. Nicknamed "Nigel" for the IndyCar-like scream of his non-traditional exhaust system, Marlin won the Daytona 500 for the second straight year. Earnhardt charged through the field after a late tire stop, but lacked the muscle to pass and finished second again. Dale Jarrett replaced the recuperating Ernie Irvan at Robert Yates' shop, but won only one race. Irvan, injured critically in a crash last season, returned to Winston Cup racing in October.

NORTH AMERICAN TOURING CARS: AN OVERFULL HOUSE?

Team sports? All of them. Professional and amateur leagues for every age and sex. Individual competitions? All of them. Motor racing? NASCAR, IndyCar, IMSA, Trans Am, USAC, NHRA (National Hot Rod Association – drag racing), World of Outlaws (sprint cars), the American Speed Association. Off-road, monster truck and motorcycle racing. Every possible machine at every possible venue.

Into this over-saturated arena, in 1996, plunges the North American Touring Car Championship (NATCC). Only one question remains: Why?

On a continent that loves big-bore V8s, there are already several small-displacement sedan series indistinguishable from it. They fill out schedules during IndyCar, IMSA and Trans Am weekends. Their drivers are unknowns and usually remain so.

Only in the last five years have NASCAR Winston Cup and IndyCar, the two top series, begun to grow. IMSA and Trans Am have barely survived. F1 has been absent from the US for four years. IndyCar has shifted its schedule to minimize conflicts with more popular baseball and football games.

Nevertheless, based on the success of touring car series elsewhere, NATCC President Roger Elliott and his partners have chosen to do battle in North America. "Sanctioned by the SCCA in association with IndyCar" is the way the banner will read. A seven-event, fourteen-race (two races each) calendar has been announced with an eighth to be added, but many promoters have made commitments contingent upon sufficient manufacturer participation. The venues are co-sited with Trans Am, IndyCar and NASCAR. Cars and drivers remain undisclosed.

The NATCC hopes to capitalize on promotions geared toward "the accessibility of the drivers and their cars to the public" which have been successful in other countries. But in the US, drivers take their roles as personalities and sponsor representatives seriously. Even Earnhardt and Andretti make frequent public appearances and attend autograph-signing sessions. Paddocks are accessible with the purchase of a pass, and drivers make time throughout the weekend for the public. The Williams F1 garage may be off-limits even for journalists and photographers, but IndyCar work is carried out under transporter awnings, and the cars are easily visible.

Only two events will be shown on live TV. The rest may be relegated to overnight time slots. Extensive promotion and top North American drivers are desirable, but most contracts prohibit racing in other series. Can the NATCC find happiness? Just this year, NASCAR introduced a "SuperTruck" series. The "trucks" are simply Winston Cup stock cars with minor roll-cage modifications and truck-like bodies, but still the class has found a following. One never knows.

ONLY IN AMERICA – 2

DRY LAKES SPEEDSTERS

John Lamm

For an auto racing fan dazzled by the carbon fiber, techno aura of Formula 1 or even the glitzy, wind tunnel world of NASCAR, El Mirage is a drive into history... a two-hour drive to be specific, east from Los Angeles over the mountains to the high desert. To dusty plains dotted with a few dry lakes, which are flat hard areas so broad the U.S. government uses one as a space shuttle landing field and makes it part of Edwards Air Force base.

As early as the 1920s, young men who were curious about their cars' top speeds would leave LA in the early morning hours to drive out to the "lakes" for speed trials. In May, 1938, racing on the lakes became more organized when the Southern California Timing Association (SCTA) was formed. There were several dry lakes from which to choose, but over the years (and after the Army Air Corps requisition one of the best) the racing settled into one expanse, El Mirage. Since then, we've had a world war, some of the racers went off and founded drag racing, a prewar lakes fan named Phil Hill raced in Europe to become a Formula 1 Champion, men walked on the moon, and the Berlin Wall fell, but to this day, six times a year, the SCTA still runs speed trials up there on El Mirage. You wouldn't want to drive a clean car or wear your best clothes to El Mirage, because it is a dry, dusty experience. Approaching the lake, kicking up a dirt cloud behind, you see a group of cars that appear to be dots at one end of the lake.

Slowly one dot leaves the crowd, heading across the dirt expanse, building speed and a trail of dust. You can hear a far-off engine roar and the speck rockets past what looks to be a tiny white semi trailer. A colorful parachute pops out behind the dot. Another run

El Mirage is a family affair, like after a run when you refold the parachute of an F Gas Lakester, a 4-cylinder machine that just went 158.8mph.

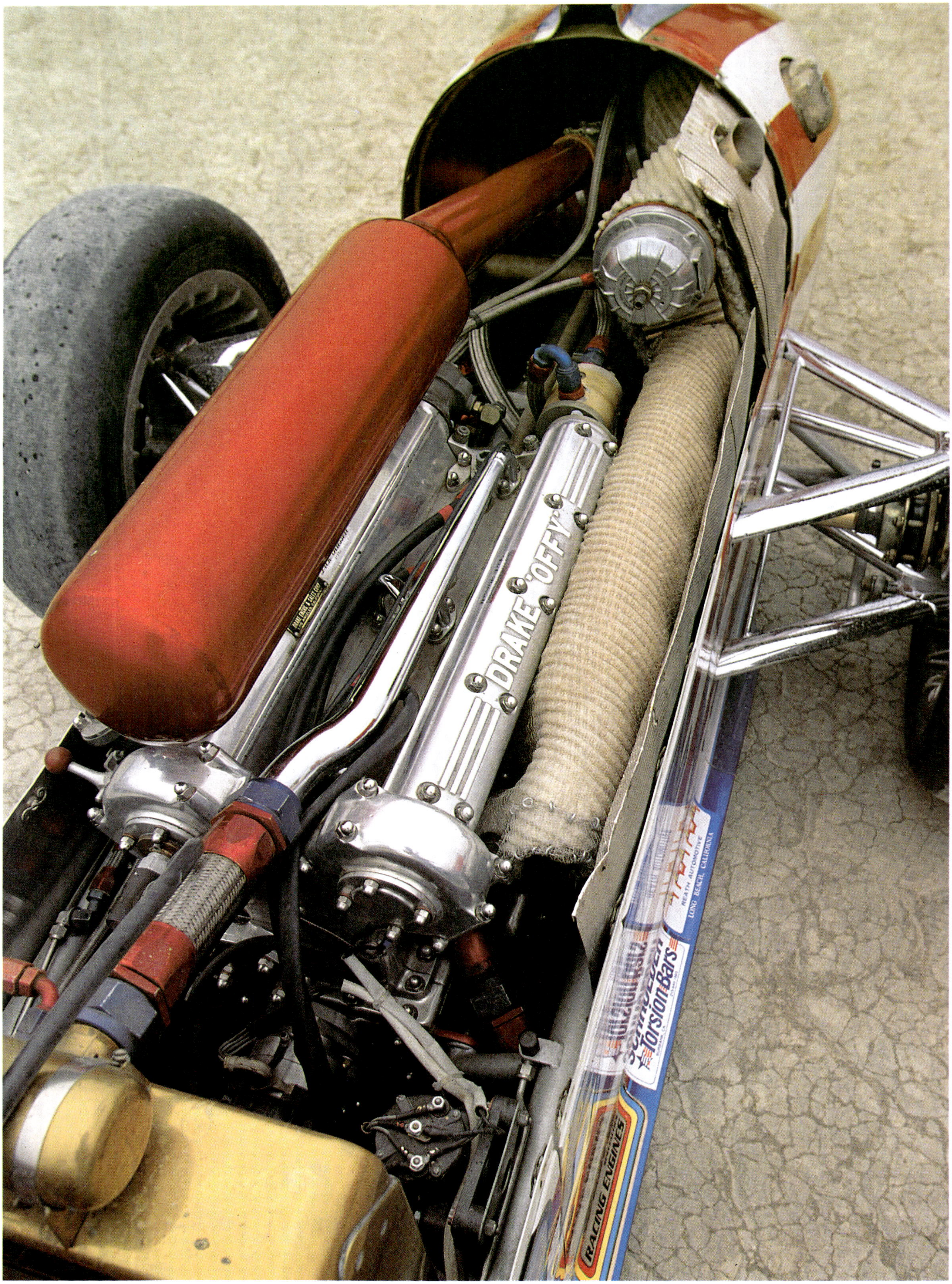
DRAKE "OFFY"
Torsion-Bars
REATH AUTOMOTIVE
LONG BEACH, CALIFORNIA
RACING ENGINES

at El Mirage, 1.3 miles from stating line to speed traps. Arriving at the pits, you park in a jumble of cars and wander over to the starting line. An amazing variety of cars are strung out in two lines, waiting their chance to run. Near the front, a tall man is encasing himself in a short, seemingly pencil-thin silver streamliner. Two young men lean on an old Chevy Monza with a big hood bulge. A smooth black '53 Studebaker waits next to a vintage sprint car with flat Moon hubcaps, a roll cage and a driver wearing a dirty Bonneville Speed Weeks baseball cap studded with pins that document how many years he's been at this sport. That's Bruce Johnson, and he's been racing at El Mirage since 1938.

You can get some sense of the dizzying array of different machines at El Mirage by running through the list of 36 major classes for cars, each with as many as 19 subcategories.

Without getting into particulars, which would fill pages, we'll start with the Special Construction Category. This is for the highest-speed vehicles, and has two basic groups, streamliners and lakesters. The rules don't care if the engine is front or rear mounted, but streamliners have four wheels and at least two of those must be covered. Lakesters have no covered wheels. Engines for these machines are separated by displacement, and can be anything from modern supercharged V-8s running on a blend of methanol and nitromethane to vintage flathead V-8s or fours using gasoline. The odd addition to this class? Electric vehicles.

The next basic group is called the Vintage Category and it is, to quote the SCTA, "... specifically intended for the lovers of antique iron." These are the classic hot rod roadsters, and the rules state you must run bodies of American cars. Street Roadsters retain most all the stock body panels or an exact replica of cars built between 1923 and 1938. Fuel-Gas Roadsters (vintage 1928-1938) allow more modifications, like removing the fenders, and while some body contour changes are permitted, the car must have a minimum grille area of 530 square inches, which is that of a '28 Ford. Modified Roadsters are those with a stock body shape aft of the firewall, but a lowered, tapered nose. There are also Vintage classes for cars built in 1948 and before, and a category for old oval track cars with pre-1948 (that is, pre-modern Detroit overhead-valve) engines.

American or imported vehicles are welcome in classes for Competition Coupes and Altered coupes that look roughly like they did when in production, but with body modifications for added speed. You can run Production cars too, though here they only allow gas-powered engines. Trucks can have a shot at record runs, whether a stock pickup (with the tailgate down for less aerodynamic drag) or big diesel cabs. There are also 15 classes for motorcycles.

If that isn't enough categories for you, the SCTA would be willing to create a class for your vehicle... they have before.

It's this amazing melange of machinery that makes El Mirage so fascinating. The racing is interesting, but basically a car leaves, disappears into a cloud of dust and soon you hear the time. But the pits are a wonderland of mechanical ingenuity. A shiny new big-block V-8 (probably a Chevy) with a massive blower (likely a GMC) in a Lakester here, a classic Ford flathead with two rows of Stromberg 97 carbs in a Roadster over there. Here's a tiny streamliner with an odd motorcycle engine concoction, there are new cars, old cars, stock cars, bizarre cars.

Know how El Mirage engineers devise some 4-cylinder engines? They use one bank of a V-8, or pull the piston and rod out of every other cylinder or, for better balance, they might leave the unnecessary pistons in and just cut the tops out of them.

Although it looks simple to point a racecar down a 1.3-mile straight line and go for top speed, it isn't. First there's the matter of getting started. Because they run a starter-less magneto ignition system, tall gearing or both, many of the cars need to be push started. This can lead to some odd pairings, like a Porsche 914 being pushed off by an aging motor home that looks like it's about to run over the German car. Then there is the matter of staying on that black 1.3-mile line. Some of the streamliners, lakesters and roadsters are so powerful they get wheelspin well down the course, so much so they carry hundreds of pounds of ballast in back. Some of the Lakesters look like dragsters with skinny tires, and in fact a few are just that. It turns out narrow tires lead to better grip on the dirt, while wide tires tend to cause the car to wander.

Drivers have to consider the climate. Meets are held in

Old Glory, the American flag, flies over the starting lane stand (above) of the Southern California Timing Association at El Mirage, as it has since the late 1930s.

Dick Russel's all-American Lakester is called the Star Spangled Banger (below), referring to its famous powerplant, a 180-cubic-inch Offenhauser (opposite). Russell's machine qualifies as a lakester, despite its closed cockpit, because the wheels are left uncovered

You can find the history of El Mirage in books that document hot rodding in America. You can also find it in the face of Bruce Johnson, who has been doing it since 1938. And in his hat, a somewhat well used cap from the Bonneville World Finals in 1990, and all the pins that decorate it. We found Johnson belted into his vintage sprint car, laughing and ready to chat about his days of racing. But before you think this is just some old guy having trouble letting go of the past, know that B. Johnson is in the record books, in class XO/Vintage Oval Track, at 157.75mph.

May, June, July, September, October and November. In August the SCTA is off running the Bonneville Speed Weeks. The June and July meets can be quite hot, so records are often set at the fall meetings. Desert winds are another hassle. Side winds can be so treacherous that when they hit 14-15mph the course is closed. At 18-19mph a tail wind becomes "El Mirage Horsepower," enough to add 3-4mph to your speed. On one recent Sunday meeting, there was a very light, occasional sprinkle of rain. A problem on the dirt surface? "No," replied one competitor, "it keeps the dust down so we can run more often, and it helps the tires hook up."

There have been accidents, of course, though for the hundreds who have driven the course there has been only a fatality or two every decade. The SCTA has strict safety rules, like a full fire suit, an approved helmet and 5-point harnesses for the driver. The cars need to be well made and fitted with a 5-or 6-point roll cage and a fire extinguishing system.

Even if your car is properly prepared you can't just arrive at El Mirage and expect to make speed runs. First you need to join one of the supporting clubs. The names are wonderful and harken back to the early years: Gear Grinders, Sidewinders, Lakers, Rod Riders, Eliminators and the San Diego Roadster Club.

It also seems a requirement that you be a friendly person. Walking through the pits or along the lines of cars waiting to make a run, the drivers, mechanics and officials are happy to answer questions. After years of races at which one has had to contend with pushy pit marshals, standoffish drivers and race organizers who seem to wish you hadn't arrived, going to El Mirage was like being welcomed by a family you never knew you had. Nice people. No complications. Great fun.

Looking like a dragster with small wheels is the 468-cubic-inch Chevrolet V-8 powered Lakester (left) that just ran 206.4mph. This car was built by Bill Summers of the famous Summers brothers record car team. These cars use narrow rear tires for better bite on the dirt surface of the 1.3-mile straight-line course. The handsome Kelly/Hall car (below) is classified as a Modified Roadster because the fiberglass body retains its stock '34 Ford shape aft of the cowling but has a tapered, modified nose. Powered by an unblown Ford flathead V-8 running on gasoline, the car went 143.2mph. Note the sturdy roll cage and the beam front axle.

Starter Bill Taylor (above) checks a streamliner driver's 5-point safety harness before he is allowed to run. Other required safety equipment includes a rollcage, onboard fire extinguishers, fire suit and helmet.

Left: Don Bjorkquist of the Gear Grinder club going 229.1mph in a B Gas Streamliner, the Shyster, thanks to a supercharged 430-cubic-inch Chevrolet V-8. Any car with the potential to get above 160mph on El Mirage must be equipped with a parachute. Below: A pair of crewmen cinch up the safety harness for the driver of a V-8 powered front-drive streamliner that has a pair of small tandem rear wheels.

According to his entry, Earl Wooden's car (opposite, top) is a 1947 Crosley, but that's only because the back of the long, long-nosed Competition Coupe looks a bit like a Crosley. Fitted with a 422-cubic-inch unblown Chevrolet V-8, Wooden's car hit 228.2mph. Curt and Bob Giovanine's Modified Roadster (left) is listed as a 1925 Chevrolet, but looks somewhat modern with that ground effects skirt around the bottom. With a non-supercharged 182-cubic-inch 4-cylinder engine, the car ran a solid 129.8mph on "fuel," which is methanol, sometimes mixed with "nitro." While many of the modern engines on El Mirage are Chevrolet V-8s, the classic Ford or Mercury flathead V-8 remains an important part of racing on the dry lakes, factored into every class right up to Blown Fuel Streamliners. Some of the flatheads, like the supercharged example (opposite, bottom), have been developed over the years into powerful contraptions. After a 196.4mph run, the pretty, new Dana Wilson, Mike Waters '29 Ford Roadster (left) comes to rest, its parachute at rest, the crew having a cold cola. The car is classed as a roadster because it retains the front profile of the original Ford. Notice the classic flat Moon spun aluminum hubcaps.

EUROPEAN TOURING CAR CHAMPIONSHIPS

NATIONAL STRENGTH, INTERNATIONAL AMBITIONS

Pierre Dieudonné

Perhaps the major political event of the year was that after negotiations with the FIA, the DTM promoters achieved the international expansion which they had been seeking. Bernie Ecclestone, having achieved the conditions he required, did not drag his feet. The FIA set in motion an International Touring Car (ITC) series which confirmed the touring car structure which the authorities had originally wanted: Class 1 cars for an high-level international championship and Class 2, or Super Tourers, as the raw material for national championships which would enter their best competitors for an annual end-of-season World Cup meeting. The position is still not finalised, however, for the ITC concept is not without problems. The enormous success of the DTM (Deutsche Tourenwagen Meisterschaft) is essentially a German phenomenon, based on the country's strong motor industry and strong national sentiment. The championship benefited from the involvement of Alfa Romeo, after internal dissension had seen BMW and Audi withdraw to concentrate Super Tourers. The involvement of manufacturers in the various national championships for this class has made them too expensive for private entrants to participate in an arena where the media exposure is insufficient to persuade sponsors to part with their money. The exception to this rule is Great Britain, but most countries are well behind in this area, but the fault is not all with the promoters, who have a hard job to do. On the other hand, the harmonisation of the regulations has enabled Super Tourers to expand internationally. Now well-established in Europe, the class has spread to Japan, Australia and South Africa, and there are plans for a US series in 1996.

One of the current problems in touring car racing lies in the rivalry between Super Touring on one side and DTM on the other, a state of affairs which splits the available resources. The creation of ITC will have profound effects, but it is not easy to forecast how things will turn out.

The convivial atmosphere which reigns among the high-tech atmosphere of DTM races is one of the ingredients in its success. There is a welcome in the paddock which makes one want to go back, a state of affairs which is not always true at FIA-controlled events, where other considerations are more important. "The DTM is oriented towards the product, while F1 is more concerned with image," says Hans Werner Aufrecht, boss of Mercedes-Benz' racing partner AMG and president of the DTM organisation. "People want to see and touch the machines, and respect for this philosophy was one of the parts of accord with Bernie Ecclestone."

It is difficult to applaud the good news of the birth of the ITC championship without remembering the sudden about-turn of the FIA on the World Touring Car Championship in 1987 and the sports car championship in 1992. Bernie Ecclestone is used to running Formula 1 through a small committee, taking rapid decisions after a discussion round a very small table. He has never hidden his dislike for negotiating with manufacturers, whose decisions are not those of a single person – and whose involvement in competition is often dependent on the policy of the moment.

One must also ask whether the three marques on whom the creation of the ITC was based (Mercedes-Benz, Alfa Romeo and Opel) will not find that involvement in the international series will affect their participation in the DTM. Each of them is committed to having six cars in the championship to maintain min-

After the opening round at Mugello, the area of the water's edge in Helsinki (opposite) was a very different venue for the new International Touring Car Championship. The series was created in haste, and the original plan to visit seven circuits, either permanent or, like the Finnish event, temporary, was modified on numerous occasions. The twisting nature of the Helsinki course combined with the slippery nature of the new surface favoured the all-wheel drive Alfas and brought wins for Danner and Larini. In the DTM, Bernd Schneider and Mercedes established their claim to the championship in the first event at Hockenheim (below).

In common with all its Class 1 competitors, the Opel Calibra was equipped with a sophisticated suspension system with centrally-mounted spring/damper units operated by pushrods. Only the fact that active suspension is forbidden limits the application of even more advanced designs. The electronically-controlled hydraulic power-steering system was developed in collaboration with Williams Grand Prix Engineering, and is based on components used in F1. Opel's engineers also worked with a number of other specialists, including Cosworth (engines), X-Trac (gearbox), Lotus Engineering (aerodynamics) and Bosch (electronics).

SCHNEIDER RULES THE CLASS 1 ROOST

By taking both Class 1 championships, the DTM and the ITC, Bernd Schneider confirmed himself as the true successor in the Mercedes team to Klaus Ludwig, who had left for Opel. The 31-year-old Schneider, who was a German Formula 1 hope in the days before Schumacher, was quick to admit that he had learned much in three years as Ludwig's partner in the AMG-Mercedes team.

He gained his first racing experience in karts, where he was successful despite his height, and made an easy transition to single-seater racing. German F3 champion in 1987, he made his debut in Formula 1 with Zakspeed the following year, while at the same time coming under the wing of Ford Germany in touring car racing. The perils presented at the back of an F1 grid persuaded him to seek a more varied motor racing career, and his results in sports-prototype racing with the Kremer team won him the Porsche Cup in 1990. 1991 saw him appearing more and more regularly in the DTM, driving a Mercedes first for Zakspeed, and then with AMG, which brought him his first victories in 1992. Although experience is of great importance in this technologically-advanced branch of the sport, Schneider's two titles did not come easily, for he had to fight not only the competition from other manufacturers, but also a number of other drivers who shared the benefits of driving the superior C-class Mercedes. Among these, Schneider not only had to beat fellow-German and contemporary Jörg van Ommen; he also had to fight off the attack from the 'young wolves' which Mercedes had nominated to follow the path of Schumacher and Frentzen. Among the youngsters, the most impressive was Jan Magnussen, a 22-year-old Dane who had a testing contract with McLaren and a bright future ahead of him. Dario Franchitti, also 22, and one of the many Scots who proudly bear an Italian name and heritage, is another future star. The retirement at the end of the year of Keke Rosberg (46), number one in his own team of Opels, underlined the success of this new wave of young DTM/ITC drivers. Another 22-year-old with an impressive record was Giancarlo Fisichella, the new wave's representative among the Alfa Romeo teams.

Next year will be an important one for the DTM, which will be absorbed into the ITC in the shape of a 13-round series to include seven 'overseas' races in such places as Japan, Brazil and the UK *and* six events in Germany. The future is hard to predict; will the ITC be successful in attracting additional entries into what promises to be a very expensive series? Or will the whole thing explode, like an over-inflated balloon? Much depends on the sport's governing body, which has control over the commercial aspects of the series, including TV rights. The way it handles the finances will be a major determining factor in the future of touring car racing. One thing is sure – for the manufacturers, already split between two classes of racing, only stability and certainty will justify the considerable expenditure required.

imum entry-levels, and this is an enormous effort in terms of capital outlay and running costs.

At the same time, there is also the consideration that if the ITC is successful, what will be the reaction of those manufacturers involved in Super Tourers, a class which is likely to become sidelined in terms of prestige.

DTM – ITC A technology shop-window

It can be seen, therefore, that the future of Touring Car racing is still far from simple, for even if the split into two classes is accepted, it still depends on so many unknowns. One cannot help but ask whether there is one class too many, for the ambitions of the leading participants in Super Tourers are not purely national. With the creation of the ITC, international recognition will come the way of Class 1, and it is likely that Super Tourers will increasingly be seen as a sort of Second Division. This deep-seated rivalry between supporters of the two clans is not new, but it could be on the verge of reaching new dimensions.

Alfa Romeo was the first manufacturer to equip its engines with pneumatic valve-control, enabling it to make the most of the maximum 12,000 revs allowed by the rules. With a compression ratio of 12.5:1, and using exhausts equipped with catalysts, the 450hp 2.5-litre four was built in two versions, with different stroke lengths, to suit different circuit characteristics. the Alfa 155 V6 Ti was also the first competing car to benefit from a semi-automatic gearbox with its complicated electro-hydraulics controlled by paddles mounted behind the steering-wheel, F1 style. The very advanced 1995 version of the car was late, under-tested, and perhaps over-endowed with electronics, and for a time it was put to one side while last year's cars carried the Alfa colours.

Later in the season, Mercedes also introduced pneumatic valve operation for its V6. It was a further addition to the C-class's high-tech specification, which included water-cooled brake callipers and an engine sub-assembly which AMG said could be changed in 12 minutes when necessary. The cars were driven through the rear wheels only, but a sophisticated traction-control system.

More spectacular than the Super Tourers, the DTM/ITC cars could possibly succeed in their search for international recognition. Battles like this one between the Opel Calibra of the veteran Keke Rosberg and the Alfa Romeo of the young Giancarlo Fisichella at Hockenheim are part of the spectacle which keeps DTM attendances high.

Could this situation be desirable for any other reason than a policy of divide-and-rule?

Now that Formula 1 has banned 'driver aids', it is the cars of the DTM which represent the cutting-edge of automobile technology. Traction-control, anti-lock brakes, all-wheel drive, electric control of differentials – and soon other systems – there is nothing available to customers which is not legal in this form of racing. Active suspension and carbon brakes are not allowed, but that is logical in view of the fact that no existing production car benefits from such systems. There is a great deal of freedom for engine modification, so long as the ground rules of 2.5-litres capacity, no more than 6 cylinders and no more than 4 valves per cylinder are respected. Engines must be derived from a production engine made in quantity by the same manufacturer, but the power unit can come from a different model and up to two cylinders may be added or subtracted from the original design. Maximum revs are electronically governed at 12,000, and a standard lead-free fuel is provided by Elf to all competitors. Exhausts carry catalysts, and there is a maximum noise-level of 98dB which is measured with a toler-

ance of only 2dB. This year, it has been possible to use suspension which differs from that of the production car, and all competitors now use pure racing designs based on wishbones and with centrally-mounted dampers operated by push-rods. Aerodynamic modifications to the bodywork are free below the centre-line of the wheels, and this has led to extensive work being carried out on lowering the car and developing spoilers and skirts which rely on sophisticated aerodynamic studies. The disadvantage of this body development is that the aerodynamic aids are often vulnerable, and drivers are therefore wary of track edges and 'rumble-strips' on corners. This 'tiptoe' driving style has taken some of the spectacle from the racing.

When they took on and beat Alfa Romeo, who dominated in 1993, Mercedes and AMG showed that all-wheel drive was not necessary for a car with more than 450hp and an overall weight of just over a metric tonne (2200lb) to achieve success in the DTM. The traction-control system fitted to the new C-class cars, was sufficient to overcome all the problems of putting the power down effectively, but all-wheel drive, used by the Alfa 155 V6 Ti's and the Opel Calibras, still showed an advantage in some combinations of circuit configuration, track conditions and weather. Driving through all four wheels also helped shorten braking distances, but the Mercedes were often faster in acceleration when conditions favoured them. Their faster straight-line speed was probably due to power and aerodynamics, coupled with their weight limit of 1020kg (2248lb), which was 40kg (8lb) lower than the all-wheel drive cars.

The design and build-quality of all the DTM cars is superb, and technical levels are close to those of F1. For instance, when necessary, it is possible to change the engine in an AMG-Mercedes in 12 minutes, thanks to a subassembly which incorporates the complete front-end, including various accessories and the radiators – including their shrouds and the front spoiler. The Calibra is equally radical in its approach, thanks to a collaboration with the Williams GP Engineering organisation. The electronically-controlled power-steering is an example, as is the development of a semi-automatic 6-speed gearbox along F1 lines to replace a sequential-change unit. Like Alfa Romeo, which had a unit available at the beginning of the season on its 'Step 2' version of the 155, Mercedes has been working hard towards the introduction of a semi-automatic box and hydraulically-controlled valve-gear. In the case of the gearbox, the aim is to reduce the time between gears to 30 milliseconds, drastically reducing the 80 milliseconds taken by the sequential box introduced when the C-class entered competition last year. The 1995 cars have also taken advantage of a change in the regulations which allows a tank of up to 70 litres (15.4 Imp. gal) capacity to be placed in the passenger compartment. This has enabled the engineers to reduce the size of the boot-mounted tank from its original 110 litres (24.2 Imp. gal) and achieve better weight distribution. The driver is positioned mid-way back in the passenger compartment, and Mercedes have paid particular attention to his (or her) protection. The driver's seat wraps round a long way on both sides, and is placed well away from the doors and the side components of the roll cage, which are heavily wrapped in foam. Mercedes was also the first manufacturer to equip all its DTM-ITC cars with airbags. Among the many examples of original technical thinking, the internal cooling system is particularly noteworthy, thanks to a system of thermostati-

The British championship continues to go from strength to strength, with manufacturers and importers fielding teams backed by F1 technology and skills. The Renault Lagunas of Alain Menu (opposite) and Will Hoy are now run by an branch of the Williams Grand Prix operation; the involvement of such organisations will push standards even higher.

cally-controlled shutters which open and close automatically, according to the temperature and the need for cooling. The brake callipers developed by AP and AMG for the Mercedes are in light alloy and are water-cooled by way of a small radiator mounted in the boot. The differential drives a small hydraulic pump which feeds the power-steering and the ABS braking system. The seven drivers charged with the factory-supported Mercedes are split between the AMG team (van Ommen, Magnussen, Schneider and Franchitti) and Zakspeed (Thiim, Grau and Ellen Lohr). Alfa Romeo's hopes of repeating their dominant form in 1993 were spoiled by a car which was too full of electronics and too late. An accident during the first test sessions meant the Italian marque had to start the season in the dark, when two years ago they had started their successful campaign with a test programme which had covered 8000km (5000 miles). The offensive soon lost its way among a mixture of differing specifications which posed organisation and logistical problems when it came to supplying the four teams running Alfas (Martini Racing/Alfa Corse, with Larini and Nannini; Schübel Engineering, with Alboreto and Danner; Euroteam, with Modena and Bartels, and Alfa Corse 2, with Fisichella, Giudici and Amthor). Alfa used 1994 chassis in its 'Step 1' cars and 1995 versions in its 'Step 2' models. In the early part of the season, which often determines the outcome of championships, it was often the earlier cars which got the better results. It was in a 'Step 1' car that Christian Danner won in Helsinki and at the Norisring; but this was not until June, after Mercedes had dominated the early part of the season.

The differences between the chassis were compounded by a choice of V6 engines, which differed between the '94 and '95 versions, and transmissions, both sequential and semi-automatic. When versions for long and short races and with and without hydraulic valvegear are considered, there were no less than eight different engine specifications! The most effective version was the short race spec. with hydraulically-operated valves in either '94 or '95 guise. This unit could rev to the 12,000 legal maximum set by the limiter, while the version with conventional valve-springs ran out of breath at 11,200rpm. Alfa reckoned on 45 minutes for an

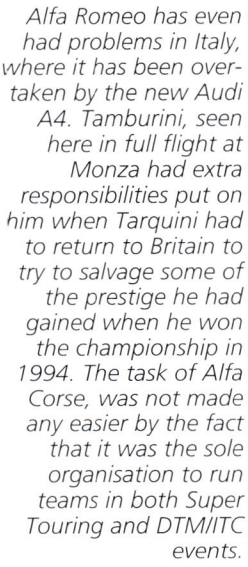

Alfa Romeo has even had problems in Italy, where it has been overtaken by the new Audi A4. Tamburini, seen here in full flight at Monza had extra responsibilities put on him when Tarquini had to return to Britain to try to salvage some of the prestige he had gained when he won the championship in 1994. The task of Alfa Corse, was not made any easier by the fact that it was the sole organisation to run teams in both Super Touring and DTM/ITC events.

emergency engine-change, and pointed out that Mercedes had rarely managed to finish the races in which they had carried out their ultra-rapid engine swaps. Developed, like the whole of the 1995 car, by Abarth, the new gearbox had electro-hydraulic control which enabled the use of a semi-automatic programme. This entailed the use of a paddle behind the steering wheel similar to those used in Formula 1, but the box – which had six speeds like the sequential unit – could also operate in a fully-automatic mode. Another complication of the 'Step 2' Alfa was the option of no less than three electronically-managed differential units. Each had six alternative programmes, and it must have been very difficult for the drivers to get the best from a solution which was excellent in theory, but which could only be used to advantage after a long setting-up session in testing. According to the circuit on which they were racing, the Alfas fed between 20 and 30% of the drive to the front wheels.

Opel, which split its forces between the Rosberg team, with Rosberg and Ludwig, and the Joest team, with Reuter, Dalmas, Lehto and Amorim, did not stint in its efforts to fight the assault of Mercedes and Alfa Romeo. Nevertheless, the elegant Calibras were often overtaken by failures in reliability or performance as they competed against teams with more experience in this type of racing. Like its two competitors, the Opel used a V6 engine with four valves per cylinder mounted longitudinally at the front of the car. The power unit is a direct development of the the Ecotec V6 used in the Calibra road car, and has the same displacement as the production version. The Mercedes engine, on the other hand, is based on the V8 used in the E240 but has two cylinders amputated. With a compression ratio of 12.5:1, this unit produces the same amount of power as its competitors; 450hp at around 11,500rpm, and with maximum torque in the region of 220lb/ft available at 9000rpm.

Bridgestone's close relationship with AMG instigated a tyre war with Michelin, who supplied both Alfa and Opel. The French manufacturer, which supplied 21 runners – bringing some 1500 tyres to each race – saw the DTM-ITC as a major field of technical development. This was thanks to the limited size of the tyres (no wider than 10 inches and no more than

In Britain, John Cleland and the Vauxhall Cavaliers fought like tigers against the powerful opposition which came from Renault and the Volvo 850s. Alfa Romeo and BMW, on the other hand, did not live up to what might have been expected from winners in the two previous years.

BIELA AND AUDI TAKE THE WORLD CUP

The third running of the FIA World Cup brought 40 entries from 15 countries to drive the products of 9 manufacturers on the Paul Ricard circuit in southern France. Qualifying, with just one second covering a dozen cars, showed that the level of competition would be high.

Run over two 100km (62-mile) legs, the race turned into a duel between Audi, with the A4, and BMW, represented by the 318i, with occasional interventions from the top competitors in the British championship.

On a circuit where the slightly lower maximum speed of the all wheel-drive Audis might be a disadvantage, the vagaries of racing turned out to give the affiliation of Audi with Dunlop tyres an advantage over the BMW/Michelin combination.

The Audi pairing of Frank Biela and Emanuele Pirro therefore finished ahead of three BMWs in the hands of Steve Soper, Yvan Muller and Johnny Cecotto.

New boy Kelvin Burt was sixth in a Mondeo, ahead of the Honda Accords of Klaus Niedzwiedz and Armin Hahne and the Renault Laguna of Alain Menu, who was forced to retire in the first leg.

The appeal of touring car racing is the element of 'same as you can buy' which attracts fans and manufacturers alike. Look inside a car, however, like this BMW 318i of the Italian Cibiemme team, and it's obvious this is far from showroom condition. The shape is 'touring car', but the technology is pure 'racing', as the electronic dash, sequential gearchange and suspension stiffness controls show.

Among their other complaints, the Alfa drivers found their cars lacking in power. The response is to abandon the twin overhead cam four-cylinder unit which has been used for some years now (right) and replace it with the Twin Spark twin-plug head unit from the 155 saloon.

Audi met some problems along the road to homologation with the new A4, but when the task was complete it was a formidable weapon. The view on the right shows the layout of the fuel tank and its lines in the car's boot. Once more, underneath the panels this is racer first and touring car second – where does the luggage go?

650 mm – 25.6 inches – in diameter) and the fact that the number of tyres available was limited. Five tyres were all that was permitted for all the practice and qualifying sessions, and four of these must be fitted to the car for the first of the two races which make up the DTM format. New tyres could not be fitted until after the end of the first lap.

Super Tourers: BTCC spells success

The 1995 season saw the progress of the Super Tourers continue, but in some countries the class has not yet reached a level where it can attract the necessary budgets. The situation in France is still delicate, but in Britain touring cars have achieved a remarkable success, with big crowds visiting the circuits to see a championship which is generously sponsored and superbly covered by TV. The teams show a professionalism worthy of the top levels of the sport, and the public relations policy maintains paddocks where the fans can wander at will. Evidence of the professionalism came with the manner in which the Williams GP Engineering operation took over the running of the two factory-backed Lagunas of Alain Menu and Will Hoy at the beginning of the season; by the end of the year Renault had the Manufacturers' Championship. Tom Walkinshaw's TWR was running Volvos for Rickard Rydell and Tim Harvey, but reverted to saloons after the station wagons of 1994. The Vauxhall Cavaliers of John Cleland and James Thompson, prepared by Ray Mallock, were seen as worthy competitors at the beginning of the season, by virtue of the experience in the team, but they were not considered as automatic winners. By the end of the year Cleland was champion once more, by virtue of that experience. The other main contenders were the Ford Mondeos of Paul Radisich and Kelvin Burt, a new team of Honda Accords in the hands of David Leslie and James Kaye, and the Toyota Carina Es of Julian Bailey and Tim Sugden. Seen as potential front-runners at the beginning of the season, the Alfa Romeo and BMW teams were both incapable of recapturing their form of earlier years. Gianpiero Simoni and Derek Warwick had a dismal year in the Alfa 155, and Johnny Cecotto and David Brabham did little better in the BMW 318i, despite a reduction in the minimum weight limit for rear-drive cars which came into force at mid-season. The rear-drive BMWs weight was cut to 1000kg (2204lb) from 1025 (2260lb), but it was still not enough to come to terms with the front-wheel drive cars running at 925kg (2039lb).

Working out just how much (if any) differential there should be between the front and rear-drive cars is a delicate business. There has been spectacular progress in front-wheel drive cars in the last few years, but the basic fact remains that when both driving and steering is being done by the same wheels, a much heavier task is imposed on the front tyres. It is often significant to see the way in which BMWs can profit from the fact that, unlike front-wheel drive cars, their grip and handling does not deteriorate over the course of a race.

BMW has decided to make Super Tourers its main priority, and was therefore present in a number of European national championships (Britain, Germany, France and Italy, and to a lesser extent, Belgium and Spain). There was also representation in Japan, in the form of the officially authorised Schnitzer team, in Australia and South Africa. Although the trend is now toward more sprint events, the marque is still strong in endurance races, and it consolidated its reputation with wins in the 24-hour events at the Nürburgring and Spa Francorchamps. The engine derived from that of the old M3 – itself an ex-F2 power unit – had reached the end of its homologation period, so it was replaced by a new development of the S42 engine fitted to production versions of the 318i. Lighter, more compact and slightly less tall than its predecessor, the 16-valve four-cylinder is placed in an almost vertical position in a chassis which was even more rigid. With a six-speed Holinger sequential gearbox, the 1996cc unit was good for 280hp at 8300rpm, with some good versions getting up to 295hp. The results were mixed; Yvan Muller dominated the French championship in his 318i, prepared by Oreca, but the Motorsports International team which contested the British BTCC championship had a very bleak year.

The Vauxhall Cavaliers were superb in Britain, and their Opel Vectra cousins, prepared by Dany Snobeck, were in good form in the French championship. Snobeck's cars used Aleon callipers with no less than 12 pistons and 6 pads on their front brakes, which were hung on a double pivot suspension system.

With the old M3's Formula 2-derived four-cylinder engine no longer eligible for use in touring car racing, BMW turned to the 16-valve S42 power unit from the 318i (above). A little more compact and lighter than its predecessor, it produced almost 300hp.

The roll-cage of a Super Tourer serves as more than a safety device. Comprehensive additions such as this, in a CIVT BMW 318i (below), serve to strengthen the original monocoque enormously.

Responding to an enquiry by Peugeot, the FIA first authorised this interpretation of the rules and then reversed their decision, an action which caused a degree of confusion. The system was still legal in France for the '95 season, and it was used by Peugeot on the 405 and Opel on the Vectra. By providing greater separation of the functions of steering and suspension, it is more favourable to the tyres.

The new Audi A4 was raced only in Germany and Italy, but it spread fear through the other competitors, despite a hitch when the overall width of the racing car, the road car and the homologation documents did not match entirely. The modern Audis are another advertisement for all-wheel drive, and thus a cause for concern to Nissan and Ford, whose Mondeos, driven by Boutsen and Patrese, were very disappointing in Germany. Honda, on the other hand, were making excellent progress with the Accord, developed in Britain with a chassis by MSD and a Neil Brown engine. Hondas competition-influenced wishbone suspension is one of the front-wheel drive cars strengths, giving it an advantage over competitors forced to go with production-based McPherson struts.

Each national championship has the right to one round each year in a neighbouring country, and Zolder traditionally welcomes the German Super Tourers early in the season. Frank Biela (above) seems to be enjoying himself in the Audi A4 which gave him first place in both ADAC Cup races run on the Belgian circuit.

There was a welcome return to the tracks by the Martini Racing colours in 1995. They adorned the official Alfa Rome entries in the ITC, and in the first race at Mugello Nannini (right) managed to keep ahead of Mercedes' two young drivers, Jan Magnussen and Dario Franchitti, for fourth place. In spite of his name, Franchitti is actually Scottish, but when he won the second race of the day the Italian crowd no doubt gave him an extra cheer.

Ford, perhaps over-attentive to Formula 1, lost out in rallying and touring car racing in 1995. In Britain, even the talents of Paul Radisich (right) could not get the Mondeo up with the Vauxhalls, Renaults and Volvos on a regular basis, while in Germany former F1 stars Boutsen and Patrese were condemned to mid-field oblivion.

GT AND ENDURANCE RACING

McLAREN FORMS A STRONG FOUNDATION

Michael Cotton

For a car that was not even tested on a racing circuit until January, the McLaren F1 GTR made an auspicious debut in 1995. McLaren won the great majority of the BPR Kärcher Global Endurance GT Cup races, and were victorious in the 24-Hours of Le Mans at their first attempt.

Grand Touring racing emerged in 1994 from the ashes of the World Sportscar Championship, and came close to maturity in 1995. Six McLarens raced on a regular basis (seven at Le Mans, the 'joker' also being the winner), the Larbre Competition team based in Caen represented Porsche, and the Ferrari Club Italia and Team Pilot Aldix teams each ran two-car Ferrari F40 teams. As usual, independent teams represented Porsche in strength, almost dominating the second category with the GT2, a further development of the Turbo road model.

Grids for the BPR's Kärcher-sponsored GT series of four-hour races were generally full of nice, colourful cars, although Venturi and Jaguar are no longer forces to be reckoned with. Endurance racing still needs more manufacturer representation, but that is now on the horizon. Reeves Callaway is preparing the GT1 version of the Chevrolet Corvette, and the ambitious Americans at Chrysler are developing a GT1 version of the thunderous V10-engined Viper. Lotus, too, will present a V8 powered Esprit with twin turbochargers for 1996, so the prospects are better than ever.

The FIA will give GT racing a higher profile in 1996 with the Triple Crown, which should comprise the GT categories at Daytona, Le Mans, and an event in Japan. However, sports car racing has polarised still further in Europe and in America. The IMSA organisation reinvented open-top, two-seater racing cars and calls them World Sports Cars. The Florida-based organisation is investing heavily in the WSC category and is prepared to handicap the marauders from Europe to ensure 'home' successes. The most successful sports car in America is the Ferrari 333 SP. However, it is hardly inexpensive – $1 million a time – and the US-based teams ran into such engine problems that they failed to win the Rolex 24 at Daytona in February. That honour went to the Kremer K8 Porsche. Laden with weight and handicapped by small air restrictors, it droned around the banking for 24 hours and won with ease.

The 'Concorde agreement' between IMSA and the Automobile Club de l'Ouest was shattered when Massimo Sigala took his Ferrari 333 SP to Le Mans in June. All the differences of opinion between the two organisations were visited upon Sigala's team, and after making a token start (a very fast one, it must be said) the 12-cylinder sports car was retired. Europe has no series for World Sports Cars, although the Interserie organisation will have a category for something similar in 1996. Interserie will adopt the ACO's regulations (which will differ from IMSA's) in order to provide an infrastructure and make it possible for European teams to run Kremer, Courage and Ferrari sports cars in preparation for Le Mans.

The Paris-based BPR Organisation arranged a 12-race series exclusively for GT cars in 1995, and secured backing from Kärcher, a German industrial cleaning company, from Shell, and from Tissot. The calendar was certainly not above criticism, with seven races arranged within 12 weeks in the early part of the season, and a potentially expensive division of the calendar between the Far East and Europe in the autumn. In general, however, it was a popular diet for the European teams which had almost no calendar at all two years before.

Three McLaren F1 GTRs were delivered to Ray Bellm, Lindsay Owen-Jones and Dr Thomas Bscher just prior to the first event at Jerez on February 26, and it was clear straight away that they would be the pacemakers. Bellm was partnered by the Brazilian, Maurizio Sala, and Owen-Jones by Pierre-Henri Raphanel. Their McLarens were run by Michael Cane's GTC Motorsports team, and sponsored by Gulf Oil (UK). Bscher secured the services of John Nielsen, and the backing of the West cigarette company, with the Davidoff subsidiary sometimes featured. After dominating qualifying in southern Spain the GTC team made short work of the 4-hour race, Bellm and Sala claiming victory. Raphanel retired when both front wheels fell off his McLaren after a pit stop, and Nielsen went out near the end when the West McLaren's six-speed gearbox failed. The transmission was soon identified as being the McLaren's Achilles heel. Centrifugal force starved the gears of oil, and designer Gordon Murray had to begin the rush development of a dry-sump lubrication system in time for Le Mans.

Neither Porsche nor Ferrari were up to strength early in the season, which made the McLaren teams look all the more formidable. Porsche developed the twin-turbo GT2 model, with 480 horsepower, to join battle in the second division, which is confusingly called GT2 at Le Mans and GT3 by the BPRO. The Porsche GT2 is based on the latest 993 chassis and effectively replaces the 350bhp 911 RSR 3.8. The bonus of 130 boosted horsepower makes the GT2 a much more potent car, which, to the chagrin of team owner Rocky Agusta, completely turned the tables on the Callaway Corvettes.

Jack Leconte, a Caen haulier, was the leading Porsche entrant through his Larbre Competition team, which developed his new GT2 for the GT1 category by using wider rear wheels and a more effective rear wing. With the services of Jean-Pierre Jarier, Bob Wollek and Christophe Bouchut, Larbre ran a most effective campaign, especially in the early part of the season. The McLaren drivers, frankly, found it difficult to believe that the Larbre Porsche had only 480 horsepower, since it kept such pressure on their 637bhp, V12 powered supercars, but Porsche's problems mounted when they stepped up the power for the fifth round.

Gordon Murray (below) designed the ultimate road car in the shape of the McLaren F1 and then turned it into the ultimate GT racing car as the GTR. The GTR was an immediate winner, but it was not perfect, and Murray and his team instituted a programme to prepare it for its greatest test, Le Mans. When it won the 24-Hours at its first attempt, it showed that although racing never sees perfection, the F1's first year was as close as it gets.

The Callaway Corvette had made a promising debut in 1994, so it was not surprising that the cars entered by Agusta Racing which first appeared at Paul Ricard (above) were among the favourites for BPR's GT3 category. Their results, however, did not fulfil their earlier promise, and the Porsche 911 GT2 proved to be the car to beat in the class.

Opposite: Of the two Gulf-sponsored McLarens, this one, driven by Lindsay Owen-Jones and Pierre-Henri Raphanel, was less successful than its team-mate, driven by Ray Bellm and Maurizio Sala, but it was always competitive at the top level. Owen-Jones and Bellm, together with Thomas Bscher, were prime examples of 'gentlemen drivers' who combined car ownership with driving skills.

Larbre Competition had some good results in 1994 with a Porsche Carrera RSR, but for 1995 it was replaced by a more powerful GT2. With the driving team of Wollek, Jarier and Bouchut mixing youth and experience, the early results were encouraging, but as the season progressed it became more difficult to combine power and reliability in the mechanism.

Manfred Freisinger already had a surfeit of power in his special 750 horsepower Porsche biturbo, which far exceeded the limitations of the six-speed (or indeed, any other) Porsche gearbox, while stalwart Franz Konrad enjoyed much more success in GT3 than with his tuned-up GT1 biturbo. The Swiss couple Enzo Calderari and Lilian Bryner quickly emerged as the top team in GT3, posting their claim by finishing third overall at Jerez. Their Porsche GT2 was immaculately prepared by Matthias Stadler, enabling Calderari and Bryner to win the category more often than not. Bryner, who represented Switzerland in equitation and holds a commercial pilot's licence, may be petite and good-looking, but she is a formidable driver greatly respected by her male competitors.

Bellm and Sala won again at the Paul Ricard circuit, the second round of the BPR series, with the Larbre Porsche second and Bscher's West McLaren third, a lap behind. This was a team that had to be watched most carefully, since Bscher seemed to be a little out of his depth at the start of the season but soon matured to claim a string of podium placings and to lead the Kärcher GT Cup series overall. The influence

SIMPLY THE BEST

In the McLaren F1, one of the world's foremost racing car designers, Gordon Murray, was given virtual carte blanche to produce the finest Grand Touring machine the world has ever seen. The chassis and body are made of lightweight carbon composite materials, and racing principles are followed throughout. McLaren turned to BMW Motorsport for the power unit, and Paul Rosche headed the design team which produced the unique 6.1 litre V12 engine. With variable valve timing, it easily exceeds the 100bhp per litre standard – maximum power is 627bhp at 7400rpm. Installed in a car weighing 1100kg (2425lb), it gives the F1 sensational performance.

From this base, Murray and his team developed a still more effective GT racing car, the GTR. Despite the installation of inlet air restrictors, power was increased to 637bhp, largely due to the efforts of the TAG Electronics engine-management specialists. Where the standard car is capable of cornering at 1g, the GTR will easily exceed a 2g cornering force on racing tyres. The six-speed McLaren-designed transverse transmission was uprated for competition, and further redesigned, with a dry sump lubrication system, for Le Mans. Carbon brakes were fitted for Le Mans and are retained by customers.

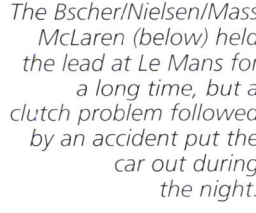

There was disappointment at Le Mans when the promised Ferrari 333 SP entry fell victim to arguments about interpretation of the rules. The car was there, (above) but it lost valuable practice time while alternative components were shipped from the USA to make what was 'IMSA-legal' 'Le Mans-legal'. It was to have been the big comeback of René Arnoux (right), but the former F1 star was left with little to do when the car retired after only seven laps.

The Bscher/Nielsen/Mass McLaren (below) held the lead at Le Mans for a long time, but a clutch problem followed by an accident put the car out during the night.

of the strong, experienced – and fast – Nielsen on the team-owner/driver was profound.

Ferrari were at full strength at Monza, where Anders Olofsson made full use of his F40's turbo power to claim pole position. The Italian team's chances were raised when the Gulf McLaren team collapsed, with Bellm miscalculating his fuel level and stopping on the circuit, and Owen-Jones' GTR losing a rear wheel. Olofsson and car owner Luciano della Noce were vying for the lead at three-quarter distance, but were delayed by a difficult brake pad change and then by a puncture. Eventually they claimed third place, behind the West McLaren and the Larbre Porsche.

No fewer than six McLarens and four Ferraris were entered for the BPR round at Jarama on April 9, raising hopes of a memorable contest. Sadly the Italian team's gearboxes proved frail, with repeated failures of the second gear ratios, and Owen-Jones did not start the race after crashing his McLaren heavily in pre-event practice. Bellm and Sala returned to the podium, joined by Bscher and Nielsen who were second. The Larbre Porsche was third, with Bouchut as the quickest driver, although the experienced Jarier and Wollek were completely reliable and hardly less fast.

Porsche's engineers at Weissach found another 70 horsepower for the Larbre Porsche in time for the Nurburgring, but the car had brake problems (probably unrelated) and retired with a transmission failure. Once again Bellm and Sala won the race, an intelligent victory in which they spared their brakes and spent less time in the pits. McLarens filled the top five positions, bad news for Porsche fans at their home event, but a testimony to the GTR's reliability. Both the Ferrari Club Italia F40s sprang water leaks, and second place was deservedly claimed by the French-owned GRT Jacadi team McLaren driven by Fabien Giroix and Olivier Grouillard.

Marcos and Lotus appeared in the GT3 division at Donington Park on May 8 and made their mark, but the calendar was now becoming impossibly crowded, with the Paris round in prospect five days later at Montlhery. There were no Ferraris at Donington and the Larbre Porsche soon retired with a broken gear-selector rod, leaving the way clear yet again for a McLaren sweep. Winners Bscher and Nielsen went to the head of the Kärcher GT Cup series, as Bellm's car was delayed by a gear selector breakage. They were

pursued by Owen-Jones' Gulf McLaren and the Mach One Racing Harrods McLaren, driven by Andy Wallace and Justin Bell.

With an unrepresentative grid and a high rate of attrition on the bumpy Montlhery circuit, Eric Graham's Venturi 600 LM was the only GT1 category car to finish… in fourth place. Porsche's GT2s filled the top three positions with Hans Muhlbauer's team taking the flag, Detlef Hubner and Stefan Oberndorfer the drivers. After a long break for Le Mans, the BPR teams went to Anderstorp for the eighth round. The Swedish airfield track has not hosted a major international race since a European Touring Car event was held there in 1986, and the big crowd was cheering for local man Anders Olofsson. He, alas, crashed into Michel Ferté's Team Pilot Aldix Ferrari early on and retired, while Ferté and Olivier Thevenin went on to give Ferrari their first victory of the season. There was an element of luck involved, due to race leader Nielsen's resistance to an unwise challenge from Fabio Mancini in the Club Italia's second F40. It caused the Ferrari's retirement and a delay for the West car, which finished second.

A win at Le Mans was the only laurel leaf missing from Mario Andretti's wreath of championships, and in the Courage-Porsche he saw an opportunity to fill the gap. Unfortunately for Mario (above, right), the weather took a hand and put victory so close, but so far away. "I'll be back", he said afterwards.

Naturally the first race at Le Mans, in 1923, was won by a manufacturer (Lorraine) at its first attempt. Since then, however, only Ferrari, in 1949, and McLaren have achieved the feat. The F1 GTR (left) was superb, but it is impossible to overestimate the part played by drivers Dalmas, Lehto and Sekiya in the 1995 victory.

Before the rain came, the prototypes were ahead at Le Mans, with a parade of two WR's and two Courages (left). It was not to last, however, and at the finish only the Courage-Porsche C 34, in third place here, would still be there, second behind a GT car.

Following a disappointing response from its customers towards GTR racing, the French Venturi factory prepared its own 600 SLM for Le Mans (right) and Suzuka. In qualifying, the car was competitive with the McLaren GTR and the Ferrari F40 GTE, but reliability was another matter.

It was an almost-perfect season for Enzo Calderari and Lilian Bryner (below). The Porsche-driving Swiss pair not only took regular honours in their category; at Jerez, they were third overall.

Nissan's Skyline GT-R is the treat Japan keeps for itself. Possibly one of the world's greatest GT cars, it dominates the Japanese GT championship, but it is not officially exported. This one, however, (right) made the trip to Le Mans. In the hands of Hideo Fukuyama, Masahiko Kondo and Shunji Kasuya it finished tenth overall.

They were not considered as pre-season favourites, but despite some problems in early races the partnership of Thomas Bscher and John Nielsen (below) and their McLaren matured into a championship-leading team.

The GTC Motorsport team moved smoothly back to the podium with a most professional victory at the Suzuka 1000kms in August, an extremely hot, humid event organised by the JAF. With last-minute backing from the Tokyo Ueno Clinic and driving help from Masanori Sekiya, who proved to be a most important element in the team, Bellm and Sala led for most of the distance. Once again Bscher and Nielsen were their shadows, the Dane proving a tower of strength in energy-sapping conditions.

The Harrods McLaren was the winner at last at Silverstone in September, Andy Wallace the star driver in wet conditions which were all but impossible at times. He started from pole and laid the foundations for victory, with Grouillard – defecting from the GRT team – providing skilful back-up in the second half. Again the Gulf team stumbled, and the West team profited from fifth. Calderari and Bryner were heavily penalised for a management error when Calderari exceeded the time allowed for any stint at the wheel. The six-minute mandatory delay dropped the Stadler Porsche from a startling second place overall to 11th! Ferraris were second and third, the Lotus Esprit S300,

in the hands of Alessandro Zanardi and Alex Portman, fourth. It was the first time in the BPR season that Porsche had been defeated in the GT3 category, and perhaps an omen for 1996.

In theory, the ACO's regulations for Le Mans (June 17/18) slightly favoured the open World Sports Cars, especially the Porsche turbo-powered Kremer K8 and Courage C34. In the event, the predominant rain and – especially – mishaps for Mario Andretti and Hans Stuck upset all calculations. The winner, by a lap, was the McLaren F1 GTR driven by Masanori Sekiya, Yannick Dalmas and JJ Lehto, whose outstanding handling of the 637bhp car on a wet track overnight was the talking-point of the race. The young Frenchman Dalmas has assembled an enviable record at Le Mans in the past four years: first, second, first, first!

McLaren was the winner, though, and the success helped to offset some disappointments for Ron Dennis and his employees in the Formula 1 arena. Taking first, third, fourth and fifth overall, and claiming the top four positions in the GT category, the Surrey-based company confounded all predictions that unforeseen problems would visit themselves on the cars. Only a handful have won the 24-Hours at their first attempt, and in June McLaren joined a very select group. Dry-sump gearboxes, new uprights, reinforced clutches, a strengthened drive-train and carbon brakes, an £80,000 list of options, turned an already fine design into a durable endurance racer. The McLaren which won the race had no problems throughout. It was in fact the 01R prototype GTR, which belongs to McLaren Cars and was leased to the Tokyo Ueno Clinic, which specialises in circumcisions! Because it was not a regular competitor, management of the Ueno McLaren was handed over to Paul Lanzante, whose Porsche GT2 team had impressed McLaren in the BPR series.

The 24-Hours was more competitive than ever, since the majority of teams had to demonstrate their mettle at the test day in April. Some factory-supported teams, including the Porsche-powered Kremer and Courage cars, the Nissan, Toyota, Honda and Mazda works entries, one McLaren, Sigala's Ferrari, a unique Lamborghini Jota prepared in England, and Chevrolet Corvettes from a little-known team in America had been invited by the ACO with guaranteed starts. For the rest, however, it was all very strange. Those

There were those who welcomed the arrival of the Ferrari F40 LM of Michel Ferté and Olivier Thévenir with incredulity – this was a museum piece, which Ferrari stopped producing in 1990! Nevertheless, after a period of development the car – which changed colour from red here at Monza to blue by Le Mans – became a potential winner. It fulfilled its promise at Anderstorp.

Derek Bell was a regular team-mate to the great Swiss driver Jo Siffert in the glory days of Porsche. In 1971, Derek and Jo were paired in a 917 L at Le Mans, and 24 years later the British driver was still there, driving with his son Justin. Siffert's son Philippe was also competing, and he met up with his father's co-driver (right, below) on the grid. The McLaren driven by the Bells and Andy Wallace was third, but Philippe's Porsche 911 GT2 was out – when he was not driving – after 2 hours.

McLarens and Ferrari F40s without an invitation could qualify with ease, but others, like the Jaguar XJ220s, the Lister Storm and the V8-powered Aston Martin DB7 were struggling all day, and in the end some notables did not make the cut.

As in 1993, the ACO designed the regulations to equalise the competitiveness between categories, limiting weights, air restrictor sizes, fuel tank capacities and wheel rim widths to balance things out. In June, the Le Mans Prototype 2 (LMP2) group proved to be the quickest of all. William David and Patrick Gonin occupied the front row in diminutive WR-Peugeot monoposto machines which, in truth, should have no place at Le Mans. All the traditions of the great event are rooted in two-seat sports-racing and Grand Touring cars, not in scantily clad single-seaters. The WR-Peugeots led after 60 minutes of racing, but Gonin had an unpleasant accident when an aerodynamic freak flipped his car over at Mulsanne and the onset of rain began to change the complexion of the race. McLarens occupied the top three positions after two hours, Andy Wallace (Harrods McLaren), John Nielsen (West McLaren) and Maurizio Sala (Gulf McLaren) having driven without respite. If rivals were looking for early signs of weakness, they were disappointed.

Hans Stuck and Mario Andretti were among relatively early victims of the soaking wet track, possibly because modern sports and GT cars have very little downforce. Underbody venturis are strictly limited, and the Sarthe track became a skating rink in places as the rain worsened. Andretti was wrong-footed by a slower driver and lost his line in the Porsche Curves, spinning gently into the wall and damaging the Courage-Porsche's rear wing. Stuck's crew never

From its first race at Jarama, the F1 GTR entered by the Giroix Racing Team was among the leaders. And yet bad luck struck too often. In Spain, at Donington (below) and finally at Suzuka a win or a podium place was denied the French team. At Le Mans, bad luck forced them to start from the pit-lane, but the car finished fifth in the hands of Giroix, Grouillard and Delétraz.

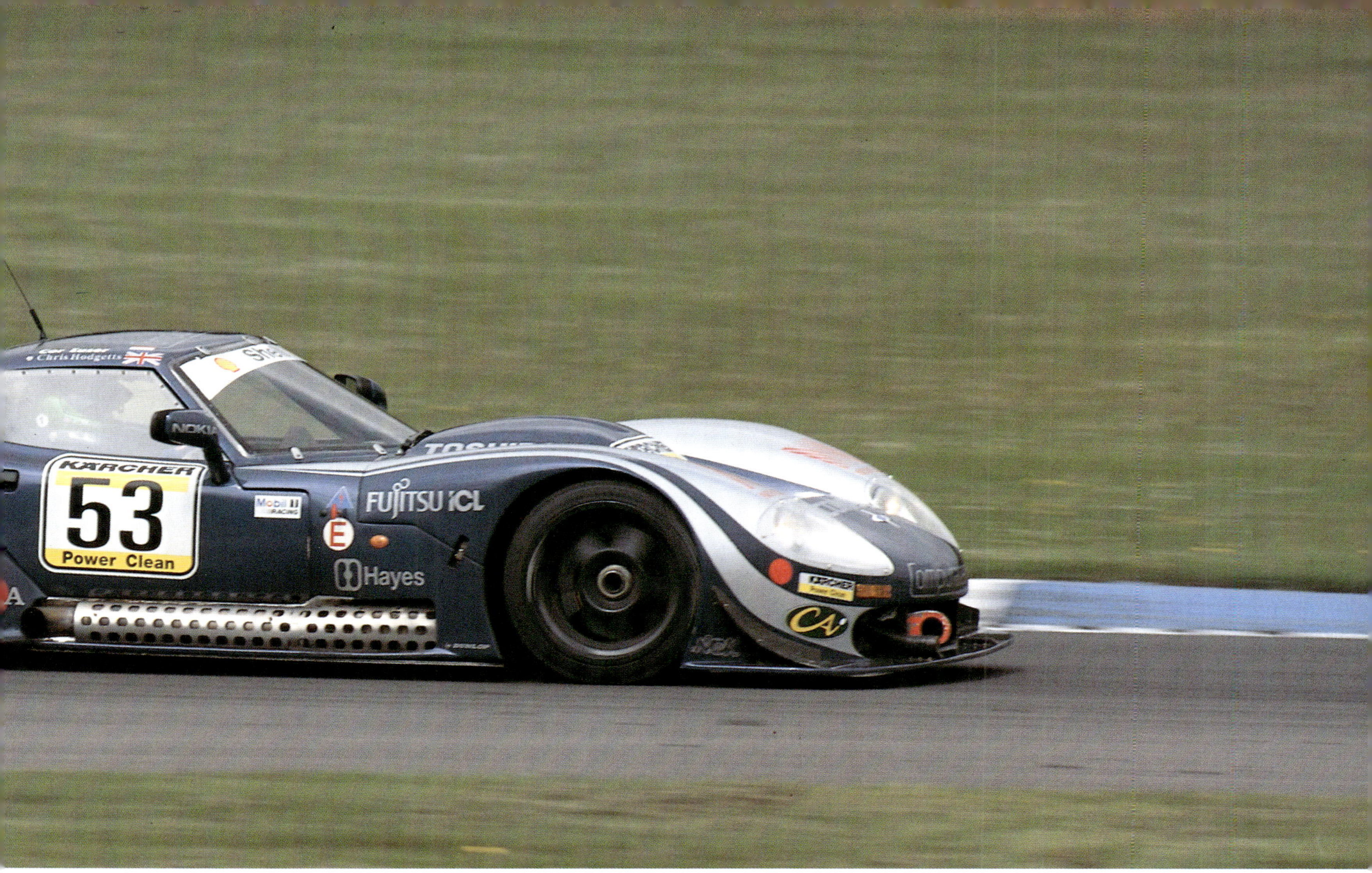

recovered from his 28-minute delay, and eventually finished eight laps behind in sixth place. Wollek, Andretti and Eric Helary pushed on throughout the race after repairs that cost six laps, and even confirmed the computed predictions by finishing one lap behind the winning McLaren. Ray Bellm crashed his Gulf McLaren and lost valuable time, Philippe Alliot crashed the other and retired.

For Porsche, the race was a fiasco. The Larbre Competition team's new GT2 Evolution models were badly damaged in separate accidents on Saturday evening, and the Kremer and Stadler teams lost their Porsches too. At midnight, in fact, Wollek, Andretti and Helary had their Courage-Porsche in eighth place and the best-positioned Porsche GT2 was 18th – far from the rosy scene usually enjoyed by the Stuttgart manufacturer.

The David Price Racing McLarens held sway during the night, the West and Harrods entries dominating the hourly bulletins. Derek Bell, the five-times winner, was rejuvenated by the experience of driving with his son, Justin, in the Mach One Racing Harrods McLaren, but they couldn't quite match the pace of Nielsen and Jochen Mass in the West entry, driving at their limit despite coping with a seized-up windscreen wiper spindle. Two Jaguar XJ220s entered by Richard Piper's PC Automotive team went well, despite a complete absence of factory support. Piper held fourth place with Tiff Needell and James Weaver at midnight, but an unexpected engine failure stopped their car, and an accident claimed the other.

The first sign of any mechanical weakness showed up on the West McLaren when the reinforced clutch broke its thrust-bearing 11 hours into the race. The DPR team changed the clutch, only for Nielsen to

Marcos styling is an acquired taste, and it always has been. The Chevrolet-powered cars which raced at Donington (above) and at Le Mans looked brutish, but demanded that you notice them among their fellow competitors in the class. They did not win, but they tried damn hard, and for many Britons, that's almost as good as winning.

Ray Bellm and Maurizio Sala had an all or nothing season in Bellm's Gulf-McLaren. 'All' came in the shape of five wins; 'nothing' came in the races at Monza, Donington (right) and Anderstorp, where the crew finished out of the points.

McLAREN AND PORSCHE ON POINTS

John Nielsen and Dr Thomas Bscher won the inaugural BPR Karcher Global GT Cup series in the West-sponsored McLaren F1 GTR, a car that failed to finish a four-hour event only once in the entire season. The GTR racing version of the McLaren supercar was tested and built just in time for the 1995 season, and started as a completely unknown factor. It soon had the more experienced Porsche and Ferrari teams on the run, proving to be extremely quick and reliable.

In the final analysis of 12 BPR rounds, Ray Bellm and Marizio Sala won five races in the GTC Motorsport Gulf McLaren, Andy Wallace and Olivier Grouillard the last three in Moody Fayed's Mach One Racing McLaren, Nielsen and Bscher two in the West McLaren also prepared by David Price Racing. Swiss couple Lilian Bryner and Enzo Calderai raced their Stadler Motorsport Porsche GT2 to second place in the BPR series, with no fewer than six straight victories in the GT3 category and three more podium finishes. BPR's scoring system was well devised to reward the class winners. As well as allocating points to the top ten finishers overall, further points were awarded for category results. By finishing fourth in the final round at Zhuhai, for instance, the Swiss team was able to score nine points overall plus 15 for winning the GT3 category, a good helping of 24 altogether.

Powerful and fast, the final version of the F40 was the GTE, or GTEvoluzione. Unfortunately, powerful and fast aren't enough; 'reliable' is the third word which counts. One or other of the Ferrari Club Italia F40s (this is that of Olofsson and della Noce) led every BPR race at some point before being forced to make a pit-stop for attention. It was sad, because the crowds love the cars in their Italian colours.

Mazda was in a transition phase in 1995. Turning towards the World Sports Cars open-topped format, it formed a good relationship with IMSA stalwart Jim Downing and his Kudzu cars (named after a quick-growing American plant). Downing drove with Franck Fréon and Yojiro Terada at Le Mans, and their seventh place made the Kudzu DG3 the best-placed Japanese entry.

crash out with cold brakes after the enforced delay. The advantage passed to Andy Wallace, with Derek and Justin Bell, but for how long, with a lead of a single lap over the Tokyo Ueno car? Some said that Lehto's eyes shone in the dark. True or not, he did the lion's share of the driving and hauled in the Harrods McLaren, going ahead for the first time at the 17-hour mark.

Wallace and Bell Senior took turns at attacking and held sway again for some hours before and after midday on Sunday, but their clutch thrust-bearing was on the way out, too. Finally, Wallace was unable to drive cleanly away from the Harrods pit and the Ueno Clinic entry swept past, with Wollek's Courage-Porsche closing quickly.

Derek Bell was denied his sixth victory and the chance to equal Jacky Ickx's record, but condolences to Bob Wollek, still denied his first victory after 25 attempts! Masanori Sekiya became the first Japanese driver to win at Le Mans, and Honda won the GT2 category with the Team Kunimitsu NSX raced by Kunimitsu Takahashi, Keiichi Tsuchiya and Akira Iida, in eighth place overall.

INTERNATIONAL F3000 CHAMPIONSHIP

SUPER NOVA MARKS THE END OF AN ERA

In this, the last season of Formula 3000 under the current rules, the Super Nova team has proved as bright a star in the firmament of the formula as its astronomical namesake is in the real heavens. In the space of just two seasons, it has risen to the heights and achieved the ultimate goal of taking the championship. David Sears, the head of the team, is part of a great British motoring family, the grandson of collector Stanley Sears and the son of Jack Sears, famed as a driver of Jaguar saloons in the Sixties. After a competent, if not distinguished, racing career of his own, David turned to team management running a team for the young Taki Inoue in Japan. Inoue's family business is called Nova, so it was natural to choose Super Nova as the name of the team. As the team and Inoue progressed, thoughts turned to F1 and its natural stepping-stone, Formula 3000.

The move to Europe and F3000 came in 1994, and the canny Sears hired Vincenzo Sospiri, one of the doyens of the championship, to partner his young Japanese protégé.

The choice of Sospiri brought immediate results, and the combination of the Italian old hand and the new team was immediately able to put up strong opposition to established outfits such as DAMS, Paul Stewart Racing and Apomatox. Having established Sospiri as a strong challenger for the championship and seen Taki Inoue established in a Formula 1 seat with Arrows, Sears kept his team busy with a comprehensive testing programme during the long F3000 winter break, stretching from October to May.

After visiting a number of European circuits, the team was well prepared for the first round of the 1995 championship, at Silverstone. It was a superb start to the year, with the win going to Inoue's successor, Brazilian Ricardo Rosset. Rosset is a man who, at 27, may no longer typical of the young generation of Brazilian drivers. Nevertheless, Silverstone was a landmark for the Sao Paolo driver, who had only scored one victory in the three previous seasons of European competition (one in the Opel Lotus Euroseries and two more in British F3). On top of Rosset's success, Sospiri was second, a position which immediately told the Italian that his new team-mate was a force to be reckoned with and a possible threat to his own title pretensions. He needed no more potent encouragement, and when the championship moved to Barcelona he celebrated his fifth anniversary in F3000 with a win. His form and that of Super Nova continued at Pau, where he won again, and at Enna-Pergusa, where Sospiri was first and Rosset second. It was the season's half-way point, and the lead of the Super Nova drivers was considerable, but it was at about this time that rumours began to circulate in the paddock about the legality of the gear-changing mechanism on the midnight-blue Reynards. There were no official moves against the team, but Sears was moved to swear on his honour that the system was totally above board. Whatever the case may be, Super Nova was not to dominate the second half of the series as it had the first. Should we see in that the confirmation of some technical trickery? Absolutely not, and for two reasons. Firstly, Sospiri had built up such a lead over his adversaries that he could afford to drive for points rather than wins, and secondly the other teams, such as Nordic and Madgwick, had all made progress.

After a faux-pas at Hockenheim, the triumphant progress of the Super Nova drivers began again at Spa. At the finish of the Belgian round Sospiri was not only the winner of the race, but was also almost con-

Eric Briquet

From the time Vincenzo Sospiri started in Formula 3000 in 1990, it took five years before he was to win a race. He achieved his goal at Barcelona, after he had been goaded to action by being beaten by his new team-mate, Ricardo Rosset, at Silverstone. Competition was obviously good for Sospiri – even before the season was complete, he had won the championship.

Its drivers Olivier Panis and Jean-Christophe Boullion had won the F3000 title in 1993 and 1994, but it all turned sour for the French DAMS team just after the start in Pau this year. The team had monopolised the front row of the grid with its drivers Guillaume Gomez and Tarso Marques, but when they took each other out in spectacular fashion (right) the way was left open for Vincenzo Sospiri. DAMS' bad luck continued until Marques won in Estoril.

firmed as the 1995 champion – the only driver who could possibly beat him was his own team-mate, Rosset! The next round of the series was in Portugal, and Sospiri played it cautiously, taking seventh place and the certainty of the championship rather than battling for an uncertain win. His victory left the final round at Magny-Cours as a race with no influence on the championship but with a great appeal for the French drivers, each eager to do his best on home ground and salvage something from the season.

Between Hockenheim in 1993 and Magny-Cours in 1994, Formula 3000 was a happy hunting ground for the French: Panis, Lagorce and Boullion had taken no less than ten wins from thirteen races. Naturally, when the 1995 season started, French teams DAMS and Apomatox were favourites together with Paul Stewart Racing. DAMS manager Jean-Paul Driot had originally said that the team would be competing in Formula 1 in 1995 and that whatever happened they would not be staying in F3000. The statement proved to be a little premature, and the team was back for the first round of the championship. However, the late decision to continue had undoubtedly reduced the pre-season preparation of its two Reynard-chassised cars. Nevertheless, a DAMS short on preparation time is still a force to be reckoned with, as a front-row qualifying time and a third place for Tarso Marques in Barcelona showed. Just 19 years old, Marques is another bright young hope from Brazil, who started in last year's championship as its youngest competitor. He had come into F3000 straight from home, skipping the normal training stage of a season in a British championship. DAMS results during the rest of the season were dogged by ill-luck, and the Pau event serves as an example of the team's misfortune. Marques had scored the first pole position of his career, and the last thing he was thinking about in a street race noted for its numerous collisions was the danger of being hit by the man next to him on the front row, team-mate Guillaume Gomez. Unfortunately for Jean-Paul Driot, his team and his drivers, that is exactly what happened; Gomez lost control and pinned Marques against the barriers. The elimination of both drivers marked an unfortunate turning point in the fortunes of the team. The two drivers were competitive, as Gomez' pole positions, fastest laps and podium finishes show, but they were not contenders. The team's recom-

Ever since the race at Brands Hatch in 1991, Reynard chassis had the monopoly on F3000 wins. Until Belgium's Marc Goossens (seen opposite on his home ground of Spa) took his Nordic team Lola to victory at Hockenheim last July. Breaking a run of 35 Reynard victories was a turning point for Lola, which has been selected by the authorities as the chassis supplier for 1996, when F3000 becomes a 'one-make' formula.

The number one driver of the Madgwick team, Kenny Bräck, has been a revelation in 1995, notably at Enna-Pergusa, where he was fastest in qualifying. In the races (here he is ahead of Belloc at Pau), he was less successful in the early season, but improved as time went on. He finished on a high note, winning at Magny-Cours, but the gloss was taken from the victory by Marco Campos' accident. Next season, Bräck will be a driver to watch.

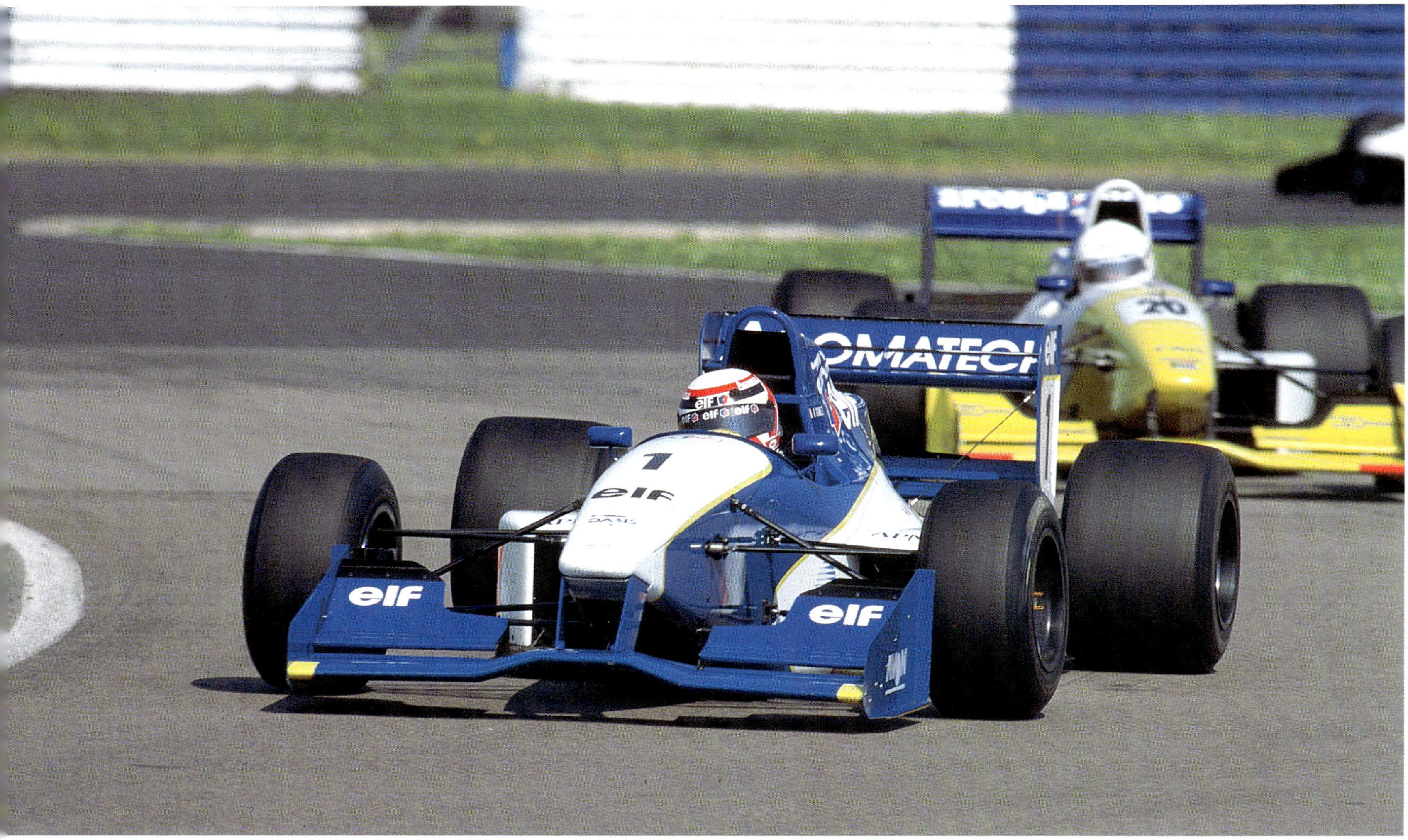

OMATECH
elf
elf
elf

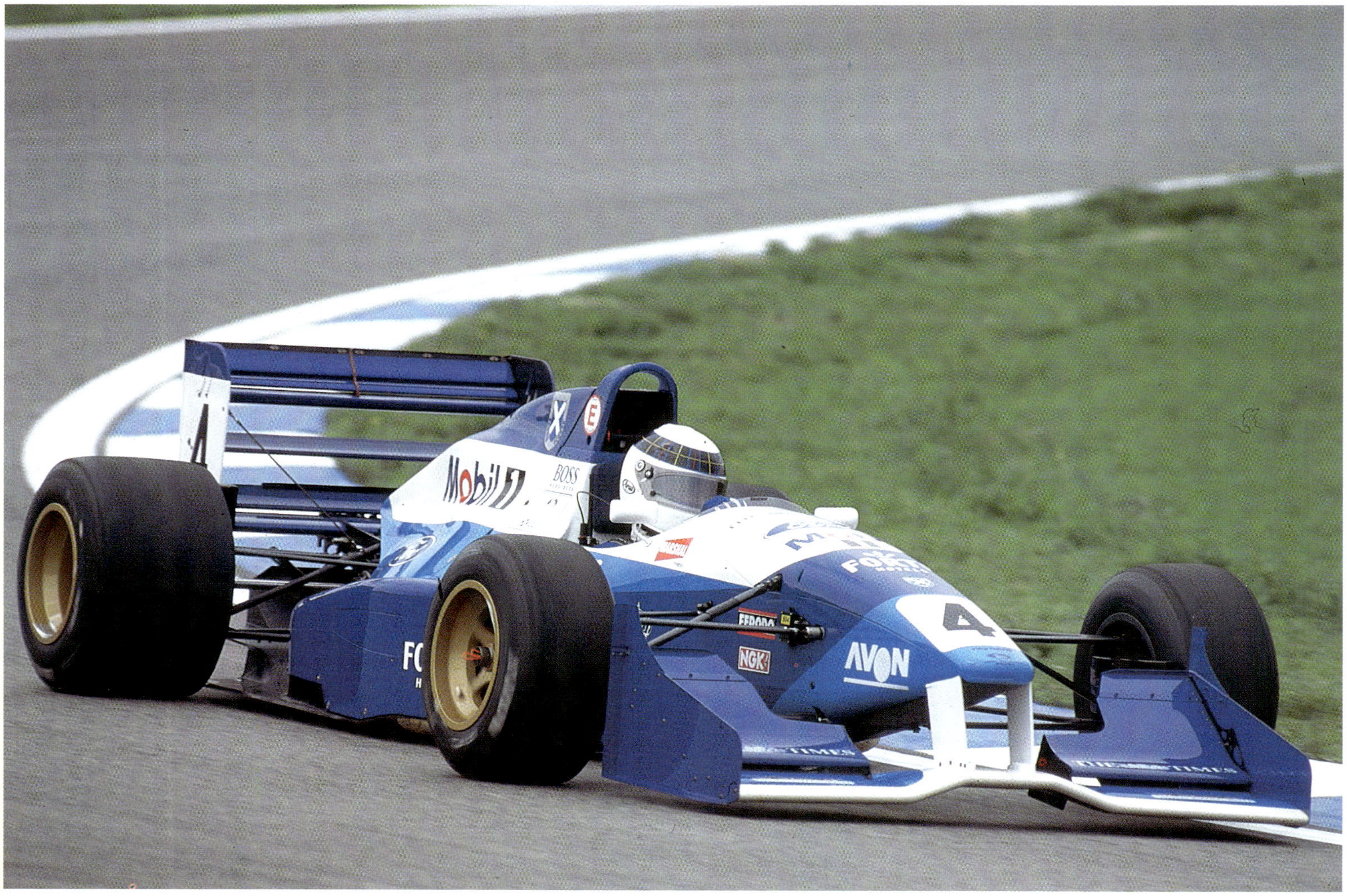

Mobil
AVON
NGK

pense came at Estoril, where Tarso Marques took his first win and brought DAMS' total of victories to 19 between 1989 and 1995 – an enviable record.

Paul Stewart and Dominique Delestre of Apomatox had plenty of time to consider the problems which faced their respective teams. Stewart's operation looked to have a very good package at the beginning of the season, with France's Didier Cottaz, the best newcomer of 1994, and the diminutive but experienced Allan McNish. Both drivers were capable of giving PSR the championship it had not yet managed to win, but from the beginning of the season misfortune was firmly attached to McNish's coat-tails, never more so than in Barcelona, where he went off while in the lead! Apart from a podium placing in Pau, McNish was not competitive, and he scored only a single point in the final five races. As for Cottaz, it seems that the reasons for his total lack of performance are unlikely to be ever fully explained. Neither the driver himself nor Paul Stewart seem ready to wash their dirty linen in public – at least not as long as they are bound by contractual obligations.

Having come so close to taking the title in 1994, Dominique Delestre could be forgiven for thinking that his Apomatox team had arrived. Franck Lagorce might have missed the title at the last moment, but he did give the team its first wins, and in Emmanuel Clérico, one of the finds of 1994, Apomatox had found a replacement for the team-leader who had gone on to be the test-driver for Ligier. However, he was to find the first half of the season hard going, collecting only three points from the Barcelona race. from Hockenheim on, he was on the pace, collecting good finishes one after another and reaching a peak with a second place in Estoril. The overall balance-sheet, however, was not what it should have been. At Magny-Cours in 1992, Jean-Marc Gounon put an end to string of 17 Reynard victories by winning in his Lola. But the cars with the sign of the fox on their noses had fought back, and between Donington in 1993 (Olivier Beretta with a Reynard-Forti) to Enna-Pergusa in 1995 (Ricardo Rosset in a Reynard Super Nova) the marque had racked up no less than 22 consecutive wins. The series was ended at Hockenheim by Marc Goossens, a driver who had gone against the tide by choosing to race one of the conventional-looking Lolas back in 1994. The Belgian had been threatening to win since the beginning of the season, returning good results which included a second place at Pau. His win in Germany made him the main threat to Sospiri and Rosset in their run for the championship, but he was unlucky to see his challenge end in the guard-rails of his home race at Spa-Francorchamps. He was one of a record number of four Belgian competitors in the race, but despite an inspired drive, luck was not with him. Sweden's Kenny Brack was another retiree at Spa, and the departure of these two contenders left the way clear for the Super Nova drivers. At the end of the season, Goossens and Brack shared third place in the championship with an equal points score and an equal tally of results.

Brack, who led the Madgwick team, alternated between good and not so good. He had a pattern of scoring in alternate races which should have sent him home from Magny-Cours empty-handed, but instead he broke the chain by not only scoring, but actually winning. Adding this to his earlier podium finishes (second at Hockenheim and third at Estoril) put Brack and Madgwick into the season's elite. The Swede was the only driver among the top twelve in the championship to use the Zytek-Judd KV as a power unit,

and it raises the question of whether his results would have been even better with a Cosworth AC behind him. To blame the engine would be a hasty verdict, and not one which would reflect the pattern of Brack's season. During the first half, he scored on only two occasions, and his tally at the mid-point was just five points. The team made real progress with the chassis and mechanical set-up during the mid-season break, and in the later races he was the best performer in the championship, scoring 19 points. As a comparison, the last four races gave Goossens 15 points, while Sospiri and Rosset scored 12 each. The presence on the podium of Christian Pescatori at Enna-Pergusa, Christophe Bouchut at Spa and Jean-Philippe Belloc at Magny-Cours were one-offs, scoring finishes certainly, but not evidence of consistency and the right to appear on the championship roll of honour. Nevertheless, many would be happy to achieve similar results. In his fourth and probably last season in the formula, Jerome Pollicand would probably have been satisfied with a bronze medal, as would Fabrizio de Simone. Apart from his Barcelona performance, de Simone was very disappointing,

SOSPIRI – ON TOP AT LAST

Vincenzo Sospiri decided to leave his native Milan for Britain after he won the World Karting Championship in 1987, at the age of 21. In his very first season in the UK, he won the prestigious Brands Hatch Formula Ford Festival, and after three years in the junior single-seater ranks he moved into F3000 full-time with Eddie Jordan's team for the 1991 season. He blotted his copybook in the last race of the year, at Nogaro, when he caused problems for his team-mate, none other than Damon Hill!

A low profile seemed the right career move, so Vincenzo returned home and kept quiet. But in 1993 he was back in F3000 with the Mythos team, with a reputation for being experienced, aggressive – and unstable. 1994 saw David Sears set up his Japanese-financed F3000 team, Super Nova, and when he needed a driver he immediately thought of the young Italian with whom he had won the British Vauxhall-Lotus championship in 1990. It was a good choice, for Sospiri was in contention for the championship right through until the final round.

Sospiri was seen as a potential champion from the beginning of the 1995 season, and he lived up to the expectations with a fine win at Barcelona. Two more victories on very different circuits – Pau and Spa-Francorchamps – underlined his ability and put him on course for a merited title.

Opposite top: "One year to learn, another to win." It's a motto that many of the drivers which Elf has nurtured have learnt by heart, but one which Guillaume Gomez (seen leading Formato) did not entirely respect. His first year showed flashes of brilliance, but not enough to make him a contender for the title. Allan McNish (opposite bottom) was making a comeback with Paul Stewart Racing after a period in the wilderness, but his results were disappointing for one who has shown real talent.

After he started the season by winning his first-ever F3000 race, Ricardo Rosset (above) went on to be the find of the year. Riding the wave of success of his team, Super Nova, the Brazilian was the only competitor able to challenge his team-mate Vincenzo Sospiri for the championship. Somewhat older than the average 'new Brazilian driver', Rosset took two wins in a year which has to be the gateway to higher things.

Marco Campos (seen above at Hockenheim, leading fellow-Brazilian Marques) was only 19 when he became the victim of a tragic accident at Magny-Cours while dashing for the flag on the last lap of the last race under the current regulations. After ten years and 110 races without a single fatal accident, it had to happen on the very last lap.

Emmanuel Clérico (below, at Enna-Pergusa) had expected better things. He had to wait until the penultimate race before ascending the podium – and that was amid comments on his driving tactics.

particularly in comparison with his team-mate, debutant Christophe Tinseau. With these two, the Mythos team was not on the same level as it had been in the early Nineties.

The organising authorities of motor sport have often been criticised for the ineffective manner in which both the promotional and the sporting aspects of Formula 3000 have been run. To answer some of those criticisms, they have created a new set of regulations and the new format will replace the current F3000 next year, ten years after it was introduced following the suppression of Formula 2 in 1984.

It was therefore the cruellest stroke of fate that the category should suffer its only fatal accident on the final lap of the very last of the 110 races run under the banner of Formula 3000. Marco Campos, the young Brazilian driver, was challenging Italy's Biaggi for eighth place on the run-in to the flag at Magny-Cours when his Lola touched the rear wheels of the Italian's Reynard. Campos' car was thrown into the air and came down across the wall bordering the track, causing injuries to the driver which even the most skilled intensive care, administered in a Paris hospital, could not relieve. There have been serious accidents and injuries, notably in 1988, when Fabien Giroix was hurt at Monza and both Michel Trollé and Johnny Herbert were injured at Brands Hatch, but this fatality – particularly because of its timing – struck everyone involved with Formula 3000 very hard. Campos was just 19; like Ayrton Senna, he was from Sao Paolo, and he was seen as one of Brazil's rising stars. His death was a cruel blow to motor sport as a whole.

F3000 has been almost a one-make championship for the last few years, but in 1996 – when it will retain the title of Formula 3000 – it will officially become one. Lola won the chassis contract in the face of Reynard, but as the end of 1995 loomed ever closer, there was still no decision about tyres (would Avon retain its monopoly or be replaced?) or engines.

Nevertheless, it seemed that the battle between the Ford-Cosworth and the Zytek-Judd would be resolved in favour of the latter, who before the season ended had sent out letters to competing teams intimating that it had the approval of the authorities to inform teams that it was ready to accept orders for engines for 1996.

The aim of the new regulations is said to reduce costs, and it is clear that firms will initially charge low to get the business and beat their competitors. *Initially*, that is certainly true – but what happens later? In a system which excludes alternative and competing suppliers, how are customers to be assured that they are buying at the best prices? The new rules go against the elementary principles of the capitalist system, and an unprecedented situation has been created. Until now, single-seater racing has been effectively in the hands of the constructors, and governed by competition between them. Can we now give over control to the authorities without competitors having the slightest question about the probity of those who make the decisions.

How and why was it decided that Reynard and Cosworth should be excluded from a sporting event whose very principle lies in clean and open competition? It is a decision which strikes at the very heart of motor sport, and causes the imagination to run riot. How about Formula 1 with a grid full of Williams-Renaults? What a sad thought – let us hope that Formula 3000, 1996-style, is not a laboratory for the future of Grand Prix racing.

INTERNATIONAL F3000 CHAMPIONSHIP

SILVERSTONE

Date: May 7, 1995. **Circuit:** 40 laps of the Silverstone circuit (5.057 km/3.142 miles), 202.28 km/125.694 miles. **Weather:** sunny.

Results:

Driver	No	Car	Laps	Time
1 Rosset	7	Reynard 95D-Cosworth AC	40	1.08'13"35
2 Sospiri	8	Reynard 95D-Cosworth AC	40	+ 7"77
3 McNish	4	Reynard 95D-Zytek Judd KV	40	+ 8"36
4 Goossens	12	Lola T95/50-Cosworth AC	40	+ 11"13
5 Bräck	15	Reynard 95D-Zytek Judd KV	40	+ 27"71
6 Pescatori	21	Reynard 95D-Cosworth AC	40	+ 50"55
7 de Simone	9	Reynard 95D-Zytek Judd KV	40	+ 1'07"77
8 Belloc	6	Reynard 95D-Cosworth AC	40	+ 1'13"06
9 Tinseau	21	Reynard 95D-Zytek Judd KV	40	+ 1'19"33
10 Eyckmans	29	Reynard 95D-Cosworth AC	40	+ 1'19"96
11 Lammers	16	Reynard 95D-Cosworth AC	40	+ 2'00"50
12 Marques	2	Reynard 95D-Cosworth AC	39	
13 Gomez	1	Reynard 95D-Cosworth AC	39	
14 Formato	20	Reynard 95D-Cosworth AC	38	
15 Gueiros*	14	Reynard 95D-Zytek Judd KV	37	
16 Filhol	24	Reynard 95D-Cosworth DFV	36	

Did not qualify: 25. Gosselin (Reynard 93D-Cosworth DFV)
Bouchut was disqualified for not observing the red flag at the end of the second qualifying session (11th row).

* Retired but classified as a finisher.

Winner's average: 177.88 kmh/110.532 mph.

Fastest lap: Marques, Reynard 95D-Cosworth AC, 1'40"95 = 180.32 kmh/112.049 mph.

Retirements:

Driver	No	Car	Laps	Reason
Campos	27	Lola T95/50-Cosworth AC	0	engine stalled
Rees	22	Reynard 95D-Zytek Judd KV	0	engine stalled
Morelli	23	Reynard 95D-Zytek Judd KV	0	engine stalled
van Hool	28	Reynard 95D-Zytek Judd KV	2	accident
Cottaz	3	Reynard 95D-Cosworth AC	2	accident
Watson	11	Lola T95/50-Cosworth AC	12	accident
Policand	18	Lola T95/50-Cosworth AC	25	accident
Clérico	5	Reynard 95D-Cosworth AC	34	gearbox selection
Gueiros	14	Reynard 95D-Zytek Judd KV	37	electrical failure

BARCELONA

Date: May 13, 1995. **Circuit:** 43 laps of the Catalunya circuit (4.727 km/2.937 miles), 203.261 km/126.304 miles. **Weather:** sunny.

Results:

Driver	No	Car	Laps	Time
1 Sospiri	8	Reynard 945-Cosworth AC	43	1.06'56"018
2 Rosset	7	Reynard 95D-Cosworth AC	43	+ 2"230
3 Marques	2	Reynard 95D-Cosworth AC	43	+ 4"197
4 Clérico	5	Reynard 95D-Cosworth AC	43	+ 7"739
5 Goossens	12	Lola T95/50-Cosworth AC	43	+ 25"658
6 Tinseau	10	Reynard 95D-Zytek Judd KV	43	+ 30"974
7 Rees	22	Reynard 95D-Zytek Judd KV	43	+ 45"566
8 van Hool	28	Reynard 95D-Zytek Judd KV	43	+ 56"355
9 Gomez	1	Reynard 95D-Cosworth AC	43	+ 56"593
10 Lammers	16	Reynard 95D-Cosworth AC	43	+ 1'22"380
11 Watson	11	Lola T95/50-Cosworth AC	42	
12 Eyckmans	29	Reynard 95D-Cosworth AC	42	
13 Bräck*	15	Reynard 95D-Zytek Judd KV	41	
14 Formato	20	Reynard 95D-Cosworth AC	41	
15 Pescatori*	21	Reynard 95D-Cosworth AC	41	
16 Belloc	6	Reynard 95D-Cosworth AC	39	
17 Filhol	24	Reynard 93D-Cosworth DFV	39	

* Retired but classified as a finisher.

Winner's average: 182.205 kmh/113.22 mph.

Fastest lap: Clérico, Reynard 95D-Cosworth AC, 1'31"597 = 185.783 kmh/115.443 mph.

Retirements:

Driver	No	Car	Laps	Reason
Campos	27	Reynard 95D-Cosworth AC	0	accident
Morelli	23	Reynard 95D-Zytek Judd KV	4	accident
McNish	4	Reynard 95D-Cosworth AC	5	accident
Cottaz	3	Reynard 95D-Cosworth AC	10	body damage following accident
de Simone	9	Reynard 95D-Zytek Judd KV	25	collision
Policand	18	Lola T95/50-Cosworth AC	25	accident
Bouchut	19	Lola T95/50-Cosworth AC	31	vibrations
Gueiros	14	Reynard 95D-Zytek Judd KV	33	spin
Bräck	15	Reynard 95D-Zytek Judd KV	41	spin
Pescatori	21	Reynard 95D-Cosworth AC	41	collision

PAU

Date: June 4, 1995. **Circuit:** 72 laps of the Pau street circuit (2.76 km/1.715 miles), 198.72 km/123.482 miles. **Weather:** cloudy.

Results:

Driver	No	Car	Laps	Time
1 Sospiri	8	Reynard 95D-Cosworth AC	72	1.26'47"82
2 McNish	4	Reynard 95D-Cosworth AC	72	+ 2"79
3 Goossens	12	Lola T95/50-Cosworth AC	72	+ 3"63
4 Bräck	15	Reynard 95D-Zytek Judd KV	72	+ 11"52
5 Belloc	6	Reynard 95D-Cosworth AC	72	+ 26"88
6 Cottaz	3	Reynard 95D-Cosworth AC	72	+ 27"94
7 Clérico	5	Reynard 95D-Cosworth AC	72	+ 28"39
8 Bouchut	19	Lola T95/50-Cosworth AC	72	+ 32"68
9 Rosset	7	Reynard 95D-Cosworth AC	72	+ 40"33
10 Lammers	16	Reynard 95D-Cosworth AC	72	+ 1'02"09
11 de Simone	9	Reynard 95D-Zytek Judd KV	72	+ 1'02"30
12 Watson	11	Lola T95/50-Cosworth AC	70	
13 Campos	27	Lola T95/50-Cosworth AC	69	

Did not qualify: Fertl (Reynard 95D-Cosworth AC), van Hool (Reynard 95D-Zytek Judd KV), Filhol (Reynard 93D-Cosworth DFV), Gosselin (Reynard 93D-Cosworth DFV).

Winner's average: 137.369 kmh/85.359 mph.

Fastest lap: Clérico, Reynard 95D-Cosworth AC, 1'10"801 = 140.337 kmh/87.204 mph.

Retirements:

Driver	No	Car	Laps	Reason
Marques	2	Reynard 95D-Cosworth AC	0	collision with Gomez
Gomez	1	Reynard 95D-Cosworth AC	0	collision with Marques
Policand	18	Lola T95/50-Cosworth AC	0	collision
Gueiros	14	Reynard 95D-Zytek Judd KV	0	spin
Formato	20	Reynard 95D-Cosworth AC	2	spin
Rees	22	Reynard 95D-Zytek Judd KV	20	suspension
Tinseau	10	Reynard 95D-Zytek Judd KV	45	accident
Pescatori	21	Reynard 95D-Cosworth AC	50	suspension
Eyckmans	29	Reynard 95D-Cosworth AC	60	transmission

ENNA-PERGUSA

Date: July 23, 1995. **Circuit:** 40 laps of the Enna-Pergusa circuit (4.950 km/3.076 miles), 198 km/123.035 miles. **Weather:** fine and warm.

Results:

Driver	No	Car	Laps	Time
1 Rosset	7	Reynard 95D-Cosworth AC	40	1.02'15"657
2 Sospiri	8	Reynard 95D-Cosworth AC	40	+ 11"914
3 Pescatori	21	Reynard 95D-Cosworth AC	40	+ 17"603
4 Campos	27	Lola T95/50-Cosworth AC	40	+ 30"513
5 de Simone	9	Reynard 95D-Zytek Judd KV	40	+ 34"601
6 Policand	18	Lola T95/50-Cosworth AC	40	+ 47"535
7 Watson	11	Lola T95/50-Cosworth AC	40	+ 49"107
8 Rees	22	Reynard 95D-Zytek Judd KV	40	+ 54"877
9 Formato	20	Reynard 95D-Cosworth AC	39	
10 Olsson	24	Reynard 93D-Cosworth AC	39	
11 Nardozi	23	Reynard 95D-Zytek Judd KV	37	

Did not qualify: Gosselin, Reynard 93D-Cosworth DFV.

Winner's average: 190.808 kmh/118.566 mph.

Fastest lap: Rosset, Reynard 95D-Cosworth AC, 1'31"149 = 195.504 kmh/121.484 mph.

Retirements:

Driver	No	Car	Laps	Reason
Gomez	1	Reynard 95D-Cosworth AC	0	car damaged in warm-up
Bräck	15	Reynard 95D-Zytek Judd KV	1	suspension
Bouchut	19	Lola T95/50-Cosworth AC	2	spin
Tinseau	10	Reynard 95D-Zytek Judd KV	5	disqualified for re-entering track after spin
Marques	2	Reynard 95D-Cosworth AC	6	engine
Belloc	6	Reynard 95D-Cosworth AC	8	collision with van Hool
van Hool	28	Reynard 95D-Zytek Judd KV	8	collision with Belloc
Cottaz	3	Reynard 95D-Cosworth AC	18	collision
Goossens	12	Lola T95/50-Cosworth AC	25	accident
Clérico	5	Reynard 95D-Cosworth AC	27	collision with McNish
McNish	4	Reynard 95D-Cosworth AC	27	collision with Clérico

HOCKENHEIM

Date: July 29, 1995. **Circuit:** 29 laps of the Hockenheim circuit (6.815 km/4.235 miles), 197.635 km/122.808 miles. **Weather:** fine and very hot.

Results:

Driver	No	Car	Laps	Time
1 Goossens	12	Lola T95/50-Cosworth AC	29	58'04"329
2 Bräck	15	Reynard 95D-Zytek Judd KV	29	+ 3"734
3 Gomez	1	Reynard 95D-Cosworth AC	29	+ 12"184
4 Clérico	5	Reynard 95D-Cosworth AC	29	+ 12"599
5 Gueiros	14	Reynard 95D-Zytek Judd KV	29	+ 24"033
6 McNish	4	Reynard 95D-Cosworth AC	29	+ 29"269
7 Tinseau	10	Reynard 95D-Zytek Judd KV	29	+ 33"918
8 Policand	18	Lola T95/50-Cosworth AC	29	+ 35"387
9 Rosset	7	Reynard 95D-Cosworth AC	29	+ 48"763
10 van Hool	8	Reynard 95D-Zytek Judd KV	29	+ 52"603
11 Cottaz	3	Reynard 95D-Cosworth AC	29	+ 1'00"418
12 Eyckmans	29	Reynard 95D-Cosworth AC	29	+ 1'58"347
13 Olsson	24	Reynard 93D-Cosworth AC	28	
14 Nardozi	23	Reynard 95D-Zytek Judd KV	28	

Did not qualify: Gosselin, Reynard 93D-Cosworth DFV.

Winner's average: 204.435 kmh/127.033 mph.

Fastest lap: Rosset, Reynard 95D-Cosworth AC, 1'58"633 = 207.048 kmh/128.657 mph.

Retirements:

Driver	No	Car	Laps	Reason
Belloc	6	Reynard 95D-Cosworth AC	0	accident
de Simone	9	Reynard 95D-Zytek Judd KV	0	accident
Fertl	17	Reynard 95D-Cosworth DFV	3	accident
Pescatori	21	Reynard 95D-Cosworth AC	10	suspension damaged in first-lap collision
Formato	20	Reynard 95D-Cosworth AC	12	engine
Watson	11	Lola T95/50-Cosworth AC	17	gearbox
Campos	27	Lola T95/50-Cosworth AC	18	collision with Marques
Bouchut	19	Lola T95/50-Cosworth AC	18	collision with Sospiri
Sospiri	8	Reynard 95D-Cosworth AC	18	collision with Bouchut
Marques	2	Reynard 95D-Cosworth AC	19	results of collision with Campos

SPA-FRANCORCHAMPS

Date: August 26, 1995. **Circuit:** 28 laps of the Spa-Francorchamps circuit (6.974 km/4.334 miles), 195.272 km/121.34 miles. **Weather:** cloudy.

Results:

Driver	No	Car	Laps	Time
1 Sospiri	8	Reynard 95D-Cosworth AC	28	59'03"485
2 Bouchut	19	Lola T95/50-Cosworth AC	28	+ 3"345
3 Gomez	1	Reynard 95D-Cosworth AC	28	+ 3"839
4 Rosset	7	Reynard 95D-Cosworth AC	28	+ 25"948
5 Marques	2	Reynard 95D-Cosworth AC	28	+ 30"597
6 Clérico	5	Reynard 95D-Cosworth AC	28	+ 38"365
7 Tinseau	10	Reynard 95D-Zytek Judd KV	28	+ 40"344
8 Campos	27	Lola T95/50-Cosworth AC	28	+ 40"934
9 van Hool	28	Reynard 95D-Zytek Judd KV	28	+ 1'16"677
10 Policand	18	Lola T95/50-Cosworth AC	28	+ 1'20"756
11 Cottaz	3	Reynard 95D-Cosworth AC	28	+ 1'40"288
12 Watson	11	Lola T95/50-Cosworth AC	28	+ 1'48"433
13 Belloc	6	Reynard 95D-Cosworth AC	27	
14 Nardozi	23	Reynard 95D-Zytek Judd KV	27	
15 Taylor	16	Reynard 95D-Cosworth AC	26	
16 Goossens*	12	Lola T95/50-Cosworth AC	25	

* Classified, but did not finish.

Winner's average: 198.386 kmh/123.275 mph.

Fastest lap: Gomez, Reynard 95D-Cosworth AC, 2'04"022 = 202.435 kmh/125.791 mph.

Retirements:

Driver	No	Car	Laps	Reason
Formato	20	Reynard 95D-Cosworth AC	1	accident
de Simone	9	Reynard 95D-Zytek Judd KV	2	spin
Bräck	15	Reynard 95D-Zytek Judd KV	2	accident
Gueiros	14	Reynard 95D-Zytek Judd KV	2	accident
Hattori	26	Reynard 95D-Cosworth AC	10	collision with Belloc
Pescatori	21	Reynard 95D-Cosworth AC	13	accident following spin by Taylor
de Groodt	17	Reynard 95D-Cosworth AC	20	accident
McNish	4	Reynard 95D-Cosworth AC	21	engine
Goossens	12	Lola T95/50-Cosworth AC	25	accident

INTERNATIONAL F3000 CHAMPIONSHIP

ESTORIL

Date: September 23, 1995. **Circuit:** 46 laps of the Estoril circuit (4.36 km/2.709 miles), 200.56 km/124.626 miles. **Weather:** fine.

Results:

	Driver	No	Car	Laps	Time
1	Marques	2	Reynard 95D-Cosworth AC	46	1.11'49"521
2	Clérico	5	Reynard 95D-Cosworth AC	46	+ 6"679
3	Bräck	15	Reynard 95D-Zytek Judd KV	46	+ 16"044
4	Policand	18	Lola T95/50-Cosworth AC	46	+ 28"229
5	Rosset	7	Reynard 95D-Cosworth AC	46	+ 29"324
6	Pescatori	21	Reynard 95D-Cosworth AC	46	+ 35"228
7	Sospiri	8	Reynard 95D-Cosworth AC	46	+ 57"043
8	Goossens	12	Lola T95/50-Cosworth AC	46	+ 1'15"449
9	Campos	27	Lola T95/50-Cosworth AC	45	
10	Tinseau	10	Reynard 95D-Zytek Judd KV	45	
11	de Simone	9	Reynard 95D-Zytek Judd KV	45	
12	Formato	20	Reynard 95D-Cosworth AC	45	
13	Olsson	25	Reynard 95D-Zytek Judd KV	45	
14	Bouchut*	19	Lola T95/50-Cosworth AC	44	
15	Nardozi	23	Reynard 95D-Zytek Judd KV	44	
16	Rostan	24	Reynard 93D-Cosworth DFY	43	
17	Taylor	16	Reynard 95D-Cosworth AC	43	

* Retired but classified as a finisher.

Did not qualify: 25. Gosselin (Reynard 93D-Cosworth DFY)

Winner's average: 167.539 kmh/104.107 mph.

Fastest lap: Gomez, Reynard 95D-Cosworth AC, 1'32"42 = 169.831 kmh/169.831 mph.

Retirements:

Driver	No	Car	Laps	Reason
Gueiros	14	Reynard 95D-Zytek Judd KV	4	accident
van Hool	28	Reynard 95D-Zytek Judd KV	4	suspension
Hattori	26	Reynard 95D-Cosworth AC	16	accident
McNish	4	Reynard 95D-Cosworth AC	17	steering
Watson	11	Lola T95/50-Cosworth AC	21	spin
Cottaz	3	Reynard 95D-Cosworth AC	25	accident
Gomez	1	Reynard 95D-Cosworth AC	35	accident
Belloc	6	Reynard 95D-Cosworth AC	36	gearbox
Bouchut	19	Lola T95/50-Cosworth AC	44	engine

MAGNY-COURS

Date: October 15, 1995. **Circuit:** 47 laps of the Magny-Cours circuit (4.25 km/2.641 miles), 199.75 km/124.145 miles. **Weather:** cloudy.

Results:

	Driver	No	Car	Laps	Time
1	Bräck	15	Reynard 95D-Cosworth AC	47	1.08'59"
2	Goossens	12	Lola T95/50-Cosworth AC	47	+ 08"50
3	Belloc	6	Reynard 95D-Cosworth AC	47	+ 14"99
4	Sospiri	8	Reynard 95D-Cosworth AC	47	+ 15"17
5	Clérico	5	Reynard 95D-Cosworth AC	47	+ 15"89
6	Pescatori	21	Reynard 95D-Cosworth AC	47	+ 30"37
7	McNish	4	Reynard 95D-Cosworth AC	47	+ 33"09
8	Gueiros	14	Reynard 95D-Zytek Judd KV	47	+ 38"03
9	Biagi	26	Reynard 95D-Cosworth AC	47	+ 1'24"96
10	Campos*	27	Lola T95/50-Cosworth AC	46	
11	Cottaz	3	Reynard 95D-Cosworth AC	46	
12	Watson	11	Lola T95/50-Cosworth AC	46	
13	Formato	20	Reynard 95D-Cosworth AC	46	
14	Tinseau	10	Reynard 95D-Zytek Judd KV	46	
15	Nardozi	23	Reynard 95D-Zytek Judd KV	45	
16	Rostan	24	Reynard 93D-Cosworth DFY	45	

* Retired but classified as a finisher.

Did not qualify: Taylor, Reynard 95D-Cosworth AC, Gomez, Reynard 95D-Cosworth AC.

Winner's average: 173.71 kmh/107.961 mph.

Fastest lap: Marques, Reynard 95D-Cosworth AC, 1'26"88 = 176.097 kmh/109.444 mph.

Retirements:

Driver	No	Car	Laps	Reason
Bouchut	19	Lola T95/50-Cosworth AC	1	clutch
Policand	18	Lola T95/50-Cosworth AC	11	engine
Rosset	7	Reynard 95D-Cosworth AC	11	accident
van Hool	8	Reynard 95D-Zytek Judd KV	20	accident
Olsson	24	Reynard 93D-Cosworth AC	20	transmission
Marques	2	Reynard 95D-Cosworth AC	33	collision with de Simone
de Simone	9	Reynard 95D-Zytek Judd KV	33	collision with Marques
Gosselin	25	Reynard 93D-Cosworth DFV	33	exhaustion
de Groodt	17	Reynard 95D-Cosworth AC	37	accident
Campos	27	Lola T95/50-Cosworth AC	46	collision with Biagi

FINAL CLASSIFICATION

	Driver	Car	Silverstone	Barcelona	Pau	Enna	Hockenheim	Spa	Estoril	Magny-Cours	Total
1	V. Sospiri (I)	Reynard 95D-Cosworth AC	6	9	9	6	—	9	—	3	42
2	R. Rosset (BR)	Reynard 95D-Cosworth AC	9	6	—	9	—	3	2	—	29
3	M. Goossens (B)	Lola T95/50-Cosworth AC	4	2	4	—	9	—	—	6	24
	K. Bräck (S)	Reynard 95D-Judd KV	2	—	3	—	6	—	4	9	24
4	E. Clérico (F)	Reynard 95D-Cosworth AC	—	3	—	—	3	1	6	2	15
	T. Marques (BR)	Reynard 95D-Cosworth AC	—	4	—	—	—	2	9	—	15
5	A. McNish (GB)	Reynard 95D-Cosworth AC	4	—	6	—	1	—	—	—	11
6	G. Gomez (F)	Reynard 95D-Cosworth AC	—	—	—	—	—	4	4	—	8
7	C. Pescatori (I)	Reynard 95D-Cosworth AC	1	—	—	4	—	—	1	1	7
8	C. Bouchut (F)	Lola T95/50-Cosworth AC	—	—	—	—	—	6	—	—	6
	J.-P. Belloc (F)	Reynard 95D-Cosworth AC	—	2	—	—	—	—	4	—	6
9	J. Policand (F)	Lola T95/50-Cosworth AC	—	—	—	1	—	—	3	—	4
10	M. Campos (BR)	Lola T95/50-Judd KV	—	—	—	—	—	3	—	—	3
11	F. de Simone (I)	Reynard 95D-Judd KV	—	—	—	—	—	2	—	—	2
	M. Gueiros (BR)	Reynard 95D-Judd KV	—	—	—	—	2	—	—	—	2
12	C. Tinseau (F)	Reynard 95D-Judd KV	—	1	—	—	—	—	—	—	1
	D. Cottaz (F)	Reynard 95D-Cosworth AC	—	—	1	—	—	—	—	—	1

FORMULA 1 WORLD CHAMPIONSHIP

	FINAL CLASSIFICATION DRIVERS	Brasil	Argentina	San Marino	España	Monaco	Canada	France	British	Deutschland	Magyarerszag	Belgique	Italia	Portugal	Europe	Pacific	Japan	Australia	Total
1	Michael SCHUMACHER	10	4	0	10	10	2	10	0	10	0	10	0	6	10	10	10	0	102
2	Damon HILL	0	10	10	3	6	0	6	0	0	10	6	0	4	0	4	0	10	69
3	David COULTHARD	6	0	3	0	0	0	4	4	6	6	0	0	10	4	6	0	0	49
4	Johnny HERBERT	0	3	0	6	3	0	0	10	3	3	0	10	0	2	1	4	0	45
5	Jean ALESI	2	6	6	0	0	10	2	6	0	0	0	0	2	6	2	0	0	42
6	Gerhard BERGER	4	1	4	4	4	0	0	0	4	4	0	0	3	0	3	0	0	31
7	Mika HÄKKINEN	3	0	2	0	0	0	0	0	0	0	0	6	0	0	0	6	0	17
8	Olivier PANIS	0	0	0	1	0	3	0	3	0	1	0	0	0	0	0	2	6	16
9	Heinz-Harald FRENTZEN	0	2	1	0	1	0	0	1	0	2	3	4	1	0	0	0	0	15
10	Mark BLUNDELL	1	0	0	0	2	0	0	2	0	0	2	3	0	0	0	0	3	13
11	Rubens BARRICHELLO	0	0	0	0	0	0	6	1	0	0	1	0	0	3	0	0	0	11
12	Eddie IRVINE	0	0	0	2	0	4	0	0	0	0	0	0	0	1	0	3	0	10
13	Mark BRUNDLE	0	0	0	0	0	0	0	0	3	0	4	0	0	0	0	0	0	7
14	Gianni MORBIDELLI	0	0	0	0	0	1	0	0	0	0	0	0	0	0	0	0	4	5
	Mika SALO	0	0	0	0	0	0	0	0	0	0	0	2	0	0	1	2	0	5
15	Jean-Christophe BOULLION	0	0	0	0	0	0	0	0	2	0	0	1	0	0	0	0	0	3
16	Aguri SUZUKI	0	0	0	0	0	0	0	0	1	0	0	0	0	0	0	0	0	1
	Pedro LAMY	0	0	0	0	0	0	0	0	0	0	0	0	0	0	0	1	0	1

	FINAL CLASSIFICATION CONSTRUCTORS	Brasil	Argentina	San Marino	España	Monaco	Canada	France	British	Deutschland	Magyarerszag	Belgique	Italia	Portugal	Europe	Pacific	Japan	Australia	Total
1	BENNETON-RENAULT	0	7	0	16	13	2	10	10	13	3	10	10	6	12	11	14	0	137
2	WILLIAMS-RENAULT	0	10	13	3	6	0	10	4	6	16	6	0	14	4	10	0	10	112
3	FERRARI	6	7	10	4	4	10	2	6	4	4	0	0	5	6	5	0	0	73
4	McLAREN-MERCEDES	4	0	2	0	2	0	0	0	0	0	0	9	0	0	0	6	3	30
5	LIGIER-MUGEN HONDA	0	0	0	1	0	3	3	3	1	1	4	0	0	0	0	2	6	24
6	JORDAN-PEUGEOT	0	0	0	2	0	4	10	1	0	0	1	0	0	4	0	3	0	21
7	SAUBER-FORD	0	2	1	0	1	0	0	1	2	2	3	5	1	0	0	0	0	18
8	FOOTWORK-HART	0	0	0	0	0	0	0	0	1	0	0	0	0	0	0	0	4	5
	TYRRELL-YAMAHA	0	0	0	0	0	0	0	0	0	0	0	2	0	0	1	2	0	5
9	MINARDI-FORD	0	0	0	0	0	0	0	0	0	0	=	0	0	0	0	1	0	1

GRANDE PRÊMIO DO BRASIL

Date:	March 26, 1995
Circuit:	71 laps of the Interlagos circuit (4.325 km/ 2.688 miles), 307.075 km/190.813 miles
Weather:	cloudy and dull
Attendance:	45,000 spectators approx.
Previous winner:	Michael Schumacher, Benetton at 192.6 kmh/ 119.679 mph (1994)
Lap record:	Michael Schumacher, Benetton, 1'18"455 = 198.4 kmh/123.283 mph (1994)

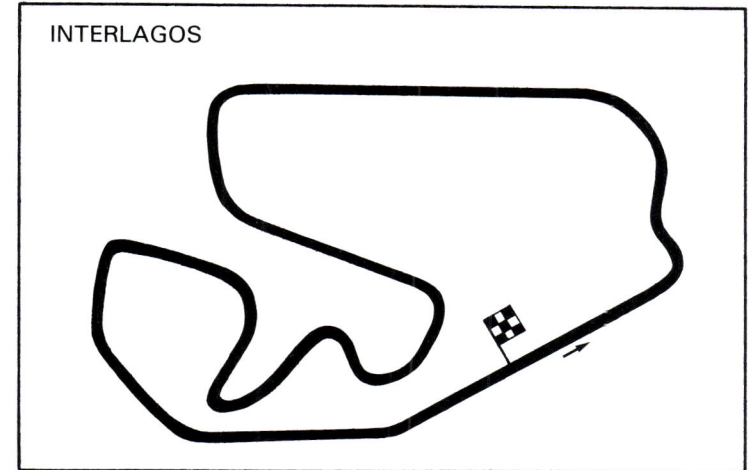

INTERLAGOS

STARTING GRID

1. SCHUMACHER 1'20"382
Benetton B195-Renault RS7 V10

5. HILL 1'20"081
Williams FW17-Renault RS7 V10

2. HERBERT 1'20"688
Benetton B195-Renault RS7 V10

6. COULTHARD 1'20"422
Williams FW17-Renault RS7 V10

27. ALESI 1'21"041
Ferrari 412T2-Ferrari V12

28. BERGER 1'20"906
Ferrari 412T2-Ferrari V12

15. IRVINE 1'21"749
Jordan 195-Peugeot V10

8. HÄKKINEN 1'21"399
McLaren MP4/10-Mercedes F0110 V10

26. PANIS 1'21"914
Ligier JS41-Mugen/Honda V10

7. BLUNDELL 1'21"779
McLaren MP4/10-Mercedes F0110 V10

4. SALO 1'22"416
Tyrrell 023-Yamaha V10

3. KATAYAMA 1'22"325
Tyrrell 023-Yamaha V10

30. FRENTZEN 1'22"872
Sauber C14-Ford Zetec-R V8

9. MORBIDELLI 1'22"468
Footwork FA16-Hart V8

14. BARRICHELLO 1'22"975
Jordan 195-Peugeot V10

25. SUZUKI 1'22"971
Ligier JS41-Mugen/Honda V10

24. BADOER 1'24"443
Minardi M195-Ford EDM V8

23. MARTINI 1'24"383
Minardi M195-Ford EDM V8

16. GACHOT 1'25"127
Pacific PR02-Ford ED V8

29. WENDLINGER 1'24"723
Sauber C14-Ford Zetec-R V8

17. MONTERMINI 1'25"886
Pacific PR02-Ford ED V8

10. INOUE 1'25"225
Footwork FA16-Hart V8

11. VERSTAPPEN 1'26"323
Simtek S951-Ford ED V8

22. MORENO 1'26"269
Forti FG01/95-Ford ED V8

12. SCHIATTARELLA 1'28"106
Simtek S951-Ford ED V8

21. DINIZ 1'27"792
Forti FG01/95-Ford ED V8

RESULTS

	Driver	Car	Laps	Time	Fastest lap
1	SCHUMACHER	Benetton	71	1.38'34"154	1'20"921
2	COULTHARD	Williams	71	+ 8"060	1'21"543
3	BERGER	Ferrari	70		1'22"679
4	HÄKKINEN	McLaren	70		1'22"495
5	ALESI	Ferrari	70		1'23"207
6	BLUNDELL	McLaren	70		1'23"252
7	SALO	Tyrrell	69		1'22"979
8	SUZUKI	Ligier	69		1'23"049
9	MONTERMINI	Pacific	65		1'27"447
10	DINIZ	Forti	64		1'28"811

Winner's average: 186.885 kmh/116.15 mph.

Fastest lap: SCHUMACHER, Benetton, 1'20"921 (192.372 kmh/119.539 mph).

RETIREMENTS

Driver	Laps	Reason	Fastest lap
MARTINI	0	gearbox	
PANIS	0	collision	
FRENTZEN	10	engine	1'24"087
SCHIATTARELLA	12	steering	1'28"487
IRVINE	15	gearbox hydraulics failure	1'23"355
KATAYAMA	15	spin	1'23"718
VERSTAPPEN	16	gearbox	1'26"017
BARRICHELLO	16	gearbox hydraulics failure	1'23"346
GACHOT	23	gearbox	1'26"826
HERBERT	30	collision with Suzuki	1'23"009
HILL	30	gearbox	1'20"982
WENDLINGER	41	electrical failure	1'24"387
MORENO	47	spin	1'27"829
BADOER	47	gearbox	1'26"249
INOUE	48	oil leak	1'26"470
MORBIDELLI	62	engine	1'22"816

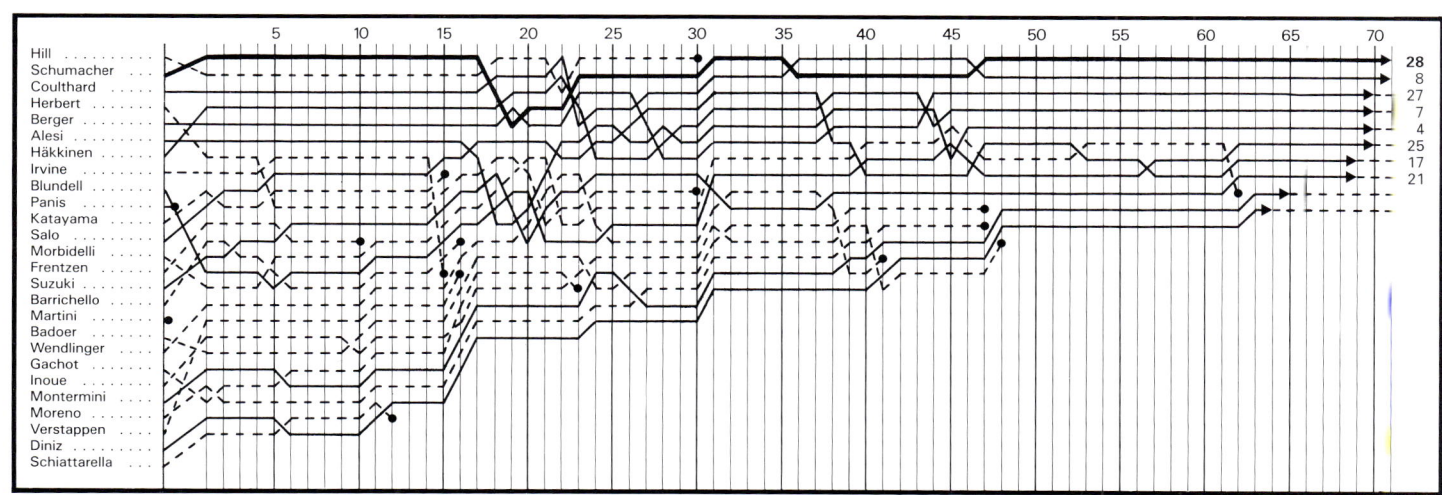

GRAN PREMIO DE ARGENTINA

Date:	April 9, 1995
Circuit:	72 laps of the Buenos Aires circuit (4.256 km/2.645 miles), 306.482 km/191.627 miles
Weather:	cloudy
Attendance:	70,000 spectators approx.
Previous winner:	Nelson Piquet, Brabham, at 200.630 kmh/124.669 mph (1981)
Lap record:	Nelson Piquet, Brabham, 1'45"287 = 204.066 kmh/126 mph (1981)

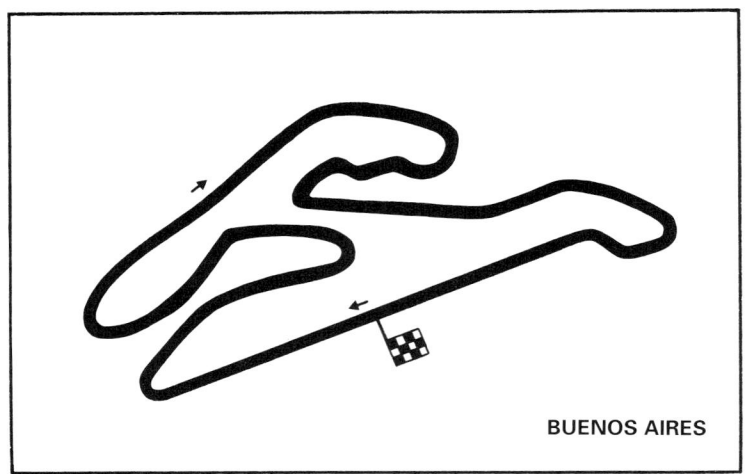

BUENOS AIRES

STARTING GRID

6. COULTHARD 1'53"241
Williams FW17-Renault RS7 V10

5. HILL 1'54"057
Williams FW17-Renault RS7 V10

1. SCHUMACHER 1'54"272
Benetton B195-Renault RS7 V10

15. IRVINE 1'54"381
Jordan 195-Peugeot V10

8. HÄKKINEN 1'54"529
McLaren MP4/10-Mercedes F0110 V10

27. ALESI 1'54"637
Ferrari 412T2-Ferrari V12

4. SALO 1'54"757
Tyrrell 023-Yamaha V10

28. BERGER 1'55"276
Ferrari 412T2-Ferrari V12

30. FRENTZEN 1'55"583
Sauber C14-Ford Zetec-R V8

14. BARRICHELLO 1'56"114
Jordan 195-Peugeot V10

2. HERBERT 1'57"068
Benetton B195-Renault RS7 V10

9. MORBIDELLI 1'57"092
Footwork FA16-Hart V8

24. BADOER 1'57"167
Minardi M195-Ford EDM V8

11. VERSTAPPEN 1'57"231
Simtek S951-Ford ED V8

3. KATAYAMA 1'57"484
Tyrrell 023-Yamaha V10

23. MARTINI 1'58"066
Minardi M195-Ford EDM V8

7. BLUNDELL 1'58"660
McLaren MP4/10-Mercedes F0110 V10

26. PANIS 1'58"824
Ligier JS41-Mugen/Honda V10

25. SUZUKI 1'58"882
Ligier JS41-Mugen/Honda V10

12. SCHIATTARELLA 1'59"539
Simtek S951-Ford ED V8

29. WENDLINGER 2'00"751
Sauber C14-Ford Zetec-R V8

17. MONTERMINI 2'01"763
Pacific PRO2-Ford ED V8

16. GACHOT 2'04"050
Pacific PRO2-Ford ED V8

22. MORENO 2'04"481
Forti FG01/95-Ford ED V8

21. DINIZ 2'05"932
Forti FG01/95-Ford ED V8

10. INOUE 2'07"298
Footwork FA16-Hart V8

RESULTS

	Driver	Car	Laps	Time	Fastest lap
1	HILL	Williams	72	1.53'14"532	1'31"253
2	ALESI	Ferrari	72	+ 6"407	1'31"453
3	SCHUMACHER	Benetton	72	+ 33"376	1'30"522
4	HERBERT	Benetton	71		1'33"082
5	FRENTZEN	Sauber	70		1'34"331
6	BERGER	Ferrari	70		1'31"868
7	PANIS	Ligier	70		1'33"953
8	KATAYAMA	Tyrrell	69		1'34"106
9	SCHIATTARELLA	Simtek	68		1'35"945
	DINIZ*	Forti	63		1'40"683
	MORENO*	Forti	63		1'40"730

* Finished, but not classified (insufficient distance).

Winner's average: 162.385 kmh/100.904 mph.

Fastest lap: SCHUMACHER, Benetton, 1'30"522 (169.377 kmh/105.249 mph) – establishes new lap record.

RETIREMENTS

Driver	Laps	Reason	Fastest lap
BADOER	0	collision with Salo and Barrichello	
WENDLINGER	0	collision with Gachot and Montermini	
GACHOT	0	collision with Wendlinger	
HÄKKINEN	0	collision with Irvine	
MONTERMINI	1	damage resulting from collision with Wendlinger	
IRVINE	6	engine	1'35"070
BLUNDELL	9	oil leak	1'34"963
COULTHARD	16	electrical failure	1'32"095
VERSTAPPEN	23	gearbox	1'35"353
BARRICHELLO	33	oil leak	1'33"810
INOUE	40	spin	1'35"325
MORBIDELLI	43	electrical failure	1'34"396
MARTINI	44	spin	1'35"837
SUZUKI	47	collision with Salo	1'34"049
SALO	48	collision with Suzuki	1'33"636

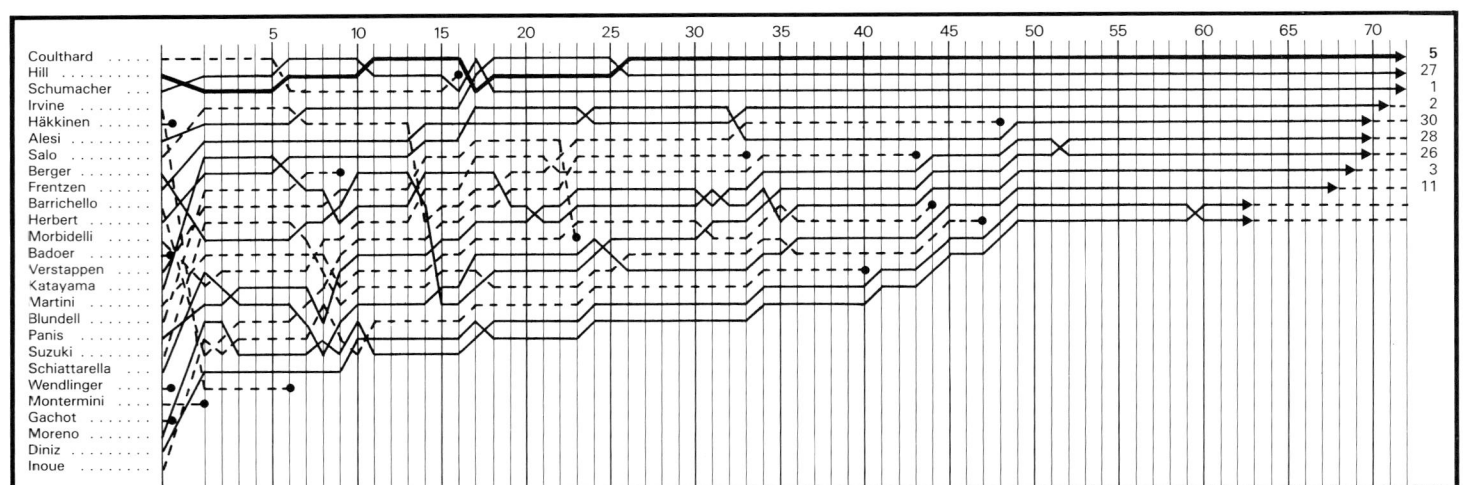

GRAN PREMIO DI SAN MARINO

Date:	April 30, 1995
Circuit:	63 laps of the Imola circuit (4.895 km/ 3.042 miles), 308.385 km/191.627 miles
Weather:	cloudy, track wet at first
Attendance:	120,000 spectators approx.
Previous winner:	Michael Schumacher, Benetton at 198.2 kmh/123.159 mph (1994)
Lap record:	Damon Hill, Williams, 1′24″335 = 215.1 kmh/133.661 mph (1994)

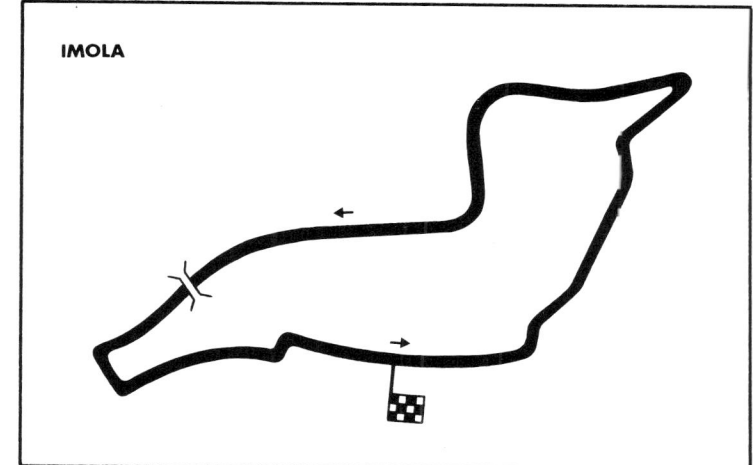

STARTING GRID

1. SCHUMACHER 1′27″274
Benetton B195-Renault RS7 V10

28. BERGER 1′27″382
Ferrari 412T2-Ferrari V12

6. COULTHARD 1′27″459
Williams FW17-Renault RS7 V10

5. HILL 1′27″537
Williams FW17-Renault RS7 V10

27. ALESI 1′27″813
Ferrari 412T2-Ferrari V12

8. HÄKKINEN 1′28″343
McLaren MP4/10-Mercedes F0110 V10

15. IRVINE 1′28″516
Jordan 195-Peugeot V10

2. HERBERT 1′29″350
Benetton B195-Renault RS7 V10

7. MANSELL 1′29″517
McLaren MP4/10-Mercedes F0110 V10

14. BARRICHELLO 1′29″551
Jordan 195-Peugeot V10

9. MORBIDELLI 1′29″582
Footwork FA16-Hart V8

26. PANIS 1′30″760
Ligier JS41-Mugen/Honda V10

4. SALO 1′31″035
Tyrrell 023-Yamaha V10

30. FRENTZEN 1′31″358
Sauber C14-Ford Zetec-R V8

3. KATAYAMA 1′31″630
Tyrrell 023-Yamaha V10

25. SUZUKI 1′31″913
Ligier JS41-Mugen/Honda V10

11. VERSTAPPEN 1′32″156
Simtek S951-Ford ED V8

23. MARTINI 1′32″445
Minardi M195-Ford EDM V8

10. INOUE 1′32″710
Footwork FA16-Hart V8

24. BADOER 1′33″071
Minardi M195-Ford EDM V8

29. WENDLINGER 1′33″494
Sauber C14-Ford Zetec-R V8

16. GACHOT 1′33″892
Pacific PRO2-Ford ED V8

12. SCHIATTARELLA 1′33″965
Simtek S951-Ford ED V8

17. MONTERMINI 1′35″169
Pacific PRO2-Ford ED V8

22. MORENO 1′36″065
Forti FG01/95-Ford ED V8

21. DINIZ 1′36″624
Forti FG01/95-Ford ED V8

RESULTS

	Driver	Car	Laps	Time	Fastest lap
1	HILL	Williams	63	1.41′42″552	1′29″710
2	ALESI	Ferrari	63	+ 18″510	1′30″008
3	BERGER	Ferrari	63	+ 43″116	1′29″568
4	COULTHARD	Williams	63	+ 51″890	1′30″049
5	HÄKKINEN	McLaren	62		1′31″029
6	FRENTZEN	Sauber	62		1′31″754
7	HERBERT	Benetton	61		1′30″055
8	IRVINE	Jordan	61		1′30″868
9	PANIS	Ligier	61		1′31″135
10	MANSELL	McLaren	61		1′31″251
11	SUZUKI	Ligier	60		1′32″280
12	MARTINI	Minardi	59		1′32″505
13	MORBIDELLI	Pacific	59		1′33″415
14	BADOER	Minardi	59		1′33″838
15	DINIZ	Forti	56		1′37″872
16	MORENO	Forti	56		1′37″529

Winner's average: 181.921 kmh/113.044 mph.

Lap record: BERGER, Ferrari, 1′29″568 (196.744 kmh/122.254 mph), new record on modified circuit.

RETIREMENTS

Driver	Laps	Reason	Fastest lap
SCHUMACHER	10	accident	1′45″701
INOUE	12	spin	1′59″717
VERSTAPPEN	14	gearbox	1′44″585
MONTERMINI	15	gearbox	1′47″102
SALO	19	engine	1′39″837
KATAYAMA	23	spin	1′37″243
BARRICHELLO	31	gearbox	1′33″540
SCHIATTARELLA	35	suspension damage after going off track	1′35″534
GACHOT	36	gearbox	1′36″136
WENDLINGER	43	wheelnut jammed	1′33″617

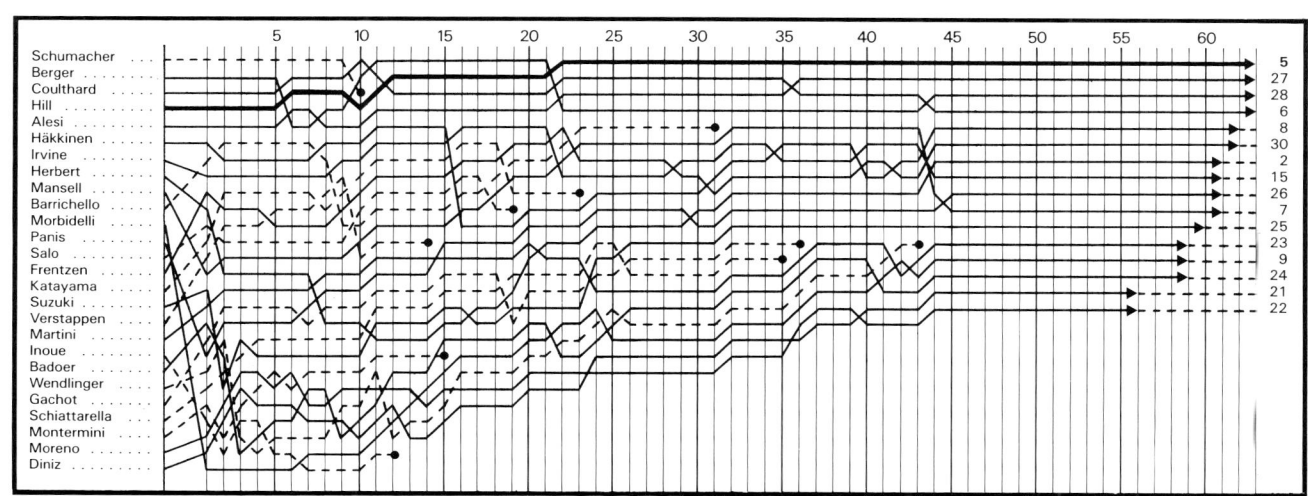

GRAN PREMIO DE ESPAÑA

Date:	May 14, 1995
Circuit:	65 laps of the Catalunya circuit (4.727 km/ 2.937 miles), 307.225 km/190.925 miles
Weather:	sunny and hot
Attendance:	53,000 spectators approx.
Previous winner:	Damon Hill, Williams, at 192.366 kmh/119.534 mph (1994)
Lap record:	Michael Schumacher, Benetton, 1'20"989 = 211.006 kmh/131.117 mph (1994)

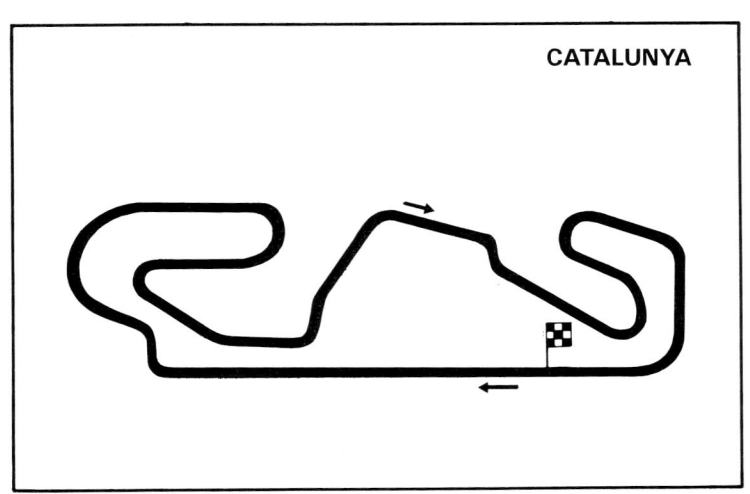

CATALUNYA

STARTING GRID

1. SCHUMACHER 1'21"452
Benetton B195-Renault RS7 V10

27. ALESI 1'22"052
Ferrari 412T2-Ferrari V12

28. BERGER 1'22"071
Ferrari 412T2-Ferrari V12

6. COULTHARD 1'22"332
Williams FW17-Renault RS7 V10

5. HILL 1'22"349
Williams FW17-Renault RS7 V10

15. IRVINE 1'23"705
Jordan 195-Peugeot V10

2. HERBERT 1'23"536
Benetton B195-Renault RS7 V10

14. BARRICHELLO 1'23"927
Jordan 195-Peugeot V10

8. HÄKKINEN 1'23"833
McLaren MP4/10-Mercedes F0110 V10

7. MANSELL 1'23"927
McLaren MP4/10-Mercedes F0110 V10

25. BRUNDLE 1'24"727
Ligier JS41-Mugen/Honda V10

30. FRENTZEN 1'24"802
Sauber C14-Ford Zetec-R V8

4. SALO 1'24"971
Tyrrell 023-Yamaha V10

17. MORBIDELLI 1'25"053
Footwork FA16-Hart V8

26. PANIS 1'25"204
Ligier JS41-Mugen/Honda V10

11. VERSTAPPEN 1'25"827
Simtek S951-Ford ED V8

3. KATAYAMA 1'25"946
Tyrrell 023-Yamaha V10

10. INOUE 1'26"059
Footwork FA16-Hart V8

23. MARTINI 1'26"619
Minardi M195-Ford EDM V8

29. WENDLINGER 1'27"007
Sauber C14-Ford Zetec-R V8

24. BADOER 1'27"345
Minardi M195-Ford EDM V8

12. SCHIATTARELLA 1'27"575
Simtek S951-Ford ED V8

17. MONTERMINI 1'28"084
Pacific PRO2-Ford ED V8

16. GACHOT 1'28"598
Pacific PRO2-Ford ED V8

22. MORENO 1'28"963
Forti FG01/95-Ford ED V8

21. DINIZ 1'29"540
Forti FG01/95-Ford ED V8

RESULTS

	Driver	Car	Laps	Time	Fastest lap
1	SCHUMACHER	Benetton	65	1.34'20"507	1'24"787
2	HERBERT	Benetton	65	+ 51"988	1'25"521
3	BERGER	Ferrari	65	+ 1'05"237	1'25"794
4	HILL	Williams	65	+ 2'01"749	1'24"531
5	IRVINE	Jordan	64		1'25"868
6	PANIS	Ligier	64		1'26"369
7	BARRICHELLO	Jordan	64		1'26"246
8	FRENTZEN	Sauber	64		1'27"328
9	BRUNDLE	Ligier	64		1'27"039
10	SALO	Tyrrell	64		1'27"823
11	MORBIDELLI	Footwork	63		1'27"284
12	VERSTAPPEN	Simtek	63		1'27"923
13	WENDLINGER	Sauber	63		1'27"991
14	MARTINI	Minardi	62		1'28"828
15	SCHIATTARELLA	Simtek	61		1'29"712

Winner's average: 195.32 kmh/121.37 mph.

Fastest lap: HILL, Williams, 1'24"531 (201.313 kmh/125.093 mph).

RETIREMENTS

Driver	Laps	Reason	Fastest lap
MONTERMINI	0	gearbox	
DINIZ	17	gearbox	1'32"423
MANSELL	18	dissatisfied with handling	1'27"054
BADOER	21	gearbox hydraulics	1'29"032
ALESI	25	engine	1'25"671
MORENO	39	spin	1'31"783
GACHOT	43	fire following refuelling	1'29"924
INOUE	43	engine fire	1'28"204
HÄKKINEN	53	fuel pressure	1'25"771
COULTHARD	54	gearbox	1'25"409
KATAYAMA	56	engine	1'27"467

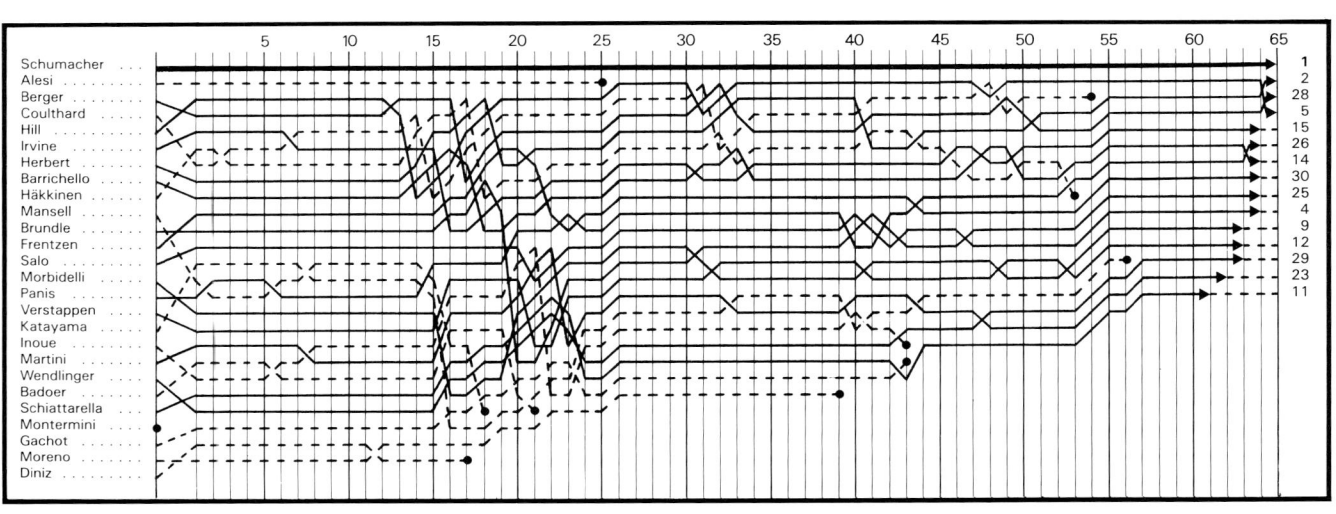

GRAND PRIX DE MONACO

Date:	May 28, 1995
Circuit:	78 laps of the Monaco street circuit (3.328 km/2.068 miles), 259.584 km/161.302 miles
Weather:	sunny and warm
Attendance:	120,000 spectators approx.
Previous winner:	Michael Schumacher, Benetton, at 141.690 kmh/88.044 mph (1994)
Lap record:	Michael Schumacher, Benetton 1'21"076 = 147.772 kmh/91.824 mph (1994)

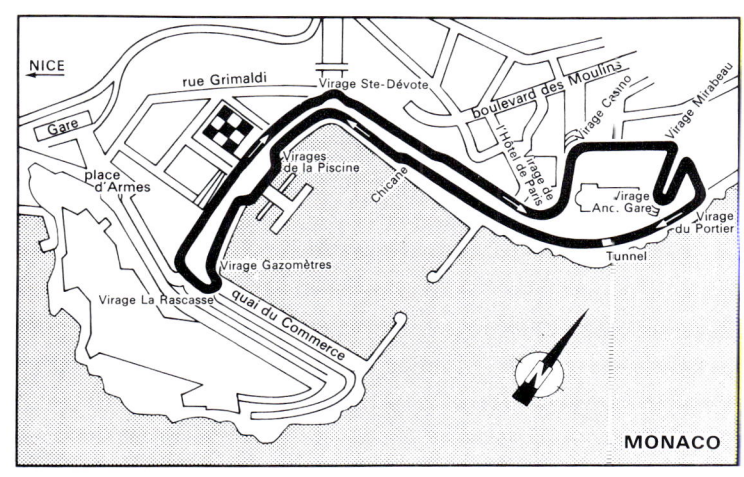

STARTING GRID

1. SCHUMACHER 1'22"742
Benetton B195-Renault RS7 V10

5. HILL 1'21"952
Williams FW17-Renault RS7 V10

28. BERGER 1'32"220
Ferrari 412T2-Ferrari V12

6. COULTHARD 1'23"109
Williams FW17-Renault RS7 V10

8. HÄKKINEN 1'23"857
McLaren MP4/10-Mercedes F0110 V10

27. ALESI 1'23"754
Ferrari 412T2-Ferrari V12

25. BRUNDLE 1'24"447
Ligier JS41-Mugen/Honda V10

2. HERBERT 1'23"885
Benetton B195-Renault RS7 V10

7. BLUNDELL 1'24"933
McLaren MP4/10-Mercedes F0110 V10

15. IRVINE 1'24"857
Jordan 195-Peugeot V10

26. PANIS 1'25"125
Ligier JS41-Mugen/Honda V10

14. BARRICHELLO 1'25"081
Jordan 195-Peugeot V10

30. FRENTZEN 1'25"661
Sauber C14-Ford Zetec-R V8

17. MORBIDELLI 1'25"447
Footwork FA16-Hart V8

24. BADOER 1'25"969
Minardi M195-Ford EDM V8

3. KATAYAMA 1'28"439
Tyrrell 023-Yamaha V10

23. MARTINI 1'26"913
Minardi M195-Ford EDM V8

4. SALO 1'26"473
Tyrrell 023-Yamaha V10

12. SCHIATTARELLA 1'28"337
Simtek S951-Ford ED V8

29. BOULLION 1'27"145
Sauber C14-Ford Zetec-R V8

21. DINIZ 1'29"244
Forti FG01/95-Ford ED V8

16. GACHOT 1'29"039
Pacific PR02-Ford ED V8

22. MORENO 1'29"608
Forti FG01/95-Ford ED V8

11. VERSTAPPEN 1'29"291
Simtek S951-Ford ED V8

10. INOUE 1'31"542
Footwork FA16-Hart V8

17. MONTERMINI 1'30"14
Pacific PR02-Ford ED V8

RESULTS

	Driver	Car	Laps	Time	Fastest lap
1	SCHUMACHER	Benetton	78	1.53'11"258	1'24"773
2	HILL	Williams	78	+ 38"817	1'24"790
3	BERGER	Ferrari	78	+ 1'11"447	1'25"379
4	HERBERT	Benetton	77		1'26"923
5	BLUNDELL	McLaren	77		1'26"717
6	FRENTZEN	Sauber	76		1'26"741
7	MARTINI	Minardi	76		1'27"761
8	BOULLION*	Sauber	75		1'28"417
9	MORBIDELLI	Footwork	74		1'27"532
10	DINIZ	Forti	72		1'30"193

* Retired but classified as a finisher.

Winner's average: 137.603 kmh/85.505 mph.

Fastest lap: ALESI, Ferrari, 1'24"621 (141.581 kmh/87.977 mph).

RETIREMENTS

Driver	Laps	Reason	Fastest lap
SCHIATTARELLA	0	gearbox control failure	
VERSTAPPEN	0	gearbox control failure	
HÄKKINEN	8	oil-pump	1'27"091
MORENO	9	accident resulting from brake problems	1'30"532
COULTHARD	16	gearbox	1'25"884
IRVINE	22	wheel failure	1'26"933
MONTERMINI	23	disqualified for non-compliance stop-and-go penalty	1'29"548
KATAYAMA	26	accident	1'27"538
INOUE	27	gearbox	1'30"174
BRUNDLE	41	spin into barrier	1'25"985
ALESI	41	collision with spinning Brundle	1'24"621
GACHOT	42	gearbox	1'30"394
BARRICHELLO	60	jammed throttle	1'26"279
SALO	63	engine	1'27"914
PANIS	65	accident	1'26"819
BADOER	68	suspension	1'27"359
BOULLION	75	collision with Morbidelli	1'28"417

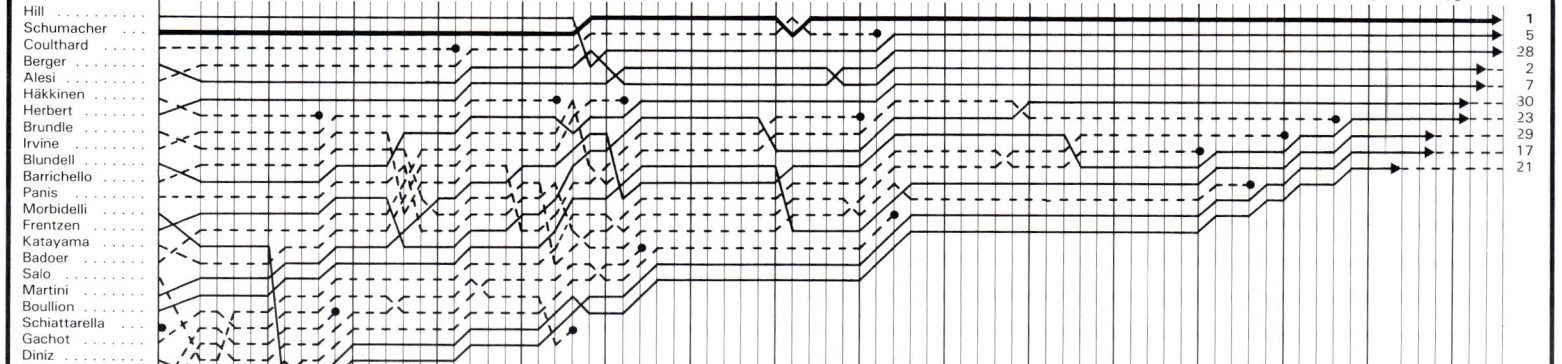

GRAND PRIX DU CANADA

Date:	June 11, 1995
Circuit:	69 laps of the Gilles Villeneuve circuit, Montreal, 4.45 km/2.765 miles, 307.05 km/190.797 miles
Weather:	cloudy
Attendance:	60,000 spectators approx.
Previous winner:	Michael Schumacher, Benetton, at 176.243 kmh/109.515 mph (1994)
Lap record:	Michael Schumacher, Benetton, 1'21"500 = 195.681 kmh/121.594 mph (1993)

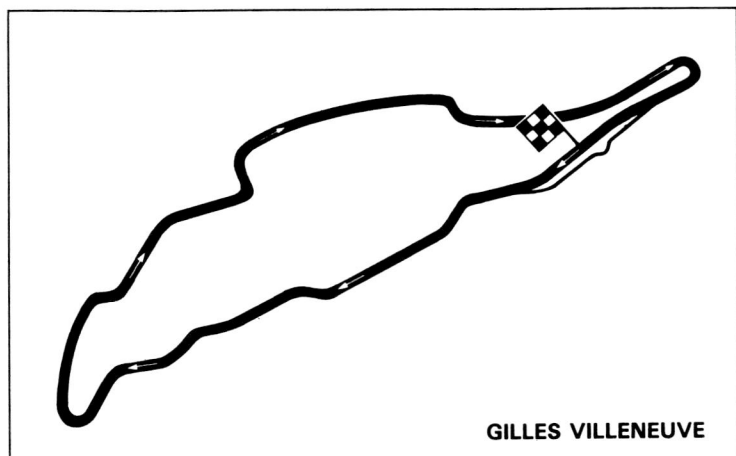

GILLES VILLENEUVE

STARTING GRID

1. SCHUMACHER 1'27"661
Benetton B195-Renault RS7 V10

5. HILL 1'28"039
Williams FW17-Renault RS7 V10

6. COULTHARD 1'28"091
Williams FW17-Renault RS7 V10

28. BERGER 1'28"189
Ferrari 412T2-Ferrari V12

27. ALESI 1'28"474
Ferrari 412T2-Ferrari V12

2. HERBERT 1'28"498
Benetton B195-Renault RS7 V10

8. HÄKKINEN 1'28"910
McLaren MP4/10-Mercedes F0110 V10

15. IRVINE 1'29"021
Jordan 195-Peugeot V10

14. BARRICHELLO 1'29"171
Jordan 195-Peugeot V10

7. BLUNDELL 1'29"641
McLaren MP4/10-Mercedes F0110 V10

26. PANIS 1'29"809
Ligier JS41-Mugen/Honda V10

30. FRENTZEN 1'30"017
Sauber C14-Ford Zetec-R V8

9. MORBIDELLI 1'30"159
Footwork FA16-Hart V8

25. BRUNDLE 1'30"255
Ligier JS41-Mugen/Honda V10

4. SALO 1'30"657
Tyrrell 023-Yamaha V10

3. KATAYAMA 1'31"382
Tyrrell 023-Yamaha V10

23. MARTINI 1'31"445
Minardi M195-Ford EDM V8

29. BOULLION 1'31"838
Sauber C14-Ford Zetec-R V8

24. BADOER 1'31"853
Minardi M195-Ford EDM V8

16. GACHOT 1'32"841
Pacific PR02-Ford ED V8

17. MONTERMINI 1'32"894
Pacific PR02-Ford ED V8

10. INOUE 1'32"995
Footwork FA16-Hart V8

22. MORENO 1'34"000
Forti FG01/95-Ford ED V8

21. DINIZ 1'34"982
Forti FG01/95-Ford ED V8

RESULTS

	Driver	Car	Laps	Time	Fastest lap
1	ALESI	Ferrari	69	1.46'31"333	1'30"398
2	BARRICHELLO	Jordan	69	+ 31"687	1'30"626
3	IRVINE	Jordan	69	+ 33"270	1'30"874
4	PANIS	Ligier	69	+ 36"506	1'31"654
5	SCHUMACHER	Benetton	69	+ 37"060	1'29"174
6	MORBIDELLI	Footwork	68		1'31"791
7	SALO	Tyrrell	68		1'32"153
8	BADOER	Minardi	68		1'33"000
9	INOUE	Footwork	67		1'33"079

Winner's average: 172.172 kmh/106.986 mph.

Fastest lap: SCHUMACHER, Benetton, 1'29"174 (178.841 kmh/111.13 mph).

Note: Positions as at the end of lap 68. Lap 69 void due to crowd invasion of track.

RETIREMENTS

Driver	Laps	Reason	Fastest lap
HERBERT	0	collision with Häkkinen	
HÄKKINEN	0	collision with Herbert	
COULTHARD	1	spin	1'40"928
MONTERMINI	5	gearbox hydraulics	1'35"588
BOULLION	19	spin	1'32"975
DINIZ	26	gearbox	1'38"055
FRENTZEN	26	engine	1'31"155
GACHOT	36	battery	1'33"607
KATAYAMA	42	engine	1'32"435
BLUNDELL	47	driveshaft	1'31"527
HILL	50	gearbox hydraulics	1'30"783
MORENO	54	fuel pump	1'36"483
MARTINI	60	throttle linkage	1'32"855
BRUNDLE	61	collision with Berger	1'31"496
BERGER	61	collision with Brundle	1'30"491

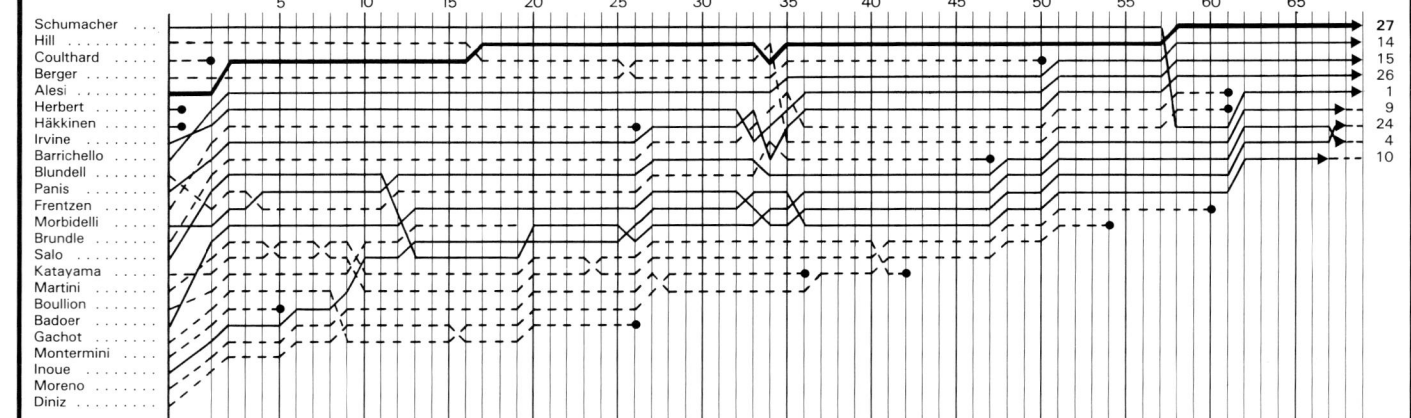

GRAND PRIX DE FRANCE

Date:	July 2, 1995
Circuit:	72 laps of the Nevers-Magny-Cours circuit (4.25 km/2.641 miles), 306 km/190.145 miles
Weather:	cloudy, light rain at mid-race
Attendance:	71,000 spectators approx.
Previous winner:	Michael Schumacher, Benetton, at 186.216 kmh/115.712 mph (1994)
Lap record:	Nigel Mansell, Williams, 1'17"070 = 198.521 kmh/123.359 mph (1992)

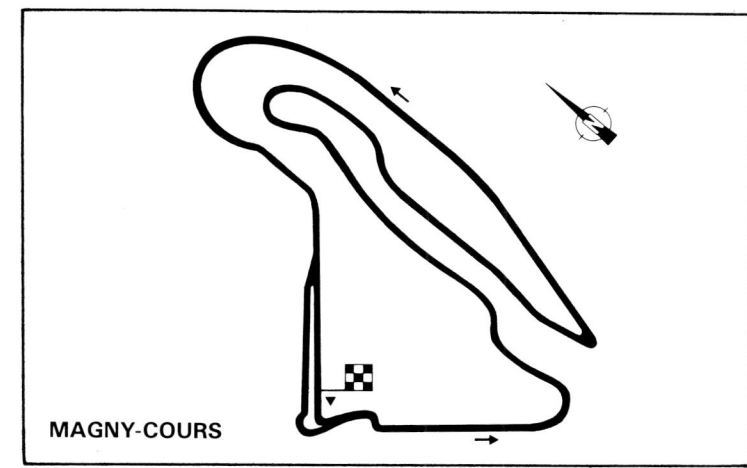

MAGNY-COURS

STARTING GRID

1. SCHUMACHER 1'17"512
Benetton B195-Renault RS7/B V10

5. HILL 1'17"225
Williams FW17-Renault RS7/B V10

27. ALESI 1'18"761
Ferrari 412T2-Ferrari 44/B V12

6. COULTHARD 1'17"925
Williams FW17-Renault RS7/B V10

26. PANIS 1'19"047
Ligier JS41-Mugen/Honda V10

14. BARRICHELLO 1'18"810
Jordan 195-Peugeot V10

8. HÄKKINEN 1'19"238
McLaren MP4/10-Mercedes F0110 V10

28. BERGER 1'19"051
Ferrari 412T2-Ferrari 44/B V12

2. HERBERT 1'19"555
Benetton B195-Renault RS7/B V10

25. BRUNDLE 1'19"384
Ligier JS41-Mugen/Honda V10

30. FRENTZEN 1'20"309
Sauber C14-Ford Zetec-R V8

15. IRVINE 1'19"845
Jordan 195-Peugeot V10

4. SALO 1'20"796
Tyrrell 023-Yamaha V10

7. BLUNDELL 1'20"527
McLaren MP4/10-Mercedes F0110 V10

9. MORBIDELLI 1'21"076
Footwork FA16-Hart V8

29. BOULLION 1'20"943
Sauber C14-Ford Zetec-R V8

10. INOUE 1'21"894
Footwork FA16-Hart V8

24. BADOER 1'21"323
Minardi M195-Ford EDM V8

23. MARTINI 1'22"104
Minardi M195-Ford EDM V8

3. KATAYAMA 1'21"930
Tyrrell 023-Yamaha V10

16. GACHOT 1'23"647
Pacific PR02-Ford ED V8

17. MONTERMINI 1'23"466
Pacific PR02-Ford ED V8

22. MORENO 1'24"865
Forti FG01/95-Ford ED V8

21. DINIZ 1'24"184
Forti FG01/95-Ford ED V8

RESULTS

	Driver	Car	Laps	Time	Fastest lap
1	SCHUMACHER	Benetton	72	1.38'28"429	1'20"218
2	HILL	Williams	72	+ 31"309	1'20"635
3	COULTHARD	Williams	72	+ 1'02"823	1'21"235
4	BRUNDLE	Ligier	72	+ 1'03"293	1'21"005
5	ALESI	Ferrari	72	+ 1'17"869	1'21"360
6	BARRICHELLO	Jordan	71		1'21"455
7	HÄKKINEN	McLaren	71		1'22"058
8	PANIS	Ligier	71		1'21"398
9	IRVINE	Jordan	71		1'21"541
10	FRENTZEN	Sauber	71		1'22"688
11	BLUNDELL	McLaren	70		1'22"698
12	BERGER	Ferrari	70		1'21"782
13	BADOER	Minardi	69		1'24"546
14	MORBIDELLI	Footwork	69		1'24"256
15	SALO	Tyrrell	69		1'23"711
16	MORENO	Forti	66		1'26"748
	MONTERMINI*	Pacific	60		1'24"812

* Finished, but did not qualify (insufficient distance covered).

Winner's average: 186.322 kmh/115.778 mph.

Fastest lap: SCHUMACHER, Benetton, 1'20"218 (190.73 kmh/118.517 mph).

RETIREMENTS

Driver	Laps	Reason	Fastest lap
DINIZ	0	collision with Martini and Montermini	
INOUE	0	collision with Katayama	
KATAYAMA	0	collision with Inoue	
HERBERT	2	hit by Alesi; spun off	1'23"080
MARTINI	23	gearbox	1'24"354
GACHOT	24	gearbox	1'26"158
BOULLION	48	driveshaft	1'22"866

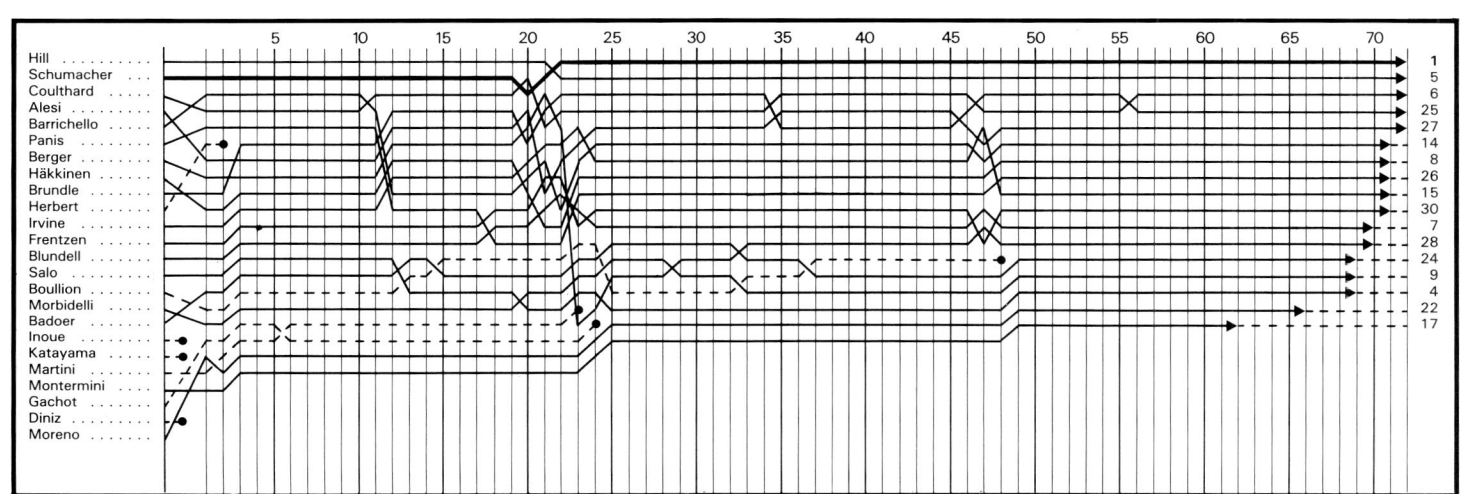

BRITISH GRAND PRIX

Date:	July 16, 1995
Circuit:	61 laps of the Silverstone circuit (5.057 km/3.142 miles), 308.477 km/191.684 miles
Weather:	cloudy
Attendance:	90,000 spectators approx.
Previous winner:	Damon Hill, Williams, at 202.143 kmh/125.609 mph (1994)
Lap record:	Damon Hill, Williams, 1'27"100 = 209.014 kmh/129.878 mph (1994 – modified circuit)

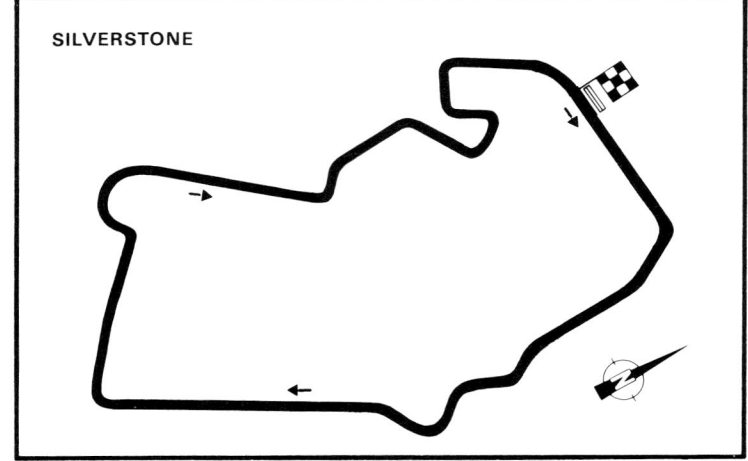

STARTING GRID

5. HILL 1'28"124
Williams FW17-Renault RS7/B V10

1. SCHUMACHER 1'28"397
Benetton B195-Renault RS7/B V10

6. COULTHARD 1'28"947
Williams FW17-Renault RS7/B V10

28. BERGER 1'29"657
Ferrari 412T2-Ferrari 44/B V12

2. HERBERT 1'29"867
Benetton B195-Renault RS7/B V10

27. ALESI 1'29"874
Ferrari 412T2-Ferrari 44/B V12

15. IRVINE 1'30"083
Jordan 195-Peugeot V10

8. HÄKKINEN 1'30"140
McLaren MP4/10-Mercedes F0110 V10

14. BARRICHELLO 1'30"354
Jordan 195-Peugeot V10

7. BLUNDELL 1'30"453
McLaren MP4/10-Mercedes F0110 V10

25. BRUNDLE 1'30"946
Ligier JS41-Mugen/Honda V10

30. FRENTZEN 1'31"602
Sauber C14-Ford Zetec-R V8

26. PANIS 1'31"842
Ligier JS41-Mugen/Honda V10

3. KATAYAMA 1'32"087
Tyrrell 023-Yamaha V10

23. MARTINI 1'32"259
Minardi M195-Ford EDM V8

29. BOULLION 1'33"323
Sauber C14-Ford Zetec-R V8

9. PAPIS 1'34"154
Footwork FA16-Hart V8

24. BADOER 1'34"556
Minardi M195-Ford EDM V8

10. INOUE 1'35"232
Footwork FA16-Hart V8

21. DINIZ 1'36"023
Forti FG01/95-Ford ED V8

16. GACHOT 1'36"076
Pacific PRO2-Ford ED V8

22. MORENO 1'36"651
Forti FG01/95-Ford ED V8

4. SALO 1'48"639
Tyrrell 023-Yamaha V10

17. MONTERMINI 1'52"398
Pacific PRO2-Ford ED V8

RESULTS

	Driver	Car	Laps	Time	Fastest lap
1	HERBERT	Benetton	61	1.34'35"093	1'31"149
2	ALESI	Ferrari	61	+ 16"479	1'30"768
3	COULTHARD	Williams	61	+ 23"888	1'30"812
4	PANIS	Ligier	61	+ 1'33"168	1'31"393
5	BLUNDELL	McLaren	61	+ 1'48"172	1'31"694
6	FRENTZEN	Sauber	60		1'33"012
7	MARTINI	Minardi	60		1'33"774
8	SALO	Tyrrell	60		1'33"061
9	BOULLION	Sauber	60		1'32"588
10	BADOER	Minardi	60		1'33"631
11	BARRICHELLO*	Jordan	59		1'30"841
12	GACHOT	Pacific	58		1'36"313

*Retired but classified as a finisher.

Winner's average: 195.682 kmh/121.594 mph.

Fastest lap: HILL, Williams, 1'29"752 (202.838 kmh/126.041 mph).

RETIREMENTS

Driver	Laps	Reason	Fastest lap
IRVINE	2	overheating	1'43"961
DINIZ	13	gearbox	1'37"859
INOUE	16	spun and stalled engine	1'35"021
BRUNDLE	16	spin	1'31"881
BERGER	20	loose left front wheel	1'31"435
HÄKKINEN	20	electrical failure	1'31"901
MONTERMINI	21	spin	1'36"445
KATAYAMA	22	out of fuel	1'33"242
PAPIS	28	broke wheel-rim on pit-lane	1'34"633
SCHUMACHER	45	collision with Hill	1'30"271
HILL	45	collision with Schumacher	1'29"752
MORENO	48	engine	1'37"734
BARRICHELLO	59	collision with Blundell	1'30"841

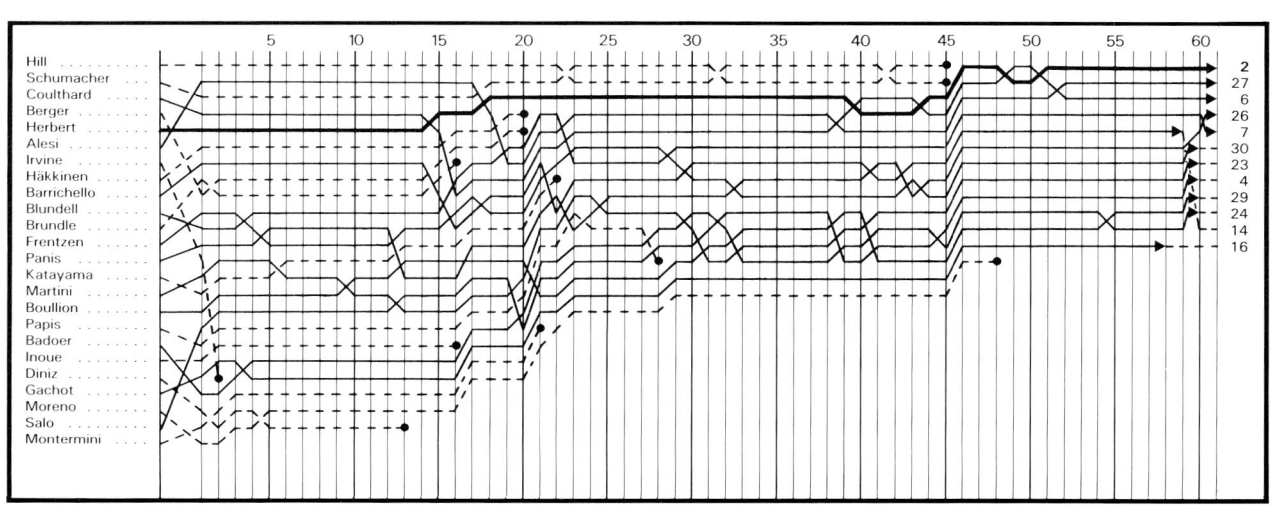

GROSSER PREIS VON DEUTSCHLAND

Date:	July 30, 1995
Circuit:	45 laps of the Hockenheim circuit (6.815 km/ 4.235 miles), 306.675 km/190.564 miles
Weather:	fine and hot
Attendance:	90,000 spectators approx.
Previous winner:	Gerhard Berger, Ferrari, at 222.97 kmh/138.551 mph (1994)
Lap record:	Riccardo Patrese, Williams, 1'41"591 = 241.498 kmh/150.064 mph (1992)

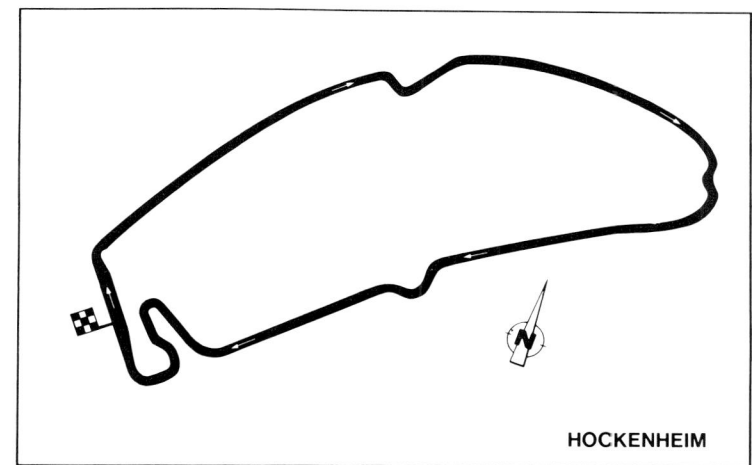

HOCKENHEIM

STARTING GRID

5. HILL 1'44"385
Williams FW17-Renault RS7/B V10

1. SCHUMACHER 1'44"465
Benetton B195-Renault RS7/B V10

6. COULTHARD 1'44"540
Williams FW17-Renault RS7/B V10

28. BERGER 1'45"553
Ferrari 412T2-Ferrari 44/B V12

14. BARRICHELLO 1'45"765
Jordan 195-Peugeot V10

15. IRVINE 1'45"846
Jordan 195-Peugeot V10

8. HÄKINNEN 1'45"849
McLaren MP4/10-Mercedes F0110 V10

7. BLUNDELL 1'46"221
McLaren MP4/10-Mercedes F0110 V10

2. HERBERT 1'46"315
Benetton B195-Renault RS7/B V10

27. ALESI 1'46"356
Ferrari 412T2-Ferrari 44/B V12

30. FRENTZEN 1'46"801
Sauber C14-Ford Zetec-R V8

26. PANIS 1'47"372
Ligier JS41-Mugen/Honda V10

4. SALO 1'47"507
Tyrrell 023-Yamaha V10

29. BOULLION 1'47"636
Sauber C14-Ford Zetec-R V8

9. PAPIS 1'48"093
Footwork FA16-Hart V8

24. BADOER 1'49"302
Minardi M195-Ford EDM V8

3. KATAYAMA 1'49"402
Tyrrell 023-Yamaha V10

25. SUZUKI 1'49"716
Ligier JS41-Mugen/Honda V10

10. INOUE 1'49"892
Footwork FA16-Hart V8

23. MARTINI 1'49"990
Minardi M195-Ford EDM V8

21. DINIZ 1'52"961
Forti FG01/95-Ford ED V8

22. MORENO 1'53"405
Forti FG01/95-Ford ED V8

17. MONTERMINI 1'53"492
Pacific PRO2-Ford ED V8

16. LAVAGGI 1'54"625
Pacific PRO2-Ford ED V8

RESULTS

	Driver	Car	Laps	Time	Fastest lap
1	SCHUMACHER	Benetton	45	1.22'56"043	1'48"824
2	COULTHARD	Williams	45	+ 5"988	1'49"714
3	BERGER	Ferrari	45	+ 1'08"067	1'49"926
4	HERBERT	Benetton	45	+ 1'23"436	1'50"929
5	BOULLION	Sauber	44		1'52"033
6	SUZUKI	Ligier	44		1'51"760
7	KATAYAMA	Tyrrell	44		1'52"791
8	MONTERMINI	Pacific	42		1'54"341
9	IRVINE*	Jordan	41		1'50"646

*Retired but classified as a finisher.

Winner's average: 222.12 kmh/138.023 mph.

Fastest lap: SCHUMACHER, Benetton, 1'48"824 (225.711 kmh/140.254 mph).

RETIREMENTS

Driver	Laps	Reason	Fastest lap
PAPIS	0	gearbox	
SALO	0	clutch	
HILL	1	spun off	1'53"989
DINIZ	8	brakes	2'02"176
INOUE	9	gearbox	1'53"541
MARTINI	11	engine	1'54"210
ALESI	12	engine	1'50"672
PANIS	13	leak in cooling system	1'50"690
BLUNDELL	17	engine	1'50"781
BARRICHELLO	20	engine	1'49"927
MORENO	27	transmission	1'56"038
LAVAGGI	27	gearbox	1'58"836
BADOER	28	gearbox oil-leak	1'52"859
FRENTZEN	32	engine	1'51"426
HÄKKINEN	33	engine	1'49"900
IRVINE	41	electrical failure	1'50"646

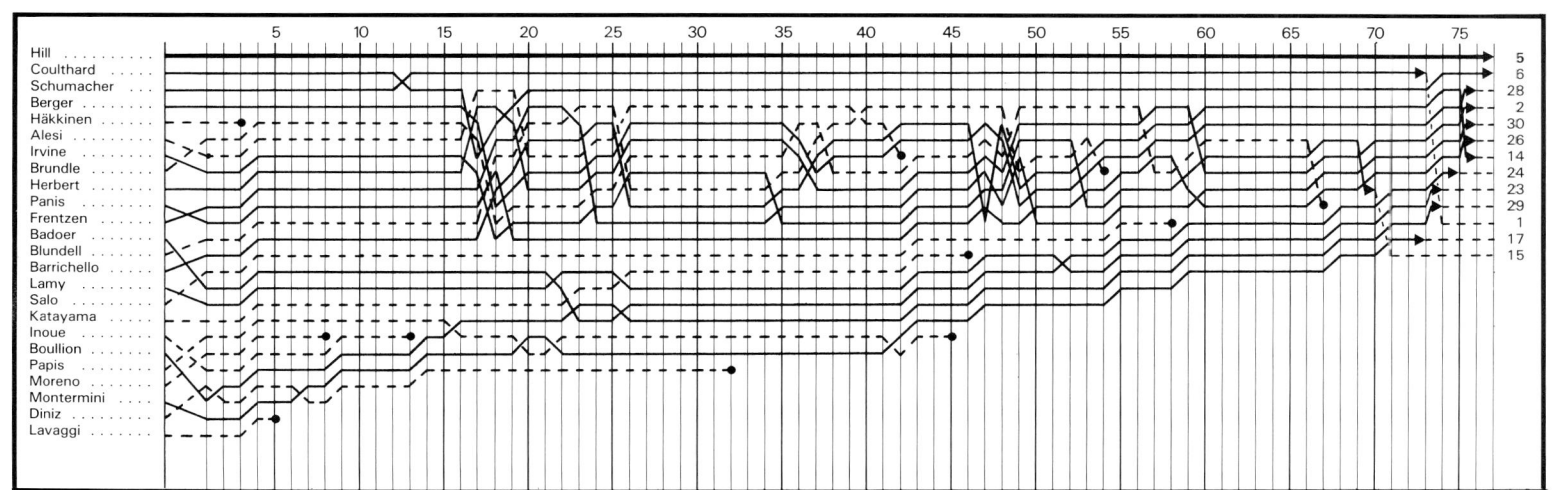

MAGYARERSZAG NAGYDIJ

Date:	August 13, 1995
Circuit:	77 laps of the Hungaroring circuit (3.968 km/ 2.466 miles), 305.536 km/189.856 miles
Weather:	light cloud cover
Attendance:	80,000 spectators approx.
Previous winner:	Michael Schumacher, Benetton, at 169.737 kmh/105.473 mph (1994)
Lap record:	Nigel Mansell, Williams, 1'18"308 = 182.418 kmh/113.352 mph (1992)

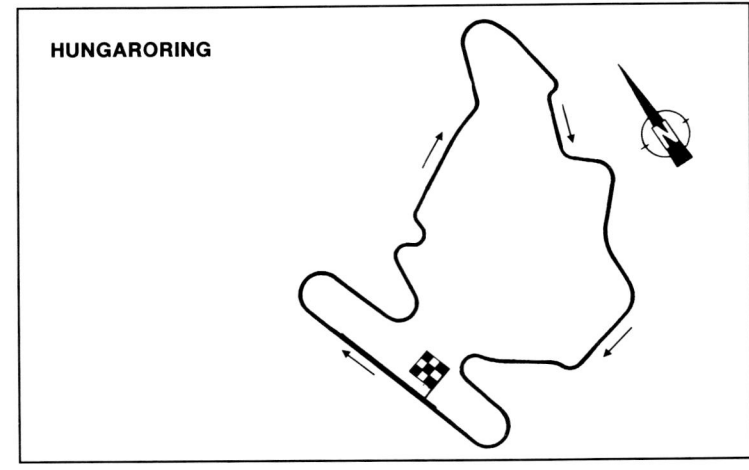

HUNGARORING

STARTING GRID

5. HILL 1'16"982
Williams FW17-Renault RS7/B V10

6. COULTHARD 1'17"366
Williams FW17-Renault RS7/B V10

1. SCHUMACHER 1'17"558
Benetton B195-Renault RS7/B V10

28. BERGER 1'18"059
Ferrari 412T2-Ferrari 44/B V12

8. HÄKKINEN 1'18"363
McLaren MP4/10-Mercedes F0110 V10

27. ALESI 1'18"968
Ferrari 412T2-Ferrari 44/B V12

15. IRVINE 1'19"499
Jordan 195-Peugeot V10

25. BRUNDLE 1'19"748
Ligier JS41-Mugen/Honda V10

2. HERBERT 1'20"072
Benetton B195-Renault RS7/E V10

26. PANIS 1'20"160
Ligier JS41-Mugen/Honda V10

30. FRENTZEN 1'20"413
Sauber C14-Ford Zetec-R V8

24. BADOER 1'20"543
Minardi M195-Ford EDM V8

7. BLUNDELL 1'20"640
McLaren MP4/10-Mercedes F0110 V10

14. BARRICHELLO 1'20"902
Jordan 195-Peugeot V10

23. LAMY 1'21"156
Minardi M195-Ford EDM V8

4. SALO 1'21"624
Tyrrell 023-Yamaha V10

3. KATAYAMA 1'21"702
Tyrrell 023-Yamaha V10

10. INOUE 1'22"081
Footwork FA16-Hart V8

29. BOULLION 1'22"161
Sauber C14-Ford Zetec-R V8

9. PAPIS 1'23"275
Footwork FA16-Hart V8

22. MORENO 1'24"351
Forti FG01/95-Ford ED V8

17. MONTERMINI 1'24"371
Pacific PRO2-Ford ED V8

21. DINIZ 1'24"695
Forti FG01/95-Ford ED V8

16. LAVAGGI 1'226"670
Pacific PRO2-Ford ED V8

RESULTS

	Driver	Car	Laps	Time	Fastest lap
1	HILL	Williams	77	1.46'25"721	1'20"247
2	COULTHARD	Williams	77	+ 33"398	1'21"126
3	BERGER	Ferrari	76		1'22"371
4	HERBERT	Benetton	76		1'22"560
5	FRENTZEN	Sauber	76		1'23"146
6	PANIS	Ligier	76		1'21"343
7	BARRICHELLO	Jordan	76		1'22"677
8	BADOER	Minardi	75		1'23"608
9	LAMY	Minardi	74		1'24"269
10	BOULLION	Sauber	74		1'23"424
11	SCHUMACHER*	Benetton	73		1'20"506
12	MONTERMINI	Pacific	73		1'22"663
13	IRVINE*	Jordan	70		1'22"211

* Retired but classified as a finisher.

Winner's average: 172.248 kmh/107.033 mph.

Fastest lap: HILL, Williams, 1'20"247 (178.010 kmh/110.613 mph), new record.

RETIREMENTS

Driver	Laps	Reason	Fastest lap
HÄKKINEN	3	engine	1'22"720
LAVAGGI	5	spin	1'27"894
MORENO	8	throttle control	1'26"556
INOUE	13	engine	1'24"804
DINIZ	32	engine	1'26"913
ALESI	42	spark plug failed	1'22"276
PAPIS	45	brake hydraulics	1'25"730
KATAYAMA	46	accident	1'23"994
BLUNDELL	54	fuel leak	1'22"235
SALO	58	electrical failure	1'23"556
BRUNDLE	67	engine	1'21"977
IRVINE	70	transmission	1'22"211
SCHUMACHER	73	engine	1'20"506

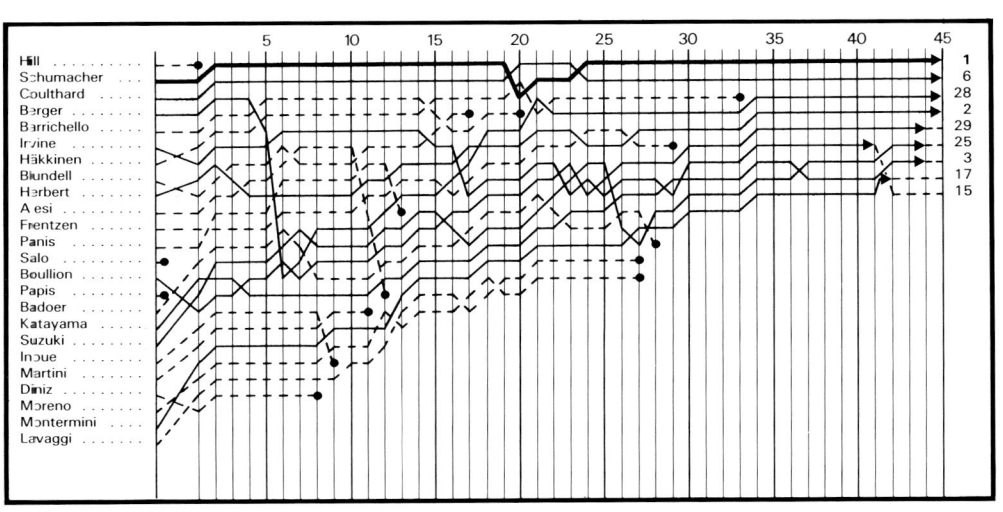

GRAND PRIX DE BELGIQUE

Date:	August 27, 1995
Circuit:	44 laps of the Spa-Francorchamps circuit (6.974 km/ 4.334 miles), 306.856 km/190.677 miles
Weather:	cloudy, occasional showers, heavy at times
Attendance:	100,000 spectators approx.
Previous winner:	Damon Hill, Williams, at 208.170 kmh/129.354 mph (1994)
Lap record:	Alain Prost, Williams, 1'51"095 = 225.990 kmh/140.427 mph (1993)

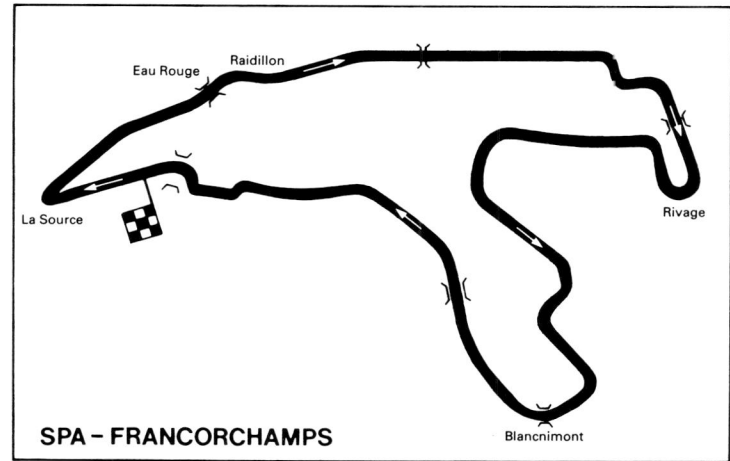

SPA – FRANCORCHAMPS

STARTING GRID

27. ALESI 1'54"631
Ferrari 412T2-Ferrari 44/B V12

28. BERGER 1'54"392
Ferrari 412T2-Ferrari 44/B V12

2. HERBERT 1'56"085
Benetton B195-Renault RS7/B V10

8. HÄKKINEN 1'55"435
McLaren MP4/10-Mercedes F0110 V10

7. BLUNDELL 1'56"622
McLaren MP4/10-Mercedes F0110 V10

6. COULTHARD 1'56"254
Williams FW17-Renault RS7/B V10

5. HILL 1'57"768
Williams FW17-Renault RS7/B V10

15. IRVINE 1'57"001
Jordan 195-Peugeot V10

30. FRENTZEN 1'58"148
Sauber C14-Ford Zetec-R V8

26. PANIS 1'58"021
Ligier JS41-Mugen/Honda V10

14. BARRICHELLO 1'58"293
Jordan 195-Peugeot V10

4. SALO 1'58"224
Tyrrell 023-Yamaha V10

29. BOULLION 1'58"356
Sauber C14-Ford Zetec-R V8

25. BRUNDLE 1'58"314
Ligier JS41-Mugen/Honda V10

1. SCHUMACHER 1'59"079
Benetton B195-Renault RS7/B V10

3. KATAYAMA 1'58"551
Tyrrell 023-Yamaha V10

10. INOUE 2'00"990
Footwork FA16-Hart V8

23. LAMY 1'59"256
Minardi M195-Ford EDM V8

9. PAPIS 2'01"685
Footwork FA16-Hart V8

24. BADOER 2'01"013
Minardi M195-Ford EDM V8

22. MORENO 2'03"817
Forti FG01/95-Ford ED V8

17. MONTERMINI 2'02"405
Pacific PR02-Ford ED V8

21. DINIZ 2'09"537
Forti FG01/95-Ford ED V8

16. LAVAGGI 2'06"407
Pacific PR02-Ford ED V8

RESULTS

	Driver	Car	Laps	Time	Fastest lap
1	SCHUMACHER	Benetton	44	1.36'47"875	1'53"613
2	HILL	Williams	44	+ 19"493	1'54"473
3	BRUNDLE	Ligier	44	+ 24"998	1'56"502
4	FRENTZEN	Sauber	44	+ 26"972	1'56"261
5	BLUNDELL	McLaren	44	+ 33"772	1'55"972
6	BARRICHELLO	Jordan	44	+ 39"674	1'56"967
7	HERBERT	Benetton	44	+ 54"048	1'55"630
8	SALO	Tyrrell	44	+ 54"548	1'57"420
9	PANIS	Footwork	44	+ 1'06"170	1'56"696
10	LAMY	Minardi	44	+ 1'19"789	1'58"312
11	BOULLION	Sauber	43		1'57"927
12	INOUE	Footwork	43		1'59"331
13	DINIZ	Forti	42		2'02"546
14	MORENO	Forti	42		2'02"603

Winner's average: 190.204 kmh/118.19 mph.

Fastest lap: COULTHARD, Williams, 1'53"412 (221.373 kmh/137.559 mph), new lap record.

RETIREMENTS

Driver	Laps	Reason	Fastest lap
HÄKKINEN	1	spin	2'07"082
ALESI	4	suspension damage	1'56"853
COULTHARD	13	gearbox	1'53"412
MONTERMINI	18	out of fuel	2'00"136
PAPIS	20	spin	1'57"866
IRVINE	21	refuelling fire	1'55"561
BERGER	22	electrical problem	1'55"462
BADOER	23	accident	1'58"395
LAVAGGI	27	gearbox	2'04"196
KATAYAMA	28	accident	1'57"229

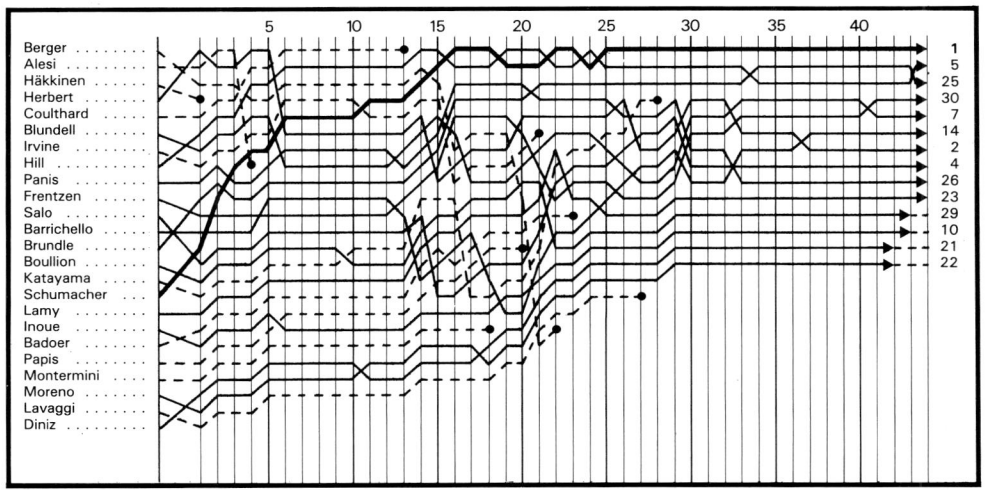

GRAN PREMIO D'ITALIA

Date:	September 10, 1995
Circuit:	53 laps of the Monza circuit (5.77 km/3.585 miles), 305.81 km/190.027 miles
Weather:	light cloud
Attendance:	75,000 spectators approx.
Previous winner:	Damon Hill, Williams, at 236.073 kmh/146.693 mph (1994)
Lap record:	Damon Hill, Williams, 1'23"575 = 249.835 kmh/155.244 mph (1993)

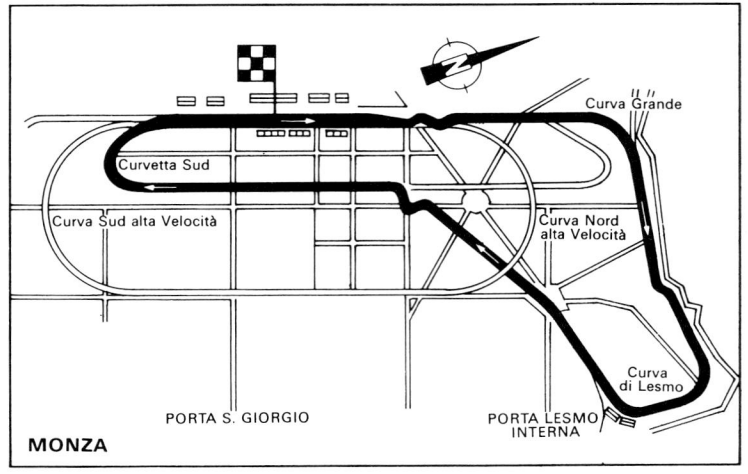

MONZA

STARTING GRID

6. COULTHARD 1'24"462
Williams FW17-Renault RS7/B V10

1. SCHUMACHER 1'25"026
Benetton B195-Renault RS7/B V10

28. BERGER 1'25"353
Ferrari 412T2-Ferrari 44/B V12

5. HILL 1'25"699
Williams FW17-Renault RS7/B V10

27. ALESI 1'25"707
Ferrari 412T2-Ferrari 44/B V12

14. BARRICHELLO 1'25"919
Jordan 195-Peugeot V10

8. HÄKKINEN 1'25"920
McLaren MP4/10-Mercedes F0110 V10

2. HERBERT 1'26"433
Benetton B195-Renault RS7/B V10

7. BLUNDELL 1'26"472
McLaren MP4/10-Mercedes F0110 V10

30. FRENTZEN 1'26"541
Sauber C14-Ford Zetec-R V8

25. BRUNDLE 1'26"XXX
Ligier JS41-Mugen/Honda V10

15. IRVINE 1'27"271
Jordan 195-Peugeot V10

26. PANIS 1'27"384
Ligier JS41-Mugen/Honda V10

29. BOULLION** 1'28"741
Sauber C14-Ford Zetec-R V8

9. PAPIS 1'28"870
Footwork FA16-Hart V8

4. SALO 1'29"028
Tyrrell 023-Yamaha V10

3. KATAYAMA 1'29"287
Tyrrell 023-Yamaha V10

24. BADOER 1'29"559
Minardi M195-Ford EDM V8

23. LAMY 1'29"936
Minardi M195-Ford EDM V8

10. INOUE 1'30"515
Footwork FA16-Hart V8

17. MONTERMINI* 1'30"721
Pacific PR02-Ford ED V8

22. MORENO* 1'30"834
Forti FG01/95-Ford ED V8

21. DINIZ 1'23"102
Forti FG01/95-Ford ED V8

16. LAVAGGI 1'32"470
Pacific PR02-Ford ED V8

* Did not participate in re-start (no spare car).
** Re-started from pit-lane.

RESULTS

	Driver	Car	Laps	Time	Fastest lap
1	HERBERT	Benetton	53	1.18'27"916	1'26"481
2	HÄKKINEN	McLaren	53	+ 17"779	1'26"869
3	FRENTZEN	Sauber	53	+ 24"321	1'27"138
4	BLUNDELL	McLaren	53	+ 28"223	1'26"784
5	SALO	Tyrrell	52		1'28"795
6	BOULLION	Sauber	52		1'28"976
7	PAPIS	Footwork	52		1'29"402
8	INOUE	Footwork	52		1'29"426
9	DINIZ	Forti	50		1'31"563
10	KATAYAMA	Tyrrell	47		1'28"909

Winner's average: 233.814 kmh/145.289 mph.

Fastest lap: BERGER, Ferrari, 1'26"419 (240.363 kmh/149.359 mph).

RETIREMENTS

Driver	Laps	Reason	Fastest lap
MONTERMINI	0	involved in collision following spin by Papis	
MORENO	0	collision with Papis	
After re-start:			
LAMY	0	driveshaft	
LAVAGGI	6	spin	1'33"023
BRUNDLE	10	damage following return to pits with punctured left rear tyre	1'29"424
COULTHARD	13	spin following front wheel-bearing failure	1'26"936
PANIS	20	spin	1'28"710
SCHUMACHER	23	hit by Hill	1'26"969
HILL	23	collision with Schumacher	1'26"936
BADOER	26	accident	1'29"175
BERGER	26	front suspension damaged by hitting camera detached from Alesi's car	1'26"419
IRVINE	40	engine	1'27"472
BARRICHELLO	43	transmission	1'26"970
ALESI	45	right rear suspension failed	1'26"818

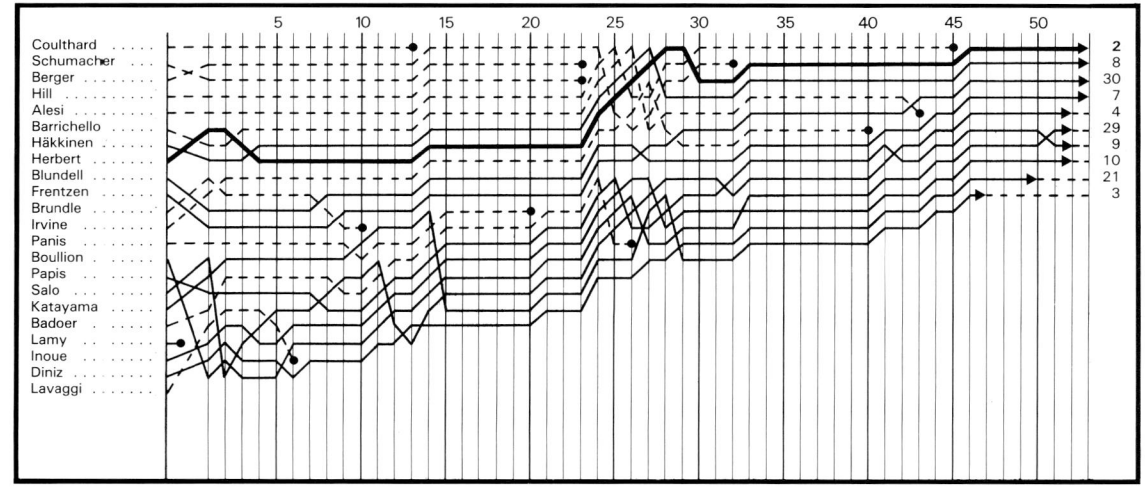

GRANDE PRÊMIO DE PORTUGAL

Date:	September 24, 1995
Circuit:	71 laps of the Estoril circuit (4.36 km/2.709 miles), 309.56 km/192.357 miles
Weather:	fine and warm
Attendance:	70,000 spectators approx.
Previous winner:	Damon Hill, Williams, at 183.589 kmh/114.08 mph (1994)
Lap record:	David Coulthard, Williams 1'22"446 = 190.379 kmh/118.299 mph (1994, new circuit)

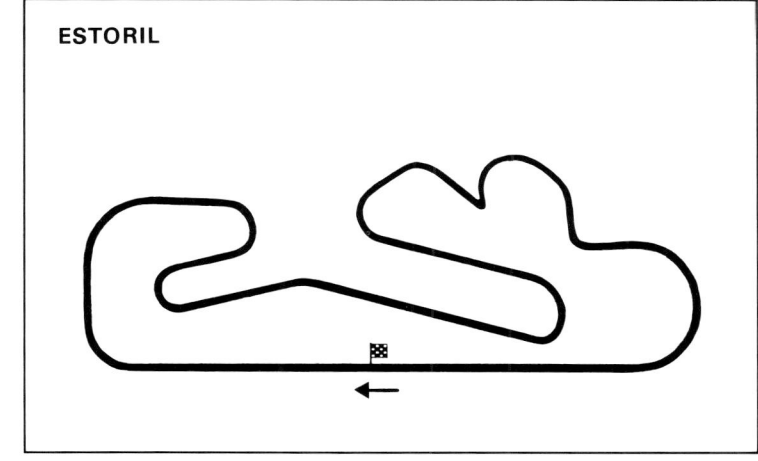

ESTORIL

STARTING GRID

6. COULTHARD 1'20"537
Williams FW17-Renault RS7/B V10

5. HILL 1'20"905
Williams FW17-Renault RS7/B V10

1. SCHUMACHER 1'21"301
Benetton B195-Renault RS7/B V10

28. BERGER 1'21"970
Ferrari 412T2-Ferrari 44/B V12

30. FRENTZEN 1'22"226
Sauber C14-Ford Zetec-R V8

2. HERBERT 1'22"322
Benetton B195-Renault RS7/B V10

27. ALESI 1'22"391
Ferrari 412T2-Ferrari 44/B V12

14. BARRICHELLO 1'22"538
Jordan 195-Peugeot V10

25. BRUNDLE 1'22"588
Ligier JS41-Mugen/Honda V10

15. IRVINE 1'22"831
Jordan 195-Peugeot V10

26. PANIS 1'22"904
Ligier JS41-Mugen/Honda V10

7. BLUNDELL 1'22"914
McLaren MP4/10-Mercedes F0110 V10

8. HÄKKINEN 1'23"064
McLaren MP4/10-Mercedes F0110 V10

29. BOULLION 1'23"934
Sauber C14-Ford Zetec-R V8

4. SALO 1'23"936
Tyrrell 023-Yamaha V10

3. KATAYAMA* 1'24"287
Tyrrell 023-Yamaha V10

23. LAMY 1'24"657
Minardi M195-Ford EDM V8

24. BADOER** 1'24"778
Minardi M195-Ford EDM V8

10. INOUE 1'24"883
Footwork FA16-Hart V8

9. PAPIS 1'25"179
Footwork FA16-Hart V8

17. MONTERMINI 1'26"172
Pacific PR02-Ford ED V8

21. DINIZ 1'27"292
Forti FG01/95-Ford ED V8

22. MORENO 1'27"523
Forti FG01/95-Ford ED V8

16. DELÉTRAZ 1'32"769
Pacific PR02-Ford ED V8

* Did not take second start.
** Started from pit-lane.

RESULTS

	Driver	Car	Laps	Time	Fastest lap
1	COULTHARD	Williams	71	1.41'52"145	1'23"220
2	SCHUMACHER	Benetton	71	+ 7"243	1'23"702
3	HILL	Williams	71	+ 22"121	1'23"737
4	BERGER	Ferrari	71	+ 1'24"879	1'24"805
5	ALESI	Ferrari	71	+ 1'25"429	1'25"544
6	FRENTZEN	Sauber	70		1'25"283
7	HERBERT	Benetton	70		1'25"128
8	BRUNDLE	Ligier	70		1'24"427
9	BLUNDELL	McLaren	70		1'25"646
10	IRVINE	Jordan	70		1'25"767
11	BARRICHELLO	Jordan	70		1'24"472
12	BOULLION	Sauber	70		1'26"193
13	SALO	Tyrrell	69		1'27"247
14	BADOER	Minardi	68		1'28"043
15	INOUE	Footwork	68		1'27"356
16	DINIZ	Forti	66		1'29"803

Winner's average: 182.319 kmh/113.291 mph.

Fastest lap: COULTHARD, Williams, 1'23"220 (188.608 kmh/117.199 mph).

RETIREMENTS

Driver	Laps	Reason	Fastest lap
KATAYAMA	0	collision with Badoer	
PAPIS	0	gearbox	
After second start:			
LAMY	7	gearbox	1'27"779
PANIS	10	spin	1'26"123
DELÉTRAZ	14	cramp in left arm	1'34"445
HÄKKINEN	44	engine	1'25"690
MONTERMINI	53	gearbox	1'27"801

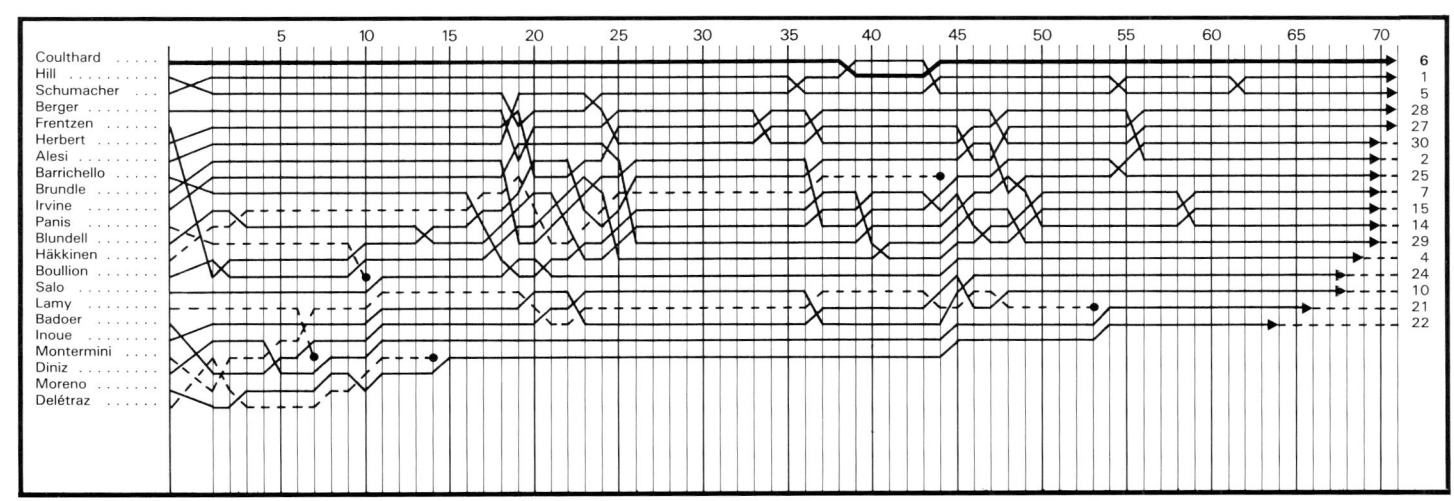

GROSSER PREIS VON EUROPA

Date:	October 1, 1995
Circuit:	67 laps of the 'New' Nurburgring circuit (4.556 km/2.831 miles), 305.252 km/189.68 miles
Weather:	cloudy and cool, wet in early stages of race
Attendance:	91,000 spectators approx.
Previous winner:	Michael Schumacher, Benetton, at 182.507 kmh/113.408 mph — Jerez (1994)
Lap record:	Niki Lauda, McLaren MP4/4-TAG Porsche V6 1'22"806 = 197.464 kmh/122.702 mph (1985)

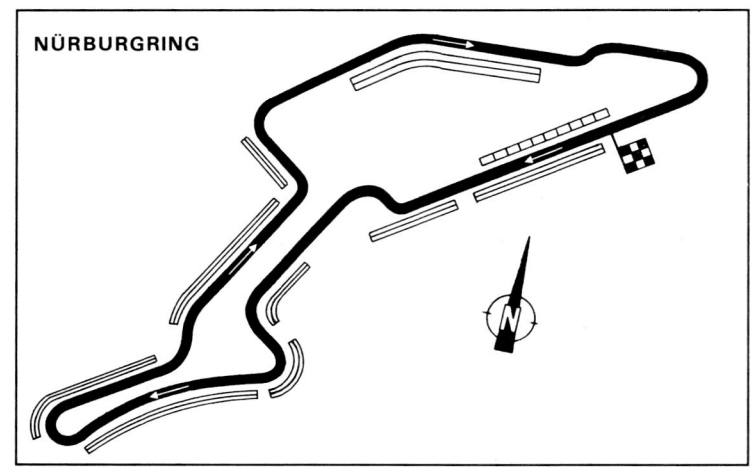

STARTING GRID

6. COULTHARD 1'18"738
Williams FW17B-Renault RS7/B V10

5. HILL 1'18"972
Williams FW17B-Renault RS7/B V10

1. SCHUMACHER 1'19"150
Benetton B195-Renault RS7/B V10

28. BERGER 1'19"821
Ferrari 412T2-Ferrari 44/B V12

15. IRVINE 1'20"488
Jordan 195-Peugeot V10

27. ALESI 1'20"510
Ferrari 412T2-Ferrari 44/B V12

2. HERBERT 1'20"653
Benetton B195-Renault RS7/B V10

30. FRENTZEN 1'20"749
Sauber C14-Ford Zetec-R V8

8. HÄKKINEN 1'20"866
McLaren MP4/10C-Mercedes F0110 V10

7. BLUNDELL 1'20"909
McLaren MP4/10C-Mercedes F0110 V10

14. BARRICHELLO 1'21"211
Jordan 195-Peugeot V10

25. BRUNDLE 1'21"541
Ligier JS41-Mugen/Honda V10

29. BOULLION 1'22"059
Sauber C14-Ford Zetec-R V8

26. PANIS 1'22"062
Ligier JS41-Mugen/Honda V10

4. SALO 1'23"058
Tyrrell 023-Yamaha V10

23. LAMY 1'23"328
Minardi M195-Ford EDM V8

9. PAPIS 1'23"689
Footwork FA16-Hart V8

24. BADOER 1'23"760
Minardi M195-Ford EDM V8

3. TARQUINI 1'24"286
Tyrrell 023-Yamaha V10

17. MONTERMINI 1'24"696
Pacific PRO2-Ford ED V8

10. INOUE* 1'24"900
Footwork FA16-Hart V8

21. DINIZ 1'25"157
Forti FG01/95-Ford ED V8

22. MORENO 1'26"098
Forti FG01/95-Ford ED V8

16. DELÉTRAZ 1'27"853
Pacific PRO2-Ford ED V8

* Did not start.

RESULTS

	Driver	Car	Laps	Time	Fastest lap
1	SCHUMACHER	Benetton	67	1.39'59"044	1'21"180
2	ALESI	Ferrari	67	+ 2"684	1'22"814
3	COULTHARD	Williams	67	+ 35"382	1'21"739
4	BARRICHELLO	Jordan	66		1'25"018
5	HERBERT	Benetton	66		1'22"544
6	IRVINE	Jordan	66		1'24"775
7	BRUNDLE	Ligier	66		1'23"801
8	HÄKKINEN	McLaren	65		1'22"760
9	LAMY	Minardi	64		1'26"832
10	SALO	Tyrrell	64		1'25"516
11	BADOER	Minardi	64		1'25"962
12	PAPIS	Footwork	64		1'26"332
13	DINIZ	Forti	62		1'27"555
14	TARQUINI	Tyrrell	61		1'26"160
15	DELÉTRAZ	Pacific	60		1'31"253

Winner's average: 183.18 kmh/113.826 mph.

Fastest lap: SCHUMACHER, Benetton, 1'21"180 (202.039 kmh/125.545 mph), new record.

RETIREMENTS

Driver	Laps	Reason	Fastest lap
INOUE	0	electrical failure	
BLUNDELL	14	accident	1'40"613
PANIS	14	spin	1'39"347
FRENTZEN	17	collision with Diniz	1'37"423
MORENO	22	driveshaft	1'37"763
BERGER	40	electrical failure	1'24"239
BOULLION	44	collision with Salo	1'25"385
MONTERMINI	45	out of fuel	1'26"566
HILL	58	accident	1'21"933

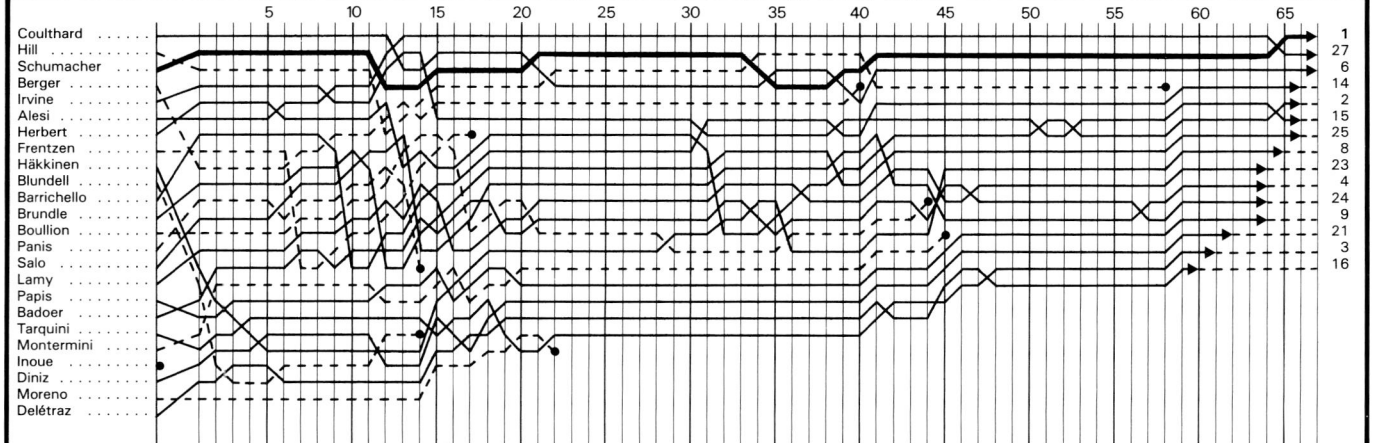

PACIFIC GRAND PRIX

Date:	October 22, 1995
Circuit:	83 laps of the Tanaka International circuit at Aïda, Japan (3.703 km/2.301 miles), 307.349 km/190.813 miles
Weather:	sunny with light cloud
Attendance:	30,000 spectators approx.
Previous winner:	Michael Schumacher, Benetton, at 173.9 kmh/108.59 mph (1994)
Lap record:	Michael Schumacher, Benetton 1′14″023 = 180.0 kmh/111.85 mph (1994)

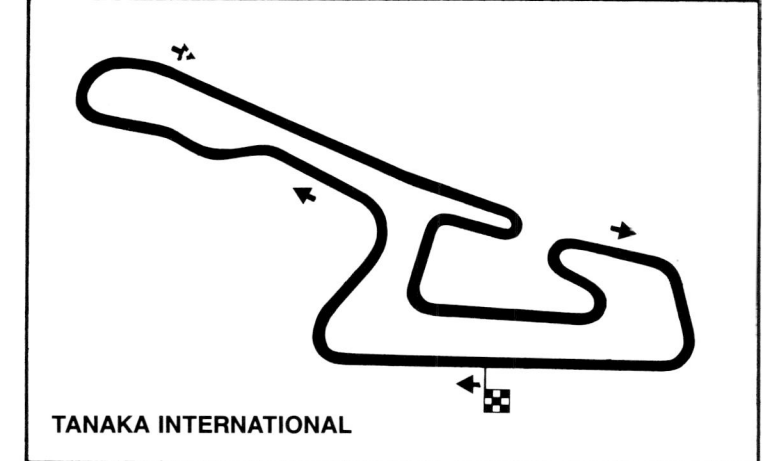

TANAKA INTERNATIONAL

STARTING GRID

6. COULTHARD 1′14″013
Williams FW17B-Renault RS7/B V10

5. HILL 1′14″213
Williams FW17B-Renault RS7/B V10

1. SCHUMACHER 1′14″284
Benetton B195-Renault RS7/B V10

27. ALESI 1′14″919
Ferrari 412T2-Ferrari 44/B V12

28. BERGER 1′14″974
Ferrari 412T2-Ferrari 44/B V12

15. IRVINE 1′15″354
Jordan 195-Peugeot V10

2. HERBERT 1′15″556
Benetton B195-Renault RS7/B V10

30. FRENTZEN 1′15″561
Sauber C14-Ford Zetec-R V8

26. PANIS 1′15″621
Ligier JS41-Mugen/Honda V10

7. BLUNDELL 1′15″652
McLaren MP4/10C-Mercedes F0110 V10

14. BARRICHELLO 1′15″774
Jordan 195-Peugeot V10

8. MAGNUSSEN 1′16″339
McLaren MP4/10C-Mercedes F0110 V10

25. SUZUKI 1′16″519
Ligier JS41-Mugen/Honda V10

23. LAMY 1′16″596
Minardi M195-Ford EDM V8

29. BOULLION 1′16″646
Sauber C14-Ford Zetec-R V8

4. SALO 1′17″213
Tyrrell 023-Yamaha V10

9. MORBIDELLI 1′18″114
Footwork FA16-Hart V8

10. INOUE 1′18″212
Footwork FA16-Hart V8

21. DINIZ 1′19″579
Forti FG01/95-Ford ED V8

22. MORENO 1′19″745
Forti FG01/95-Ford ED V8

17. MONTERMINI 1′20″093
Pacific PR02-Ford ED V8

16. GACHOT 1′21″405
Pacific PR02-Ford ED V8

RESULTS

	Driver	Car	Laps	Time	Fastest lap
1	SCHUMACHER	Benetton	83	1.48′49″972	1′16″374
2	COULTHARD	Williams	83	+ 14″920	1′16″674
3	HILL	Williams	83	+ 48″333	1′16″444
4	BERGER	Ferrari	82		1′17″795
5	ALESI	Ferrari	82		1′17″654
6	HERBERT	Benetton	82		1′18″164
7	FRENTZEN	Sauber	82		1′17″913
8	PANIS	Ligier	81		1′18″335
9	BLUNDELL	McLaren	81		1′18″983
10	MAGNUSSEN	McLaren	81		1′18″631
11	IRVINE	Jordan	81		1′16″927
12	SALO	Tyrrell	80		1′19″878
13	LAMY	Minardi	80		1′20″055
14	KATAYAMA	Tyrrell	80		1′19″574
15	BADOER	Minardi	80		1′20″299
16	MORENO	Forti	78		1′22″102
17	DINIZ	Forti	77		1′22″528

Winner's average: 169.442 kmh/105.308 mph.

Fastest lap: SCHUMACHER, Benetton, 1′16″374 (174.546 kmh/108.481 mph).

RETIREMENTS

Driver	Laps	Reason	Fastest lap
GACHOT	2	gearbox hydraulics	1′26″608
BOULLION	7	accident	1′20″099
SUZUKI	10	accident	1′19″816
MONTERMINI	14	transmission	1′21″355
INOUE	38	engine failed	1′21″503
MORBIDELLI	53	engine	1′19″975
BARRICHELLO	67	engine failed	1′18″326

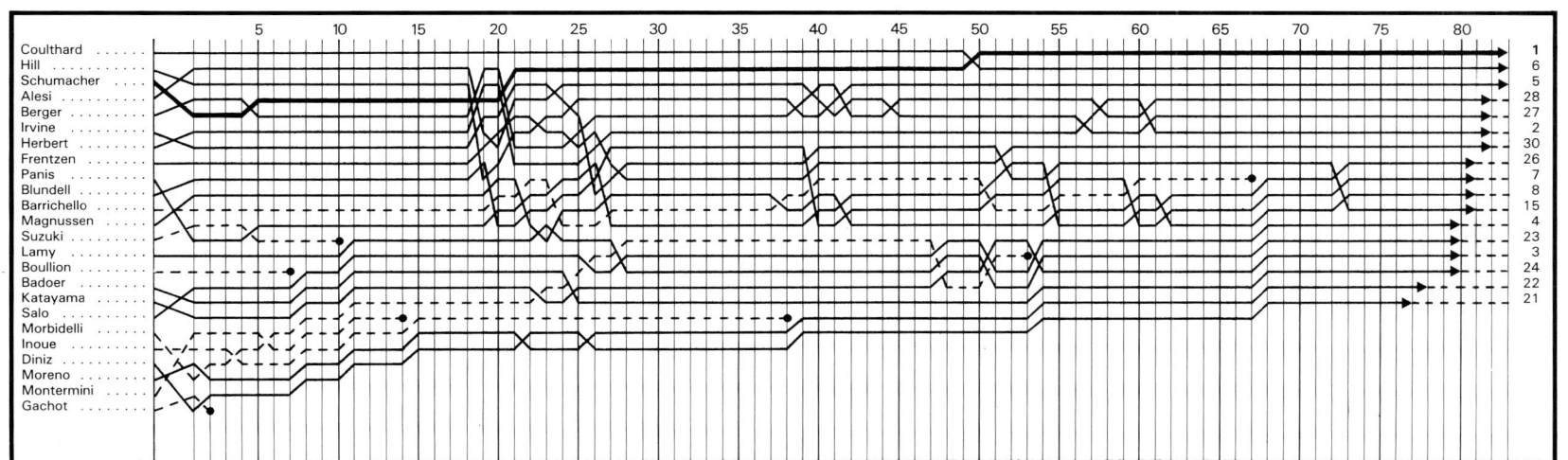

JAPANESE GRAND PRIX

Date:	October 29, 1995
Circuit:	53 laps of the Suzuka circuit (5.864 km/ 3.66 miles), 310.793 km/193.98 miles
Weather:	cloudy after earlier rain, light rain during race
Attendance:	90,000 spectators approx.
Previous winner:	Damon Hill, Williams, at 151.796 kmh/94.341 mph
Lap record:	Nigel Mansell, Williams, 1'40"646 = 209.749 kmh/130.359 mph (1992)

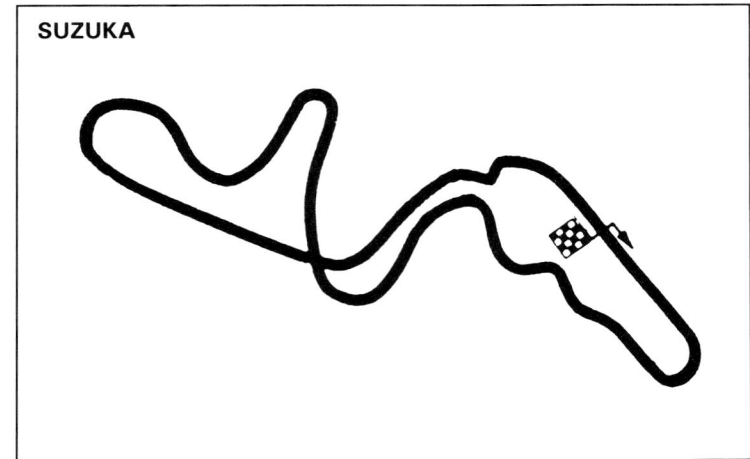
SUZUKA

STARTING GRID

1. SCHUMACHER 1'38"023
Benetton B195-Renault RS7/B V10

27. ALESI 1'38"888
Ferrari 412T2-Ferrari 44/B V12

8. HÄKKINEN 1'38"954
McLaren MP4/10B-Mercedes F0110 V10

5. HILL 1'39"032
Williams FW17-Renault RS7/B V10

28. BERGER 1'39"040
Ferrari 412T2-Ferrari 44/B V12

6. COULTHARD 1'39"155
Williams FW17-Renault RS7/B V10

15. IRVINE 1'39"621
Jordan 195-Peugeot V10

30. FRENTZEN 1'40"010
Sauber C14-Ford Zetec-R V8

2. HERBERT 1'40"349
Benetton B195-Renault RS7/B V10

14. BARRICHELLO 1'40"381
Jordan 195-Peugeot V10

26. PANIS 1'40"838
Ligier JS41-Mugen/Honda V10

4. SALO 1'41"365
Tyrrell 023-Yamaha V10

25. SUZUKI* 1'41"592
Ligier JS41-Mugen/Honda V10

3. KATAYAMA 1'41"977
Tyrrell 023-Yamaha V10

9. MORBIDELLI 1'42"059
Footwork FA16-Hart V8

29. WENDLINGER 1'42"912
Sauber C14-Ford Zetec-R V8

23. LAMY 1'43"102
Minardi M195-Ford EDM V8

24. BADOER 1'43"542
Minardi M195-Ford EDM V8

10. INOUE 1'44"074
Footwork FA16-Hart V8

17. MONTERMINI 1'46"097
Pacific PR02-Ford ED V8

21. DINIZ 1'46"654
Forti FG01/95-Ford ED V8

22. MORENO 1'48"267
Forti FG01/95-Ford ED V8

16. GACHOT 1'48"289
Pacific PR02-Ford ED V8

7. BLUNDELL 16'42"640
McLaren MP4/10B-Mercedes F0110 V10

*Did not start: injured in practice.

RESULTS

	Driver	Car	Laps	Time	Fastest lap
1	SCHUMACHER	Benetton	53	1.36'52"930	1'42"976
2	HÄKKINEN	McLaren	53	+ 19"337	1'43"369
3	HERBERT	Benetton	53	+ 1'23"804	1'43"404
4	IRVINE	Jordan	53	+ 1'42"136	1'43"477
5	PANIS	Ligier	52		1'45"661
6	SALO	Tyrrell	52		1'45"625
7	BLUNDELL	McLaren	52		1'44"287
8	FRENTZEN	Sauber	52		1'44"211
9	BADOER	Minardi	51		1'47"025
10	WENDLINGER	Sauber	51		1'45"824
11	LAMY	Minardi	51		1'46"924
12	INOUE	Footwork	51		1'46"600

Winner's average: 192.349 kmh/119.545 mph.

Fastest lap: SCHUMACHER, Benetton, 1'42"976 (205.003 kmh/127.410 mph), new record.

RETIREMENTS

Driver	Laps	Reason	Fastest lap
MORBIDELLI	0	spin after collision with Wendlinger	
MORENO	1	gearbox	
GACHOT	6	driveshaft bearing	2'06"927
KATAYAMA	12	accident	1'56"404
BARRICHELLO	15	collision with Irvine	1'51"343
BERGER	16	electronic failure	1'52"165
MONTERMINI	23	spin	1'49"985
ALESI	24	differential	1'44"370
DINIZ	32	spin	1'50"261
COULTHARD	39	accident	1'43"079
HILL	40	spin	1'43"193

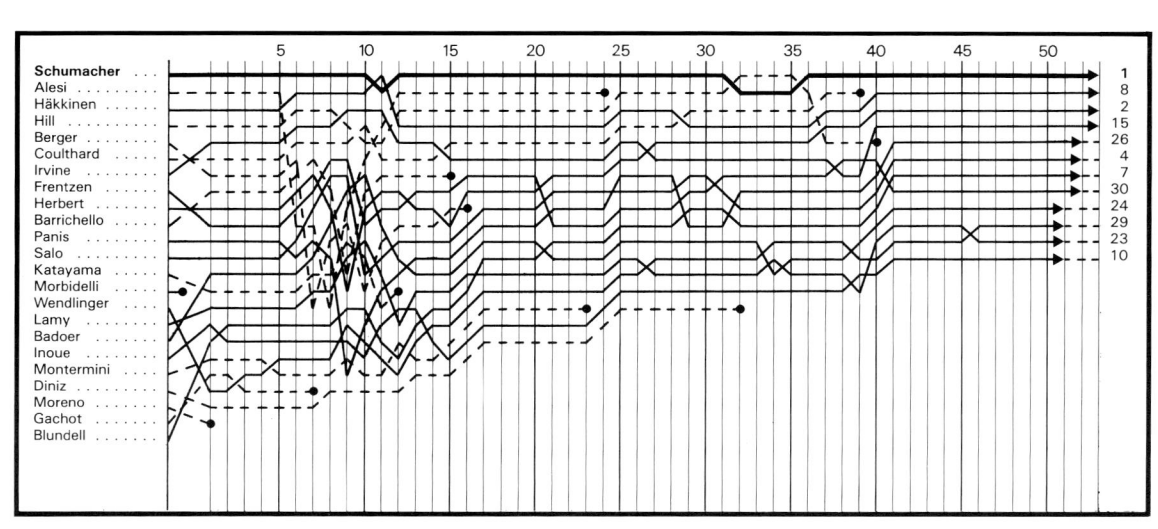

AUSTRALIAN GRAND PRIX

Date:	November 12, 1995
Circuit:	81 laps of the Adelaide circuit (3.78 km/2.36 miles), 306.180 km/191.16 miles
Weather:	sunny
Attendance:	205,000 spectators approx.
Previous winner:	Nigel Mansell, Williams, at 170.323 kmh/105.856 mph
Lap record:	Damon Hill, Williams, 1'15"381 = 180,523 km/h (1993)

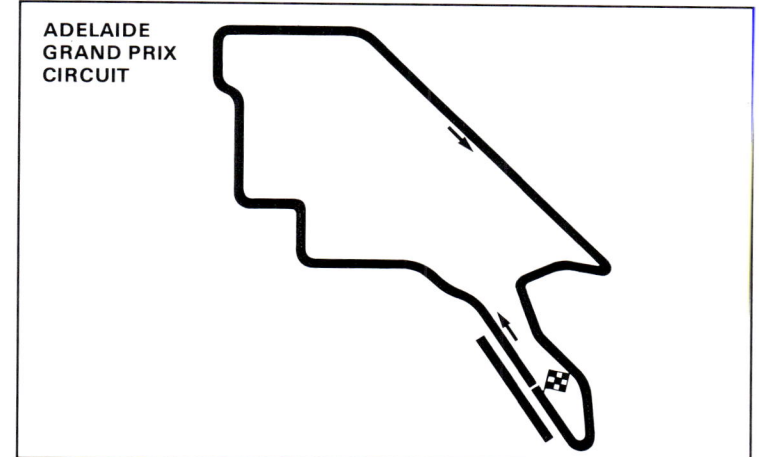

STARTING GRID

5. HILL 1'15"505
Williams FW17-Renault RS7/B V10

6. COULTHARD 1'15"628
Williams FW17-Renault RS7/B V10

1. SCHUMACHER 1'15"839
Benetton B195-Renault RS7/B V10

28. BERGER 1'15"932
Ferrari 412T2-Ferrari 44/B V12

27. ALESI 1'16"305
Ferrari 412T2-Ferrari 44/B V12

30. FRENTZEN 1'16"647
Sauber C14-Ford Zetec-R V8

14. BARRICHELLO 1'16"725
Jordan 195-Peugeot V10

2. HERBERT 1'16"950
Benetton B195-Renault RS7/B V10

15. IRVINE 1'17"110
Jordan 195-Peugeot V10

7. BLUNDELL 1'17"348
McLaren MP4/10B-Mercedes F0110 V10

25. BRUNDLE 1'17"624
Ligier JS41-Mugen/Honda V10

26. PANIS 1'18"033
Ligier JS41-Mugen/Honda V10

9. MORBIDELLI 1'18"391
Footwork FA16-Hart V8

4. SALO 1'18"604
Tyrrell 023-Yamaha V10

24. BADOER 1'18"810
Minardi M195-Ford EDM V8

3. KATAYAMA 1'18"828
Tyrrell 023-Yamaha V10

23. LAMY 1'18"875
Minardi M195-Ford EDM V8

29. WENDLINGER 1'19"561
Sauber C14-Ford Zetec-R V8

10. INOUE 1'19"677
Footwork FA16-Hart V8

22. MORENO 1'20"657
Forti FG01/95-Ford ED V8

21. DINIZ 1'20"878
Forti FG01/95-Ford ED V8

17. MONTERMINI 1'21"659
Pacific PRO2-Ford ED V8

16. GACHOT 1'21"998
Pacific PRO2-Ford ED V8

RESULTS

	Driver	Car	Laps	Time	Fastest lap
1	HILL	Williams	81	1.49'15"943	1'17"943
2	PANIS	Ligier	79		1'20"305
3	MORBIDELLI	Footwork	79		1'21"418
4	BLUNDELL	McLaren	79		1'21"363
5	SALO	Tyrrell	78		1'21"392
6	LAMY	Minardi	78		1'21"677
7	DINIZ	Forti	77		1'23"253
8	GACHOT	Pacific	76		1'24"139

Winner's speed: 168.129 kmh/104.492 mph.

Fastest lap: Hill, Williams, 1'17"943 (174.589 kmh/108.507 mph).

RETIREMENTS

Driver	Laps	Reason	Fastest lap
BADOER	0	would not start	
MONTERMINI	2	gearbox and spin	1'25"242
WENDLINGER	8	sore neck	1'22"784
INOUE	15	accident	1'22"641
COULTHARD	19	accident	1'18"025
BARRICHELLO	20	accident	1'20"643
MORENO	21	spin	1'22"944
ALESI	23	collision damage after collision with Schumacher	1'19"503
SCHUMACHER	25	collision damage after collision with Alesi	1'18"199
BRUNDLE	29	spin	1'20"835
BERGER	34	engine	1'19"493
FRENTZEN	39	gearbox	1'19"861
IRVINE	62	engine	1'20"563
HERBERT	69	hydraulic leak	1'19"056
KATAYAMA	70	engine	1'22"790

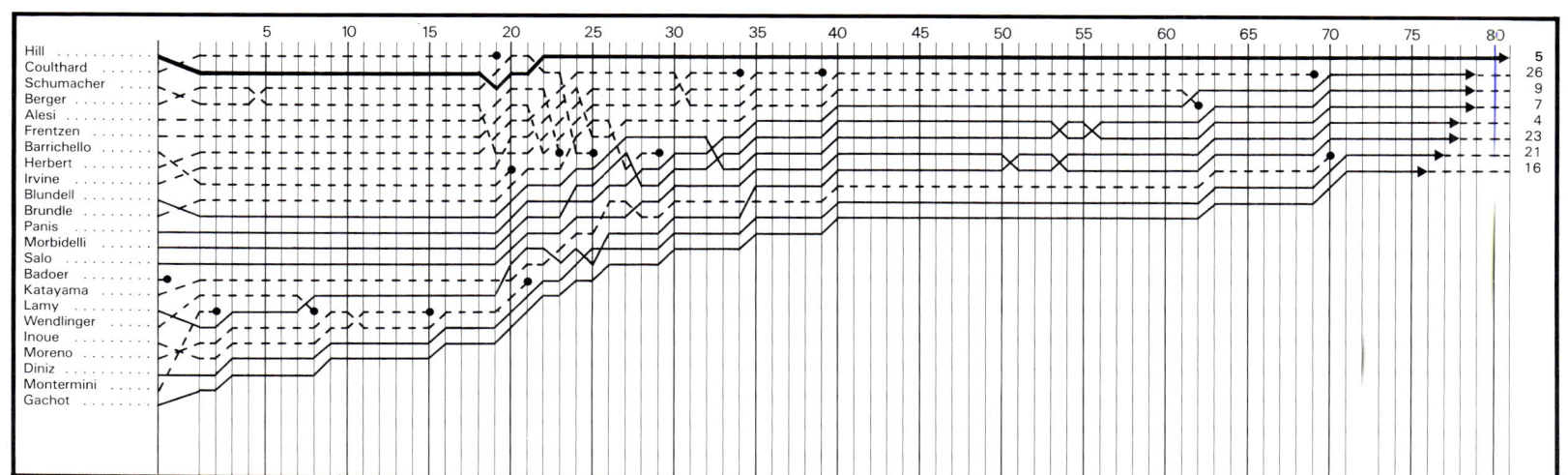

TOURING CAR CHAMPIONSHIPS

BRITISH TOURING CAR CHAMPIONSHIP

Final classification/Drivers:

Driver	Car	Points
1 John CLELAND (GB)	Vauxhall Cavalier	348
2 Alain MENU (CH)	Renault Laguna	305
3 Richard RYDELL (S)	Volvo 850	255
4 Will HOY (GB)	Renault Laguna	195
5 Tim HARVEY (GB)	Volvo 850	176
6 Paul RADISICH (NZ)	Ford Mondeo	130
7 James THOMPSON (GB)	Vauxhall Cavalier	124
8 Kelvin BURT (GB)	Ford Mondeo	117
9 Julian BAILEY (GB)	Toyota Carina	94
10 Patrick WATTS (GB)	Peugeot 405 Mi 16	61
David LESLIE (GB)	Honda Accord	61

Final classification/Makes:

1	RENAULT	419
2	VAUXHALL	414
3	VOLVO	359
4	FORD	236
5	TOYOTA	172
6	BMW	144

BELGIAN PROCAR

Final classification/Drivers:

Driver	Car	Points
1 Thierry TASSIN	BMW 318i	98
2 Marc DUEZ	BMW 318i	72
3 Philippe ADAMS	Audi 80 Quattro + Audi A4	66
4 Eric BACHELART	Peugeot 405 Mi 16	45
5 Didier DE RADIGUES	Honda Accord	36
6 Pierre-Alain THIBAUT	Opel Vectra	19
7 Vincent VOSSE	Honda Accord	13
8 Philip VERELLEN	Peugeot 405 Mi 16	10
9 Patrick SNIJERS	Honda Accord	6
10 Wolfgang HAUGG	Audi 80 Quattro	4

Final classification/Makes:

1	BMW	148
2	AUDI	79
3	HONDA	54
4	PEUGEOT	45
5	OPEL	19

D1 ADAC SUPER-TOURENWAGEN-CUP (GERMANY)

Final classification/Drivers:

Driver	Car	Points
1 Joachim WINKELHOCK	BMW 318i	418
2 Peter KOK	BMW 318i	397
3 Frank BIELA	Audi A4	391
4 Hans-Joachim STUCK	Audi A4	353
5 Alfred HEGER	Audi A4	315
6 Roberto RAVAGLIA	BMW 318i	309
7 Alex BURGSTALLER	BMW 318i	280
8 Roland ASCH	Ford Mondeo	267
9 Tamara VIDALI	Audi A4	258
10 Keith ODOR	Nissan Primera	225

Final classification/Makes:

1	BMW	945
2	AUDI	905
3	FORD	438
4	HONDA	367
5	NISSAN	365

JAPANESE TOURING CAR CHAMPIONSHIP

Final classification/Drivers:

Driver	Car	Points
1 Steve SOPER	BMW 318i	124
2 Masanori SEKIYA	Toyota Corona	117
3 Kazuyoshi HOSHINO	Nissan Primera	98
4 Anthony REID	Opel Vectra	87
5 Tom KRISTENSEN	Toyota Corona	82
6 Akira IIDA	Nissan Sunny	67
7 Hidetoshi MITSUSADA	Toyota Corona	57
8 Michael KRUMM	Toyota Corona	52
9 Joachim WINKELHOCK	BMW 318i	41
10 Masami KAGEYAMA	Toyota Corona	34

SUPERTOURISME (FRANCE)

Final classification/Drivers:

Driver	Car	Points
1 Yvan MULLER	BMW 318i	131
2 Eric HELARY	Opel Vectra	128
3 Laurent AIELLO	Peugeot 405 Mi 16	88
4 Jacques LAFFITE	Opel Vectra	71
5 Alain CUDINI	Opel Vectra	66
6 Philippe ALLIOT	Peugeot 405 Mi 16	53
7 William DAVID	Peugeot 405 Mi 16	40
8 Stéphane ORTELLI	BMW 318i	31
9 Philippe GACHE	Alfa Romeo 155 TS	30
10 Marcel TARRES	BMW 318i	19

Final classification/Makes:

1	OPEL	298
2	BMWL	285
3	PEUGEOT	218
4	ALFA ROMEO	59

DEUTSCHE TOURENWAGEN-MEISTERSCHAFT (GERMANY)

Final classification/Drivers:

Driver	Car	Points
1 Bernd SCHNEIDER (D)	AMG-Mercedes C Class	138
2 Jörg VAN OMMEN (D)	AMG-Mercedes C Class	113
3 Klaus LUDWIG (D)	Opel Calivra V6	80
4 Kurt THIIM (DK)	AMG-Mercedes C Class	78
5 Dario FRANCHITTI (I)	AMG-Mercedes C Class	74
6 Nicola LARINI (I)	Alfa Romeo 155 V6 Ti	71
7 Alexander GRAU (D)	AMG-Mercedes C Class	68
8 Jan MAGNUSSEN (DK)	AMG-Mercedes C Class	49
9 Christian DANNER (D)	Alfa Romeo 155 V6 Ti	48
10 Michael BARTELS (D)	Alfa Romeo 155 V6 Ti	47

Final classification/Makes:

1	MERCEDES-BENZ	224
2	ALFA ROMEO	150
3	OPEL	107

INTERNATIONAL TOURING CAR CHAMPIONSHIP (ITC)

Final classification/Drivers:

Driver	Car	Points
1 Bernd SCHNEIDER (D)	AMG-Mercedes C Class	155
2 Jan MAGNUSSEN (DK)	AMG-Mercedes C Class	83
3 Dario FRANCHITTI (I)	AMG-Mercedes C Class	80
4 Nicola LARINI (I)	Alfa Romeo 155 V6 Ti	59
5 Manuel REUTER (D)	Opel Calivra V6	50
6 Jörg VAN OMMEN (D)	AMG-Mercedes C Class	50
7 Stefano MODENA (I)	Alfa Romeo 155 V6 Ti	49
8 Kurt THIIM (D)	AMG-Mercedes C Class	45
9 Alexander GRAU (D)	AMG-Mercedes C Class	39
10 Giancarlo FISICHELLA (I)	Alfa Romeo 155 V6 Ti	37

FIA WORLD CUP (PAUL RICARD)

Final classification/Drivers:

Driver	Car	Points
1 Frank BIELA (D)	Audi A4	70
2 Emanuele PIRRO (I)	Audi A4	54
3 Steve SOPER (GB)	BMW 318i	54
4 Yvan MULLER (F)	BMW 318i	44
5 Johnny CECOTTO (VEZ)	BMW 318i	35
6 Kelvin BURT (GB)	Ford Mondeo	23
7 Klaus NIEDZWIEDZ (D)	Honda Accord	22
8 Armin HAHNE (D)	Honda Accord	22
9 Hans Joachim STUCK (D)	Audi A4	16
10 Alain MENU (CH)	Renault Laguna	16

SUPERTURISMO (ITALY)

Final classification/Drivers:

Driver	Car	Points
1 Emanuele PIRRO	Audi A4	317
2 Rinaldo CAPELLO	Audi A4	253
3 Antonio TAMBURINI	Alfa Romeo 155 Ts	179
4 Fabrizio GIOVANARDI	Alfa Romeo 155 Ts	179
5 Gianni MORBIDELLI	BMW 318i	149
6 Emanuele NASPETTI	BMW 318i	135
7 Gabriele TARQUINI	Alfa Romeo 155 Ts	88
8 Roberto COLCIAGO	Opel Vectra	61
9 Yolanda SURER	BMW 318i	59
10 Oscar LARRAURI	Alfa Romeo 155 Ts	48

Final classification/Makes:

1	AUDI	352
2	ALFA ROMEO	265
3	BMW	217
4	OPEL	61

AUSTRALIAN TOURING CAR CHAMPIONSHIP

Final classification/Drivers:

Driver	Car	Points
1 Paul MORRIS	BMW 318i	286
2 Geoff BRABHAM	BMW 318i	232
3 Brad JONES	Audi 80 Quattro	232
4 Greg MURPHY	Audi 80 Quattro	132
5 Graham MOORE	Opel Vectra	84
6 Steven ELLERY	BMW 318i	79
7 Jeff ALLAM	Ford Mondeo	62
8 Tony SCOTT	Volvo 850	57
9 Steven RICHARDS	Alfa Romeo 155 Ts	56
10 Charlie O'BRIEN	BMW 318i	30

Final classification/Makes:

1	BMW	386
2	AUDI	294
3	FORD	140
4	VOLVO	130
5	HYUNDAI	64

SOUTH AFRICAN TOURING CAR CHAMPIONSHIP

Final classification/Drivers:

Driver	Car	Points
1 Michael BRIGGS	Opel Vectra	109
2 Grant McCLEERY	Opel Vectra	83
3 Deon JOUBERT	BMW 318i	82
4 Shaun VAN DER LINDEN	BMW 318i	40
5 Terry MOSS	Audi 80 Quattro	33
6 Anthony TAYLOR	Toyota Camry	28
7 Mike WHITE	Toyota Camry	20
8 Steve WINDHAM	Ford Mondeo	20
9 Sarel VAN DER MERWE	Ford Mondeo	16
10 Shaun WATSON-SMITH	Opel Vectra	15

SWISS TOURING CAR TROPHY

Final classification/Drivers:

Driver	Car	Points
1 Rolf KUHN	Peugeot 405 Mi 16	122
2 Eddy KAMM	Mitsubishi Lancer	85
3 Philip MULLER	Toyota Carina E	80
4 Josef KOCH	Opel Vectra + TGoyota Carina E	72
5 Walter BRENY	Toyota Celica	62
6 Peter STECK	BMW M3	44
7 Sven FRIESECKE	Mercedes 190E	32
8 Rüdi SCHURTER	Opel Vectra GT	30
9 Beat WEBER	BMW M3	30
10 Johnny HAUSER	Ford Mondeo	20

R.A.C. RALLY

Date: November 21-24, 1994
Total distance: 2364 km/1469 miles
29 special stages: 520 km/323 miles
178 starters, 97 finishers

	Team	No	Car	Group	Time
1	**C. McRae-D. Ringer**	4	Subaru Impreza 555	A	5.17'25"
2	J. Kankkunen-N. Grist	1	Toyota Celica GT-Four	A	+ 3'33"
3	B. Thiry-S. Prevot	11	Ford Escort RS Cosworth	A	+10'12"
4	S. Blomqvist-B. Melander	12	Ford Escort RS Cosworth	A	+12'48"
5	A. Vatanen-F. Pons	7	Ford Escort RS Cosworth	A	+17'00"
6	D. Auriol-B. Occelli	6	Toyota Celica Turbo 4WD	A	+30'32"
7	G. Evans-H. Davis*	27	Ford Escort RS 2000	A	+34'59"
8	J. Habig-D. Judd	38	Ford Escort RS Cosworth	A	+35'52"
9	T. Mäkinen-S. Harjanne	18	Nissan Sunny GTi	A	+36'00"
10	G. de Mevius-W. Lux	17	Opel Astra GSi 16v	A	+36'29"
.../...					
12	**J. Milner-S. Turvey**	32	Ford Escort RS Cosworth	N	+40'12"
.../...					
16	*I. Holderied-C. Thörner*	30	Mitsubishi Lancer Evolution 2	N	+47'58"

Group winners in bold type
Ladies' winners in italics
* Winners of Formula 2

Principal retirements

Team	No	Car	Reason	Stages completed
F. Delecour-D. Grataloup	3	Ford Escort RS Cosworth	disqualified	6
A. McRae-D. Senior	16	Nissan Sunny GTi	electrics	8
R. Burns-R. Reid	9	Subaru Impreza 555	accident damage to suspension	9
M. Biasion-T. Siviero	5	Ford Escort RS Cosworth	electrics	14
Y. Fujimoto-A. Hertz	14	Toyota Celica Turbo 4WD	accident	18
C. Sainz-L. Moya	2	Subaru Impreza 555	accident	24
M. Wilson-B. Thomas	10	Ford Escort RS Cosworth	accident	25

Successive leaders:
SS 1 & 2: Sainz; SS 3 to 29: McRae.

Stage winners:
McRae, 16 (3 tied); Kankkunen, 9 (2 tied); Sainz, 5 (1 tied); Auriol, 1; Blomqvist, 1; Biasion, 1 tied.

MONTE CARLO RALLY

Date: January 23-26, 1995
Total distance: 2617 km/1626 miles
21 special stages: 547 km/340 miles
199 starters, 83 finishers

	Team	No	Car	Group	Time
1	**C. Sainz-L. Moya**	5	Subaru Impreza 555	A	6.32'31"
2	F. Delecour-C. François	7	Ford Escort RS Cosworth	A	+ 2'25"
3	J. Kankkunen-N. Grist	2	Toyota Celica GT-Four	A	+ 3'57"
4	T. Mäkinen-S. Harjanne	11	Mitsubishi Lancer Evolution 2	A	+ 4'41"
5	B. Thiry-S. Prevot	8	Ford Escort RS Cosworth	A	+ 6'47"
6	A. Aghini-S. Farnocchia	12	Mitsubishi Lancer Evolution 2	A	+10'46"
7	J. Ragnotti-G. Thimonier*	14	Renault Clio Williams Maxi	A	+31'55"
8	P. Liatti-A. Alessandrini	6	Subaru Impreza 555	A	+37'23"
9	**P. Camandona-G. Crausaz**	24	Ford Escort RS Cosworth	N	+40'30"
10	*I. Holderied-C. Thörner*	17	Mitsubishi Lancer Evolution 2	N	+41'03"

Principal retirements

Team	No	Car	Reason	Stages completed
C. McRae-D. Ringer	4	Subaru Impreza 555	accident	11
D. Auriol-B. Occelli	1	Toyota Celica GT-Four	accident	15
A. Schwarz-K. Wicha	3	Toyota Celica GT-Four	engine	15
P. Bugalski-T. Renaud	15	Renault Clio Williams Maxi	accident	16

Successive leaders:
SS 1: McRae; SS 3 to 8: Sainz; SS 9 & 10: Delecour; SS 11 to 21: Sainz.

Stage winners:
Sainz, 7; Delecour, 6; Kankkunen, 3; Thiry, 3; McRae, 2.

SWEDISH RALLY

Date: February 10-12, 1995
Total distance: 1633 km/1015 miles
25 special stages: 501 km/311 miles
95 starters, 49 finishers

	Team	No	Car	Group	Time
1	**K. Eriksson-S. Parmander**	10	Mitsubishi Lancer Evolution 2	A	4.51'37"
2	T. Mäkinen-S. Harjanne	11	Mitsubishi Lancer Evolution	A	+ 12"
3	T. Rådström-L. Bäckman	14	Toyota Celica GT-Four	A	+ 1'07"
4	J. Kankkunen-N. Grist	2	Toyota Celica GT-Four	A	+ 2'18"
5	D. Auriol-B. Occelli	1	Toyota Celica GT-Four	A	+ 2'20"
6	B. Thiry-S. Prevot	8	Ford Escort RS Cosworth	A	+ 5'31"
7	S. Blomqvist-B. Melander	9	Ford Escort RS Cosworth	A	+ 6'49"
8	T. Jansson-I. Algerstedt	15	Toyota Celica GT-Four	A	+ 8'02"
9	A. Schwarz-K. Wicha	3	Toyota Celica GT-Four	A	+ 9'45"
10	**K. Bäcklund-T. Andersson**	12	Mitsubishi Lancer Evolution 2	N	+12'44"
.../...					
12	P. Svan-J. Olsson*	18	Opel Astra GSi	A	+18'07"

* Winners of Formula 2

Principal retirements

Team	No	Car	Reason	Stages completed
C. Sainz-L. Moya	5	Subaru Impreza 555	engine	9
F. Delecour-C. François	7	Ford Escort RS Cosworth	engine	11
C. McRae-D. Ringer	4	Subaru Impreza 555	engine	18
M. Jonsson-J. Johansson	6	Subaru Impreza 555	engine	18
M. Grönholm-V. Silander	17	Toyota Celica Turbo 4WD	gearbox	22

Successive leaders:
SS 1: Auriol, Mäkinen & Rådström; SS 2: Mäkinen; SS 3 & 4: Eriksson; SS 5: Eriksson & Mäkinen; SS 6: Mäkinen; SS 7: Eriksson & Mäkinen; SS 8: Eriksson; SS 9: Mäkinen; SS 10 to 18: Eriksson; SS 19 to 24: Mäkinen; SS 25: Eriksson.

Stage winners:
Mäkinen, 9 (2 tied); Eriksson, 8 (2 tied); Kankkunen, 3 (1 tied); Jansson, 3 (1 tied); McRae, 2; Rådström, 2 tied; Auriol, 2 tied; Blomqvist & Sainz, 1.

PORTUGUESE RALLY

Date: March 8-10, 1995
Total distance: 1706 km/1060 miles
31 special stages: 467 km/290 miles
114 starters, 39 finishers

	Team	No	Car	Group	Time
1	**C. Sainz-L. Moya**	5	Subaru Impreza 555	A	5.32'37"
2	J. Kankkunen-N. Grist	2	Toyota Celica GT-Four	A	+ 12"
3	C. McRae-D. Ringer	4	Subaru Impreza 555	A	+ 3'14"
4	A. Schwarz-K. Wicha	3	Toyota Celica GT-Four	A	+ 4'59"
5	D. Auriol-B. Occelli	1	Toyota Celica GT-Four	A	+ 6'13"
6	B. Thiry-S. Prevot	8	Ford Escort RS Cosworth	A	+ 8'46"
7	R. Burns-R. Reid	6	Subaru Impreza 555	A	+14'21"
8	A. Fiorio-V. Brambilla	9	Ford Escort RS Cosworth	A	+25'37"
9	**R. Madeira-N. Silva**	12	Mitsubishi Lancer Evolution 2	N	+30'59"
10	J. Recalde-M. Christie	11	Mitsubishi Lancer Evolution 2	N	+34'45"
11	*I. Holderied-C. Thörner*	25	Mitsubishi Lancer Evolution 2	N	+40'56"
.../...					
16	P. Deila-P. Scalvini*	57	Peugeot 306 XSi	A	+55'18"

* Winner of Formula 2

Principal retirements

Team	No	Car	Reason	Stages completed
F. Delecour-D. Grataloup	7	Ford Escort RS Cosworth	engine failure following accident	4
J.-C. Macedo-M. Borges	18	Renault Clio Williams Maxi	gearbox	9
P. Sibera-P. Gross	19	Skoda Felicia 1500	gearbox	15
E. Triner-P. Stanc	22	Skoda Felicia 1300	gearbox	16
G. de Mevius-J.-M. Fortin	15	Nissan Sunny GTi	gearbox	25
M. Grönholm-V. Silander	16	Toyota Celica Turbo 4WD	accident	28
P. Camandona-G. Crausaz	21	Ford Escort RS Cosworth	differential	31

Successive leaders:
SS 1 to 10: Kankkunen; SS 11 & 12: Sainz; SS 13: Kankkunen & Sainz; SS 14 to 23: Kankkunen; SS 24: cancelled; SS 25 & 26: Kankkunen; SS 27: cancelled; SS 28 & 29: Kankkunen; SS 30: Kankkunen & Sainz; SS 31 to 33: Sainz.

Stage winners:
Kankkunen, 13 (2 tied); Sainz, 12; Auriol, 4 (1 tied); McRae, 2; Schwarz, 2 (1 tied); Delecour, 1 tied.

SAFARI RALLY

Date: April 13-16, 1995
Total distance: 2995 km/1861 miles
45 time controls
45 starters, 21 finishers

	Team	No	Car	Group	Time
1	**Y. Fujimoto-A. Hertz**	3	Toyota Celica Turbo 4WD	A	17.38'27"
2	K. Shinozuka-P. Kuukala	2	Mitsubishi Lancer Evolution 3	A	+ 42'22"
3	I. Duncan-D. Williamson	1	Toyota Celica Turbo 4WD	A	+ 1.22'43"
4	**H. Miyoshi-M. Verjee**	9	Subaru Impreza 555	N	+ 3.58'35"
5	M. Brighetti-P. Stone	14	Subaru Impreza 555	N	+ 5.04'53"
6	R. Hellier-S. Haji	15	Mitsubishi Galant VR4	A	+ 5.35'34"
7	M. Galanti-H. Thiede	7	Toyota Celica Turbo 4WD	A	+ 5.39'59"
8	J. Toroitich-I. Choge	8	Toyota Celica Turbo 4WD	A	+ 5.50'00"
9	R. Stohl-J. Bertl	6	Audi Coupé S2	A	+ 6.15'01"
10	C. Tundo-W. Luckhurst	49	Subaru Impreza 555	N	+ 8.13'14"
.../...					
18	A. Anwar-S. Shah*	12	Daewoo Cielo 1.8	N	+15.19'17"

* Winners of Formula 2

Principal retirements

Team	No	Car	Reason	Stages completed
P. Njiru-A. Sidi	4	Subaru Impreza 555	accident	16
R. Burns-R. Reid	5	Subaru Impreza 555	accident	20

Successive leaders:
TC 2: Numerous competitors without penalty; TC 3 and 4: Duncan; TC 5 to 45: Fujimoto.

TOUR DE CORSE

Date: May 3-5, 1995
Total distance: 1227 km/762 miles
22 special stages: 489 km/304 miles
92 starters, 44 finishers

Team	No	Car	Group	Time
1 **D. Auriol-D. Giraudet**	1	Toyota Celica Turbo 4WD	A	5.14′19″
2 F. Delecour-C. François	7	Ford Escort RS Cosworth	A	+ 15″
3 A. Aghini-S. Farnocchia	12	Mitsubishi Lancer Evolution 3	A	+ 57″
4 C. Sainz-L. Moya	5	Subaru Impreza 555	A	+ 1′18″
5 C. McRae-D. Ringer	4	Subaru Impreza 555	A	+ 1′43″
6 P. Liatti-A. Alessandrini	6	Subaru Impreza 555	A	+ 2′27″
7 P. Bernardini-J.-M. Andrié	9	Ford Escort RS Cosworth	A	+ 3′05″
8 T. Mäkinen-S. Harjanne	11	Mitsubishi Lancer Evolution 2	A	+ 4′50″
9 P. Bugalski-J.-P. Chiaroni*	21	Renault Clio Maxi kit-car	A	+ 5′36″
10 J. Kankkunen-N. Grist	2	Toyota Celica Turbo 4WD	A	+10′01″
.../...				
18 *R. Madeira-N. Silva*	14	Mitsubishi Lancer Evolution 2	N	+28′54″
19 *I. Holderied-C. Thörner*	30	Mitsubishi Lancer Evolution 2	N	+30′00″

* Winners of Formula 2

Principal retirements

Team	No	Car	Reason	Stages completed
E. Triner-P. Stanc	16	Skoda Felicia kit-car	accident	1
Y. Loubet-B. Brissart	22	Ford Escort RS Cosworth	gearbox	6
P. Sibera-P. Gross	19	Skoda Felicia kit-car	engine	7
A. Schwarz-K. Wicha	3	Toyota Celica GT-Four	alternator	9
B. Thiry-S. Prevot	8	Ford Escort RS Cosworth	wheel-bearing	20

Successive leaders:
SS 1: Delecour & Thiry; SS 2 to 20: Thiry; SS 21 & 22: Auriol.

Stage winners:
Thiry, 12 (3 tied); Auriol, 6 (1 tied); Delecour, 2 (2 tied); Aghini, 1; Liatti, 1; McRae, 1.

ACROPOLIS RALLY

Date: May 28-30, 1995
Total distance: 1307 km/812 miles
25 special stages: 455 km/283 miles
75 starters, 36 finishers

Team	No	Car	Group	Time
1 **A. Vovos-K. Stefanis**	11	Lancia HF Integrale	A	6.37′19″
2 R. Stohl-P. Müller	8	Audi Coupé S2	A	+ 3′01″
3 E. Weber-M. Hiemer*	4	Seat Ibiza GTi 16v	A	+ 3′09″
4 A. Rius-M. Casanova	6	Seat Ibiza GTi 16v	A	+ 6′09″
5 "Stratissino"-T. Pavli	14	Nissan Sunny GTi	A	+11′11″
6 P. Moshoutis-N. Mouzakis	20	Mazda 323 GT-R	A	+14′29″
7 E. Panagiotopoulos-N. Panou	12	Nissan Sunny GTi-R	A	+16′10″
8 P. Sibera-P. Gross	5	Skoda Felicia kit-car	A	+20′56″
9 F. Loix-S. Smeets	9	Opel Astra GSi 16v	A	+35′37″
10 A. Kolokithas-G. Karavangelis	21	Mazda 323 GT-X	A	+40′45″

* Winners of Formula 2

Principal retirements

Team	No	Car	Reason	Stages completed
E. Triner-P. Stanc	3	Skoda Felicia kit-car	suspension	6
P. Snijers-D. Colebunders	2	Ford Escort RS Cosworth	radiator	8
M. Biasion-T. Siviero	1	Lancia HF Integrale	engine	15
L. Kirkos-J. Stavropoulos	7	Ford Escort RS Cosworth	injection system	19

Successive leaders:
SS 1: Biasion; SS 2: Biasion & Kirkos; SS 3: Kirkos; SS 4 to 14: Biasion; SS 15 to 19: Kirkos; SS 20 to 25: Vovos.

Stage winners:
Biasion, 8 (1 tied); Vovos, 7; Kirkos, 4 (1 tied); Loix, 3; Snijers, 2; Rius & Weber, 1.

ARGENTINE RALLY

Date: July 6-8, 1995
Total distance: 1146 km/712 miles
23 special stages: 458 km/285 miles
47 starters, 17 finishers

Team	No	Car	Group	Time
1 **J. Recalde-M. Christie**	5	Lancia HF Integrale	A	5.22′21″
2 G. Trelles-J. del Buono	4	Lancia HF Integrale	A	+ 9′33″
3 M. Galanti-V. Zucchini	3	Toyota Celica Turbo 4WD	A	+ 15′39″
4 P. Sibera-P. Gross*	2	Skoda Felicia kit-car	A	+ 17′19″
5 M. Torras-E. Gatt	32	Renault 18 GTX	A	+ 35′47″
6 E. Triner-P. Stanc	1	Skoda Felicia kit-car	A	+ 38′07″
7 R. Sufan-D. Rama	10	Peugeot 405 Mi16	A	+ 45′37″
8 **S. Reininger-R. Czosz**	18	Renault Clio Williams	N	+ 55′35″
9 L.-A. Oxoteguy-M. Olhaberry	12	Renault 18 GTX	A	+ 56′21″
10 A. Sailen-C. Henin	26	Renault 18 GTX	N	+1.22′31″

* Winners of Formula 2

Principal retirements

Team	No	Car	Reason	Stages completed
G. Raies-J.-M. Volta	6	Renault Clio Williams	accident	2
J. Bescham-J. Garcia	7	Peugeot 405 Mi16	broken piston	8

Successive leaders:
SS 1-23: Recalde.

Stage winners:
NA.

RALLY OF NEW ZEALAND

Date: July 27-30, 1995
Total distance: 2056 km/1278 miles
30 special stages: 499 km/310 miles
86 starters, 56 finishers

Team	No	Car	Group	Time
1 **C. McRae-D. Ringer**	4	Subaru Impreza 555	A	5.33′06″
2 D. Auriol-D. Giraudet	1	Toyota Celica GT-Four	A	+ 44″
3 J. Kankkunen-N. Grist	2	Toyota Celica GT-Four	A	+ 1′09″
4 A. Schwarz-K. Wicha	3	Toyota Celica GT-Four	A	+ 1′45″
5 K. Eriksson-S. Parmander	10	Mitsubishi Lancer Evolution 3	A	+ 2′32″
6 F. Delecour-C. François	7	Ford Escort RS Cosworth	A	+ 4′24″
7 P. Bourne-T. Sircombe	6	Subaru Impreza 555	A	+ 8′55″
8 N. Allport-C. Vincent	9	Ford Escort RS Cosworth	A	+21′41″
9 **J. Recalde-M. Christie**	18	Mitsubishi Lancer Evolution 2	N	+24′39″
10 R. Madeira-N. Silva	17	Mitsubishi Lancer Evolution 2	N	+25′10″
.../...				
28 *V. Slee-S. Haldane*	53	Subaru Impreza 555	N	+50′49″
29 D. Black-J. Black*	60	Toyota Corolla GT	A	+53′27″

* Winners of Formula 2

Principal retirements

Team	No	Car	Reason	Stages completed
I. Holderied-C. Thörner	20	Mitsubishi Lancer Evolution 2	accident	1
B. Thiry-S. Prevot	8	Ford Escort RS Cosworth	electrical failure	6
R. Burns-R. Reid	14	Subaru Impreza 555	damaged radiator	20

Successive leaders:
SS 1: Schwarz; SS 2: Auriol; SS 3: Auriol & Schwarz; SS 4-9: Mäkinen; SS 10-33: McRae (SS 16, 17 and 22 cancelled).

Stage winners:
Auriol, 10 (4 tied); McRae, 10 (5 tied); Mäkinen, 5; Schwarz, 5 (1 tied); Kankkunen, 4 (2 tied); Delecour, 2 (1 tied); Eriksson, 2 (1 tied).

THOUSAND LAKES RALLY

Date: August 22-27, 1995
Total distance: 1539 km/956 miles
31 special stages: 530 km/329 miles
83 starters, 43 finishers

Team	No	Car	Group	Time
1 **T. Mäkinen-S. Harjanne**	1	Mitsubishi Lancer Evolution 3	A	4.39′25″
2 M. Grönholm-T. Rautiainen	9	Toyota Celica Turbo 4WD	A	+ 9′31″
3 J. Kytölehto-A. Kapanen*	11	Opel Astra GSi 16v	A	+20′41″
4 P. Svan-J. Olsson	7	Opel Astra GSi 16v	A	+21′43″
5 A. McRae-D. Senior	8	Nissan Sunny GTi	A	+24′48″
6 **M. Korhonen-L. Heinonen**	14	Mitsubishi Lancer Evolution	N	+27′28″
7 M. Ipatti-H. Kiesi	31	Mitsubishi Lancer Evolution	N	+27′52″
8 J. Ahvenlammi-T. Leino	23	Toyota Celica GT-Four	N	+30′08″
9 M. Utria-M. Lehtinen	32	Mitsubishi Lancer Evolution	N	+34′43″
10 P. Sibera-P. Gross	4	Skoda Felicia kit-car	A	+37′32″

* Winners of Formula 2

Principal retirements

Team	No	Car	Reason	Stages completed
J. Kankkunen-N. Grist	2	Toyota Celica GT-Four	accident	0
G. de Mevius-J.-M. Fortin	6	Nissan Sunny Gti	accident	1
S. Lindholm-T. Hantunen	10	Ford Escort RS Cosworth	engine	3
J. Puhakka-K. Eerola	13	Mitsubishi Lancer Evolution 2	accident	5

Successive leaders:
SS 1 to SS 32: Mäkinen (SS 16 cancelled).

Stage winners:
Mäkinen, 29; Grönholm, 2.

RALLY AUSTRALIA

Date: September 15-18, 1995
Total distance: 1621 km/1007 miles
30 special stages: 504 km/313 miles
94 starters, 47 finishers

	Team	No	Car	Group	Time
1	**K. Eriksson-S. Parmander**	10	Mitsubishi Lancer Evolution 3	A	5.36'17"
2	C. McRae-D. Ringer	4	Subaru Impreza 555	A	+ 19"
3	J. Kankkunen-N. Grist	2	Toyota Celica GT-Four	A	+ 1'55"
4	T. Mäkinen-S. Harjanne	11	Mitsubishi Lancer Evolution 3	A	+ 3'27"
5	A. Schwarz-K. Wicha	3	Toyota Celica GT-Four	A	+ 4'11"
6	B. Thiry-S. Prevot	8	Ford Escort RS Cosworth	A	+16'52"
7	Y. Fujimoto-A. Hertz	14	Toyota Celica GT-Four	A	+22'37"
8	**E. Ordynski-M. Stacey**	12	Mitsubishi Lancer Evolution 3	N	+27'06"
9	N. Bates-C. Taylor	16	Toyota Celica GT-Four	A	+30'42"
10	J. Recalde-M. Christie	15	Mitsubishi Lancer Evolution 2	N	+31'54"
...					
19	*I. Holderied-C. Thörner*	19	Mitsubishi Lancer Evolution 2		+48'36"

Principal retirements

Team	No	Car	Reason	Stages completed
P. Bourne-T. Sircombe	6	Subaru Impreza 555	accident	2
C. Sainz-L. Moya	5	Subaru Impreza 555	engine	9
D. Auriol-D. Giraudet	1	Toyota Celica GT-Four	accident	12
F. Delecour-C. François	7	Ford Escort RS Cosworth	accident	17
R. Madeira-N. Silva	17	Mitsubishi Lancer Evolution 2	electrical failure	17

Successive leaders:
SS1 to 3: Auriol; SS4 to 14: Kankkunen; SS15: Eriksson; SS16: Eriksson & McRae; SS17 & 18: Eriksson; SS19: McRae; SS20 & 21: Eriksson & McRae; SS22 to 30: Eriksson.

Stage winners:
Eriksson, 11 (2 tied); McRae, 7 (2 tied); Kankkunen, 7 (3 tied); Mäkinen, 5 (2 tied); Auriol, 3; Schwarz, 2 (1 tied).

SAN REMO RALLY

Date: October 8-11, 1995
Total distance: 2207 km/1371 miles
24 special stages: 463 km/287 miles
70 starters, 36 finishers

	Team	No	Car	Group	Time
1	**P. Liatti-A. Alessandrini**	6	Subaru Impreza 555	A	5.33'25"
2	A. Dallavilla-D. Fappani	20	Toyota Celica GT-Four	A	+ 1'20"
3	G. Cunico-S. Evangelisti	5	Ford Escort RS Cosworth	A	+ 4'28"
4	M. Biasion-T. Siviero	7	Subaru Impreza 555	A	+ 5'30"
5	G. Grossi-A. Borri	19	Toyota Celica Turbo 4WD	A	+ 10'42"
6	G. Trelles-J. del Buono	4	Subaru Legacy	A	+ 11'50"
7	V. Pasquali-L. Tedeschini	2	Subaru Impreza 555	A	+ 17'00"
8	F. Loix-S. Smeets*	14	Opel Astra GSi 16v	A	+ 20'26"
9	E. Mannarino-D. Vernuccio	21	Toyota Celica Turbo 4DW	A	+ 23'58"
10	P. Andreucci-S. Fedeli	11	Peugeot 306 S16	A	+ 27'26"
...					
12	J. Schachinger-R. Kaufmann	30	Mazda 323 4WD	N	+ 46'13"
...					
15	*L. Zumelli-S. Mantovani*	27	Ford Escort RS Cosworth	N	+1.05'53"

* Winners of Formula 2

Principal retirements

Team	No	Car	Reason	Stages completed
P. Longhi-L. Pirollo	18	Ford Escort RS Cosworth	accident	4
A. Aghini-S. Farnocchia	8	Peugeot 306 Maxi kit-car	lost a wheel	5
B. Béguin-P. Pivato	15	Peugeot 306 Maxi kit-car	accident	10
R. Travaglia-F. Zanella	24	Renault Clio Williams kit-car	transmission	17
P. Snijers-D. Colebunders	1	Ford Escort RS Cosworth	gearbox	19

Successive leaders:
SS 1: Longhi; SS 2 to 16: Cunico; SS 17 to 24: Liatti.

Stage winners:
Dalavilla, 11 (1 tied); Liatti, 9 (3 tied); Cunico, 6 (2 tied); Longhi, 1.

RALLY OF SPAIN

Date: October 23-25, 1995
Total distance: 1664 km/1034 miles
23 special stages: 474 km/294 miles
81 starters, 42 finishers

	Team	No	Car	Group	Time
1	**C. Sainz-L. Moya**	5	Subaru Impreza 555	A	5.05'58"
2	C. McRae-D. Ringer	4	Subaru Impreza 555	A	+ 51"
3	P. Liatti-A. Alessandrini	6	Subaru Impreza 555	A	+ 1'58"
4	F. Delecour-C. François	7	Ford Escort RS Cosworth	A	+ 2'40"
5	A. Aghini-S. Farnocchia	12	Mitsubishi Lancer Evolution 3	A	+ 2'54"
6	G. Trelles-J. del Buono	16	Toyota Celica GT-Four	A	+ 5'56"
7	O. Gomez-M. Marti	19	Renault Clio Williams	A	+12'03"
8	A. Navarra-R. Casazza	22	Toyota Celica GT-Four	A	+12'22"
9	J. Bassas-A. Rodriguez	31	BMW M3	A	+22'08"
10	I. Postel-O. Peyret	14	Subaru Impreza 555	A	+26'40"
11	**R. Madeira-N. Silva**	14	Mitsubishi Lancer Evolution 3	N	+27'54"

Principal retirements

Team	No	Car	Reason	Stages completed
B. Thiry-S. Prevot	8	Ford Escort RS Cosworth	wheel bearing	0
J. Recalde-M. Christie	17	Mitsubishi Lancer Evolution 3	lost a wheel	1
I. Holderied-C. Thörner	20	Mitsubishi Lancer Evolution 3	accident	1
J. Kankkunen-N. Grist	2	Toyota Celica GT-Four	accident	15
T. Mäkinen-S. Harajanne	11	Mitsubishi Lancer Evolution 3	accident	18
D. Auriol-D. Giraudet	1	Toyota Celica GT-Four	disqualified	23

Successive leaders:
SS 1: Schwarz; SS 2 to 15: Kankkunen; SS 16 to 19: Sainz; SS 20 to 22: McRae; arrival: Sainz.

Stage winners:
Kankkunen, 8 (3 tied); Sainz, 6 (2 tied); McRae, 5 (2 tied); Schwarz, 4; Auriol, 4 (2 tied); Aghini, 1.

CONSTRUCTORS' WORLD CUP (2-LITRE CARS)

	FINAL CLASSIFICATION*	Monte Carlo	Sweden	Portugal	Safari	Corsica	Acropolis	Argentina	New Zealand	1000 Lakes	San Remo	Total	Total retained
	OPEL	(25)	(64)	(29)	—	(18)	(29)	—	—	(64)	(57)	0	286
1	PEUGEOT	28	(9)	54	—	46	11	21	43	9	45	257	266
2	RENAULT	65	—	24	—	64	—	22	—	13	39	227	
3	SKODA	—	33	—	—	21	60	—	39	21		174	
4	SEAT	—	—	25	—	64	—	—	26	—		115	
5	NISSAN	18	—	19	—	25	—	—	25	—		87	
6	SUZUKI	—	7	—	—	—	24	44	—	—		75	
7	TOYOTA	—	—	—	—	—	28	—	35	—		63	
8	FIAT	20	—	9	—	4	—	—	—	—	22	55	
9	RENAULT RA	—	—	—	—	—	—	45	—	—		45	
10	CITROËN	4	13	24	—	—	—	—	—	3		44	
11	VOLKSWAGEN	2	17	—	—	—	—	—	—	17		36	
12	DAEWOO	—	—	—	35	—	—	—	—	—		35	
	HONDA	—	—	—	—	—	—	—	35	—		35	
13	FORD	—	21	—	—	—	—	—	—	—		21	
14	DAIHATSU	—	—	—	—	—	—	—	20	—		20	
15	FIAT RA	—	—	—	—	—	15	—	—	—		15	
16	MITSUBISHI	—	8	—	—	—	—	—	13	—		13	

* Only the 8 best results are taken into consideration (discarded scores are shown in brackets). In order for a marque to qualify for the world championship title, points must have been scored in at least one event outside Europe. Opel did not fulfil this requirement and was therefore not eligible.

WORLD RALLY CHAMPIONSHIP FOR DRIVERS

	FINAL CLASSIFICATION**	Monte Carlo	Sweden	Portugal	Corsica	New Zealand	Australia	Spain	RAC	Intermediate total	Total
1	C. SAINZ	20	0	20	10	—	0	20		70	
2	C. McRAE	0	0	12	8	20	15	15		70	
3	J. KANKKUNEN	12	10	15	1	12	12	0		62	
4	D. AURIOL	0	8	8	20	15	0	D		51	
5	K. ERIKSSON	—	20	—	—	8	20	—		48	
6	F. DELECOUR	15	0	—	15	6	0	10		46	
7	T. MÄKINEN	10	15	—	3	0	10	0		38	
8	A. SCHWARZ	0	2	10	0	10	8	0		30	
9	B. THIRY	8	6	6	0	0	6	0		26	
	A. AGHINI	6	—	—	12	—	—	8		26	
10	P. LIATTI	3	—	—	6	—	—	12		21	
11	T. RÅDSTRÖM	—	12	—	—	—	—	—		12	
12	G. TRELLES	—	—	—	—	—	—	6		6	
13	J. RAGNOTTI	4	—	—	00	—	—	—		4	
	S. BLOMQVIST	—	4	—	—	—	—	—		4	
	R. BURNS	—	—	4	—	0	—	—		4	
	P. BERNARDINI	—	—	—	4	—	—	—		4	
	P. BOURNE	—	—	—	—	4	0	—		4	
	Y. FUJIMOTO	—	—	—	—	—	4	—		4	
	J. RECALDE	—	—	1	00	2	1	0		4	
	O. GOMEZ	—	—	—	—	—	—	4		4	
14	T. JANSSON	—	3	—	—	—	—	—		3	
	A. FIORIO	—	—	3	—	—	—	—		3	
	R. MADEIRA	00	—	2	00	1	0	00		3	
	N. ALLPORT	—	—	—	—	3	—	—		3	
	E. ORDYNSKI	—	—	—	—	00	3	—		3	
	A. NAVARRA	—	—	00	0	0	00	3		3	

** At the time of going to press, the RAC had not yet taken place. The results will be given in the next edition of *Automobile Year*, but columns have been provided for readers to complete the results table, while points scores can be inserted in the "Total" column.
0 = Retired. 00 = Did not finish in first ten. D = Disqualified.

FIA CUP FOR PRODUCTION CARS' DRIVERS

	FINAL CLASSIFICATION**	Monte Carlo	Sweden	Portugal	Corsica	New Zealand	Australia	Spain	RAC	Intermediate total	Total
1	R. MADEIRA	7	—	13	13	10	0	13		56	
2	J. RECALDE	—	—	10	7	13	10	0		40	
3	I. HOLDERIED	10	—	7	10	0	00	0		27	
4	E. ORDYNSKI	—	—	—	—	7	13	—		20	
5	M. KAMIOKA	—	—	5	—	0	5	—		10	
6	M. BIN SULAYEM	—	2	0	5	0	0	—		7	
	K. SINGH	—	—	—	—	3	4	—		7	
	M. LIEU	—	—	—	—	0	7	—		7	
7	K. INOUE	—	—	—	—	5	—	—		5	
8	H. MIYOSHI	—	—	4	—	0	0	—		4	
	A. NAVARRA	—	—	3	0	0	1	—		4	
	H. TESHIGAWARA	—	—	—	—	4	—	—		4	
9	M. BECKTON	—	—	—	—	—	3	—		3	
10	K. TAGUCHI	—	—	—	—	2	—	—		2	
	D. WEST	—	—	—	—	—	2	—		2	
11	A. GRANT	—	—	—	—	1	—	—		1	

** At the time of going to press, the RAC had not yet taken place. The results will be given in the next edition of *Automobile Year*, but columns have been provided for readers to complete the results table, while points scores can be inserted in the "Total" column.
0 = Retired. 00 = Did not finish in first eight.

WORLD RALLY CHAMPIONSHIP

	FINAL CLASSIFICATION**	Monte Carlo	Sweden	Portugal	Corsica	New Zealand	Australia	Spain	RAC	Intermediate total	Total
1	MITSUBISHI	36	64	32	36	31	56	33		288	
2	SUBARU	10	—	—	10	10	6			286	
3	TOYOTA	—	10	5	—	—	8			260	
4	FORD	—	—	6	8	—	10			205	

** At the time of going to press, the RAC had not yet taken place. The results will be given in the next edition of *Automobile Year*, but columns have been provided for readers to complete the results table, while points scores can be inserted in the "Total" column.

LADIES' CUP

	FINAL CLASSIFICATION*	Monte Carlo	Sweden	Portugal	Corsica	New Zealand	Australia	Spain	RAC	Intermediate total	Total
1	I. Holderied	11	—	10	11	0	9	0		41	

* At the time of going to press, the RAC had not yet taken place. The results will be given in the next edition of *Automobile Year*, but columns have been provided for readers to complete the results table, while points scores can be inserted in the "Total" column.

LES 24 HEURES DU MANS

Date:	June 17-18, 1995
Weather:	cloudy, wet and misty from 5.00pm to 9.00am, track dry from 10.00am to finish
Circuit:	13.6 km/8.45 miles
Starters:	48
Finishers:	20 classified out of 23
Winners:	Dalmas-Lehto-Sekiya, McLaren F1 GTR, 4055.8 km/2521.16 miles at 168.992 kmh/105.006 mph
1994 Winners:	Dalmas-Haywood-Baldi, Dauer-Porsche 962 LM, 4678.4 km/2907.1 miles at 195.265 kmh/121.335 mph
Fastest lap:	Gonin-Petit-Rostan, WR LM 95-Peugeot, in 3'51"41, at 211.573 kmh/131.465 mph

RESULTS

	No	Drivers	Car	Laps
1	59	**Dalmas-Lehto-Sekiya**	McLaren F1 GTR	298
2	13	**Wollek-Andretti-Hélary**	Courage C34-Porsche	298
3	51	Wallace-J. Bell-D. Bell	McLaren F1 GTR	297
4	24	Bellm-Sala-Blundell	McLaren F1 GTR	293
5	50	Giroix-Grouillard-Delétraz	McLaren F1 GTR	291
6	4	Stuck-Boutsen-Bouchut	Kremer K8-Porsche	290
7	5	Terada-Downing-Fréon	Mazda DG3	283
8	84	**Takahashi-Tsuchiya-Iida**	Honda NSX GT	276
9	73	Unser-Jelinski-Bertaggia	Callaway Corvette	273
10	22	Fukuyama-Kondo-Kasuya	Nismo GT-R LM	272
11	75	Agusta-O'Brien-Donovan	Callaway Corvette	271
12	34	M. Ferté-Thévenin-Palau	Ferrari F40 LM	271
13	42	Maury Laribière-Sourd-Poulain	McLaren F1 GTR	267
14	27	Krosnoff-Martini-Apicella	Toyota GT LM	265
15	77	Kuster-Dolejsi-Seikel	Porsche 911 GT2	264
16	78	van de Vyver-Ortion-Veroux	Porsche 911 GT2	263
17	81	Jones-Adams-McQuillan	Porsche 911 GT2	251
18	41	Mancini-Monti-Ayles	Ferrari F40	238
19	54	Kaufmann-Hane-Ligonnet	Porsche RSR GT1	230
20	14	**Roussel-Santal-Sezionale**	Debora LMP2 95-Ford	223
	44	Gounon-Belmondo-Trévisiol*	Venturi 600 LM	
	71	Marsh-Migault-Leslie*	Marcos LM500	
	46	Favre-Okada-Hattori*	Honda NSX GT1	

Category winners in **bold** * Finished, but not classified (insufficient distance).

RETIREMENTS

No	Drivers	Car	Time*	Reason
1	Cochran-Arnoux-Sigala	Ferrari 333 SP	16.32	gearbox
82	Margueron-Siffert-de Thoisy	Porsche 911 GT2	18.10	accident
47	Gachot-Hahne-Capelli	Honda NSX GT1	18.10	clutch
8	Gonin-Petit-Rostan	WR LM 95-Peugeot	18.57	accident
11	Pescarolo-Lagorce-Bernard	Courage C41-Chevy	19.38	oil pump
55	Yver-Chéreau-Lecomte	Porsche RSR GT1	20.30	accident
52	Lees-Kegan-Chappell	Lister Storm-Jaguar	21.15	transmission
40	della Noce-Olofsson-Ota	Ferrari F40 GTE	21.40	gearbox
36	Jarier-Comas-Pareja	Porsche RSR GT1	21.54	accident
91	Saldana-de Orléans-de Castro	Porsche 911 GT2	21.58	accident
25	Owen Jones-Raphanel-Alliot	McLaren F1 GTR	23.23	accident
79	Calderari-Bryner-Fuchs	Porsche 911 GT2	23.55	collision with Collard
37	Dupuy-Collard-Ortelli	Porsche RSR GT1	02.03	collision with No 79
76	Coppelli-Thyrring-Bourdais	Callaway Corvette	02.50	accident
26	A. Ferté-Acheson	Sard MC8R	03.07	clutch
49	Nielsen-Bscher-Mass	McLaren F1 GTR	04.28	accident
57	Piper-Needell-Weawer	Jaguar XJ 220	04.50	engine
43	Clérico-Chauvin-Lecuyer	Venturi 600 LM	06.00	fire
23	Hoshino-T. Suzuki-Kageyama	Nismo GT-R LM-Nissan	06.57	gearbox
58	Percy-Iacobelli-Thuner	Jaguar XJ 220	07.50	accident
3	Lässig-Konrad-Hermann	Kremer K8-Porsche	08.28	electrical failure
9	David-Bouvet-Balandras	WR LM 94-Peugeot	10.55	ingnition/battery
70	Hodgetts-Euser-Erdos	Marcos LM 500	11.42	transmission
45	Graham-Birbeau-de Lesseps	Venturi 600 LM	12.17	electrical failure
30	J. Paul Jr-McDougall-Mero	Corvette ZR1	13.30	engine

* Times supplied by the organisers.

HOUR-BY-HOUR POSITIONS

No	Drivers	Car	Cat.	Grid	1	2	3	4	5	6	7	8	9	10	11	12	13	14	15	16	17	18	19	20	21	22	23	24	Result
9	David-Bouvet-Balandras	WR LM 94-Peugeot	2	1	9	51	49	49	49	25	49	49	49	49	51	51	51	51	51	59	59	51	51	51	51	59	59		**59**
8	Gonin-Petit-Rostan	WR LM 95-Peugeot	2	2	8	49	51	13	25	49	51	51	51	51	51	59	59	59	59	51	59	59	59	59	51	13			**13**
13	Wollek-Andretti-Hélary	Courage C34-Porsche	1	3	13	24	13	25	51	51	59	59	59	59	13	13	13	13	13	13	13	13	13	13	13	51			**51**
11	Pescarolo-Lagorce-Bernard	Courage C41-Chevy	1	4	49	13	25	51	36	59	37	57	4	50	50	50	50	24	24	24	24	24	24	24	24	24			**24**
4	Stuck-Boutsen-Bouchut	Kremer K8-Porsche	1	5	51	9	59	36	59	37	57	50	4	50	13	24	24	50	50	50	50	50	50	50	50	50			**50**
41	Mancini-Monti-Ayles	Ferrari F40 GTE	3	6	11	4	36	59	57	57	79	3	13	13	4	57	4	4	4	4	4	4	4	4	4	4			**4**
34	M. Ferté-Thévenin-Palau	Ferrari F40 LM	3	7	24	25	91	23	3	4	50	24	24	4	5	5	5	5	5	5	5	5	5	5	5	5			**5**
40	della Noce-Olofsson-Ota	Ferrari F40 GTE	3	8	25	11	79	91	37	79	23	13	24	57	57	5	34	34	34	34	34	84	84	84	84	84			**84**
59	Dalmas-Lehto-Sekiya	McLaren F1 GTR	3	9	59	59	57	34	23	3	50	58	5	5	49	22	22	22	73	84	84	73	73	73	73	73			**73**
44	Gounon-Belmondo-Trévisiol	Venturi 600 SLM	3	10	3	40	37	79	50	25	24	58	58	22	22	73	73	75	22	73	75	22	73	22	22	22			**22**
24	Bellm-Sala-Blundell	McLaren F1 GTR	3	11	4	3	37	57	3	58	4	22	75	22	3	84	73	73	84	22	34	22	75	75	75	75			**75**
49	Nielsen-Bscher-Mass	McLaren F1 GTR	3	12	36	54	34	23	27	76	58	9	75	22	73	73	75	75	84	75	75	75	75	34	34	34			**34**
51	Wallace-J. Bell-D. Bell	McLaren F1 GTR	3	13	40	57	91	79	76	4	13	22	73	73	75	75	84	42	9	9	42	42	42	42	42	42			**42**
25	Owen Jones-Raphanel-Alliot	McLaren F1 GTR	3	14	58	27	23	5	54	34	24	73	34	58	3	23	54	54	42	42	54	77	77	77	78	27			**27**
50	Giroix-Grouillard-Delétraz	McLaren F1 GTR	3	15	82	34	24	75	50	13	22	75	3	3	84	84	42	42	9	54	54	42	78	78	27	77			**77**
3	Lässig-Konrad-Hermann	Kremer K8-Porsche	1	16	27	36	40	27	5	5	9	34	76	9	3	3	77	78	78	78	78	78	27	77	78	78			**78**
1	Cochran-Arnoux-Sigala	Ferrari 333 SP	1	17	23	23	76	76	58	22	5	43	78	78	23	42	9	77	77	77	77	54	81	81	81	81			**81**
37	Dupuy-Collard-Ortelli	Porsche RSR GT1	3	18	34	79	54	54	70	9	73	78	70	54	9	54	77	77	23	81	81	81	81	54	41	54	54	41	**41**
5	Terada-Downing-Fréon	Mazda-Kudzu DG3	1	19	84	37	75	58	75	78	78	76	43	84	42	9	78	27	27	27	9	14	54	41	54	54			**54**
42	Maury Laribière-Sourd-Poulain	McLaren F1 GTR	3	20	54	5	27	50	4	73	75	84	84	42	54	77	81	81	45	45	14	41	14	14	14	14			**14**
36	Jarier-Comas-Pareja	Porsche RSR GT1	3	21	70	75	78	70	34	70	43	54	54	23	43	45	45	27	3	3	14	45	45	71	44	44			
57	Piper-Needell-Weawer	Jaguar XJ 220	3	22	37	91	58	22	22	24	34	70	9	43	77	81	27	45	45	23	14	41	71	44	71	71			
76	Coppelli-Thyrring-Bourdais	Callaway Corvette	4	23	5	76	70	78	73	75	54	42	81	81	78	43	14	14	23	71	44	46	46	46	46				
52	Lees-Keegan-Chappell	Lister Storm-Jaguar	3	24	79	22	9	4	78	43	76	37	23	77	78	58	70	14	41	41	71	70	70	30					
58	Percy-Iacobelli-Thuner	Jaguar XJ 220	3	25	76	58	22	40	13	54	70	77	77	70	45	27	27	58	58	70	70	70	44	46					
23	Hoshino-T. Suzuki-Kageyama	Nismo GT-R LM-Nissan	3	26	50	55	55	73	9	91	84	23	81	45	27	45	14	70	70	71	44	46	30						
54	Kaufmann-Hane-Ligonnet	Porsche RSR GT1	3	27	57	78	50	14	43	27	77	81	45	27	70	41	71	44	44	46	30								
47	Gachot-Hahne-Capelli	Honda NSX GT1	3	28	91	73	8	77	81	81	79	27	76	14	41	71	45	46	30										
43	Clérico-Chauvin-Lecuyer	Venturi 600 LM	3	29	14	8	4	43	24	77	42	45	14	41	44	44	46	30	30										
27	Krosnoff-Martini-Apicella	Toyota GT LM	3	30	75	70	73	9	77	84	45	27	41	71	71	71	46	46	30										
26	A. Ferté-Acheson	Sard MC8R	3	31	73	52	43	81	84	45	14	14	71	44	44	30	30												
79	Calderari-Bryner-Fuchs	Porsche 911 GT2	4	32	55	43	77	45	45	42	27	44	44	44	46	46													
55	Yver-Chéreau-Lecomte	Porsche RSR GT1	3	33	46	77	14	55	14	14	41	71	46	46	26	26													
22	Fukuyama-Kondo-Kasuya	Nismo GT-R LM-Nissan	3	34	78	42	52	42	41	71	46	26	26	30	30														
45	Graham-Birbeau-de Lesseps	Venturi 600 LM	3	35	81	50	81	24	40	46	55	44	30	30															
84	Takahashi-Tsuchiya-Iida	Honda NSX GT	4	36	45	81	45	84	41	55	46	26																	
73	Unser-Jelinski-Bertaggia	Callaway Corvette	4	37	43	45	84	42	55	71	44	30																	
14	Roussel-Santal-Sezionale	Debora LMP 295-Ford	2	38	52	71	42	41	52	46	26																		
75	Agusta-O'Brien-Donovan	Callaway Corvette	4	39	77	46	11	8	71	44	30																		
91	Saldana-de Orléans-de Castro	Porsche 911 GT2	4	40	83	84	41	71	46	26																			
82	Margueron-Siffert-de Thoisy	Porsche 911 GT2	4	41	71	42	41	46	44	30																			
70	Hodgetts-Euser-Erdos	Marcos LM500	4	42	41	41	46	82	26																				
71	Marsh-Migault-Leslie	Marcos LM500	4	43	1	82	82	26	30																				
46	Favre-Okada-Hattori	Honda NSX GT1	3	44	42	1	26	44																					
81	Jones-Adams-McQuillan	Porsche 911 GT2	4	45	47	47	44	30																					
47	Kuster-Dolejsi-Seikel	Porsche 911 GT2	4	46	44	26	30																						
78	Van de Vyver-Ortion-Veyroux	Porsche 911 GT2	4	47	30	44																							
30	J. Paul Jr-McDougall-Mero	Corvette ZR1	3	48	26	30																							

INTERNATIONAL BPR SERIES

JEREZ – FEBRUARY 26, 1995

	Driver	No	Car	Category
1	Bellm-Sala	1	McLaren F1 GTR	GT1
2	Wollek-Jarier-Bouchut	86	Porsche 911 GT2	GT2
3	Bryner-Calderari	55	Porsche 911 GT2	GT2
4	Altenbach-Leineman	30	Porsche 911 GT2	GT2
5	Ploeg-Rebai	20	Porsche 993 Bi-Turbo	GT1
6	Chereau-Leconte-Yver	47	Porsche 911 RSR 3,8	GT3
7	Hübner-Palmberger-Oberndorfer	70	Porsche 911 RSR 3,8	GT3
8	Maury Laribière-Lecuyer-Fabre	56	Venturi 600 LM	GT1
9	Saldara-d'Orléans	10	Porsche 911 GT2	GT2
10	Konrad-de Lesseps	21	Porsche 911 Bi-Turbo	GT1

PAUL RICARD – MARCH 12, 1995

	Driver	No	Car	Category
1	Bellm-Sala	1	McLaren F1 GTR	GT1
2	Wollek-Jarier-Bouchut	86	Porsche 911 GT2	GT1
3	Nielsen-Bscher	8	McLaren F1 GTR	GT1
4	Kaufmann-Ligonnet-Albera	50	Porsche 911 Bi-Turbo	GT1
5	Maury Laribière-Lecuyer-Fabre	5	McLaren F1 GTR	GT1
6	Grohs-Angelastri	25	Porsche Turbo	GT1
7	Owen Jones-Raphanel	3	McLaren F1 GTR	GT1
8	Burdell-Roessledr-Langton	20	Porsche 993 Bi-Turbo	GT3
9	Chereau-Leconte-Yver	47	Porsche 911 RSR	GT3
10	Guiod-Bacle	26	Venturi 600 LM	GT1
16	Grassi-Passerini-Colombo	36	Porsche 993	GT4
20	Guillot-Brarda-Muller	29	Porsche Carrera	GT2

MONZA – MARCH 26, 1995

	Driver	No	Car	Category
1	Nielsen-Bscher	8	McLaren F1 GTR	GT1
2	Wollek-Jarier	86	Porsche 911 GT2	GT2
3	Della Noce-Olofsson	60	Ferrari F40 GTE	GT1
4	Konrad-Ploeg	20	Porsche 993	GT3
5	Keegan-Kaufmann	50	Porsche 911 Bi-Turbo	GT1
6	Bryner-Calderari	55	Porsche 911 GT2	GT3
7	Angelastri-von Gartzen	25	Porsche Turbo 2	GT1
8	Maury Laribière-Lecuyer	5	McLaren F1 GTR	GT1
9	Mastropietro-Rossi	12	Porsche RSR 3.	GT3
10	Thirring-Wallace	37	de Tomaso Pantera	GT1
15	Monti-Giovenzana	35	Porsche Carrera Cup	GT4

JARAMA – APRIL 9, 1995

	Driver	No	Car	Category
1	Bellm-Sala	1	McLaren F1 GTR	GT1
2	Nielsen-Bscher	8	McLaren F1 GTR	GT1
3	Wollek-Jarier-Bouchut	86	Porsche 911 GT2	GT2
4	Wallace-Bell	9	McLaren F1 GTR	GT1
5	Giroix-Grouillard	7	McLaren F1 GTR	GT1
6	Lässig-von Gartzen	25	Porsche 911 Turbo	GT1
7	Bryner-Calderari	55	Porsche 911 GT2	GT3
8	Margueron-Less-Neugarten	22	Porsche 91 GT2	GT3
9	Saldana-d'Orléans	10	Porsche 911 GT2	GT1
10	Seiler-Reis	20	Porsche 993	GT3
19	Ried-Bovenstepen	58	Porsche 911 RSR	GT4

NÜRBURGRING – APRIL 23, 1995

	Driver	No	Car	Category
1	Bellm-Sala	1	McLaren F1 GTR	GT1
2	Giroix-Grouillard	7	Mclaren F1 GTR	GT1
3	Nielsen-Bscher	8	McLaren F1 GTR	GT1
4	Owen Jones-Raphanel	16	McLaren F1 GTR	GT1
5	Wallace-Bell	9	McLaren F1 GTR	GF1
6	Bryner-Calderari	55	Porsche 911 GT2	GT3
7	Hübner-Oberndorfer	70	Porsche 911 GT2	GT3
8	Kaufmann-Giacomelli	50	Porsche 911 Bi-Turbo	GT1
9	Burdell-Roessler-Langton	6	Porsche 911 GT2	GT3
10	von Gartzen-Angelastri	25	Porsche 911 Turbo	GT1
17	Bliz-Rosterg	31	Porsche RSR 3,8	GT4

DONINGTON – MAY 8, 1995

	Driver	No	Car	Category
1	Nielsen-Bscher	1	McLaren F1 GTR	GT1
2	Raphanel-Owen Jones	16	McLaren F1 GTR	GT1
3	Wallace-Bell	9	McLaren F1 GTR	GT1
4	Mastropietro-König	65	Porsche 911 GT2	GT3
5	Kaufmann-Albera-Ligonnet	50	Porsche 911 Bi-Turbo	GT1
6	Bryner-Calderari	55	Porsche 911 GT2	GT3
7	Farmer-Edwards	14	Porsche 911 GT2	GT3
8	Hardman-Dean	80	Jaguar XJ 220	GT1
9	Greasley-Morrison	46	Porsche 911 GT2	GT3
10	Agusta-O'Brien-Donovan	4	Callaway Corvette	GT3

MONTLHÉRY – MAY 14, 1995

	Driver	No	Car	Category
1	Oberndorfer-Hübner	70	Porsche 911 GT2	GT3
2	Farmer-Edwards-Nearn	14	Porsche 911 GT2	GT3
3	Quargentan-Auvray	33	Porsche 911 GT2	GT3
4	Graham-Birbeau-Faraut	44	Venturi 600 LM	GT1
5	Touroul-Perrier-Tardif	57	Porsche RSR	GT2
6	Coudert-Jurasz-Sanguiolo	31	Porsche RSR 3,8	GT4
7	Grassi-Passerini-Colombo	36	Porsche 911 Cup	GT4
8	Vuillaume-Ried-Bovensiep	58	Porsche RSR 3,6	GT3
9	Monti-de Castro-Morini	35	Porsche 911 Cup	GT4
10	Heinkele-O'Born	11	Ferrari F355	GT3

ANDERSTORP – JULY 2, 1995

	Driver	No	Car	Category
1	Ferté-Thévenin	40	Ferrari F40 LM	GT1
2	Nielsen-Bscher	8	McLaren F1 GTR	GT1
3	Owen Jones-Raphanel	16	McLaren F1 GTR	GT1
4	Konrad-Spinelli-Seiler	21	Porsche 911 GT2	GT3
5	Bryner-Calderari	55	Porsche 911 GT2	GT3
6	de Lesseps-Margueron-Charriol	22	Porsche 911 GT2	GT3
7	Burdell-Roessler-Langton	6	Porsche 911 GT2	GT3
8	Capra-Quargentan-Sanguiolo	33	Porsche 911 GT2	GT3
9	Veerte-Wirdheim	42	Porsche 911 Bi-Turbo	GT1
10	Hardman-Dean	80	Jaguar XJ 220	GT1
11	de Creane-de Puysseleyr	59	Porsche Carrera Cup	GT4

SUZUKA – AUGUST 27, 1995

	Driver	No	Car	Category
1	Bellm-Sala-Sekiya	1	McLaren F1 GTR	GT1
2	Nielsen-Bscher	8	McLaren F1 GTR	GT1
3	della Noce-Olofsson-Mancini	60	Ferrari F40 GTE	GT1
4	Wollek-Jarier	86	Porsche 911 GT2 Evo. Proto. 1 Class	
5	Takahashi-Tsuchiya-Iida	100	Honda NSX/M1	GT1
6	Ota-Monti-Ayles	61	Ferrari F40 GTE	Suzuka Super GT
7	Gounon-Gache-Trevisol	90	Venturi 600 SLM	GT1
8	Bryner-Calderari-Ratel	55	Porsche 911 GT2	GT3
9	Jonai-Tanigawa	19	Samos FS951	Suzuka Super GT
10	Konrad-Hermann	20	Porsche 911 GT2	Suzuka GT-1 Class

SILVERSTONE SEPTEMBER 17, 1995

	Driver	No	Car	Category
1	Wallace-Grouillard	9	McLaren F1 GTR	GT1
2	Ferté-Thévenin	40	Ferrari F40 LM	GT1
3	Olofsson-Della Noce	60	Ferrari F40 GTE	GT1
4	Zanardi-Portman	45	Lotus Esprit Sport	GT3
5	Nielsen-Bscher	8	McLaren F1 GTR	GT1
6	Roessler-Burdell-Langton	6	Porsche 911 GT2	GT3
7	Morrison-Greasley	3	Porsche 911 GT2	GT3
8	Raphanel-Owen Jones	16	McLaren F1 GTR	GT1
9	Wirdheim-Veerte	30	Porsche 911 LM GT	GT2
10	Sala-Bellm	1	McLaren F1 GTR	GT1

NOGARO – OCTOBER 8, 1995

	Driver	No	Car	Category
1	Wallace-Grouillard	9	McLaren F1 GTR	GT1
2	Nielsen-Bscher	8	McLaren F1 GTR	GT1
3	Bellm-Sala	1	McLaren F1 GTR	GT1
4	Owen Jones-Raphanel	16	McLaren F1 GTR	GT1
5	Drudi-Ayles	61	Ferrari F40 GTE	GT1
6	Jarier-Wollek-Bouchut	86	Porsche 911 GT2	GT1
7	Bryner-Calderari	55	Porsche 911 GT2	GT3
8	Chereau-Yver-Hélary	47	Porsche 911 GT2	GT1
9	Konrad-Seiler-Spinelli	21	Porsche 911 GT2	GT3
10	Puig-Belmondo-Chatriot	41	Ferrari F40	GT1
12	Bilz-Seikel	31	Porsche RSR 3.8	GT4
14	Touroul-Ortion-Jakubowski	57	Porsche Carrera 2	GT2

ZHUHAI – NOVEMBER 5, 1995

	Driver	No	Car	Category
1	Wallace-Grouillard	9	McLaren F1 GTR	GT1
2	Nielsen-Bscher	8	McLaren F1 GTR	GT1
3	Giroix-Delétraz	7	McLaren F1 GTR	GT1
4	Bryner-Calderari	55	Porsche 911 GT2	GT3
5	Laribière-Libert	5	McLaren F1 GTR	GT1
6	Ligonnet-Albera	51	Porsche 911 Biturbo	GT1
7	Li-Lo-Whillock	93	Porsche 911 3.6 RS	GT4
8	Guido-Smaniotto	29	Venturi 600 LM	GT1
9	Ma-Pickup-Goddard	89	Porsche 911 3.8 RS	GT4
10	Schmickler-Schuster	42	Porsche 911	GT1

Final classification:

1	John Nielsen-Thomas Bscher	McLaren F1 GTR	West Competition	252
2	Lilian Bryner-Enzo Calderari	Porsche 911 GT2	Stadler Motorsport	205
3	Ray Bellm-Maurizio Sala	McLaren F1 GTR	Gulf Racing/GTC	201
4	Andy Wallace	McLaren F1 GTR	Mach One Racing	154
5	Jean-Pierre Jarier-Bob Wollek	Porsche 911 GT2	Larbre Competition	124
6	Franz Konrad	Porsche 911 GT2	Konrad Motorsport	110

IndyCar World Series

MIAMI

Date: March 5, 1995. **Circuit:** 90 laps of the 2.942 km/1.828 mile Bicentennial Park, Miami circuit, 264.78 km/164.531 miles. **Winner's time:** 1.59'16". **Winner's average speed:** 133.226 kmh/82.785 mph.

Results:

Driver	No	Car	Laps
1 Villeneuve	27	Reynard 951-Ford Cosworth XB	90
2 Gugelmin	18	Reynard 951-Ford Cosworth XB	90
3 Rahal	9	Lola T95/00-Ford Cosworth XB	90
4 Pruett	20	Lola T95/00-Ford Cosworth XB	90
5 C. Fittipaldi	15	Reynard 951-Ford Cosworth XB	90
6 Boesel	11	Lola T95/00-Mercedes V8	90
7 Danner	64	Reynard 94-Ford Cosworth XB	90
8 Vasser	12	Reynard 951-Ford Cosworth XB	90
9 Sullivan	17	Reynard 951-Ford Cosworth XB	89
10 Herta	4	Reynard 951-Ford Cosworth XB	87
11 Fernandez	10	Lola T95/00-Mercedes V8	86
12 Hall	99	Lola T95/00-Ford Cosworth XB	86
Cheever*	14	Lola T95/00-Ford Cosworth XB	81
Unser*	1	Penske PC24-Mercedes V8	79

*Finished, but did not score points.

Retirements:

Driver	No	Car	Laps	Reason
Tracy	3	Lola T95/00-Ford Cosworth XB	0	accident
Matsushita	25	Lola T94/00-Ford Cosworth XB	10	accident
de Ferran	8	Reynard 951-Mercedes V8	14	gearbox
E. Fittipaldi	2	Penske PC24-Mercedes V8	24	engine
Zampredi	34	Lola T94/00-Ford Cosworth XB	34	accident
Johansson	16	Penske PC23-Mercedes V8	46	gearbox
Ribeiro	31	Reynard 951-Honda V8	47	collision with Fernandez
Andretti	6	Lola T95/00-Ford Cosworth XB	49	suspension damaged in collision
Bachelart	19	Lola T94/00-Ford Cosworth XB	54	damaged suspension
Vitolo	21	Reynard 951-Mercedes V8	55	turbo
Salazar	7	Lola T95/00-Ford Cosworth XB	71	engine
Fabi	33	Reynard 951-Ford Cosworth XB	72	radiator
Gordon	5	Reynard 951-Ford Cosworth XB	83	accident

PHOENIX

Date: April 2, 1995. **Circuit:** 200 laps of the 1.609 km/1 mile Phoenix International Raceway circuit, 321.8 km/200 miles. **Winner's time:** 1.29'33"930. **Winner's average speed:** 215.573 kmh/133.954 mph.

Results:

Driver	No	Car	Laps
1 Gordon	5	Reynard 951-Ford Cosworth XB	200
2 Andretti	6	Lola T95/00-Ford Cosworth XB	200
3 E. Fittipaldi	2	Penske PC24-Mercedes V8	200
4 Tracy	3	Lola T95/00-Ford Cosworth XB	200
5 Villeneuve	27	Reynard 951-Ford Cosworth XB	200
6 Boesel	11	Lola T95/00-Mercedes V8	198
7 Fabi	33	Reynard 951-Ford Cosworth XB	198
8 Unser	1	Penske PC24-Mercedes V8	197
9 Pruett	20	Lola T95/00-Ford Cosworth XB	197
10 C. Fittipaldi	15	Reynard 951-Ford Cosworth XB	195
11 de Ferran	8	Reynard 951-Mercedes V8	195
12 Fernandez	10	Lola T95/00-Mercedes V8	195
Gugelmin	18	Reynard 951-Ford Cosworth XB	194
Cheever	14	Lola T95/00-Ford Cosworth XB	194
Salazar	7	Lola T95/00-Ford Cosworth XB	192
Guerrero	21	Reynard 94-Mercedes V8	190
Hall	99	Lola T95/00-Ford Cosworth XB	189
Bachelart	19	Lola T94/00-Ford Cosworth XB	188
Zampredi	34	Lola T94/00-Ford Cosworth XB	185

Retirements:

Driver	No	Car	Laps	Reason
Sullivan	17	Reynard 951-Ford Cosworth XB	21	brakes
Ribeiro	31	Reynard 951-Honda V8	38	accident
Luyendyk	22	Lola T95/00-Ford Cosworth XB	71	handling
Johansson	16	Penske PC23-Mercedes V8	112	collision with Villeneuve
Vasser	12	Reynard 94-Ford Cosworth XB	131	gearbox
Matsushita	25	Reynard 94-Ford Cosworth XB	143	handling
Rahal	9	Lola T95/00-Mercedes V8	160	gearbox
Herta	4	Reynard 951-Ford Cosworth XB	170	handling

NAZARETH

Date: April 23, 1995. **Circuit:** 200 laps of the 1.609 km/1 mile Nazareth oval circuit, 321.8 km/200 miles. **Winner's time:** 1.31'23"410. **Winner's average speed:** 211.269 kmh/131.28 mph.

Results:

Driver	No	Car	Lap
1 E. Fittipaldi	2	Penske PC24-Mercedes V8	200
2 Villeneuve	27	Reynard 951-Ford Cosworth XB	200
3 Johansson	16	Penske PC23-Mercedes V8	200
4 Gordon	5	Reynard 951-Ford Cosworth XB	200
5 Cheever	14	Lola T95/00-Ford Cosworth XB	199
6 Rahal	9	Lola T95/00-Mercedes V8	199
7 Fabi	33	Reynard 951-Ford Cosworth XB	199
8 Pruett	20	Lola T95/00-Ford Cosworth XB	199
9 Fernandez	10	Lola T95/00-Mercedes V8	199
10 Boesel	11	Lola T95/00-Mercedes V8	199
11 Ribeiro	31	Reynard 951-Honda V8	199
12 Salazar	7	Lola T95/00-Ford Cosworth XB	198
Unser	1	Penske PC24-Mercedes V8	198
Guerrero	22	Lola T95/00-Ford Cosworth XB	196
Zampredi	34	Lola T94/00-Ford Cosworth XB	196
Hall	99	Lola T95/00-Ford Cosworth XB	194
Gugelmin	18	Reynard 951-Ford Cosworth XB	186
Sullivan	17	Reynard 951-Ford Cosworth XB	185
Greco	55	Lola T95/00-Mercedes V8	179

Retirements:

Driver	No	Car	Lap	Reason
Tracy	3	Lola T95/00-Ford Cosworth XB	30	collision with Vasser
Lazier	19	Lola T94/00-Ford Cosworth XB	38	accident
Vasser	12	Reynard 951-Ford Cosworth XB	67	overheating
Herta	4	Reynard 951-Ford Cosworth XB	155	engine
Andretti	6	Lola T95/00-Ford Cosworth XB	172	accident
C. Fittipaldi	15	Reynard 951-Ford Cosworth XB	179	electrical failure
de Ferran	8	Reynard 951-Mercedes V8	183	accident

QUEENSLAND (AUS)

Date: March 19, 1995. **Circuit:** 65 laps of the 4.498 km/2.795 mile Surfers Paradise street circuit, 292.37 km/181.675 miles. **Winner's time:** 1.58'26"054. **Winner's average speed:** 147.93 kmh/91.922 mph.

Results:

Driver	No	Car	Laps
1 Tracy	3	Lola T95/00-Ford Cosworth XB	65
2 Rahal	9	Lola T95/00-Mercedes V8	65
3 Pruett	20	Lola T95/00-Ford Cosworth XB	65
4 Gugelmin	18	Reynard 951-Ford Cosworth XB	65
5 Sullivan	17	Reynard 951-Ford Cosworth XB	65
6 Unser	1	Penske PC24-Mercedes V8	65
7 Cheever	14	Lola T95/00-Ford Cosworth XB	65
8 Boesel	11	Lola T95/00-Mercedes V8	65
9 Andretti*	6	Lola T95/00-Mercedes V8	64
10 Salazar	7	Lola T95/00-Ford Cosworth XB	64
11 Matsushita	25	Lola T94/00-Ford Cosworth XB	62
12 Hall	99	Lola T95/00-Ford Cosworth XB	61
Fabi	33	Reynard 951-Ford Cosworth XB	60
Zampredi	34	Lola T94/00-Ford Cosworth XB	51

*Retired, but classified as a finisher.

Retirements:

Driver	No	Car	Laps	Reason
Fernandez	10	Lola T95/00-Mercedes V8	3	accident
C. Fittipaldi	15	Reynard 951-Ford Cosworth XB	11	gearbox
Vasser	12	Reynard 951-Ford Cosworth XB	19	gearbox
Ribeiro	31	Reynard 951-Honda V8	23	gearbox
Bachelart	19	Lola T94/00-Ford Cosworth XB	31	gearbox
Lazier	64	Lola T93/00-Ford Cosworth XB	32	gearbox
Villeneuve	27	Reynard 951-Ford Cosworth XB	38	gearbox
E. Fittipaldi	2	Penske PC24-Mercedes V8	52	electrical failure
Johansson	16	Penske PC23-Mercedes V8	53	gearbox
de Ferran	8	Reynard 951-Mercedes V8	54	gearbox
Herta	4	Reynard 951-Ford Cosworth XB	58	accident
Gordon	5	Reynard 951-Ford Cosworth XB	59	electrical failure
Andretti	6	Lola T95/00-Ford Cosworth XB	64	accident

LONG BEACH

Date: April 9, 1995. **Circuit:** 105 laps of the 2.558 km/1.59 mile Long Beach street circuit, 268.59 km/166.899 miles. **Winner's time:** 1.49'32"667. **Winner's average speed:** 147.130 kmh/91.425 mph.

Results:

Driver	No	Car	Laps
1 Unser	1	Penske PC24-Mercedes V8	105
2 Pruett	20	Lola T95/00-Ford Cosworth XB	105
3 Fabi	33	Reynard 951-Ford Cosworth XB	105
4 Cheever	14	Lola T95/00-Ford Cosworth XB	104
5 Gugelmin	18	Reynard 951-Ford Cosworth XB	104
6 Johansson	16	Penske PC23-Mercedes V8	104
7 Bachelart	19	Lola T94/00-Ford Cosworth XB	104
8 Zampredi	34	Lola T94/00-Ford Cosworth XB	104
9 Andretti	6	Lola T95/00-Ford Cosworth XB	104
10 Sullivan	17	Reynard 951-Ford Cosworth XB	104
11 Guerrero	22	Lola T95/00-Ford Cosworth XB	104
12 Ribeiro	31	Reynard 951-Honda V8	104
Greco	55	Lola T95/00-Mercedes V8	104
Fréon	64	Reynard 94-Ford Cosworth XB	103
Boesel	11	Lola T95/00-Mercedes V8	100
Hall	99	Lola T95/00-Ford Cosworth XB	99
Fernandez	10	Lola T95/00-Mercedes V8	99
Matsushita	25	Reynard 94-Ford Cosworth XB	86

Retirements:

Driver	No	Car	Laps	Reason
Tracy	3	Lola T95/00-Ford Cosworth XB	16	collision with de Ferran
de Ferran	8	Reynard 951-Mercedes V8	16	collision with Tracy
Herta	4	Reynard 951-Ford Cosworth XB	28	accident
Villeneuve	27	Reynard 951-Ford Cosworth XB	34	gearbox
Salazar	7	Lola T95/00-Ford Cosworth XB	39	electrical failure
Vasser	12	Reynard 94-Ford Cosworth XB	45	engine
Gordon	5	Reynard 951-Ford Cosworth XB	57	engine
Rahal	9	Lola T95/00-Mercedes V8	77	gearbox
E. Fittipaldi	2	Penske PC24-Mercedes V8	85	engine
C. Fittipaldi	15	Reynard 951-Ford Cosworth XB	103	gearbox

INDIANAPOLIS

Date: May 28, 1995. **Circuit:** 200 laps of the 4.023 km/2.5 mile Indianapolis Speedway circuit, 804.60 km/500 miles. **Winner's time:** 3.15'17"561. **Winner's average speed:** 247.168 kmh/153.587 mph.

Results:

Driver	No	Car	Laps
1 Villeneuve	27	Reynard 951-Ford Cosworth XB	200
2 C. Fittipaldi*	15	Reynard 951-Ford Cosworth XB	200
3 Rahal	9	Lola T95/00-Mercedes V8	200
4 Salazar*	7	Lola T95/00-Ford Cosworth XB	200
5 Gordon	5	Reynard 951-Ford Cosworth XB	200
6 Gugelmin	18	Reynard 951-Ford Cosworth XB	200
7 Luyendyk	40	Lola T95/00-Menard	200
8 Fabi	33	Reynard 951-Ford Cosworth XB	199
9 Sullivan	17	Reynard 951-Ford Cosworth XB	199
10 Matsushita	25	Reynard 951-Ford Cosworth XB	199
11 Zampredi	34	Lola T94/00-Ford Cosworth XB	198
12 R. Guerrero	21	Reynard 94-Mercedes V8	198
Herta	4	Reynard 951-Ford Cosworth XB	198
Goodyear	24	Reynard 951-Honda V8	195
Matsuda	54	Lola T94/00-Ford Cosworth XB	194
Johansson	16	Penske PC23-Ford Cosworth XB	192
Brayton	60	Lola T95/00-Menard	190
Ribeiro*	31	Reynard 951-Honda V8	187

*Rookie driver

Retirements:

Driver	No	Car	Laps	Reason
C. Guerrero*	22	Lola T95/00-Ford Cosworth XB	0	collision
St. James	90	Lola T95/00-Ford Cosworth XB	0	collision
Cheever	14	Lola T95/00-Ford Cosworth XB	0	collision
Fox	91	Reynard 951-Ford Cosworth XB	0	collision
de Ferran*	8	Reynard 951-Mercedes V8	0	collision
Bachelart	19	Lola T94/00-Ford Cosworth XB	6	mechanical problem
Lazier	80	Lola T95/00-Menard	45	fuel pump
Sharp	41	Lola T95/00-Ford Cosworth XB	74	accident
Andretti	6	Lola T95/00-Ford Cosworth XB	77	suspension
Tracy	3	Lola T95/00-Ford Cosworth XB	136	electrical failure
Jones	77	Lola T95/00-Ford Cosworth XB	161	accident
Vasser	12	Reynard 94-Ford Cosworth XB	170	accident
Fernandez	10	Lola T95/00-Mercedes V8	176	engine
Boesel	11	Lola T95/00-Mercedes V8	184	engine
Pruett	20	Lola T95/00-Ford Cosworth XB	184	spin

INDYCAR WORLD SERIES

MILWAUKEE

Date: June 4, 1995. **Circuit:** 200 laps of the 1.609 km/1.0 mile West Allis circuit, 321.8 km/200 miles. **Winner's time:** 1.27'23"853. **Winner's average speed:** 220.922 kmh/137.278 mph.

Results:

Driver	No	Car	Laps
1 Tracy	3	Lola T95/00-Ford Cosworth XB	200
2 Unser	1	Penske PC24-Mercedes V8	200
3 Andretti	6	Lola T95/00-Ford Cosworth XB	199
4 Fabi	33	Reynard 951-Ford Cosworth XB	198
5 Gordon	5	Reynard 951-Ford Cosworth XB	197
6 Villeneuve	27	Reynard 951-Ford Cosworth XB	197
7 C. Fittipaldi	15	Reynard 951-Ford Cosworth XB	196
8 de Ferran	8	Reynard 951-Mercedes V8	195
9 Vasser	12	Reynard 94-Ford Cosworth XB	195
10 Fernandez	10	Lola T95/00-Mercedes V8	195
11 Boesel	11	Lola T95/00-Mercedes V8	194
12 Pruett	20	Lola T95/00-Ford Cosworth XB	194
Rahal	9	Lola T95/00-Mercedes V8	193
Gugelmin	18	Reynard 951-Ford Cosworth XB	193
C. Guerrero	22	Lola T95/00-Ford Cosworth XB	191
Salazar	7	Lola T95/00-Ford Cosworth XB	191
Sullivan	17	Reynard 951-Ford Cosworth XB	188
Lazier	19	Lola T94-Ford Cosworth XB	188
Matsushita	25	Reynard 94-Ford Cosworth XB	184
St. James	90	Lola T95/00-Ford Cosworth XB	184
Johansson	16	Penske PC23-Mercedes V8	177
Zampredi	34	Lola T9400-Ford Cosworth XB	173

Retirements:

Driver	No	Car	Laps	Reason
Cheever	14	Lola T95/00-Ford Cosworth XB	32	handling
Ribeiro	31	Reynard 951-Honda V8	35	suspension
E. Fittipaldi	2	Penske PC24-Mercedes V8	122	minor collision

PORTLAND

Date: June 25, 1995. **Circuit:** 102 laps of the 3.15 km/1.957 mile Portland circuit, 321.8 km/199.652 miles. **Winner's time:** 1.55'17"971. **Winner's average speed:** 166.537 kmh/103.484 mph.

Results:

Driver	No	Car	Laps
Unser*	1	Penske PC24-Mercedes V8	102
1 Vasser	12	Reynard 951-Ford Cosworth XB	102
2 Rahal	9	Lola T95/00-Mercedes V8	102
3 Andretti	6	Lola T95/00-Ford Cosworth XB	102
4 Boesel	11	Lola T95/00-Mercedes V8	102
5 Johansson**	16	Penske PC23-Mercedes V8	101
6 Gugelmin	18	Reynard 951-Ford Cosworth XB	101
7 Gordon	5	Reynard 951-Ford Cosworth XB	101
8 Fernandez	10	Lola T95/00-Mercedes V8	101
9 de Ferran	8	Reynard 951-Mercedes V8	100
10 Greco	99	Lola T95/00-Mercedes V8	100
11 C. Fittipaldi	15	Reynard 951-Ford Cosworth XB	100
12 Pruett	20	Lola T95/00-Ford Cosworth XB	99
Ribeiro	31	Reynard 951-Honda V8	99
Salazar	7	Lola T95/00-Ford Cosworth XB	99
Zampredi	34	Lola T94/00-Ford Cosworth XB	97
Matsushita	25	Reynard 951-Ford Cosworth XB	96
Bachelart	19	Lola T94/00-Ford Cosworth XB	95

* Disqualified – below minimum height.
** Retired but classified as a finisher.

Retirements:

Driver	No	Car	Laps	Reason
Herta	4	Reynard 94-Ford Cosworth XB	49	collision with Andretti
Cheever	14	Lola T94/00-Ford Cosworth XB	60	overheating
C. Guerrero	22	Lola T95/00-Ford Cosworth XB	62	collision with Fabi
Fabi	33	Reynard 951-Ford Cosworth XB	62	collision with C. Guerrero
Sullivan	17	Reynard 951-Ford Cosworth XB	63	pit fire
E. Fittipaldi	2	Penske PC24-Mercedes V8	69	engine
Villeneuve	27	Reynard 951-Ford Cosworth XB	70	suspension
Tracy	3	Lola T95/00-Ford Cosworth XB	95	gearbox
Johansson	16	Penske PC23-Mercedes V8	101	out of fuel

TORONTO

Date: July 16, 1995. **Circuit:** 98 laps of the 2.86 km/1.777 mile Toronto street circuit, 280.28 km/174.163 miles. **Winner's time:** 1.50'25"202. **Winner's average speed:** 152.512 kmh/94.769 mph.

Results:

Driver	No	Car	Laps
1 Andretti	6	Lola T95/00-Ford Cosworth XB	98
2 Rahal	9	Lola T95/00-Mercedes V8	98
3 Villeneuve	27	Reynard 951-Ford Cosworth XB	98
4 Fabi	33	Reynard 951-Ford Cosworth XB	98
5 Gordon	5	Reynard 951-Ford Cosworth XB	98
6 Boesel	11	Lola T95/00-Mercedes V8	98
7 Fernandez	10	Lola T95/00-Mercedes V8	98
8 Tracy	3	Lola T95/00-Ford Cosworth XB	98
9 C. Fittipaldi	15	Reynard 951-Ford Cosworth XB	98
10 E. Fittipaldi	2	Penske PC24-Mercedes V8	98
11 Cheever	14	Lola T95/00-Ford Cosworth XB	97
12 Gugelmin	18	Reynard 951-Ford Cosworth XB	96
Ribeiro	31	Reynard 951-Honda V8	96
Johansson	16	Penske PC23-Mercedes V8	94
Lazier	64	Reynard 951-Ford Cosworth XB	93

Retirements:

Driver	No	Car	Laps	Reason
Herta	4	Reynard 951-Ford Cosworth XB	0	accident
Unser	1	Penske PC24-Mercedes V8	17	accident
Pruett	20	Lola T95/00-Ford Cosworth XB	19	cooling system
C. Guerrero	22	Lola T95/00-Ford Cosworth XB	22	collision
Zampredi	34	Lola T94/00-Ford Cosworth XB	22	collision
Bachelart	19	Lola T94/00-Ford Cosworth XB	22	collision
Salazar	7	Lola T95/00-Ford Cosworth XB	23	accident
Greco	55	Lola T95/00-Mercedes V8	45	gearbox
Matsushita	25	Reynard 951-Ford Cosworth XB	66	cooling system
Sullivan	17	Reynard 951-Ford Cosworth XB	83	engine
Vasser	12	Reynard 94-Ford Cosworth XB	85	exhaust
de Ferran	8	Reynard 951-Mercedes V8	89	clutch

DETROIT

Date: June 11, 1995. **Circuit:** 77 laps of the 3.37 km/2.094 mile Belle Isle Park street circuit, 259.49 km/161.244 miles. **Winner's time:** 1.56'11". **Winner's average speed:** 134.349 kmh/83.483 mph.

Results:

Driver	No	Car	Laps
1 Gordon	5	Reynard 951-Ford Cosworth XB	77
2 Vasser	12	Reynard 94-Ford Cosworth XB	77
3 Pruett	20	Lola T95/00-Ford Cosworth XB	77
4 Andretti	6	Lola T95/00-Ford Cosworth XB	77
5 Unser	1	Penske PC24-Mercedes V8	77
6 Fernandez	10	Lola T95/00-Mercedes V8	77
7 Fabi	33	Reynard 951-Ford Cosworth XB	77
8 Tracy	3	Lola T95/00-Ford Cosworth XB	77
9 Villeneuve	27	Reynard 951-Ford Cosworth XB	77
10 E. Fittipaldi	2	Penske PC24-Mercedes V8	77
11 Johansson	16	Penske PC23-Mercedes V8	77
12 Sullivan	17	Reynard 951-Ford Cosworth XB	77
Greco	55	Lola T95/00-Mercedes V8	77
Matsushita	25	Reynard 951-Ford Cosworth XB	75
Gugelmin	18	Reynard 951-Ford Cosworth XB	75
de Ferran	8	Reynard 951-Mercedes V8	73
C. Fittipaldi	15	Reynard 951-Ford Cosworth XB	72

Retirements:

Driver	No	Car	Laps	Reason
Boesel	11	Lola T95/00-Mercedes V8	0	engine
Herta	4	Reynard 94-Ford Cosworth XB	1	fire
Zampredi	34	Lola T94/00-Ford Cosworth XB	12	collision with Cheever
Cheever	14	Lola T95/00-Ford Cosworth XB	13	collision with Zampredi
Rahal	9	Lola T95/00-Mercedes V8	16	accident
Bachelart	19	Lola T94/00-Ford Cosworth XB	33	gearbox
Danner	64	Reynard 94-Ford Cosworth XB	35	collision with Guerrero
C. Guerrero	22	Lola T95/00-Ford Cosworth XB	35	collision with Danner
Salazar	7	Lola T95/00-Ford Cosworth XB	47	collision with Johnstone
Johnstone	49	Reynard 951-Honda V8	47	collision with Salazar
Ribeiro	31	Reynard 951-Honda V8	52	gearbox

ELKHART LAKE

Date: July 9, 1995. **Circuit:** 50 laps of the 6.436 km/4 mile Elkhart Lake Road America circuit, 321.8 km/200 miles. **Winner's time:** 1.55'29"659. **Winner's average speed:** 167.176 kmh/103.881 mph.

Results:

Driver	No	Car	Laps
1 Villeneuve	27	Reynard 951-Ford Cosworth XB	50
2 Tracy	3	Lola T95/00-Ford Cosworth XB	50
3 Vasser	12	Reynard 94-Ford Cosworth XB	50
4 Ribeiro	31	Reynard 951-Honda V8	50
5 Rahal	9	Lola T95/00-Mercedes V8	50
6 Fernandez	10	Lola T95/00-Mercedes V8	50
7 Pruett	20	Lola T95/00-Ford Cosworth XB	50
8 C. Fittipaldi	15	Reynard 951-Ford Cosworth XB	50
9 Fabi	33	Reynard 951-Ford Cosworth XB	50
10 Johansson	16	Penske PC23-Mercedes V8	50
11 Bachelart	19	Lola T94/00-Ford Cosworth XB	50
12 Johnstone	49	Reynard 951-Honda V8	50
Matsushita	25	Reynard 951-Ford Cosworth XB	50
Herta	4	Reynard 94-Ford Cosworth XB	49
E. Fittipaldi	2	Penske PC24-Mercedes V8	49
Stromberger	64	Reynard 94-Ford Cosworth XB	48
Cheever	14	Lola T95/00-Ford Cosworth XB	48
Salazar	7	Lola T95/00-Ford Cosworth XB	48
C. Guerrero	22	Lola T95/00-Ford Cosworth XB	48
Zampredi	34	Lola T94/00-Ford Cosworth XB	47
Greco	99	Lola T95/00-Mercedes V8	38

Retirements:

Driver	No	Car	Laps	Reason
Unser	1	Penske PC24-Mercedes V8	2	collision with Andretti
Andretti	6	Lola T95/00-Ford Cosworth XB	2	collision with Unser
Gordon	5	Reynard 951-Ford Cosworth XB	17	gearbox
Sullivan	17	Reynard 951-Ford Cosworth XB	29	collision with Gugelmin
Gugelmin	18	Reynard 951-Ford Cosworth XB	29	collision with Sullivan
Boesel	11	Lola T95/00-Mercedes V8	41	gearbox
de Ferran	8	Lola T9400-Ford Cosworth XB	45	accident

CLEVELAND

Date: July 23, 1995. **Circuit:** 90 laps of the 3.79 km/2.355 mile Burke Lakefront Airport circuit, 341.1 km/211.955 miles. **Winner's time:** 1.38'19"151. **Winner's average speed:** 209.351 kmh/130.088 mph.

Results:

Driver	No	Car	Laps
1 Villeneuve	27	Reynard 951-Ford Cosworth XB	90
2 Herta	4	Reynard 94-Ford Cosworth XB	90
3 Vasser	12	Reynard 951-Ford Cosworth XB	90
4 Rahal	9	Lola T95/00-Mercedes V8	90
5 Sullivan	17	Reynard 951-Ford Cosworth XB	90
6 Gordon	5	Reynard 951-Ford Cosworth XB	90
7 Andretti	6	Lola T95/00-Ford Cosworth XB	90
8 Johansson	16	Penske PC23-Mercedes V8	89
9 Zampredi	34	Lola T94/00-Ford Cosworth XB	89
10 Salazar	7	Lola T95/00-Ford Cosworth XB	88
11 Johnstone	49	Reynard 951-Honda V8	88
12 Fernandez*	10	Lola T95/00-Mercedes V8	87
Matsushita	25	Reynard 951-Ford Cosworth XB	86
Greco	55	Lola T95/00-Mercedes V8	84
Guerrero	22	Lola T95/00-Ford Cosworth XB	82

* Retired but classified as a finisher.

Retirements:

Driver	No	Car	Laps	Reason
Ribeiro	31	Reynard 951-Honda V8	1	accident
Tracy	3	Lola T95/00-Ford Cosworth XB	17	handling problems
E. Fittipaldi	2	Penske PC24-Mercedes V8	22	cooling-system
C. Fittipaldi	15	Reynard 951-Ford Cosworth XB	22	engine
Gugelmin	18	Reynard 951-Ford Cosworth XB	35	fuel pressure
Cheever	14	Lola T95/00-Ford Cosworth XB	48	engine
Bachelart	19	Lola T94/00-Ford Cosworth XB	63	accident
Boesel	11	Lola T95/00-Mercedes V8	65	electrical failure
Fabi	33	Reynard 951-Ford Cosworth XB	67	exhaust system
Unser	1	Penske PC24-Mercedes V8	70	gearbox
Pruett	20	Lola T95/00-Ford Cosworth XB	83	accident
de Ferran	8	Reynard 951-Mercedes V8	85	accident
Fernandez	10	Lola T95/00-Mercedes V8	87	engine

INDYCAR WORLD SERIES

BROOKLYN

Date: July 30, 1995. **Circuit:** 250 laps of the 3.218 km/2.0 mile Michigan International Speedway oval track, 804.5 km/500 miles. **Winner's time:** 3.07′52″826. **Winner's average speed:** 256.918 kmh/159.646 mph.

Results:

Driver	No	Car	Laps
1 Pruett	20	Lola T95/00-Ford Cosworth XB	250
2 Unser	1	Penske PC24-Mercedes V8	250
3 Fernandez	10	Lola T95/00-Mercedes V8	249
4 Fabi	33	Reynard 951-Ford Cosworth XB	247
5 E. Fittipaldi	2	Penske PC24-Mercedes V8	245
6 Johansson	16	Penske PC23-Mercedes V8	244
7 Vasser	12	Reynard 951-Ford Cosworth XB	241
8 Rahal	9	Lola T95/00-Mercedes V8	240
9 C. Fittipaldi	15	Reynard 951-Ford Cosworth XB	239
10 Villeneuve	27	Reynard 951-Ford Cosworth XB	235
11 Gugelmin	18	Reynard 951-Ford Cosworth XB	232
12 de Ferran*	8	Reynard 951-Mercedes V8	226
Lazier	19	Lola T94/00-Ford Cosworth XB	223

*Retired but classified as a finisher.

Retirements:

Driver	No	Car	Laps	Reason
C. Guerrero	22	Lola T95/00-Ford Cosworth XB	5	accident
Andretti	6	Lola T95/00-Ford Cosworth XB	40	electrical failure
Boesel	11	Lola T95/00-Mercedes V8	57	engine
Tracy	3	Lola T95/00-Ford Cosworth XB	91	engine
Johnstone	49	Reynard 951-Honda V8	100	brakes
Ribeiro	31	Reynard 951-Honda V8	130	electrical failure
Matsushita	25	Reynard 951-Ford Cosworth XB	139	accident
Cheever	14	Lola T95/00-Ford Cosworth XB	163	gearbox
Salazar	7	Lola T95/00-Ford Cosworth XB	175	engine
St. James	90	Lola T95/00-Ford Cosworth XB	188	collision with Sullivan
Sullivan	17	Reynard 951-Ford Cosworth XB	189	collision with St. James
Herta	4	Reynard 94-Ford Cosworth XB	193	accident
Zampredi	34	Lola T94/00-Ford Cosworth XB	225	accident
de Ferran	8	Reynard 951-Mercedes V8	226	hit debris on track

LOUDON

Date: August 20, 1995. **Circuit:** 200 laps of the 1.609 km/1 mile New Hampshire International Speedway circuit, 321.8 km/200 miles. **Winner's time:** 1.34′36″192. **Winner's average speed:** 215.932 kmh/134.178 mph.

Results:

Driver	No	Car	Laps
1 Ribeiro	31	Reynard 951-Honda V8	200
2 Andretti	6	Lola T95/00-Ford Cosworth XB	200
3 Unser	1	Penske PC24-Mercedes V8	199
4 Villeneuve	27	Reynard 951-Ford Cosworth XB	199
5 E. Fittipaldi	2	Penske PC24-Mercedes V8	199
6 Vasser	12	Reynard 951-Ford Cosworth XB	198
7 de Ferran	8	Reynard 951-Mercedes V8	198
8 C. Fittipaldi	15	Reynard 951-Ford Cosworth XB	198
9 Gordon	5	Reynard 951-Ford Cosworth XB	197
10 Rahal	9	Lola T95/00-Mercedes V8	197
11 Gugelmin	18	Reynard 951-Ford Cosworth XB	196
12 Fabi	33	Reynard 951-Ford Cosworth XB	196
Salazar	7	Lola T95/00-Ford Cosworth XB	196
Zampredi	32	Lola T95/00-Ford Cosworth XB	195
J. M. Fangio II	17	Reynard 951-Ford Cosworth XB	194
C. Guerrero	22	Lola T95/00-Ford Cosworth XB	193
Cheever	14	Lola T95/00-Ford Cosworth XB	191
Boesel	11	Lola T95/00-Mercedes V8	191
Herta	4	Reynard 94-Ford Cosworth XB	189
Matsushita	25	Reynard 951-Ford Cosworth XB	184

Retirements:

Driver	No	Car	Laps	Reason
Fernandez	10	Lola T95/00-Mercedes V8	0	accident
Johansson	16	Penske PC23-Mercedes V8	17	oil leak
Pruett	20	Lola T95/00-Ford Cosworth XB	40	accident
Tracy	3	Lola T95/00-Ford Cosworth XB	101	oil leak
Lazier	19	Lola T94/00-Ford Cosworth XB	184	collision with Greco
Greco	55	Lola T95/00-Mercedes V8	184	collision with Lazier

MONTEREY

Date: September 10, 1995. **Circuit:** 84 laps of the 3.562 km/2.214 mile Laguna Seca Raceway circuit, 299.208 km/185.976 miles. **Winner's time:** 1.53′17″579. **Winner's average speed:** 158.475 kmh/98.493 mph.

Results:

Driver	No	Car	Laps
1 de Ferran	8	Reynard 951-Mercedes V8	84
2 Tracy	3	Lola T95/00-Ford Cosworth XB	84
3 Gugelmin	18	Reynard 951-Ford Cosworth XB	84
4 Andretti	6	Lola T95/00-Ford Cosworth XB	84
5 Pruett	20	Lola T95/00-Ford Cosworth XB	84
6 Unser	1	Penske PC24-Mercedes V8	84
7 Rahal	9	Lola T95/00-Mercedes V8	84
8 Vasser	12	Reynard 951-Ford Cosworth XB	84
9 Fabi	33	Reynard 951-Ford Cosworth XB	84
10 Fernandez	10	Lola T95/00-Mercedes V8	84
11 Villeneuve	27	Reynard 951-Ford Cosworth XB	83
12 Boesel	11	Lola T95/00-Mercedes V8	83
J.M. Fangio II	17	Reynard 951-Ford Cosworth XB	83
Johansson	16	Penske PC23-Mercedes V8	83
E. Fittipaldi	2	Penske PC24-Mercedes V8	83
Johnstone	49	Reynard 951-Honda V8	83
C. Guerrero	22	Lola T95/00-Ford Cosworth XB	83
Zampredi	34	Lola T94/00-Ford Cosworth XB	82
Schiattarella	64	Reynard 94-Ford Cosworth XB	81
Matsushita	25	Reynard 951-Ford Cosworth XB	81
Greco	55	Lola T95/00-Mercedes V8	80

Retirements:

Driver	No	Car	Laps	Reason
Fréon	19	Lola T94/00-Ford Cosworth XB	0	did not start
Salazar	7	Lola T95/00-Ford Cosworth XB	0	did not start
Ribeiro	31	Reynard 951-Honda V8	63	accident
Herta	4	Reynard 94-Ford Cosworth XB	66	accident
C. Fittipaldi	15	Reynard 951-Ford Cosworth XB	70	mechanical failure

MID-OHIO

Date: August 13, 1995. **Circuit:** 83 laps of the 3.62 km/2.25 mile Mid-Ohio circuit, 300.46 km/186.75 miles. **Winner's time:** 1.44′04″774. **Winner's average speed:** 172.339 kmh/107.089 mph.

Results:

Driver	No	Car	Laps
1 Unser	1	Penske PC24-Mercedes V8	83
2 Tracy	3	Lola T95/00-Ford Cosworth XB	83
3 Villeneuve	27	Reynard 951-Ford Cosworth XB	83
4 Fernandez	10	Lola T95/00-Mercedes V8	83
5 Herta	4	Reynard 94-Ford Cosworth XB	83
6 Gugelmin	18	Reynard 951-Ford Cosworth XB	83
7 J. M. Fangio II	17	Reynard 951-Ford Cosworth XB	83
8 Gordon	5	Reynard 951-Ford Cosworth XB	83
9 Vasser	12	Reynard 951-Ford Cosworth XB	83
10 Cheever	14	Lola T95/00-Ford Cosworth XB	83
11 Pruett	20	Lola T95/00-Ford Cosworth XB	82
12 Goodyear	24	Reynard 951-Honda V8	82
Salazar	7	Lola T95/00-Ford Cosworth XB	82
Zampredi	34	Lola T94/00-Ford Cosworth XB	81
Matsushita	25	Reynard 951-Ford Cosworth XB	81
Bachelart	19	Lola T94/00-Ford Cosworth XB	81
Fabi	33	Reynard 951-Ford Cosworth XB	80
C. Guerrero	22	Lola T95/00-Ford Cosworth XB	80

Retirements:

Driver	No	Car	Laps	Reason
Johnstone	49	Reynard 951-Honda V8	0	minor collision
Ribeiro	31	Reynard 951-Honda V8	32	fire
Rahal	9	Lola T95/00-Mercedes V8	38	accident
C. Fittipaldi	15	Reynard 951-Ford Cosworth XB	46	fire
de Ferran	8	Reynard 951-Mercedes V8	49	engine
Johansson	16	Penske PC23-Mercedes V8	61	engine
Greco	55	Lola T95/00-Mercedes V8	62	engine seized
E. Fittipaldi	2	Penske PC24-Mercedes V8	65	engine
Boesel	11	Lola T95/00-Mercedes V8	74	engine
Andretti	6	Lola T95/00-Ford Cosworth XB	79	engine

VANCOUVER

Date: September 3, 1995. **Circuit:** 100 laps of the 2.741 km/1.703 mile Vancouver street circuit, 274.173 km/170.322 miles. **Winner's time:** 1.46′54″900. **Winner's average speed:** 160.209 kmh/99.552 mph.

Results:

Driver	No	Car	Laps
1 Unser	1	Penske PC24-Mercedes V8	100
2 de Ferran	8	Reynard 951-Mercedes V8	100
3 Gordon	5	Reynard 951-Ford Cosworth XB	100
4 Johansson	16	Penske PC23-Mercedes V8	100
5 Rahal	9	Lola T95/00-Mercedes V8	100
6 Pruett	20	Lola T95/00-Ford Cosworth XB	100
7 E. Fittipaldi	2	Penske PC24-Mercedes V8	100
8 Tracy	3	Lola T95/00-Ford Cosworth XB	99
9 Zampredi	34	Lola T94/00-Ford Cosworth XB	99
10 Boesel	11	Lola T95/00-Mercedes V8	99
11 Johnstone	49	Reynard 951-Honda V8	99
12 Villeneuve	27	Reynard 951-Ford Cosworth XB	98
Salazar	7	Lola T95/00-Ford Cosworth XB	98
Goodyear	24	Reynard 951-Honda V8	98
C. Guerrero	22	Lola T95/00-Ford Cosworth XB	97
Herta	4	Reynard 94-Ford Cosworth XB	96
Matsushita	25	Reynard 951-Ford Cosworth XB	95

Retirements:

Driver	No	Car	Laps	Reason
J.M. Fangio II	17	Reynard 951-Ford Cosworth XB	8	accident
Vasser	12	Reynard 951-Ford Cosworth XB	9	engine
Till	14	Lola T95/00-Ford Cosworth XB	26	accident
Greco	55	Lola T95/00-Mercedes V8	46	gearbox
C. Fittipaldi	15	Reynard 951-Ford Cosworth XB	49	exhaust
Ribeiro	31	Reynard 951-Honda V8	55	accident
Fernandez	10	Lola T95/00-Mercedes V8	61	handling
Andretti	6	Lola T95/00-Ford Cosworth XB	63	gearbox
Gugelmin	18	Reynard 951-Ford Cosworth XB	65	accident
Fabi	33	Reynard 951-Ford Cosworth XB	73	cooling system

FINAL CLASSIFICATION

	Driver	Car	Points	Wins	Poles	Laps led	Laps completed	Miles completed
1	J. Villeneuve	Reynard 951-Ford Cosworth XB	173	4	6	304	2042	3525
2	Al Unser Jr.	Penske PC24-Mercedes V8	140	4	—	343	1726	2707
3	B. Rahal	Lola T95/00-Ford Cosworth XB	130	—	—	2	1999	3470
4	M. Andretti	Lola T95/00-Mercedes V8	125	1	3	478	1700	2715
5	R. Gordon	Reynard 951-Ford Cosworth XB	122	2	2	69	1842	3067
6	P. Tracy	Lola T95/00-Ford Cosworth XB	115	2	—	136	1443	2570
7	S. Pruett	Lola T95/00-Ford Cosworth XB	113	1	—	66	1913	3431
8	J. Vasser	Reynard 951-Ford Cosworth XB	96	—	—	27	1725	3101
9	T. Fabi	Reynard 951-Ford Cosworth XB	83	—	1	103	2065	3565
10	M. Gugelmin	Reynard 951-Ford Cosworth XB	82	—	—	70	2027	34[illegible]1
11	E. Fittipaldi	Penske PC24-Mercedes V8	67	1	—	116	1690	27[illegible]5
12	A. Fernandez	Lola T95/00-Mercedes V8	67	—	—	—	1843	3264
13	S. Johansson	Penske PC23-Mercedes V8	62	—	—	6	1800	3300
14	G. de Ferran	Reynard 951-Mercedes V8	57	1	1	127	1707	2793
15	C. Fittipaldi	Reynard 951-Ford Cosworth XB	55	—	—	10	19[illegible]8	3230
16	R. Boesel	Lola T95/00-Mercedes V8	50	—	—	2	1840	3082
17	A. Ribeiro	Reynard 951-Honda V8	38	1	1	164	1411	2506
18	E. Cheever	Lola T95/00-Ford Cosworth XB	33	—	—	40	1378	2257
19	D. Sullivan	Reynard 951-Ford Cosworth XB	32	—	—	—	1332	2541
20	B. Herta	Reynard 94-Ford Cosworth XB	30	—	1	30	1554	2816
21	E. Salazar	Lola T95/00-Ford Cosworth XB	19	—	—	—	1811	3093
22	A. Zampredi	Lola T94/00-Ford Cosworth XB	15	—	—	—	1891	3261
23	E. Bachelart	Lola T94/00-Ford Cosworth XB	8	—	—	—	727	1[illegible]78
24	J.M. Fangio II	Reynard 951-Ford Cosworth XB	6	—	—	—	368	588
25	C. Danner	Reynard 94-Ford Cosworth XB	6	—	—	—	125	238
26	A. Luyendyk	Lola T95/00-Ford Cosworth XB	6	—	—	7	271	571
27	P. Johnstone	Reynard 951-Honda V8	6	—	1	52	469	1062
28	H. Matsushita	Reynard 951-Ford Cosworth XB	5	—	—	—	1637	3014
29	M. Greco	Lola T95/00-Mercedes V8	3	—	—	—	999	1720
30	C. Guerrero	Lola T95/00-Ford Cosworth XB	2	—	—	—	1199	1916
31	D. Hall	Lola T95/00-Ford Cosworth XB	2	—	—	—	329	368
32	S. Goodyear	Reynard 951-Honda V8	1	—	—	42	375	837
33	R. Guerrero	Reynard 94-Mercedes V8	1	—	—	—	388	685
34	S. Brayton	Lola T95/00-Menard	1	—	1	—	190	475

European Hill Climb Championship

FINAL CLASSIFICATION		Cat. I	Rechberg (A)	Jaizkibel (E)	Rampa da Falperra (E)	Trier (D)	Ecce Homo (CZ)	Coppa Carotti Rieti (I)	Vale Camonica (I)	Le Mont Dore (F)	Les Rangiers (CH)	Turck-heim 3 Epis (F)	Slovakia Matador (SZ)	Subida al Fito (E)	Total
1	O. Kramsky (CS)	BMW M3 Sport Evo	A	(15)	20	20	20	(10)	20	20	20	15	(—)	10	(—)	145
2	G. Rossi (F)	BMW M3 Sport Evo	A	12	10	(—)	12	20	(—)	(—)	(—)	20	20	20	12	126
3	T. Vavrinec (CS)	Ford Escort Cosworth	N	20	(—)	(—)	20	15	12	(6)	8	20	10	20	(—)	125
4	M. Nydrle (CS)	BMW M3 E36	N	12	(—)	20	15	10	(—)	(—)	1	15	2	15	(—)	90
5	P. Vojacek (CS)	Ford Escort Cosworth	N	20	(—)	10	(—)	15	—	(—)	2	8	12	15	(—)	82
6	G. de la Casa (AND)	BMW M3 Sport Evo	A	(10)	12	12	15	12	(—)	(—)	(—)	—	—	—	—	51
7	M. Lamiscarre (F)	BMW M3	N	(—)	10	15	(—)	—	—	(1)	1	12	1	(—)	12	51
8	X. Riera (E)	BMW M3 Sport Evo	A	(—)	15	15	(—)	—	—	(—)	(—)	—	—	—	20	50
9	A. Hidalgo Herrero (E)	Ford Escort Cosworth	N	(—)	20	12	(—)	—	—	(—)	(—)	—	—	—	15	47
10	R. Wanek (D)	BMW M3	N	(—)	(—)	—	12	8	—	(—)	4	(—)	8	—	—	32
11	H. D. Meckel (D)	BMW M3 E36	N	(—)	(—)	—	10	12	—	(—)	(—)	—	—	8	—	30
12	P. Jurena (SK)	Ford Escort Cosworth	N	6	(—)	(—)	—	6	—	(—)	(—)	—	—	12	—	24
13	M. France (F)	Peugeot 306 S16	A	(—)	(—)	—	8	—	—	(—)	3	(—)	8	—	—	19
14	B. Gassler (A)	Opel Kadett GSi	N	8	(—)	(—)	—	1	—	(—)	(—)	—	—	6	—	15
15	A. Studenic (SK)	VW Golf GTi 16v	A	6	(—)	(—)	—	—	—	(—)	(—)	3	—	6	—	15
16	C. Pin (F)	Renault Clio Williams	N	(—)	(—)	—	8	—	—	(—)	2	(—)	3	—	—	13
17	J.-L. Fritsch (F)	Peugeot 205 Rallye	A	(—)	(—)	—	3	—	—	(—)	4	(—)	2	—	—	9
18	C. Strell (A)	Renault 5 GT Turbo	N	4	(—)	(—)	—	1	—	(—)	(—)	—	—	1	—	6

FINAL CLASSIFICATION		Cat. II	Rechberg (A)	Jaizkibel (E)	Rampa da Falperra (E)	Trier (D)	Ecce Homo (CZ)	Coppa Carotti Rieti (I)	Vale Camonica (I)	Le Mont Dore (F)	Les Rangiers (CH)	Turck-heim 3 Epis (F)	Slovakia Matador (SZ)	Subida al Fito (E)	Total
1	F. Danti (I)	Lucchini P3 BMW	CN	20	20	20	20	(—)	(—)	(—)	20	20	20	(10)	20	160
2	R. Faustmann (D)	Faust BMW P94	C3	15	(12)	20	(—)	20	20	20	(15)	20	15	20	(7.5)	150
3	F. Dosières (F)	Lucchini SP390	CN	(—)	15	15	15	20	(—)	(—)	15	15	15	(—)	15	125
4	R. Koeppel (D)	PRC M87 BMW	C3	12	(—)	(—)	10	10	12	(—)	4	12	8	12	(—)	80
5	G. Regosa (I)	Rebo BMW	CN	(—)	(—)	12	12	15	—	12	(—)	10	(—)	6	10	77
6	J. Micanek (CZ)	Lucchini P3 BMW	CN	12	(—)	(—)	10	12	—	—	8	(6)	12	7.5	12	73.5
7	M. Krisam Jr (D)	URD Replica C391	C3	10	(—)	(—)	15	15	—	(—)	(—)	—	—	15	—	55
8	A. Zabaleta (E)	Lola T 298	C3	(—)	20	15	(—)	—	—	(—)	(—)	—	—	—	10	45
9	G. de la Casa (AND)	Osella PA9	C3	(—)	(—)	—	—	—	—	12	(—)	15	12	(—)	6	45
10	F. Bormolini (I)	Lucchini+Osella	CN	(—)	(—)	—	—	—	—	10	12	(8)	10	(5)	8	40
11	E. Öppinger (D)	Osella PA9	C3	(—)	(—)	—	8	12	—	10	(—)	(—)	—	10	—	40
12	G. Olbrich (D)	Rigol Sport	C3	(—)	(—)	—	6	8	—	(—)	1	8	4	8	(—)	35
13	R. Napione (I)	Lucchini SP 91	CN	10	12	(—)	3	(—)	—	(—)	(—)	3	6	—	—	34
14	C. Sinopoli (F)	PRC Alfa Romeo	CN	(—)	10	(—)	4	—	—	—	6	(—)	4	—	—	24
15	L. Bormolini (I)	Osella+Lucchini	C3	6	(—)	(—)	—	—	—	(—)	(—)	10	3	—	—	19

European Championship for Rallycross Drivers

Division 1 — Production cars (Group N)			A	P	F	S	GB	IRL	B	NL	N	FIN	CZ	D	Total
1	E. Opland (N)	Mitsubishi Lancer Evo.	20	20	E	20	17	20	(13)	17	20	(12)	15	(15)	149
2	J. Kuypers (NL)	Mitsubishi Lancer Evo.	12	15	17	(—)	20	—	20	E	(9)	13	20	17	134
3	G. Svan (S)	Toyota Celica GT Four	15	(12)	20	17	15	(10)	15	15	(11)	17	17	(13)	131
4	L. Hunsbedt (N)	Ford Escort RS Cosworth	11	0	(10)	13	(4)	15	11	20	(7)	20	13	20	123
5	I. Carlsson (S)	Toyota Celica GT Four	13	17	12	(10)	(6)	0	17	12	17	15	11	(11)	114
6	L. Sällström (S)	Ford Escort RS Cosworth	9	13	(8)	15	10	17	(6)	0	13	11	—	9	97
7	B. Leinemann (D)	Ford Escort RS Cosworth	(6)	10	13	8	11	13	12	(7)	(8)	10	(7)	10	87
8	P. Koutny (CZ)	Ford Escort RS Cosworth	10	—	15	0	12	9	(3)	10	(2)	8	12	7	83
9	J. Becker (D)	Nissan Sunny GTi-R	8	11	7	12	9	(6)	7	9	(5)	—	(6)	12	75
10	G. Kittilsen (N)	Ford Escort RS Cosworth	0	—	10	6	8	12	10	13	12	0	0	0	61
11	J. Franssen (B)	Subaru Impreza 555	0	7	6	5	(1)	—	9	6	10	13	9	8	60
12	H. Sulberg (N)	Ford Escort RS Cosworth	17	0	0	9	5	11	0	—	4	6	—	—	52

Division 2 — Touring cars (Group A) with modifications			A	P	F	S	GB	IRL	B	NL	N	FIN	CZ	D	Total
1	M. Schanche (N)	Ford Escort RS 2000 T16 4x4	E	(11)	20	17	17	(15)	20	20	20	20	20	(11)	154
2	K. Hansen (S)	Citroën ZX 16v Turbo 4x4	15	17	(15)	20	20	20	17	(12)	(13)	(11)	20	146
3	J.-L. Pailler (F)	Citroën Xantia T16 4x4	20	12	17	—	15	13	(11)	13	—	(12)	15	17	122
4	P. Eklund (S)	Subaru Impreza 555	17	0	12	15	(10)	(9)	13	12	17	(11)	17	15	118
5	W. Gollop (GB)	Peugeot 306 16S Turbo 4x4	12	15	13	0	13	17	(5)	0	6	10	12	(6)	98
6	T. Kristoffersson (S)	Audi Coupé S2 20v	13	0	0	13	7	11	12	0	11	17	0	13	97
7	M. Jernberg (S)	Ford Escort RS Cosworth	—	—	—	12	(9)	10	15	11	10	15	10	12	95
8	B. Skogstad (N)	Ford Escort RS Cosworth	11	20	0	(8)	12	(1)	0	14	13	9	9	9	93
9	M. Iversen (N)	Ford Escort RS Cosworth	10	9	7	—	(6)	12	—	15	15	(6)	13	10	91
10	B. Squibb (GB)	Ford Escort RS Cosworth	9	13	8	11	11	6	7	8	—	—	—	—	73
11	S. Andersson (S)	Audi Coupé S2 10v	0	10	11	10	8	0	6	6	(5)	(4)	8	8	67
12	K. Vereeken (B)	Ford Escort Cosworth 4x4	(1)	8	10	4	2	—	(2)	3	4	3	6	0	40

Division 3 — 2WD Production (Group N) cars below 1400cc			A	P	F	S	GB	IRL	B	NL	N	FIN	CZ	D	Total
1	K. Kasse (NL)	Citroën AX GTi	15	17	20	20	(9)	—	20	17	17	(12)	(9)	17	143
2	M. Beck (A)	Citroën AX Sport	17	(12)	17	15	15	(13)	(10)	20	20	20	(12)	15	139
3	P. Novotny (CZ)	Citroën AX GTi	(7)	13	9	10	20	20	(8)	(7)	(3)	10	17	11	110
4	J.-M. Laurant (B)	Peugeot 106 XSi	—	—	15	—	17	—	17	12	15	—	13	13	102
5	R. Bergvall (S)	Citroën AX Sport/AX GTi	0	10	0	17	12	17	3	0	10	13	0	6	88
6	S. Seeliger (D)	Citroën AX Sport	20	—	13	12	—	—	2	11	8	—	15	0	81
7	V. Bohacek (CZ)	Citroën AX Sport	(4)	6	(2)	(4)	8	11	7	10	7	15	0	10	74
8	J. Boone (NL)	Citroën AX GTi	—	—	—	—	—	—	13	15	—	—	20	20	68
9	P. Nielsen (DK)	Rover Metro GTi	3	8	10	0	6	—	0	6	13	11	10	(3)	67
10	L. Hagestig (S)	Citroën AX Sport	13	—	0	7	0	—	11	5	5	—	—	12	53
11	E. Branden (S)	Citroën AX Sport	9	20	0	—	10	—	0	0	—	—	—	8	47
12	J. van de Ven (NL)	Citroën AX GTi	—	7	—	11	0	—	12	3	—	—	0	9	42

— = Did not compete.   0 = Did not qualify for finals.   ( ) = Dropped score.   E = Exclusion.